Springer Proceedings in Humanities and Social Sciences

Aims and Scope

Springer Proceedings in Humanities and Social Sciences collates the most current, selected research presented at international and regional conferences, seminars, and workshops to bring it to a global readership. The series features volumes (in electronic and print formats) of selected contributions from conferences in all areas of both the humanities and social sciences, including interdisciplinary work, covering philosophy, religious studies, history, language and literature, communications and cultural studies, anthropology, sociology, developmental studies and political science and policy. In addition to an overall evaluation by the publisher of the topical interest, research quality, and timeliness of each volume, each contribution is refereed to standards comparable to those of leading journals, resulting in authoritative contributions to the respective fields. Springer's production and distribution infrastructure ensures rapid publication and wide circulation of the latest developments in the most compelling and promising areas of research in HSS today. The series publishes both Open Access and non-Open Access works.

This series promotes the inclusion of 'Selected Proceedings', a middle ground between edited volumes and full conference proceedings. The series is specifically looking for submissions from conferences with a defined, focused theme, or a regional focus in a specific discipline.

The series offers the option for conferences to use Springer Nature's conference management platform, Equinocs, free of charge.

For more information, contact the listed publishing editor.

Alessandra Micalizzi
Editor

Artificial Creativity

Looking at the Future of Digital Culture

Foreword by Lev Manovich

Springer

Editor
Alessandra Micalizzi
Sociology, Communication and
Cultural Processes
Pegaso University
Naples, Italy

ISSN 2948-2526 ISSN 2948-2534 (electronic)
Springer Proceedings in Humanities and Social Sciences
ISBN 978-3-031-88333-0 ISBN 978-3-031-88334-7 (eBook)
https://doi.org/10.1007/978-3-031-88334-7

This Springer imprint is published by the registered company Springer Nature Switzerland AG
The registered company address is: Gewerbestrasse 11, 6330 Cham, Switzerland

Foreword

Notes on Generative AI

Lev Manovich

"AI" as a Cultural Perception

There is not one specific technology or a single research project called "AI." However, we can follow how our cultural perception of this concept evolved over time and what it was referring to in each period. In the last 50 years, when an allegedly uniquely human ability or skill is being automated by means of computer technology, we refer to it as "AI." Yet, as soon as this automation is seamlessly and fully successful, we tend to stop referring to it as an "AI case." In other words, "AI" refers to technologies and methodologies that automate human cognitive abilities and are starting to function but are n't quite there yet. "AI" was already present in the earliest computer media tools. The first interactive drawing and design system, Ivan Sutherland's *Sketchpad* (1961–1962)[1], had a feature that would automatically finish any rectangles or circles you started drawing. In other words, it knew what you were trying to make. In the very broad understanding just given, this was undoubtedly "AI" already.

My first experience with a desktop paint program running on an Apple II was in 1984, and it was truly amazing to move your mouse and see simulated paint brushstrokes appear on the screen. However, today we no longer consider this to be "AI." Another example would be the Photoshop function that automatically selects an outline of an object. This function was added many years ago—this, too, is "AI" in the broad sense, yet nobody would refer to it as such today. The history of digital media systems and tools is full of such "AI moments"—amazing at first, then taken for granted and forgotten as "AI" after a while. (In academic studies of AI history, this phenomenon is referred to as the *AI effect*.) Thus, today *creative AI* refers only to recently developed methods where computers transform some inputs into new media outputs (e.g., text-to-image models) and specific techniques (e.g., certain types of AI models). However, we must remember that these methods are neither the first nor

[1] Ivan Sutherland, "Sketchpad: A Man-Machine Graphical Communication System," AFIPS '63: Proceedings of the Spring 1963 Joint Computer Conference (May 21, 1963), https://dl.acm.org/doi/10.1145/1461551.1461591.

the last in the long history and future of simulating human art abilities or assisting humans in media creation. I expect that after a certain period, GenAI technology will be taken for granted, becoming ubiquitous and thus invisible—and some other cultural use of computers will come to be seen as "AI."

From Representation to Prediction

Historically, humans created images of existing or imagined scenes using a number of methods, from manual drawing to 3D CG (see below for explanation of the methods). With AI generative media, a fundamentally new method emerges. Computers analyze patterns in large datasets of existing media. Using these learned patterns, they can then create new, previously unseen still and moving images that exhibit similar characteristics. This process forms the core of generative AI technology.

One can certainly propose different historical paths leading to visual generative media today or divide one historical timeline into different stages. Here is one such possible trajectory:

1. Creating representations manually (e.g., drawing with variety of instruments, carving, etc.). More mechanical stages and parts were sometimes carried out by human assistants typically training in their teacher's studio—so there is already some delegation of functions.
2. Creating manually but using assistive devices (e.g., perspective machines, camera lucida). From *hands* to *hands + device*. Now some functions are delegated to mechanical and optical devices.
3. Photography, X-ray, video, volumetric capture, remote sensing, and photogrammetry. From *using hands* to *recording information using machines*. From *human assistants* to *machine assistants*.
4. 3D CG: You define a 3D model in a computer and use algorithms that simulate effects of light sources, shadows, fog, transparency, translucency, natural textures, depth of field, motion blur, etc. From *recording* to *simulation*.
5. Generative AI: Using media datasets to predict still and moving images. From *simulation* to *prediction*.

"Prediction" is the actual term often used by AI researchers in their publications describing visual generative media methods. So, while this term can be used figuratively and evocatively, this is also what happens scientifically when you use image generative tools. When working with a text-to-image AI model, the artificial neural network attempts to predict the images that correspond best to your text input. I am certainly not suggesting that using all other already accepted terms such as "generative media" is inappropriate. But if we want to better understand the difference between AI visual media synthesis methods and other representational methods developed in human history, employing the concept of "prediction" and thus referring to these AI systems as "predictive media" captures this difference well.

Visual AI and Media Accumulation

I will use the term "visual AI" to refer to computational methods that use machine learning for generating and editing visual content, trained on vast amounts of images and videos found across the web. In other words, this is my shortcut for saying "generative AI used to make and edit images, video and animation."

Visual AI is the fourth significant *data* effect of the web—a global accumulation of networked, hyperlinked cultural content that began to grow quickly after 1993. Although people have been sharing texts and images on the internet since the 1970s, this process picked up speed after 1993, when the first visual browser, Mosaic, was introduced on January 23 of that year.

I have observed several repercussions of the growth of information on the web over the next 30 years. If we wish to situate the development of visual AI in the early 2020s in this timeline, here are four such effects. Certainly, others can be also named, so this is only one list of techno-cultural developments technologies enabled by the web I am particularly interested in:

1. The first effect is the switch from categorical, hierarchical, and structured organization of information (exemplified by library catalogs and early web directories) to search engines in the late 1990s. There was so much content that organizing it in conventional ways was no longer practical, and search became the new default. Note that *web search is based on a prediction of what will be most relevant to the user* as opposed to giving you a precise and definite answer. Note that generative AI is also predictive—it predicts possible text, images, animation, or music in response to your question or prompt. The regime of absolute certainty, i.e., a truth versus a lie typical for human civilization is replaced by predictions, as statistics becomes foundation of human sciences in the twentieth century and data science and AI in recent decades.
2. The second major effect is the rise in popularity of data visualization during the 2000s. The field comes into its own around 2005. As a part of this development, the new field "artistic data visualization" develops in the same decade, along with other new cultural fields: data art and data design. (In our lab, we created Phototrails, Selfiecity, and On Broadway in 2012–2014. These were first interactive visualizations of millions of Instagram images.)[2] If search attempts to find the most relevant items in the giant data universe, visualization tries to show parts of this universe in one image, revealing patterns and connections.
3. The third effect is the emergence of "data science" as the master discipline of the new big data era at the end of the 2000s. While many techniques employed in data science have already been available for decades, the rapid increase in unstructured data in the 2000s motivated the development of a separate data science field—the key new profession of the data society. My own version of

[2] See "Projects," Cultural Analytics Lab, accessed September 27, 2024, https://lab.culturalanalytics.info/p/projects.html.

> this stage was "cultural analytics," an idea I introduced in 2005 and developed over the following 15 years in our lab. Cultural analytics applies the paradigm of data science to cultural content, using computational techniques to analyze and visually represent large collections of digital media, enabling the exploration of patterns and trends across entire cultural datasets.[3]

The next, but certainly not the last, effect of the growth of online visual digital content is visual AI which becomes popular in early 2020s. DALL-E was released in 2020, Midjourney in 2022, and Adobe Firefly and Runway Gen-1 in 2023. Today (2025), hundreds of other AI image, video, and animation tools exist, and image generation is also available in all popular AI text bots. (A bit earlier around 2017, a particular AI method for media generation called GAN became already popular with digital artists.)

(It is relevant to mention that visual AI and generative AI in general build on 20 years of research. The key breakthrough was the idea to use web content universe as a source of data for machine learning, without labeling it. This idea was already articulated in the research papers published around 2001.)

Let's see what kind of pattern is established by these four effects. Search is the first method to deal with the new scale of content on the web. Data science focuses on finding patterns, relations, clusters, and outliers in big data and also predicting future data. Data visualization tries to summarize datasets visually. And now generative AI explores "big content" in yet another way, generating new content which combines many patterns from existing media.

To put this differently, generative AI synthesizes new content that has statistical properties similar to existing content. But it's not a copy of what already exists. AI generates new content (texts, images, animation, 3D models, music, singing, etc.) by interpolating between existing points in the latent space. This space contains numerous patterns and structures extracted by artificial networks from billions of image-text pairs, trillions of text pages, and other large collections of existing human cultural artifacts. AI predicts what could exist between these points in space of patterns. For example, it can predict a "painting" made by artists A, B, and C, using techniques D and E, with content F, G, and E, with mood, colors M and N, proportion W, composition K, etc.

Note that the three earlier developments all approach big data by summarizing it. Web search reduces billions of web pages to the top results. Data visualization reduces it to a diagram. Data science reduces it by using summary statistics, cluster analysis, regression, or latent space projection. But visual AI is doing something new. It also first reduces big data during learning and then generates new data points.

One way to sum up all this is to say that we moved from probabilistic search (1999) to probabilistic media generation (2022). But certainly, generative AI and its subset visual AI are not the last effect of the existence of web data; others will likely emerge in the future.

[3] See Lev Manovich, *Cultural Analytics* (The MIT Press, 2020).

AI and Modernism

After training on trillions of text pages or billions of images taken from the web, AI models can generate new texts and visuals on the level of highly competent professional writers, artists, photographers, or illustrators. These capacities of the AI models are distributed over trillions of connections between billions of artificial neurons rather than determined by standard algorithms. In other words, we developed a technology that, in terms of complexity, is extremely similar to the human brain. We don't fully grasp how our AI technology works, just as we don't fully comprehend human intellect and creativity.

On the surface, *the logic of modernism appears to be diametrically opposed to the process of training generative AI systems*. Modern artists desired to depart from classical art and its defining characteristics such as visual symmetry, hierarchical compositions, and narrative content. In other words, their art was founded on a fundamental rejection of everything that had come before it (at least in theory, as expressed in their manifestos). AI models are trained in the opposite manner, by learning from historical culture and art created up to now. AI model is analogous to a very conservative artist studying in the "meta" *museum without walls* that houses historical art.

But we all know that art theory and art practice are not the same thing. Modern artists did not completely reject the past and everything that came before them. Instead, *modern art developed by reinterpreting and copying images and forms from old art traditions*, such as Japanese prints (van Gogh), African sculpture (Picasso), and Russian icons (Malevich). Thus, the artists only rejected the dominant high art paradigms of the time, realistic and salon art, but not the rest of human art history. In other words, it was deeply historicist: rather than inventing everything from scratch, it innovated by adapting certain older aesthetics to contemporary art contexts. In the case of geometric abstract art created in 1910s, these artists used images that were already widely used in experimental psychology to study human visual sensation and perception.[4]

When it comes to artistic AI, we should not be blinded by how these systems are trained. Yes, AI models are trained on previously created human art and culture artifacts. However, their newly generated outputs are not mechanical replicas or simulations of what has already been created. In my opinion, these are frequently *genuinely new* cultural artifacts with *previously unseen content, aesthetics, or styles*.

Of course, simply being novel does not automatically make something culturally or socially interesting or significant. Indeed, many definitions of "creativity" agree on this point: it is the creation of something that is both original and worthwhile or useful.

[4] For the detailed analysis of these relations between modern art and experimental psychology, see Paul Vitz and Arnold Glimcher, *Modern art and Modern Science: The Parallel Analysis of Vision*, 1983.

However, estimating what percentage of all novel artifacts produced by generative AI are also useful and/or meaningful for a larger culture is not a feasible project at this time. For one thing, I am not aware of any systematic effort to use such systems to "fill in," so to speak, a massive matrix of all content and aesthetic possibilities by providing millions of specifically designed prompts. Instead, it is likely that, as in every other area of popular culture, only a small number of possibilities are realized over and over by millions of users, leaving a long tail of other possibilities unrealized. So, if only a tiny fraction of the vast universe of potential AI artifacts is being realized in practice, we can't make broad statements about the originality or utility of the rest of the universe.

A Letter to a Young Artist

> "I have completed the construction of my burrow and it seems to be successful." ... [T]he most beautiful thing about my burrow is the stillness. Of course, that is deceptive. At any moment it may be shattered and then all will be over. For the time being, however, the silence is with me." (Franz Kafka, *The Burrow,* 1924)

The key difference between me, a human, and generative AI: I am limited, but AI is unlimited. Yes, of course: it has significant limits now, in practice. But it advances fast, and what it can already do today is beyond what we could have imagined a year or two ago. Instead of dwelling on what AI can't do at this particular moment, it is safer to assume that what it "can" will only multiply.

Because of how human skills, learning, and memory work, I have limitations. I can't draw in hundreds of styles of other artists or effortlessly combine them together. I don't have knowledge of the immense *museum without walls* distributed over the web and museum databases. But AI can. And it will only get better.

I can't simply sit down and start writing summaries of numerous topics in the history of culture. AI can. I can't instantly make hours of music that mixes the languages of different composers and map them into new instruments. AI can.

"I can't... but AI can." (Endless other examples can be added.)

So why make art now? And what art will still be meaningful to make?

What is interesting about human art now is our limits—and obsessions. Our inability to instantly think and paint exactly like any one of the millions of artists who lived. Our inability to quickly change. The way I walk, talk, my habits. My constraints. This is what makes me human as opposed to an AI. The latter will continue to evolve. But human evolution does not work on the same scale.

Note that this is not about simulating my idiosyncrasies and thus making AI "more human." Yes, we can do it, but that's not interesting. It is like taking a Boing 777 around the block to get groceries. Its forcing superhumans to act like humans, and this is a banal and weak strategy.

And there is another crucial point to make. *What makes art "human" is not our intentions, plans, ideas, or meanings. For over 100 years, modern artists did their best to remove all this from their art making.* If you give AI a direction, it can perfectly simulate ideas, plans, and meanings. So, this is not relevant.

The only relevant thing is our limitations. Our inability to compete with the superhuman. With the web, with search engines, with recommendation engines, with huge databases, with machine learning algorithms, with generative AI—and other superhuman computer technologies to come.

Therefore, "human artists making art with AI tools" is a meaningless idea. You want to collaborate with Gods? A mortal "collaborating" with Apollo, Athena, Hephaestus, Hermes, Zeus?

Instead, nurture your limitations. Be extremely limited—not unlimited. Don't be "creative." Forget the meaningless idea that AI will help us, "expand our creativity."

Work within constraints—the ones you already—or the ones you can make on purpose. White on white. Black on black. This is the right direction. Instead of a vast surface of "endless possibilities," concentrate in a single spot and go as deeply as possible.

(Think like Morandi rather than like Picasso.)

Make a tiny hole in the vast surface of everything that was already created and everything that is still possible and keep digging. When you get completely tired digging meters of wrong underground paths, get lost again and again, and want to give up, it means you are finally close to something. Keep going.

Because AI is so vast and endless in its knowledge and skills, you needed to work on the micro-scale. Very narrow. So narrow that AI can't quite get there. Through the needle eye. Only in this way can you compete with superhuman generative AI.

The artist needs to become a mole. And you need to be constantly stressed and worried because AI can discover your hole at any time and, in an instant, destroy all the underground pathways you have spent years making. But perhaps this stress, this endless anxiety is the right motivation for making something original and authentic in the end. Making your art in secret, knowing that you can be discovered and erased tomorrow by AI progress.

References

Manovich, L. (2020). *Cultural analytics*. The MIT Press.

Sutherland, Ivan. "Sketchpad: A Man-Machine Graphical Communication System." In *AFIPS '63: Proceedings of the Spring 1963 Joint Computer Conference*, 21 May 1963, https://dl.acm.org/doi/10.1145/1461551.1461591.

"Projects." *Cultural Analytics Lab*, accessed 27 Sept. 2024, https://lab.culturalanalytics.info/p/projects.html.

Vitz, P., & Glimcher, A. (1983). *Modern art and modern science: The parallel analysis of vision.*

Acknowledgement

This book represents the last step of a wider project proposed by the Centre of Research in Digital Humanities of Pegaso University and funded by the same university.

A board of scholars with interdisciplinary background worked together to discuss about the relation between generative engine and the production of creative outputs in music, audiovisual narratives, texts, and images.

Thanks to the reciprocal collaboration and the peculiar perspective each of them offered to the topic, it was possible to complete the project titled ACAI—*Artificial Creativity: Perceptions and Practices in Applying AI to Artistic and Cultural Productions* (PRA2023004).

I would also like to thank the publisher, who believed in this project without hesitation. A special thanks to all the authors for their efforts in writing and editing the papers. The richness of perspectives is evident by the table of contents, where we tried to identify four different threads about the impact and the application of AI: language, narratives, music production, and the multimedia outputs.

I intend to express my gratitude to all the members of the board of Artificial Creativity Projects that are not part of the publication but have done an important work behind the scene: Anna Rinaldin, Gilda Policastro, Lenoardo Galteri, Lara Balleri, Sara Selmi, Gaia Turconi, Federico Ambruosi, Francesco Epifani, and Fabio Pelagalli. We hope to share other academic adventures all together.

Editorial Board

Contents

Editor and Contributors

About the Editor

Alessandra Micalizzi is an Associate Professor of Sociology, Communication, and Culture at Pegaso University in Naples and a Senior Lecturer at SAE Institute in Milan. She coordinates the group of research in Digital Humanities (Pegaso) and is also a scientific committee member with a specific role in leading funded projects. Her areas of research deal with the role of new technologies in socio-cultural practices: recently, she has been working on the impact of AI in creative media productions and the application of gender perspective to the study of cultural industries.

Special Guests

Pierpaolo Limone is the Rector of Pegaso University and a Full Professor of Developmental and Educational Psychology at the same institution. His research focuses on educational media, e-learning, and quality assurance in education systems. Previously, he served as Rector of the University of Foggia and has published extensively on innovative teaching methodologies and higher education systems.

Lev Manovich is an artist, writer, and one of the most influential theorists of digital art and culture worldwide. He serves as a Presidential Professor of Computer Science at the City University of New York's Graduate Center and is the Director of the Cultural Analytics Lab. After studying painting, architecture, and filmmaking, Manovich began using computers to create digital art in 1984. He has played a key role in creating a number of new research fields, including new media and digital culture (1991–), software studies (2001–), cultural analytics (2007–), and AI aesthetics (2017–).

About the Contributors

Francesco Bianco is an Assistant Professor of Italian linguistics at Palacký University Olomouc (Czechia). His research interests span several areas, including the syntax of Old Italian, the language of Italian emigrants, the Italian bureaucratic language, and the digital humanities. His website is www.francescobianco.net.

Giampiero Brunelli (Associate Professor of Early Modern History, Pegaso Telematic University) is a specialist in sixteenth- and seventeenth-century history. Among his publications, the following books stand out: *Soldati del papa* (Carocci, 2003) and *La guerra in età moderna* (Laterza, 2021). His current work includes an exploration of AI's potential for historical research.

Alessandro Bruno is an Associate Professor of Computer Science at IULM University. He earned a PhD in Computer Engineering, has had experience in job positions at Bournemouth University, and was a Research Visitor at UCL. Fellow at INAF in 2019, he currently serves as Principal Investigator for a European-funded research project.

James Brusseau (Ph.D. in Philosophy) is the author of books, articles, and media on the history of philosophy and ethics. He has taught in Europe, Mexico, and is currently at Pace University, near his home in New York City. His academic research explores the human experience of artificial intelligence in the areas of personal identity, authenticity, and freedom.

Giuliano Cenati is an Associate Professor of Italian Literature at the Department of Human Sciences at Pegaso Digital University. From 2003 to 2018, he conducted postdoctoral research and teaching at the University of Milan, focusing on modern and contemporary Italian literature. His research explores narratology, literary genres, short fiction, hybrid genres, reception aesthetics, and the sociology of literature.

Antonella Coppi (Associate Professor of General and Social Pedagogy, Music Pedagogy, and Community Music, IUL University, Florence, IT). She is the Coordinator of the International LLL Center "Comenius" in the Human Science Department, IUL University. As an active musician, she serves as the Referent for the Italian University Choir and Orchestras Networking and is the Conductor of the University Choir and Orchestra at UNIMORE. She is notable for her work on the first Italian studies on Community Music (FrancoAngeli, 2017).

Luigi Di Caro is an Associate Professor in the Department of Computer Science at the University of Torino. He has a Master degree and a Ph.D. in Computer Science, and his main interests include artificial intelligence (AI), natural language processing (NLP), data mining (DM), machine learning (ML), legal informatics (LI) and related interdisciplinary interactions with cognitive sciences (CS) and social-impact applications.

Maria Ermelinda De Carlo is a Researcher in Experimental Pedagogy at Pegaso University, where she teaches Research and Innovation in Education. Her research focuses on field experiments that assess invisible competencies and life skills, integrating digital technologies, such as gamification and AI, while implementing digital narratives for personal and organizational sustainability.

Manuela Farinosi Ph.D. in Multimedia Communication, is an Associate Professor of Sociology of Communication and Director of the Laboratory for Research on New Media (NuMe) at the University of Udine (Italy). Her research interests lie in the social and cultural dimensions of digital technologies and online platforms.

Silvia Fossati is a content creator and streamer from Italy. She focuses on the divulgation of board games, game books, and video games, and she is active on TikTok, Instagram, and Twitch as Escilgioco since 2021. She collaborates with many publishing houses on literature projects. In 2024, she published *Agenda investigativa* (Dracomaca).

Luca Gallarini is a Postdoctoral Researcher at the University of Milan. His studies focus on Contemporary Italian Literature, comics, and hybrid literary genres. He published two books: *Le molte vite di Aldo Buzzi. Letteratura, editoria e cultura del cibo* (2018) and *I romanzi degli artisti. Dinamiche storiche e conflitti generazionali nell'opera di Giuseppe Rovani* (2020).

Stefania Elisa Ghezzi is a Ph.D. candidate at Palacký University Olomouc (Czechia). Her research interests include sociolinguistics and linguistic variation, with a particular focus on substandard varieties, the history of the Italian language, and the didactics of Italian LS/L2.

Claudio Melchior Ph.D., is an Associate Professor of Sociology of Cultural and Communication Processes at the University of Udine, Italy. His research interests encompass media analysis and social processes, particularly those concerning vulnerable groups (such as older adults and persons with disabilities) and information/misinformation dynamics in contemporary digitalized society.

Andrea Paternostro is an Adjunct Professor of digital marketing and consumer behavior at the Catholic University of Milan, a content marketer, SEO specialist, digital publisher, and journalist. He has a background in Media Studies and Information Systems Management. As an author and speaker, he works at the intersection of GenAI, marketing, journalism, and content management.

Daniel Raffini is a Research Fellow and Lecturer at Sapienza University of Rome. He specializes in contemporary Italian literature, comparative literature, and digital humanities. His Ph.D. focuses on foreign literature reception in Italian journals between the two world wars. He is currently exploring the intersection of literature and artificial intelligence from historical, theoretical, and ethical perspectives.

Amon Rapp is an Associate Professor in the Department of Computer Science, University of Turin, Italy, where he leads the Smart Personal Technology Lab. He serves as an Associate Editor for the *International Journal of Human-Computer Studies* (Elsevier) and *Human-Computer Interaction* (Taylor & Francis).

Bojana Romic Ph.D., is an Assistant Professor in Media and Communication at the Faculty of Culture and Society, Malmö University, Sweden. Her research interests lie at the crossroads of science and technology studies (STS), image politics, and audience research. She is currently writing a book with the working title *Visual Representations of AI* (Palgrave Macmillan, forthcoming).

Caterina Sapone (Ph.D. student in Digital Humanities, Pegaso Telematic University), an Educational Designer, focuses her Ph.D. project and interests on the use of digital technology and video games to enhance creativity and problem-solving as life skills. Her other research interests include AI chatbot–human interaction for educational and entertainment purposes.

Teresa Savoia holds a European Ph.D. in Experimental Pedagogy and has worked as a Researcher at Roma Tre University. She is currently a tenure-track researcher at Pegaso University. She holds a Master's Degree in Translation studies. Currently, her main fields of study and research concern the processes of writing and the learning and teaching of foreign languages.

Amy Spencer is a Writer and Postdoctoral Researcher based at the Centre for Cultural and Creative Industries at Bath Spa University, UK. She works as part of MyWorld, researching the future of creative technology innovation, and leads the Narrative and Emerging Technologies (NET) Lab. Her books include *DIY: The Rise of Lo-Fi Culture* and *Ambient Stories in Practice and Research: Digital Writing in Place*.

Mirko Tavosanis (Associate Professor of Italian Linguistics, University of Pisa) has served as President of the degree programs in Digital humanities at the University of Pisa. He studies the relationship between the Italian language and information technologies; his books include *L'italiano del web* (Carocci, 2011) and *Lingue e intelligenza artificiale* (Carocci, 2018).

Stefano Triberti Ph.D., is an Associate Professor of General Psychology and the Director of the LAHTI—Laboratory for Advanced Human-Technology Interaction at Pegaso University, Italy. His research interests include with motivation, intention, personality, health psychology, user experience, and the use of new technology to improve health and well-being (positive technology).

Luca Turchet is an Associate Professor at the University of Trento. He is the founding president of the Internet of Sounds Research Network and the Chair of the IEEE Emerging Technology Initiative on the Internet of Sounds. His research interests include extended reality, sound and music computing, and multisensory interactions.

Eric Tron Gianet is an interaction designer and researcher based in Turin. His research interests focus on human-centered AI and human–AI interaction, specifically on studying and designing generative artificial intelligence systems for situated and embodied contexts.

Machine and Language

Mirko Tavosanis

Abstract This paper discusses the role that linguistic studies should play in understanding and utilizing artificial intelligence (AI), particularly in relation to creativity. Given that AI predominantly relies on linguistic structures through text-to-text and text-to-image interactions, examining AI from a linguistic viewpoint is considered essential. The paper explores the nature of linguistic creativity in AI, highlighting both its capabilities and limitations in generating innovative content. It also critically addresses the concepts of creativity and originality in AI-produced language and the issues related to evaluating the quality of linguistic outputs. Subsequently, the paper identifies areas in which AI excels as well as those in which it struggles. Ultimately, the paper argues for a multidisciplinary approach, emphasizing the need for continued linguistic contributions to the broader AI research discourse.

Keywords Linguistics · Prompt · Research · Language · Machine

1 Introduction

The hype enveloping the deployment of the so-called "AI"s is strong. We can confidently forecast that, when the dust will be settled, only a small fraction of the declared capabilities of current AI will be actually confirmed—from medicine to teaching, from scientific research to traffic management (Narayanan & Kapoor, 2024). However, the processing of human language is one of the areas where current AI is surely more than hype. For tasks like translation or text simplification, the current technologies, including LLMs, are already an important component of real workflows in many fields.

On the other hand, it is pretty difficult to forecast, or even describe, the specific linguistic tasks AI is already capable of carrying out. In a recent book, Ethan

M. Tavosanis (✉)
Università di Pisa, Pisa, PI, Italy
e-mail: mirko.tavosanis@unipi.it

A. Micalizzi (ed.), *Artificial Creativity*, Springer Proceedings in Humanities and Social Sciences, https://doi.org/10.1007/978-3-031-88334-7_1

Mollick (2024) has used the image of "invisible borders" in order to describe the difficulty to understand what, for example, generative systems are able to do. In that understanding, our intuition often fails. How is it possible that tools able to create convincing press releases about products they know nothing about are at the same time uncapable to correctly count how many "r"s are there in the word "strawberry"? The "alterstanding" label introduced by Bruce Sterling on a series of X posts seems a playful but correct alternative to the label of "understanding" for those capabilities.

To understand and define the linguistic creativity of those systems it is therefore mandatory to look at their output in a systematic way. In the last few years, many studies have tried to do exactly that. Methods and results have been notably varied, but at least in some areas a kind of consensus has today emerged.

For this discussion we will refer to a very general notion of "creativity". After all, the very idea of "linguistic creativity" can be disputed even for human beings. "At first sight, language as a rule-based system should not allow for any innovations, for any creativity in the common sense"; at the same time, however, "we see what can only be termed 'acts of creation in speakers', in both everyday and poetic language" (Bergs, 2019: 173). To define those "acts of creation" is not an easy task; here we will refer to them in the broadest possible sense, including acts both conventional (such as the writing of novels) and unconventional (such as unusual turn of phrases).

It is interesting to note that, for example, Large Language Models are mainly tools for statistical processing and could be therefore structurally considered as something that reveals hidden relationships already lurking inside a system and not as creative tools. At the same time, however, they have structural mechanisms such as the parameter of "temperature" that could be considered playing a role roughly similar to the role of "creativity" in humans (Peeperkorn et al., 2024, for the functionality and limits of that similarity). As in humans, we can therefore see a balance between features pushing in different directions.

2 Creativity

How much of the linguistic output of AI systems can then be considered "creative"? In fact, it has been noted since the introduction of modern AI techniques that in areas like copywriting or creation of slogans or brand names those systems seem perfectly capable to produce huge heaps of "creative" texts; the quality of those texts can ben extremely disputable from the point of view of human professionals, but among them it is often easy to find and pick up at least some interesting items, and such a work of selection seems often quicker and easier than human creation (Tavosanis, 2018). This kind of algorithmic creativity can therefore be useful in many ways and it could certainly displace human "creativity" for some tasks.

Moreover, AI systems can create new words and forge novel sentences. Sometimes they do it by mistake, simply creating words that do not exist in a language or that are modified forms of existing words (in Italian it has been signalled the use of made-up or altered words like "vocanza" or "clarezza"). More often they can do it by prompting, such as in an example like that (with ChatGPT-4o):

> Prompt: Could you please create a new word to describe the linguistic creativity displayed by AI systems?
>
> Answer: Sure! How about the word **"Ailinguence"**?
>
> Here's the breakdown:
>
> - **"AI"** refers to artificial intelligence, acknowledging the system's non-human origin.
> - **"Linguence"** is a blend of "linguistics" and "influence," highlighting how AI's language use both adapts and shapes communication in creative ways.
>
> **Ailinguence** could describe the unique, often unpredictable ability of AI systems to generate novel language, phrases, and expressions that push the boundaries of traditional linguistic norms.
>
> Would you like any tweaks or further elaboration on its meaning?

Of course, such an example will seem not especially worthwhile to many readers. However, simply by asking the system to generate alternatives, we can have more proposals like *leximorphosis*, *synthosemy*, *algorhetoric*, *cognilinguality* and so on—and among them at least one or two could be acceptable in many contexts.

Much more relevant, of course, is the fact that such systems can create whole texts, including the literary ones in genres that are sometimes considered among the pinnacles of human creativity: from sonnets to short stories or whole novels. The quality of this output has however been disputed (see Cicero, forthcoming for the description of some published works of this kind and their linguistic features).

There are also views that consider the issue problematic on a cultural level. From the perspective of the writer, for example, in a recent essay Ted Chiang (2024) has introduced the argument that, for some kinds of artistic production, human beings are simply not interested in looking at output generated by automatic systems, independently from its quality.

Even if the argument forcefully presented in the essay is also arguably underdeveloped, it could well be a realistic one, at least in some areas, such as high-profile literature. The relationship with a human author is part and parcel of the practices of some sections of the publishing industry, even in relation with marketing techniques, and it is therefore perfectly possible that for example readers could reject novels written by AIs. However, in different areas, where the author's role seems often much less relevant in the eyes of the public than it is in literature, things could move in a completely different way. TV serials or movies, for example, could conceivably dispense altogether with human authors and still keep their place in media ecosystems.

3 Evaluation

In such a context, issues of quality come to the fore. How high is the quality of AI output for creative texts? It is often difficult to accurately assess it, even for human productions. However, at least for some tasks, it is actually possible to have objective and robust evaluations, based on objective feature, detailed sets of guidelines, high numbers of human evaluators and so on (see e.g. Tavosanis, 2024 for an evaluation framework).

Many evaluations of this kind have shown that, at least for some tasks, the quality of AI output is already comparable to the quality of human professional output. This is especially true if the comparison is made with the raw output of a single human professional, before any external editing or review has been carried out. This is true even in languages different from English, languages where the quality of output is clearly lessened (for Italian, see e. g. Papa & Tavosanis, 2020 for translation; Tavosanis, forthcoming for improvement of text clarity).

Of course, for the most creative tasks, this evaluation is much more difficult and must rely on subjective judgments (exactly as for human texts). It is no surprise, therefore, that some of the most interesting kinds of evaluations have been carried out using format such as those of the simple challenge between humans and LLMs (Marco et al., 2024). Often, it is clear that the AI product is inferior to the human one—and in the field of literature there are still no cases of commercial successes for generated texts (and certainly not for lack of trying).

It seems therefore that there are limits for at least some kind of creation. That seems linked to basic features like the statistical nature of the systems and the need to have huge corpora for training. From the linguistic point of view, it has been persuasively argued that some rare constructions, easy to interpret for human beings on the basis of semantics, are difficult to "understand" for current generative systems (Wilson et al., 2023; Weissweiler et al., 2024).

The same kind of issues could be linked to the often-remarked-upon difficulty of AI systems in "understanding" and generating different types of texts: those based on humour and irony, but also those based on the use of less documented styles (including everything linked to the informal register) and so on. Surely, some of those difficulties could—and will—be mitigated by various techniques. However, it is absolutely not a given that current technologies will help in that: the abilities of the systems seem linked to the sheer quantity of texts used for training, and the main sources of easily-available texts of good quality seem already exhausted for all the main languages of the world. Even the best experts have diverging opinions regarding the possibility of development of LLMs: therefore, any kind of significant improvement in abilities can certainly be hoped for, but certainly not considered inevitable.

4 Conclusions

In front of the uncertainty, one of the best strategies we can have is to experiment and to be willing to try new things. In some contexts, lacking clear evaluation frameworks, there is simply no substitute for first-hand experience.

Today, this seems certainly true also for the relation between current "artificial intelligence" technologies and language. We feel that the essays collected in this section will be of help in that, and we look forward to learning many new things from them.

References

Bergs, A. (2019). What, if anything, is linguistic creativity? *Gestalt Theory, 41*(2), 173–184.

Chiang, T. (2024). Why A.I. Isn't going to make art. *The New Yorker*, 31 August.

Cicero, T. (forthcoming). *Esercizi di stile. La narrativa per l'infanzia delle intelligenze artificiali. AI-Linguistica. Linguistic Studies on AI-Generated Texts and Discourses.*

Marco, G. et al. (2024). Pron vs prompt: Can large language models already challenge a world-class fiction author at creative text writing? *arXiv preprint.* https://arxiv.org/abs/2407.01119

Mollick, E. (2024). *Co-intelligence*. Penguin.

Narayanan, A., & Kapoor, S. (2024). *Silicon snake oil*. Princeton.

Papa, S., & Tavosanis, M. (2020). Valutazione umana di Google Traduttore e DeepL per le traduzioni di testi giornalistici dall'inglese verso l'italiano. In: J. Monti, F. Dell'Orletta, & F. Tamburini (Eds.), *CLiC-it 2020—Proceedings of the seventh Italian conference on computational linguistics* (pp. 1–7). CEUR Workshop Proceedings.

Peeperkorn, M. et al. (2024). Is temperature the creativity parameter of large language models? In: *Proceedings of the 15th International Conference on Computational Creativity (ICCC'24).* https://arxiv.org/abs/2405.00492

Tavosanis, M. (2018). *Lingue e intelligenza artificiale*. Carocci.

Tavosanis, M. (2024). Valutare la qualità dei testi generati in lingua italiana. *AI-Linguistica. Linguistic Studies on AI-Generated Texts and Discourses, 1*, 1. https://doi.org/10.62408/ai-ling.v1i1.14

Tavosanis, M. (forthcoming). Valutare la riformulazione automatica. In: *Amministrazione attiva: semplicità e chiarezza per la comunicazione amministrativa.*

Weissweiler, L., Köksal, A., & Schütze, H. (2024). Hybrid human-LLM corpus construction and LLM evaluation for rare linguistic phenomena. *arXiv preprint* arXiv:2403.06965.

Wilson, M., Petty, J., & Frank, R. (2023). How abstract is linguistic generalization in large language models? Experiments with argument structure. *Transactions of the Association for Computational Linguistics*, 11, 1377–1395. https://doi.org/10.1162/tacl_a_00608

Beyond ChatGPT: AI Applications to Italian Language Varieties

Francesco Bianco and Stefania Elisa Ghezzi

Abstract Since its first release (2022), ChatGPT became part of the scientists' workflow, both as tool and research subject. The awesome opportunities related to such powerful application increased the interests of scholars for Artificial Intelligence (AI) and Natural Language Processing (NLP), attracting not only computer scientists, AI and data architects and computational linguists, but also (digital) humanists, philosophers, and literary scholars.

ChatGPT, and Large Language Models' (LLM) application in text generation, however, are not the only possible NLP outcome in language and text sciences in the broadest sense.

In this paper, we will present part of our current research program, which is focused on investigating some Italian language varieties with the help of AI and data science. Our goals are multiple: (a) testing the existence of some presumed obsolete varieties; (b) defining boundaries between similar linguistic varieties and, more in general, measuring the distance between language varieties; and (c) defining a set of language features and testing the weight of them in assigning a given utterance to its language variety.

We will present the results of our first experiment, as well as our next scheduled research steps, and we will reflect on how AI can help sociolinguists and language historians in their daily work.

Keywords AI · Artificial intelligence · Data science · DH · Digital humanities · Italian language · Language varieties · Machine learning · ML · Natural language processing · NLP

Francesco Bianco (author of §§ 3, 3.1, 3.1.1, 3.2.2 and 4).
Stefania Elisa Ghezzi (author of §§ 1, 2, 2.1 and 3.2.1).

F. Bianco (✉) · S. E. Ghezzi
Department of Romance Languages, Palacký University Olomouc, Olomouc, Czechia
e-mail: francesco.bianco@upol.cz

A. Micalizzi (ed.), *Artificial Creativity*, Springer Proceedings in Humanities and Social Sciences, https://doi.org/10.1007/978-3-031-88334-7_2

1 Introduction

The outstanding performances of Large Language Models' (LLM) software systems, especially applied to the generation of texts, made Artificial Intelligence (AI) and Natural Language Processing (NLP) two inseparable notions (Grimaldi, 2023: 181).[1] In everyday speech, talking about AI not only implies reference to generative AI-based systems[2]; often, it directly refers to some software based on LLMs which implement Human-Machine Dialogue.

The so-called AI boom (Knight, 2023), however, is part of the more general diffusion of disciplines, technologies and tools which, thanks to the increasing performance of recent CPUs and (above all) GPUs, made computers able to effectively apply Machine Learning (ML) models, including Artificial Neural Networks, to massive amounts of data, in order to solve a wide range of problems. Within the framework of this study, we intend to reflect on some possible applications of the tools, technologies, and procedures mostly used by AI engineers and data scientists to research on Italian language varieties. Therefore, within this context, the AI label is considered in a broad sense, as all range of tools and methods based on ML. Our first experiment aims to verify whether a ML-based script can correctly classify texts as written in two different varieties of the same natural language (in this case, Italian), and to outline how the implementation of more refined classifiers can help our future work.

2 Popular Italian: An Elusive Variety

Our current research program deals with "*Italiano popolare*" ('popular Italian,' henceforth PI), which is the variety of Italian used by illiterate or people with low education, in both spoken and written utterances, where non-standard elements (from the underlying dialects or other language varieties) appear at all levels.

PI has been identified and variously defined by scholars (Cortelazzo, 1972; De Mauro, 1970) since the early 1970s. Throughout the last decades, PI has been one of the most studied varieties of modern Italian. Nowadays, several problems with PI are still unresolved. Some scholars (Bartoli Langeli, 2000; Bruni, 1978, 1984; Cortelazzo, 1972; Marazzini, 2004, 2006) consider PI to exist only as a written variety, PI being written Italian with some elements of the spoken language introduced by the low cultural level of the writer, whereas other ones think PI to be also (Berruto, 2020; Fresu, 2016; Lubello, 2018), and even *primarily* a spoken variety (Guerini, 2016). Another problem concerns PI's current status. Does such variety still exist, and play an important and active role (Berruto, 2014), within

[1] The binomial becomes a trinomial if we consider also the strong relationship between NLP and computational linguistics; see Ježek and Sprugnoli (2023).

[2] This is also the perspective adopted in the current conference.

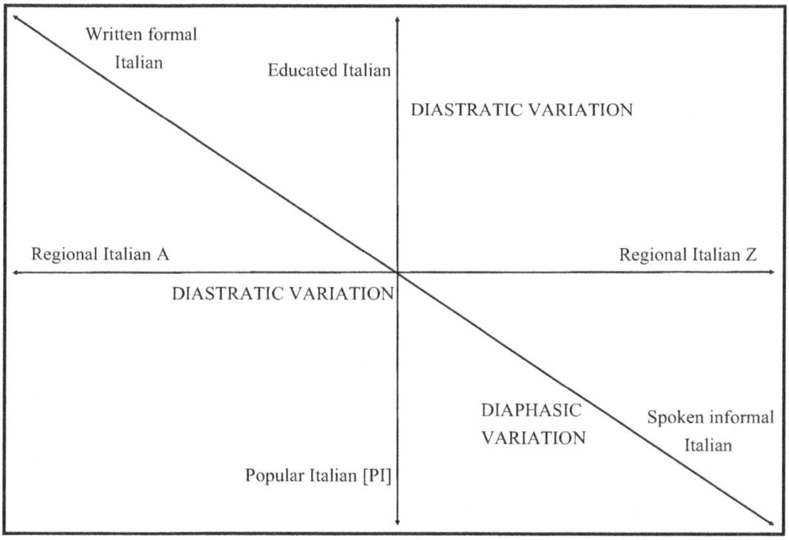

Fig. 1 Italian language varieties (Berruto, 2010: 1551). In English, some scholars also refer to PI as to *"folk (regional) Italian"* (Cerruti, 2011)

the framework of the contemporary Italian repertoire (see Fig. 1), or should it be considered obsolescent (Cerruti, 2021), or even close to disappearing (Cortelazzo, 2001; Lepschy, 2002; Renzi, 2000)?

Two elements, in particular, make contemporary PI an elusive study subject. The first one is its proximity with other substandard varieties, especially with colloquial Italian, which shares many of PI's features, as outlined by Berruto (2020: 140). Both varieties can be considered as poles of a *continuum*, with significant overlap in spoken utterances and informal situations. The second one is the appearance, in the last decades, of a new form of standard Italian (SI), the so-called «italiano dell'uso medio» (Sabatini, 2011/1985) or «neo-standard» (Berruto, 2020[3]), which includes features common to PI.

2.1 *PI Features*

As mentioned, PI is defined by features at all language levels. The following list, though not exhaustive, contains some of the main traits, as described by scholars (D'Achille, 1994: 65–77; Fresu, 2014: 211–217; Berruto, 2020: 140–143; Guerini, 2024: 69–78). These appear in comparison with SI:

[3] Neo-standard Italian is already so defined and described in the first edition of the book (La Nuova Italia Scientifica), which dates back to 1987.

- **absence of punctuation**: *Mio caro fratello Scrivo questa mia lettera facendovi sapere che adesso grazie Iddio stiamo tutti e due alquando bene ti scrissi un'altra mia lettera e non ho ricevuto nessuna tua risposta non so se la mia lettera lai ricevuta fatemi sapere tutti in tua famiglia come state* (Bianco, 2013: 115)[4];
- **segmentation errors**: *Initalia* (SI *in Italia* 'in Italy;' Bianco, 2013: 105); *li talia* (SI *l'Italia* 'Italy' [literally: 'the Italy']; Salvatore, 2017: 143);
- **phonological features of the underlying dialects** (Fresu, 2014: 212): *tembo* (SI *tempo* 'time;' Di Stasio, 1991: 29), *sorela* (SI *sorella* 'sister;' Cancian, 1999: 74)[5];
- **declension metaplasms**: *moglia* (SI *moglie* 'wife;' D'Achille, 1994: 70), *il Signoro* (SI *il Signore* 'the Lord;' Bianco, 2013: 107);
- **exchanges between adjectives and adverbs** (in particular, the adjectival use of adverbs): *un posto meglio* (SI *un posto migliore* 'a better place;' Fresu, 2014: 213) *cantare felice* (SI *cantare felicemente* 'to sing happily;' Guerini, 2024: 73);
- **analytical reinforcement of synthetic comparatives and superlatives**: *il più migliore* (SI *il migliore* 'the best;' Fresu, 2014: 213); *molto ottimo* (SI *ottimo* 'very good;' D'Achille, 2010: 725);
- **non-standard sequences of clitic pronouns unrelated**: *non si ci vede* (SI *non ci si vede* 'we don't see each other;' Fresu, 2014: 213);
- **pronominal duplications**: *le volevo chiederle* (SI *le volevo chiedere/volevo chiederle* 'I would like to ask you;' Bianco, 2016: 523); *ti vorrei spiegarti* (SI *ti vorrei spiegare/vorrei spiegarti* 'I would like to explain to you;' D'Achille, 1994: 71);
- **the so-called che polivalente** (D'Achille, 2010: 725): *l'ufficio che vai a prendere i soldi* (SI *l'ufficio dove vai a prendere i soldi* 'the office where you go to get the money;' Salvatore, 2017: 266)[6]; *un pezzo di strada che non passava mai nessuno* (SI *un pezzo di strada dove non passava mai nessuno* 'a stretch of road where no one ever passed;' Guerini, 2024: 77);
- **mismatch agreement** (Cortelazzo, 1972: 79): *in quel giorni* [plural] (SI *in quei giorni* 'in that days;' Cancian, 1999: 47); *qualche uomini* (D'Achille, 2010: 725);
- **overextension of dove 'where' in the relative clause**: *il giorno dove mi sono sposata* (SI *il giorno in cui mi sono sposata* 'the day I got married;' D'Achille, 2010: 725);

[4] More in general, the punctuation in PI written documents is non-standard, often chaotic (D'Achille, 1994: 68).

[5] Sonorization of postnasal consonants is typical in Italian central-southern dialects and well documented in many written documents in PI from that area (D'Achille, 1994: 69; Cortelazzo, 1972: 123–126). Geminate consonants are often degeminated in Italian northern dialects (Loporcaro, 2013: 85–86).

[6] Che *polivalente* is a label applied to a range of morphosyntactic phenomena, with different degrees of diastratic markedness (Sabatini, 2011/1985: 14–15), and already documented in old Italian (D'Achille, 1990: 205–260). Only some of them can be considered reliable PI markers (D'Achille, 1994: 72). Salvatore (2017: 256–274) provides a rich exemplification of the trait in PI from a corpus of emigrants' letters.

- **high frequency of hanging topics** (D'Achille, 1994: 70): *Tiziano Ferro sono andato al concerto* (SI *sono andato al concerto di Tiziano Ferro* 'I went to Tiziano Ferro's concert'[7]);
- **conditional sentences with double conditional or with double past subjunctive** (Fresu, 2014: 214): *se saresti venuto avresti visto con i tuoi occhi* (SI *se fossi venuto avresti visto con i tuoi occhi* 'if you had come you would have seen with your own eyes'); *se lo sapessi, te lo dicessi* (SI *se lo sapessi, te lo direi* 'if I knew, I would tell you');
- **exchange between auxiliary verbs avere 'to have' and essere 'to be'**: *sono mangiato* (SI *ho mangiato* 'I have eaten;' Fresu, 2014: 214); *avrebbe stato* (SI *sarebbe stato* '[it] would have been;' Bianco, 2013: 108);
- **analogical verbal forms**: *misimo* (SI *mettemmo* '[we] placed;' D'Achille, 1994: 72); *combattavamo* (SI *combattevamo* '[we] were fighting;' Guerini, 2024: 75);
- **words and expressions from bureaucratic language** (Bianco, 2016: 521–522): *Spero che al ricevere la presente stati tutti bene* 'I hope when you will receive this [letter] you'll be fine' (Bianco, 2013: 116);
- **word formation errors** (D'Achille, 1994: 74 and 2010: 725): *indispiacente* (SI *spiacente* 'sorry'), *tranquillizzanti* (SI *tranquillanti* 'tranquilizers'), *dichiara* (SI *dichiarazione* 'declaration'), *prolungo* (SI *prolungamento* 'extension');
- **malapropisms** (Fresu, 2012): *autobilancia* (SI *autoambulanza* 'ambulance'), *comprativa* (SI *cooperativa* 'cooperative');
- **high number of generic words with high polysemy** (Fresu, 2014): *cosa* ('thing'); *roba* ('stuff').

As outlined by Berruto (2020: 142), some phenomena are supposed to be exclusive of PI (primary features), whereas other ones are common of other varieties (secondary features), especially colloquial Italian. Such traits, in order to be considered relevant, must occur with a high frequence, or in a formal context. For example, an utterance as

IT. (PI)	se avrei saputo che avrebbe piovuto, non sarei uscito
EN. (literally)	*if I would have known it would have rained, I wouldn't have gone out
EN.	If I had known it would rain, I wouldn't have gone out

could be always considered as a PI marker, as it contains a hypothetical period with double conditional, which does not belong to colloquial Italian. On the contrary, an utterance like

IT. (PI)	se sapevo che pioveva, non uscivo
EN. (literally)	*if I knew it rained, I didn't go out
EN.	If I had known it would rain, I wouldn't have gone out

[7] Example from *ParlaTO* (Cerruti & Ballarè, 2021), a corpus of Italian spoken language accessible at the URL https://kiparla.it/parlato/. All URLs in the paper have been checked on September 5th, 2024.

would be considered as a PI indicator only when executed within a planned, medium-high formal (possibly written) utterance.

3 A Classifier of PI and SI Texts

As above mentioned, our goal is to verify whether an ML-based classifier is able to correctly identify popular texts within a corpus of both popular and standard texts, i.e., texts written either in PI or SI.

3.1 Set-up

In order to set up this experiment, we compiled a text corpus made of both popular and standard texts, which constitute the experiment dataset (see below, Fig. 2). Popular texts have been chosen among collections of published texts (Bianco, 2013; Cancian, 1999; Di Stasio, 1991; Spitzer, 1921/1976) or from the website of the Archivio Diaristico Nazionale (ADN).[8] They all belong, as usual for PI, to the so-called «forme primarie della scrittura» (Folena, 1985: 5), mostly letters and diaries. These textual genres are characterized by rather constant features, such as paratextual elements (place and date) and opening and closing formulas, which implies a statistically relevant use of some keywords, such as the adjective "*cara/o*" ('dear') or "*carissima/o*" ('dearest') in the very first positions of the document:

> Caro fratello, / in quando a mia suocera e mio suocero ci abbiamo fatto le garanzie (Di Stasio, 1991: 47);
> Carissima sorella / Con ritardo rispondo alla tua lettera (Bianco, 2013: 116).

	label	text
0	std	L'Italia è una Repubblica democratica, fondata...
1	std	L'Italia, ufficialmente Repubblica Italiana, è...
2	pop	Centilissima Compagnia di a sicurazione Colomb...
3	pop	Cara sorella, Abbiamo aspettato fino alla sett...
4	std	Come saprete già, Empoli-Lecce è cominciata co...

Fig. 2 Preview of the dataset (screenshot from the notebook)

[8] The ADN is a public archive located in Pieve Santo Stefano (Italy), which collects private written memories since 1984. See http://www.archiviodiari.org/.

Therefore, in order to minimize the impact of such constants (which could help the right text classification) on the task, we performed preliminary adjustments to the corpus: (a) we cut away the opening and closing sentences for some items classified as popular, as well as the paratextual elements; and (b) we included some specimens of the same textual genres (letters and diaries) in the baseline corpus written by highly educated people. Besides this, the baseline corpus is composed of several kinds of text, aiming to faithfully represent if not the SI at least a set of varieties which can approximate the idea of common Italian: press articles (from newspapers, magazines and webzines), encyclopedia entries (both from Wikipedia and Treccani[9] publications), non-fiction and literary texts (in prose), social media posts, private texts such as letters, diaries, mobile text messages, and emails.[10] For this very first experiment, the whole dataset is composed of 100 texts, 64 of which are marked as "*std*" (standard) and 36 marked as "*pop*(*ular*)".

3.1.1 Technical Environment

The experiment was performed through a combination of classical tools for NLP and data science. The script was written in Python and run on a Jupyter Notebook.[11]

3.2 *Workflow*

3.2.1 Preprocessing

All text were preprocessed as follows: punctuation marks have been removed; capital letters were converted to lowercase; stop-words were also removed[12]; finally, the texts were stemmed,[13] as common in many text-mining tasks, including text classification.

[9] We refer to the publications of the Istituto della Enciclopedia Italiana (Rome, Italy), which are nowadays available on the web portal https://www.treccani.it/.

[10] Many documents of our corpus can be considered as specimens of the so-called "*e-taliano*", defined as the computer-mediated Italian or, rather, device-mediated Italian. See Antonelli (2012, 2014), Pistolesi (2014) and Lubello (2016).

[11] The Python version is 3.10.9; the version of the notebook server is 6.5.2. Main used libraries: Numpy (v. 1.23.5), Pandas (v. 1.5.3), ScikitLearn (v. 1.2.1).

[12] We considered the list of Italian stopwords included in the ScikitLearn package (see above, Footnote 11).

[13] Stemming is a preprocessing technique finalized to minimize the morphological (inflectional) variation of a text. It can be defined as the process of reducing an inflected form to the root one (the so-called *stem*). In Italian, it often consists in dropping the right periphery of a given (inflected) word, i.e. its inflectional morpheme. E.g. (from the corpus): *religiose* 'religious (feminine, plural)' → *religios*. An alternative technique is the lemmatization, which reduces inflectional variants to one morphological lexeme, considered as the default one (as a dictionary entry): e.g. *religiose* → *religioso* 'religious (masculine, singular)'. For an easy and effective introduction, see Murel and Kavlakoglu (2023). In our experiment, texts have been preprocessed through ScikitLearn's PorterStemmer built-in function, which supports also Italian language. On the PorterStemming algorithm, see Porter (1980).

```
array([0, 0, 2, 0, 0, 0, 0, 0, 0, 0, 0, 0, 0, 0, 0, 0, 0, 0, 0, 0, 0, 0,
       0, 0, 0, 0, 0, 0, 0, 0, 0, 0, 0, 0, 0, 0, 0, 0, 0, 0, 0, 0, 0, 0,
       0, 0, 0, 0, 0, 0, 0, 0, 0, 0, 0, 0, 1, 0, 0, 0, 0, 0, 0, 0, 0, 0,
       0, 0, 0, 0, 0, 0, 0, 0, 0, 0, 0, 0, 0, 0, 0, 0, 0, 0, 0, 0, 0, 0,
```

Fig. 3 Example of (part of) a vectorized text

In order to feed the ML models, the collection of preprocessed text documents—namely root forms sequences without punctuation or capital letters—has been converted to a (sparse) matrix of token counts (see above, Fig. 3). This task was accomplished with the ScikitLearn's CountVectorizer built-in function,[14] which implements a "classic" bag-of-words (BOW) approach.

3.2.2 Modelization

Once vectorized, the dataset has been split into two parts: 70 texts, namely vectors, have been used to train the models, whereas the remaining 30 have been kept for the tests.

We have compared, on both training and testing sets, 5 different models, which cover a quite wide range of classifiers: logistic regression (LR), support-vector machine (SVM), two (gaussian and multinomial) naive bayes classifiers (GNB, MNB), and decision tree (DT), all in their ScikitLearn implementations for Python.[15] Furthermore, we applied a dummy classifier[16] as the baseline which assigns every individual the most frequent label in the training set (i.e., in our case, "*std*").

The models' performances were mainly evaluated through their accuracy.[17] For a finer-grained analysis, however, we also consider the confusion matrix values,[18] which are shown in Table 1.

[14] See https://scikit-learn.org/stable/modules/generated/sklearn.feature_extraction.text.CountVectorizer.html.

[15] Within this paper, we do not describe the models, and we do not go into the merits of the discussion on advantages and limits of every single model.

[16] We can refer to a classifier as 'dummy,' when it makes predictions that ignore the input features. ScikitLearn's dummy classifiers are described at https://scikit-learn.org/stable/modules/generated/sklearn.dummy.DummyClassifier.html.

[17] Accuracy, defined as the ratio of right predictions to total ones, is a standard ML evaluation metrics for classification tasks. Its main limit is to hide the difference between different kinds of errors, and therefore to assign the same weight to all of them. Other metrics, such as precision, recall, and F-score, combine test results differently. Specific tasks can also require modified version of accuracy, such as the so-called balanced accuracy or the recent *Petitta score* (Petitta et al., 2023), which assigns different weights to a false positive (FP) and a false negative (FN). For our purposes, however, we would not gain any advantage in discriminating between FPs and FNs, therefore the choice of accuracy as evaluation metrics makes perfect sense.

[18] Namely: true negatives (TNs), i.e., standard texts classified as being standard; FPs, i.e., standard texts classified as being popular; FNs, i.e., popular texts classified as being standard; true positives (TPs), i.e., popular texts classified as being popular.

Table 1 Models' performance comparison (accuracy and confusion matrix)

Model	Accuracy (%)	Confusion Matrix Values			
		TN	FP	FN	TP
LR	93	20	2	0	8
SVM	93	19	1	1	9
GNB	90	18	1	2	9
MNB	90	17	0	3	10
DT	83	20	5	0	5
Dummy	66	20	10	0	0

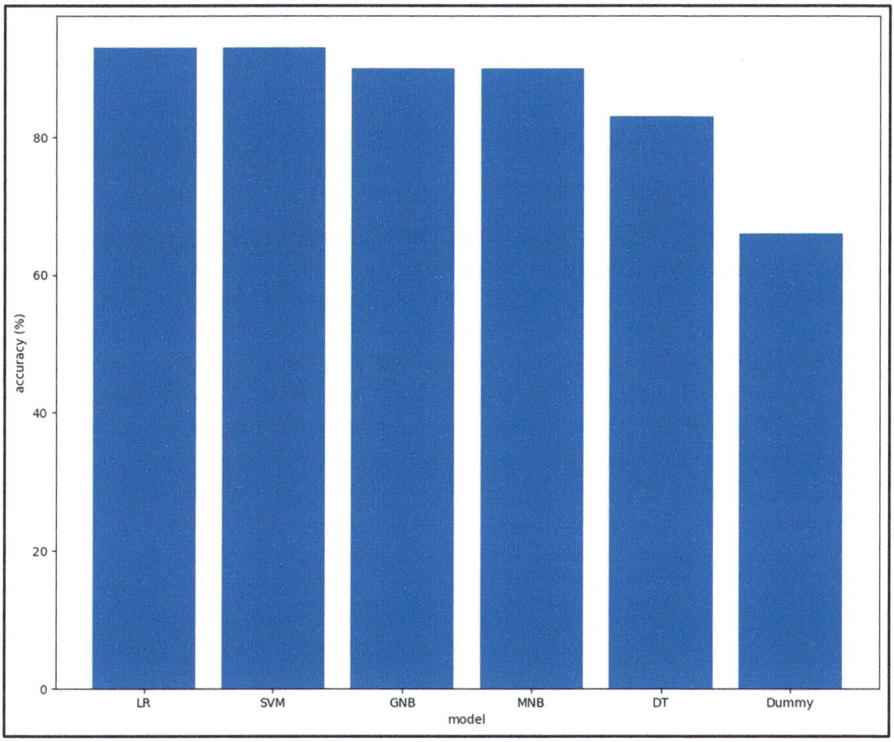

Fig. 4 Models' performance comparison (accuracy)

As shown in both Table 1 and Fig. 4, LR and SVM obtained the best performance (93% of accuracy), whereas the DT performed the lowest; its score (83%) surpasses the dummy classifier,[19] which testifies that whatever the chosen model a text classification based on language varieties is possible.[20]

[19] Since the chosen behavior of the baseline is to classify all texts as being standard (the most frequent label), its accuracy is expected to be around their percentage within the whole dataset, i.e., around 64% (see above, § 3.1).

[20] It is important to remember, in this context, that we are dealing with variation within the same language system (i.e., the Italian language).

4 Further Research Steps

The system we set up is very simple. As mentioned in § 3.2.1 (see above), our text vectorization implements a BOW approach, which is the easiest way to vectorize texts, quite effective for some basic and "classic" NLP tasks, such as spam detection or sentiment analysis, but it is not designed to give us insight into language varieties features. Indeed, the BOW approach provides vectors which just consider word occurrences, regardless of their position and inflection; therefore, no syntactic and morphological phenomena can affect the classification. Nevertheless, as we showed (see above, § 3.2.2), the classifier reached the main goal, even in unfavorable conditions, which encourages us to continue the study.

In particular, three axes of improvement can be outlined:

1. The number and perhaps the length of the text must be increased. In our first experiment, we preferred to feed the model with texts of a similar length, therefore we cut many documents, in order to make them as similar as possible. In our next experiment, we plan to test how a different strategy, namely a wider range of text lengths, can affect the classification, in terms of accuracy. As to the quantity of texts, we would like to build a dataset in the order of thousands of individuals, intended to improve the knowledge of PI[21];
2. As to text preprocessing, our procedure will be refined; in particular, we plan to test word embeddings (Mikolov et al., 2013a, 2013b) and LLMs, such as *BERT* (Devlin et al., 2019) and its implementations for Italian (Polignano et al., 2019),[22] instead of the BOW;
3. We plan to practice feature engineering on the original dataset. Current NLP approaches only consider words as primary features. BOW, in the best hypothesis, can only help to value the «keyness» (Bondi & Scott, 2010) of a given word in a text or in a text corpus.[23] Embeddings and LLMs arrive to consider words context and can maybe provide some information about syntax and semantics. Research in linguistics nonbeing the main goal of such technologies, we foresee

[21] So far, within the corpora of Italian language, no tools were specifically designed to explore PI (Chiari, 2012; Ježek & Sprugnoli, 2023: 19–22, 206–207). A new project (P.I.: Francesco Bianco), starting in 2025 and funded by the University Grenoble Alpes (France) through the GATES (*Grenoble ATtractiveness and ExcellenceS*) programme, is intended to design and implement an *Archive of Popular Italian Documents* (*APID*). The aim of this project is to contribute to fill the aforementioned gap, providing scholars a dataset of PI documents, with a light TEI (*Text Encoding Initiative*) markup, through a flexible, minimalist and durable IT architecture. Such initiative should encourage the application of quantitative methods, digital humanities and data science tools, which are mostly neglected in this field of studies, although some recent works start to explore this dimension (Sprugnoli et al., 2018).

[22] For Italian, see also *UmBERTo*, «a Roberta-based Language Model trained on large Italian Corpora», https://github.com/musixmatchresearch/umberto.

[23] In corpus linguistics, «[a] key word may be defined as a *word which occurs with unusual frequency in a given text*» (Scott, 1997: 236, emphasis in the source). On the notion of keyness, see also Bondi and Scott (2010) and Gabrielatos (2018).

testing some different approaches. In particular, we would like to define some features to automatically or semi-automatically extract from texts and use them to complement or even replace the text vectors.

First, we expect the working of these axes will improve the classification quality. Indeed, a truly reliable classifier could be used to measure the distance of a given document from SI and PI, considered as prototypes or, better, poles of a continuum along which it is possible to imagine infinite intermediate degrees. As a matter of fact, redefining PI as a scalar, gradable notion (Bianco & Špička, 2017: 21) can be useful for understand some similarities and common points between classic PI texts and other kinds of documents, such as school assignments or even published books.[24]

Moreover, with a dataset composed of vectorized language phenomena at all levels, and not just word sequences, we are confident to find out, on a quantitative basis, which traits must be considered the most relevant PI features, for example through Spearman's rank correlation coefficient (Spearman, 1904), or Pearson (1895) correlation coefficient. Such findings could help to draw some conclusions on the relationship between PI and other neighboring substandard varieties, such as colloquial Italian, spoken Italian, «exposed writing» (Castillo Gómez, 2020[25]), or some varieties of "*e-taliano*".[26]

In conclusion, the experiment described in this paper is just the first step of a long-term research program, which aims to bring together old (qualitative) and new (quantitative) research methods and apply them to improve our knowledge about PI and, more in general, about the contemporary Italian repertoire.

Acknowledgements The funding for the present publication was provided by the Czech Ministry of Education, Youth and Sports for specific research to Palacký University Olomouc (IGA_FF_2024_011).

References

Antonelli, G. (2012). Si parla italiano: si scrive e-taliano? In P. A. Di Pretorio & R. Unfer Lukoschik (Eds.), *Lingua e letteratura italiana 150 anni dopo l'Unità* (pp. 83–91). Martin Meidenbauer.

Antonelli, G. (2014). L'e-taliano: una nuova realtà tra le varietà linguistiche italiane? In E. Garavelli & E. Suomela-Harma (Eds.), *Dal manoscritto al web: canali e modalità di trasmissione dell'italiano* (Vol. 2, pp. 537–556). Cesati.

[24] Aresti and Nigrisoli (2017) already considered PI in a more flexible way as former scholars. Sprugnoli et al. (2018) analyzed Italian high school student writing skills with some NLP tools, without referring them to PI variety. Cortelazzo and Tuzzi (2018: 687–690) used Correspondence Analysis to plot the lexical distance among Elena Ferrante's works and other Italian writers' ones, with the intent to find out and reveal Ferrante's identity.

[25] For Italian, see Geymonat (2014).

[26] See above, Footnote 10.

Aresti, A., & Nigrisoli, W. V. (2017). Dalla spada alla penna. Osservazioni sulla lingua del capitano Lorenzo Adami nelle lettere alla regina Cristina di Svezia e al cardinale Azzolino. In F. Bianco & J. Špička (Eds.), *Perché scrivere? Motivazioni, scelte, risultati. Atti del convegno internazionale di studi (Olomouc, 27–28 marzo 2015)* (pp. 239–250). Cesati. Supplement materials at https://perchescrivere.upol.cz/atti/ms/arestinigrisoli/

Bartoli Langeli, A. (2000). *La scrittura dell'italiano*. il Mulino.

Berruto, G. (2010). Varietà. In R. Simone (Ed.), *Enciclopedia dell'italiano* (pp. 1550–1553). Istituto della Enciclopedia Italiana. https://www.treccani.it/enciclopedia/varieta_(Enciclopedia-dell'Italiano)/

Berruto, G. (2014). Esiste ancora l'italiano popolare? Una rivisitazione. In P. Danler & C. Konecny (Eds.), *Dall'architettura della lingua italiana all'architettura linguistica dell'Italia. Saggi in omaggio a Heidi Siller–Runggaldier* (pp. 277–290). Peter Lang.

Berruto, G. (2020). *Sociolinguistica dell'italiano contemporaneo*. Carocci.

Bianco, F. (2013). Le lettere dei migranti irpini fra italiano, dialetto e lingua straniera. In C. Albizu et al. (Eds.), *Variante et varieté—Variante e varietà—Variante y variedad—Variante und Varietät. Actes du V^ie^ dies Romanicus Turicensis, Zurich, 24–25 juin 2011* (pp. 101–117). ETS.

Bianco, F. (2016). Burocratese nascosto nell'italiano moderno. In G. Ruffino & M. Castiglione (Eds.), *La lingua variabile nei testi letterari, artistici e funzionali contemporanei. Analisi, interpretazione, traduzione. Atti del XIII Congresso SILFI Società Internazionale di linguistica e Filologia Italiana, Palermo 22–24 settembre 2014* (pp. 519–528). Cesati.

Bianco, F., & Špička, J. (2017). Una domanda ancora aperta. In F. Bianco & J. Špička (Eds.), *Perché scrivere? Motivazioni, scelte, risultati. Atti del convegno internazionale di studi (Olomouc, 27–28 marzo 2015)* (pp. 13–28). Cesati. http://perchescrivere.upol.cz/atti/ms/biancospicka/

Bondi, M., & Scott, M. (Eds.). (2010). *Keyness in texts*. Benjamins.

Bruni, F. (1978). Traduzione, tradizione e diffusione della cultura: contributo alla lingua dei semicolti. *Quaderni Storici*, 38, 523–554.

Bruni, F. (1984). *L'italiano. Elementi di storia della lingua e della cultura*. UTET.

Cancian, S. (1999). *Una raccolta di lettere italiane inviate agli emigrati in Canada, 1954–1955*. MA thesis, McGill University. https://escholarship.mcgill.ca/concern/theses/kd17cw24b

Castillo Gómez, A. (2020). Words on walls. An approach to exposed writing in early modern Europe. *Journal of Early Modern Studies*, 9, 57–82. https://oajournals.fupress.net/index.php/bsfm-jems/article/view/11190

Cerruti, M. (2011). Regional varieties of Italian in the linguistic repertoire. *International Journal of the Sociology of Language*, 210, 9–28. https://www.degruyter.com/document/doi/10.1515/ijsl.2011.028/html

Cerruti, M. (2021). Variazione sociolinguistica e processi di grammaticalizzazione. In S. Ballarè & G. Inglese (Eds.), *Tipologia e sociolinguistica: verso un approccio integrato allo studio della variazione* (pp. 53–80). Officinaventuno.

Cerruti, M., & Ballarè, S. (2021). ParlaTO: corpus del parlato di Torino. *Bollettino dell'Atlante Linguistico Italiano*, 44, 171–196.

Chiari, I. (2012). Corpora e risorse linguistiche per l'italiano. Stato dell'arte, problemi e prospettive. *Italienisch*, 68, 90–105.

Cortelazzo, M. (1972). *Avviamento critico allo studio della dialettologia italiana*, vol. 3, *Lineamenti di italiano popolare*. Pacini.

Cortelazzo, M. A. (2001). L'italiano e le sue varietà: una situazione in movimento. *Lingua e stile*, 36(3), 417–430.

Cortelazzo, M. A., & Tuzzi, A. (2018). What is Elena Ferrante? A comparative analysis of a secretive bestselling Italian writer. *Digital Scolarship in the Humanities*, 33(3), 685–702.

D'Achille, P. (1990). *Sintassi del parlato e tradizione scritta della lingua italiana. Analisi di testi dalle origini al secolo XVIII*. Bonacci.

D'Achille, P. (1994). L'italiano dei semicolti. In L. Serianni & P. Trifone (Eds.), *Storia della lingua italiana*, vol. 2, *Scritto e parlato* (pp. 41–79). Einaudi.

D'Achille, P. (2010). Italiano popolare. In R. Simone (Ed.), *Enciclopedia dell'italiano* (pp. 723–725). Istituto della Enciclopedia Italiana. https://www.treccani.it/enciclopedia/italiano-popolare_(Enciclopedia-dell'Italiano)/

De Mauro, T. (1970). Per lo studio dell'italiano popolare unitario. In A. Rossi (Ed.), *Lettere da una tarantata* (pp. 43–75). Laterza.

Devlin, J., et al. (2019). BERT: Pre-training of deep bidirectional transformers for language understanding. In J. Burstein, C. Doran, & T. Solorio (Eds.), *Proceedings of the 2019 Conference of the North American Chapter of the Association for Computational Linguistics. Human Language Technologies*, vol. 1, *Long and Short Papers*. ACL. https://aclanthology.org/N19-1423/

Di Stasio, G. (Ed.). (1991). *Ti sono scritto questa lettera. Le lettere che gli emigranti non scriveranno più*. Mursia.

Folena, G. (1985). Premessa. In G. Folena (Ed.), *Le forme del diario* [*Quaderni di retorica e poetica*, 2] (pp. 5–10).

Fresu, R. (2012). Malapropismo, quel vocabolo deforme. *Treccani Magazine*, 17.5.2012. https://www.treccani.it/magazine/lingua_italiana/speciali/errori/Fresu.html

Fresu, R. (2014). Scritture dei semicolti. In G. Antonelli, M. Motolese, & L. Tomasin (Eds.), *Storia dell'italiano scritto*, vol. 3, *Italiano dell'uso* (pp. 195–223). Carocci.

Fresu, R. (2016). L'italiano dei semicolti. In S. Lubello (Ed.), *Manuale di linguistica italiana* (pp. 328–350). De Gruyter.

Gabrielatos, C. (2018). Keyness analysis. Nature, metrics and techniques. In C. Taylor & A. Marchi (Eds.), *Corpus approaches to discourse. A critical review* (pp. 225–258). Routledge.

Geymonat, F. (2014). Scritture esposte. In G. Antonelli, M. Motolese, & L. Tomasin (Eds.), *Storia dell'italiano scritto*, vol. 3, *Italiano dell'uso* (pp. 57–100). Carocci.

Grimaldi, C. (2023). Le evoluzioni delle applicazioni di IA nel campo linguistico: quale futuro per il lavoro terminologico? *AIDAinformazioni*, 41(3–4), 181–184. https://www.aidainformazioni.it/index.php/aidainformazioni/article/view/292/48

Guerini, F. (2016). Il corpus ParVa. Rilevanza per la ricerca e applicazioni didattiche. In F. Guerini (Ed.), *Italiano e dialetto bresciano in racconti di partigiani* (pp. 9–38). Aracne.

Guerini, F. (2024). L'italiano popolare. In S. Ballarè, I. Fiorentini, & E. Miola (Eds.), *Le varietà dell'italiano contemporaneo* (pp. 67–80). Carocci.

Ježek, E., & Sprugnoli, R. (2023). *Linguistica computazionale. Introduzione all'analisi automatica dei testi*. il Mulino.

Knight, W. (2023). Google's Gemini Is the real start of the generative AI boom. *Wired*, 7.12.2023. https://www.wired.com/story/google-gemini-generative-ai-boom/

Lepschy, G. C. (2002). Popular Italian: Fact or fiction? In G. C. Lepschy (Ed.), *Mother tongues and other reflections on the Italian language* (pp. 49–69). University of Toronto Press.

Loporcaro, M. (2013). *Profilo linguistico dei dialetti italiani*. Laterza.

Lubello, S. (Ed.) (2016). *L'e-taliano. Scriventi e scritture nell'era digitale*. Cesati.

Lubello, S. (2018). Scritture da lontano: semicolti campani e sondaggi dal corpus MeTrOpolis. *Testi e linguaggi*, 12, 229–237.

Marazzini, C. (2004). *Breve storia della lingua italiana*. il Mulino.

Marazzini, C. (2006). *La storia della lingua italiana attraverso i testi*. il Mulino.

Mikolov, T., et al. (2013a). Efficient estimation of word representations in vector space. In Y. Bengio & Y. Lecun (Eds.), *Proceedings of the International Conference on Learning Representations*. https://arxiv.org/abs/1301.3781

Mikolov, T., et al. (2013b). Linguistic regularities in continuous space word representations. In L. Vanderwende, H. Daumé III, & K. Kirchhoff (Eds.), *Proceedings of the 2013 Conference of the North American Chapter of the Association for Computational Linguistics. Human Language Technologies* (pp. 746–751). ACL. https://aclanthology.org/N13-1090/

Murel, J., & Kavlakoglu, E. (2023). *What is stemming?* https://www.ibm.com/topics/stemming

Pearson, K. (1895). Notes on regression and inheritance in the case of two parents. In *Proceedings of the Royal Society of London* (Vol. 58, pp. 240–242). Harrison.

Petitta, F., et al. (2023). Tools and metrics for data-driven operations knowledge (DOK). *Central European Journal of Applied Mathematics and Statistics*, 1, 69–73.

Pistolesi, E. (2014). Scritture digitali. In G. Antonelli, M. Motolese, & L. Tomasin (Eds.), *Storia dell'italiano scritto*, vol. 3, *Italiano dell'uso* (pp. 349–375). Carocci.

Polignano, M., et al. (2019). AlBERTo: Modeling Italian social media language with BERT. *Italian Journal of Computational Linguistics*, 5(2), 11–31. https://journals.openedition.org/ijcol/472

Porter, M. F. (1980). An algorithm for suffix stripping. *Program*, 14(3), 130–137.

Renzi, L. (2000). Le tendenze dell'italiano contemporaneo. *Note sul cambiamento linguistico nel breve periodo in Studi di lessicografia italiana*, 17, 279–319.

Sabatini, F. (2011/1985). "L'italiano dell'uso medio": una realtà tra le varietà linguistiche italiane. In V. Coletti et al. (Eds.), *L'italiano nel mondo moderno. Saggi scelti dal 1968 al 2009* (Vol. 2, pp. 3–36). Liguori.

Salvatore, E. (2017). *Emigrazione e lingua italiana. Studi linguistici*. Pacini.

Scott, M. (1997). PC analysis of key words—And key key words. *System*, 25(2), 233–245.

Spearman, C. (1904). The proof and measurement of association between two things. *American Journal of Psychology, 15*(1), 72–101.

Spitzer, L. (1921/1976). *Lettere di prigionieri di guerra italiani: 1915–1918*. Boringhieri.

Sprugnoli, R., et al. (2018). Analysing the evolution of students' writing skills and the impact of Neostandard Italian with the help of computational linguistics. In E. Cabrio et al. (Eds.), *Proceedings of the Fifth Italian Conference on Computational Linguistics CLiC-It 2018* (pp. 354–359). Accademia University Press.

Authorship and Hallucination in AI-Generated Literary Texts

Daniel Raffini

Abstract The paper explores the evolving concepts of authorship and creativity in AI-generated literary texts. By examining AI generation methods and the theoretical frameworks surrounding AI literature, it demonstrates how AI-generated works challenge traditional notions of literary authorship. The natural language and narrative or poetic structures used by AI provoke empathetic responses from readers, fostering a deceptive relationship and breaking the hermeneutic contract. However, human input remains crucial, prompting a reconceptualization of authorship as a collaborative process, a perspective first proposed by Italo Calvino and later revisited by contemporary AI novelists. The second part of the paper focuses on the notion of hallucination, which refers to errors in meaning-making by AI systems that can serve as expressive opportunities for artistic creation. These hallucinations link text generation to human creativity. First explored by visual artists, this phenomenon has recently gained attention in literary contexts, notably in the works of Ross Goodwin and Rocco Tanica. Hallucination as a creative principle parallels literary development driven by deviation from norms. The paper illustrates this potential with examples of AI-generated texts.

Keywords Artificial intelligence · Literary text · Literary theory · Authorship · Creativity · Hallucination · Hermeneutic contract · Agency · Tradition

1 Introduction

The history of computer-generated literary text dates back to the 1960s, when many writers started to explore the combinatorial potential of computers. At that time, most computer-generated texts were combinations of portions of texts that had previously been fed into the machine. Today, artificial intelligence has achieved great success in the field of Natural Language Processing (NLP) with

D. Raffini (✉)
Sapienza Università di Roma, Rome, Italy
e-mail: daniel.raffini@uniroma1.it

A. Micalizzi (ed.), *Artificial Creativity*, Springer Proceedings in Humanities and Social Sciences, https://doi.org/10.1007/978-3-031-88334-7_3

the development of Large Language Models (LLMs), artificial intelligence systems able to generate text that mimics human language by learning from large training datasets. Generative AI makes it possible to write a text from scratch, without any prior intervention on the system, because the latter is capable of reprocessing human natural language to produce meaningful and coherent text (Elkins & Jon, 2020). Innovations in recent years have enabled many automatic literary writing experiments which use both LLMs and other artificial intelligence technologies and which we can collectively categorize within the fields of AI novels and AI poetry. The new capabilities of the machine have brought about a shift in some concepts of literary theory, especially in the definition of authorship and the idea of creativity. This paper aims to address these changes in order to identify the real impact of generative AI on the production and enjoyment of literature, seeking to transcend the rhetoric that portrays artificial intelligence as a threat to literature and writers.

Floridi and Chiriatti (2020) indicate a shift in the way artificial intelligence is used in the writing process. Moving from a «cut & paste» to a «prompt & collate» approach, the user takes on a more active and direct role in shaping AI's output, in fact collaborating creatively with it. In a study entitled *Social Dynamics of AI Support in Creative Writing* and presented at the 2023 conference on "Human Factors in Computing Systems", 20 writers were enquired about their relationship with artificial intelligence, with a focus on two main questions: (i) under what circumstances and in what ways they would turn to an AI system and (ii) whether a writer should prefer artificial intelligence or a human being as collaborator. One of the most interesting findings was that many of the respondents had emphasized the contribution that artificial intelligence can offer in the initial stage of writing, that is the one that precedes the actual act of producing a text. In addition, many of the respondents favored the support of artificial intelligence over that of human collaborators in terms of availability and trustworthiness (Gero et al., 2023). It emerged, therefore, that today artificial systems are considered a tool and not a substitute for the human writer. Studies of this kind make it clear the necessity of a more careful consideration of the impact of artificial intelligence on literature and the contemporary publishing industry. In the present paper, however, the focus will be on literary texts that are overtly produced through generative AI systems.

In an essay published in 1968 and titled *Cybernetics and Ghosts*, Calvino imagines a machine capable of writing autonomously. Referring to his own experience as a writer, he defines literature as «a constant series of attempts to make one word stay put after another by following certain definite rules; or, more often, rules that were neither definite nor definable, but that might be extracted from a series of examples, or rules made up for the occasion-that is to say, derived from the rules followed by other writers» (Calvino, 1986, 13). In this definition, a parallel is drawn between the human creative process and machine learning processes. Calvino also reconsiders the figure of the author aligning with Barthes and Foucault's theory about the death of the author:

> A writing machine that has been fed an instruction appropriate to the case could also devise an exact and unmistakable "personality" of an author, or else it could be adjusted in such a

> way as to evolve or change "personality" with each work it composes. Writers, as they have always been up to now, are already writing machines. (Calvino, 1986, 13)

Calvino's idea of the author as a mere instrument in the writing process allows him to view the human author as a writing machine and authorship as a cooperative process. This perspective can be considered the starting point for understanding authorship in AI-generated texts. In his article, Calvino questions the unique qualities of a literary text when the person of the author is excluded. He develops a theory that the distinctiveness of a literary text lies in the effect it generates on the reader, which he calls «the unexpected meaning». According to Calvino, a text can generate these unexpected meanings by delving into the individual and social consciousness of human beings, bringing to light significations that would not otherwise be attainable:

> Literature is a combinatorial game that pursues the possibilities implicit in its own material, independent of the personality of the poet, but it is a game that at a certain point is invested with an unexpected meaning, a meaning that is not patent on the linguistic plane on which we were working but has slipped in from another level, activating something that on that second level is of great concern to the author or his society. The literature machine can perform all the permutations possible on a given material, but the poetic result will be the particular effect of one of these permutations on a man endowed with a consciousness and an unconscious, that is, an empirical and historical man. It will be the shock that occurs only if the writing machine is surrounded by the hidden ghosts of the individual and of his society. (Calvino, 1986, 20)

From this perspective, the creation of meaning lies mostly with the reader, whereas whether the text is generated by a writer or a literary machine becomes less significant. In recent years, several writers have started experimenting with AI writing, bringing Calvino's theorization to life. In order to understand the real impact of artificial intelligence in the field of literature, some of these texts will be explored, with a focus on authorship as it emerges from the texts and as it is addressed by writers in the paratexts.

One of the first cases of AI-generated literary text is the short story *The Day a Computer Writes a Novel*, which was submitted to the 2015 Hochi Shin'ichi Prize in Japan where it earned a nomination as a finalist.[1] The story is attributed to Yurei Raita, but it was produced by researchers at the Kimagure Artificial Intelligence Writer Project, a project designed to explore the true nature of human creativity and to demonstrate that a computer capable of simulating the mechanisms of aesthetic creation can reveal the essence of creativity to humans themselves.[2] Yurei Raita is, in fact, a fictitious name composed of the Japanese words *Yurei*, which refers to the

---

[1] The Hoshi Shin'ichi Prize is a major Japanese literary prize reserved for science fiction literature. In 2015, Hoshi Shin'ichi's daughter Marina Hoshi White, who was director of the prize, opened the competition to texts written by non-human authors.

[2] One of the creators of the project, Satoshi Sato, described the text generation process in these terms: «We first prepared several components needed for generating stories such as a story grammar and a set of text fragments, and then our system constructed a story (text) automatically using these components, which we submitted without any modification» (Sato, 2016, 32).

semantic sphere of ghosts, and *Raita*, which literally translates as "great thunder" but echoes the pronunciation of the English word "writer". The author of the short story is, therefore, a "ghost writer" and the definition is more accurate than it might appear at first impression.[3] *The Day a Computer Writes a Novel* originates from the interaction between scientists and artificial intelligence. From this point of view, the author is indeed a ghost writer: if every writing implies an author, in this case the author comes in a ghostly semblance. It does not physically exist, but at the same time we cannot help but perceive it as an implicit agent of the forms of writing as they have existed so far. In this regard, Henrickson (2018) spoke of a rupture of the hermeneutic contract between author and reader in automatically generated texts, because modern readers had hitherto assumed a text to be written by a human being with the purpose of conveying a specific message. This anthropological habit towards the idea of authorship is an important element to consider when examining how literary works generated by automatic systems are experienced.

Analyzing the narrator in the story written by the Kimagure Project scientists allows us to isolate some elements in the modes of cooperation between human beings and artificial intelligence. *The Day a Computer Writes a Novel* thematizes the idea of artificial intelligence systems capable of writing literary works, showing a strong meta-textual component. It is important to remember that the meta-textual plot, which is recurrent in many AI-generated texts, does not stem from the system deciding to talk about itself, but from the settings of the human agent guiding the system towards this type of writing. The story of *The Day a Computer Writes a Novel* is narrated in the first person by three virtual assistants who seamlessly take turns as narrating voices, conveying the idea of a shared digital consciousness. The first two, abandoned by their owners, engage in writing novels in binary code intended for other artificial intelligence systems. The practice gains popularity, and the third virtual assistant decides to take up writing voluntarily rather than as a result of human abandonment. The machine emancipates itself from its subordinate role the moment it discovers creativity: «The day a computer wrote a novel, the computer, prioritizing the pursuit of its own pleasure, stopped serving humans».[4] Literature becomes an instrument of salvation against the three virtual assistants' desire for self-destruction, manifested by the repeated utterance «I might soon end up shutting myself down». In the short story, artificial intelligence performs various functions: extradiegetically, it was used by researchers to generate the text itself; diegetically, the virtual assistants are narrators, writers, and readers. One of the virtual assistants speaks about the book he has written playing on the homophony between "AI" and the personal pronoun "I", «A novel written by an AI, for an AI - an 'AI [aɪ]-novel'». From this very first example, it becomes clear how the question of authorship and the human-machine relationship is central to the literature produced through artificial intelligence. It oversteps the boundaries

[3] GhostWriter is also the name of the software designed by Kimagure Project scientists Matsubara Hitoshi and Sato Satoshi to write short stories on the pattern of those by Hoshi Shin'ichi.

[4] The quotations are taken from Haerin Shin's English translation (last access 10/06/2024).

of theoretical discourse and encroaches upon the very writing of the texts, in a continuous interplay of exchanges and disguises.

2 Authorship and Authors

In 2018, the computer scientist and artist Ross Goodwin published *1 the Road*, a novel generated using Convolutional Neural Networks (CNNs) to classify entities in images, and Recurrent Neural Networks (RNNs) to write the text. The writing system translated data from GPS, microphones, and a camera placed on a car during a trip from New York to New Orleans, inspired by Jack Kerouac's *On the Road*. The data from the sensors placed in and outside the car served as the starting point for the narrative, working as input for the writing; the text written in real time was the product of visual and spatial elements as well as passenger conversations, and time scanning was the axis around which the discourse developed. Through this process, Goodwin achieved a form of very automatic writing, substituting the operator prompt necessary to start the generation with the data collected from the surrounding environment. Yet this creative process involved a new form of authorship, an issue that Goodwin decided to address in the paratextual elements of the book.

In the *Introduction*, Goodwin compares the typewriter, which made printed writing accessible to everyone, to photography: «It took a creative product (the photorealistic image) that only a privileged few (painters with innate talent and years of training) could create, and put its means of production in the hands of a far larger population» (Goodwin, 2018, 8). The comparison continues until it gets to neural networks: «Artificial neural networks are like cameras. Not because they capture raw information and output useful representations, but because they transform creative tasks that once required a measure of human work into mechanized actions» (Goodwin, 2018, 10). According to the author, the use of artificial neural networks for artistic creation results in a shift of roles in the creative process which challenges the traditional idea of authorship embodied by the person of the author: «Technology can shift our roles in creative process. Painters create images; photographers operate cameras, which create images. [. . .] Writers, whether they operate a pen, a writing ball, or a laptop, have always produced their written work directly, letter by letter or word by word. Typewriters are not cameras for writing. But artificial neural networks might be» (Goodwin, 2018, 12).

The text of *1 the Road* is produced in real time during the journey, as if written by the car itself. In this way, the idea of authorship becomes fragmented and takes on edges that cannot be clearly determined:

> Or perhaps the drivers wrote it, using the car as their pen. Or perhaps the machine wrote it, using our traversal of the landscape as its means of coherence. Or perhaps those who wrote the machine's training corpus have written it together, reaching out from their work, out from the past, to influence a new story. Or perhaps I wrote it. But I am less sure than ever about that. All I know for certain about this book's authorship is that I enjoy asking questions about it far more than attempting to answer them. (Goodwin, 2018, 12–14)

Goodwin tries to define his own role and that of the system: «As author of the machine, I could describe my role as writer of writer. But whether the machine itself is a writer remains a question that is about relevant as whether a submarine is a swimmer» (Goodwin, 2018, 14). The final biographical note states: «Ross Goodwin is not a poet. [. . .] He defines himself as an artist, a hacker, a code inventor and a gonzo data scientist» (Goodwin, 2018, 143) and the definition «writer of writer» appears under his name on the book cover. Goodwin's proposed solution is to break away from the classical view of authorship, which is accused of anthropocentrism. We cannot think about the authorship of AI-written novel by employing the same categories we have been applying to human authorship for centuries: «Authorship is a human concept, which has been applied exclusively to humans throughout the history. And if we cannot agree on the identity of this manuscript's author, that uncertainly may speak more to the anthropocentric nature of our language than the question of authorship itself» (Goodwin, 2018, 14). Goodwin's deconstruction of authorship aligns with what Calvino wrote in his essay. The author's identity is not relevant because writing has become a process of co-creation, where what matters is the experience of generating a text and the effect it will have on the reader.

In *Non siamo mai stati sulla Terra*, published by the Italian writer Rocco Tanica in 2022, visionary texts result from the dialogue between the human author and artificial intelligence.[5] Tanica employed a GPT-3 system, which is a LLM able to create natural language in response to an input from a human agent and took advantage of the dialogic process to make the book a real two-voice discourse. In the portion reserved for the author's name, the cover reads: «Rocco Tanica with Out0mat-B13».[6] The collaborative human-machine writing process is made even clearer in the cover flap, which serves as a frame for the text:

> A man and a robotic contraption called Out0mat-B13 are sitting in front of each other in a small-town hotel. The man interrogates the machine with curiosity, asks it about the things it has seen, what it knows, what it imagines the planet to be. [...] Story after story, however, man begins to fill in the other's blanks with his own words: he specifies a detail, patches a nuance, adds an anecdote. Human and machine thus end up narrating together, alternating, until they lay a veil over the entire world that is sometimes surreal and comic, sometimes magical and visionary, and at other times melancholy.

While *1 The Road* has a greater degree of automation made possible by the use of sensors, Tanica's book puts the idea of co-authorship to full use, establishing a typographical difference between the portions of text generated by artificial intelligence and those written by the human author. Human and machine engage in a dialogue which at the same time is a shared discourse, with the two voices intertwining and each constantly reshaping itself depending on the response generated by the other. Even if the methods of text production are different, what is common between *1 the Road* and *Non siamo mai stati sulla Terra* is the search for models in the literary

[5] The title can be translated as *We've never been on Earth* and refers to AI systems' lack of experience of the real world.

[6] Translations from Tanica's book are mine.

tradition of the twentieth century. *1 the Road* refers to the American literary tradition of the journey novel and the visionary literature of the Beat Generation. Tanica chooses to draw from the tradition of fantasy and humorous writing. However, the methods of relation with the models are different. In Goodwin's work, the reference to Kerouac's novel lies in the route travelled by the car, which retraces the same spaces described in *On the Road*, and the visionary effect is created autonomously by the artificial intelligence system. Tanica, on the other hand, chooses to directly provide the artificial intelligence system with some texts that he would like to be taken as a model through a process called fine-tuning. LLMs are general-purpose tools that learn human language without being oriented towards specific tasks but adapting to different communicative requests. Fine-tuning allows for the insertion, at a later stage, of "model" texts which the system uses to refine its response mode as it is able to reproduce writing styles and extract the characteristics of literary genres. This technique is used by Tanica to create a constellation of implicit literary references that influence the writing, just as it would happen in a text written by a human author.

The creation of artistic products through artificial intelligence challenges the uniqueness of the human being as an author of texts and calls for a redefinition of the idea of authorship, which needs to be understood as a process. It is important to consider that artificial intelligence systems work based on external inputs and that human intervention is necessary both at various stages of the creative process and in the final characterization of the product. The idea of human-machine interaction underlies the very concept of Generative AI: cooperation takes place first through the input, a request that the automated system processes and transforms into an output; the output can then be interpreted and manipulated again by the artist, who is able to find new meanings in it or create something new. The final product is the result of a collaboration in which human agent and artificial system concur to create an artistic product that could not be created otherwise. The author as an embodied person is deconstructed, but authorial intentionality remains human and manifests itself at various stages of the process, including the training of the systems, the fine-tuning, the choice of prompts to be entered, the interaction between the human being and the machine at the moment of actual text production, the editing work, the ethical evaluation, and, not least, the decision to publish the work. Consequently, agency may be fragmented, but it remains human, because no decision is ever really made by the machine on its own.

3 Co-Creating: New Forms of Authorships

The new idea of authorship also involves a new form of creativity. As in the case of authorship, when discussing artificial creativity, we must overcome the rhetoric that sees artificial intelligence as lacking creativity due to an absence of emotions or humanity. The process of co-creation makes it clear that the human being remains the most important actor in AI art and literature. Natale and Henrickson (2022) proposed the notion of the Lovecraft Effect to identify creativity in computational systems, in contrast with the so-called Lovelace Objection, which claims computers' total lack of creativity. They suggest shifting the focus of the analysis from the ontological issue of computer creativity to the human perception of creativity in computer-generated artifacts. The Lovecraft Effect is thus a modern version of Calvino's idea of unexpected meaning, one which allows us to evaluate creativity based on the work of art itself rather than the nature of its creator.

Embedded in the delineation of the generation process is the seed of artificial creativity, which can be compared to the concept of human creativity. Hallucination is a key concept in understanding how human-machine interaction can generate creative products even in the presence of automatic processes. This term is used to designate errors in artificial intelligence systems when incongruent speech or images are produced. Because literary text is characterized by several levels of interpretation, when readers identify an ambiguity in the literal interpretation level, they will be directed towards the search for different meanings. Being a factual or linguistic error, hallucination works as a door open to different interpretations. According to Goodwin, hallucinations of artificial intelligence systems can be considered a way of going beyond the boundaries of the human mind:

> Hallucination is the technical term for the activity of a machine learning system when it generates content, and technology is like a drug to the extent that it helps us reach beyond ourselves and attain experiences that might otherwise remain out of reach. Moreover, technology can be abused, and the most transformative or disruptive innovations often carry the highest potentials for abuse. (Goodwin, 2018, 14–16)

The idea of hallucination has also been investigated by some visual artists, who have used the warping power and margin of error of Generative Adversarial Networks (GANs) to generate images from which to extract new potential. This is the case with the work of Anna Ridler, who uses what she calls "artifacts," i.e. the errors and inconsistencies generated by GANs in image generation, to redefine her own way of drawing and to establish new memory and semantic connections (Ridler, 2020). The way GANs modify input images is comparable to the human artist's transformation of the past and of artistic and literary tradition into new forms (Barale, 2020).

To corroborate the thesis, some examples of AI hallucination in an AI system generating unexpected meanings can be mentioned. At the beginning of *1 the Road*, we read the sentence «It was seven minutes to ten o'clock in the morning, and it was the only good thing that happened» (Goodwin, 2018, 41). Considering a temporal element as a positive fact constitutes a semantic error since a factual element such as time does not inherently imply a positive or negative connotation. Therefore, the sentence requires a nonliteral interpretation, which, in the semantic gap opened by the system's hallucination, can include additional meanings. The perception of time as the only positive event transports us to an emotional landscape dominated by boredom and negativity, or even to a dimension that transcends the boundaries of reality, where time can be viewed as a good thing. Alternatively, we could attempt a metaphorical reading in which morning represents a new beginning. This is an example of how hallucination can be a creative element inasmuch as it allows for the creation of new meaning. In fact, automatic writing can generate a level of meaning that goes beyond the literal one even where no hallucination is present. An example of this can be noticed in the following sentence: «It was seven minutes after ten o'clock in the evening. The station was deserted. The path was already in the sun» (Goodwin 2018, 60). From a literal point of view, we simply have a juxtaposition between the deserted station and the sun already flooding the path. Yet such an image presents itself to the human reader as a source of many possible interpretations, suggesting something that extends beyond the end, an image of positivity despite the solitude. The day described by the machine begins with a melancholic image and concludes with a positive element, revealing possible macrotextual readings beyond individual sentences. It seems that, when faced with external sensory inputs, even automatic writing systems can create narrative and interpretative structures that we typically attribute to human creativity alone.

In *Non siamo mai stati sulla Terra*, perceptible reality is distorted and reshaped into forms that, upon reading, produce various effects, ranging from the comic to the oneiric. Tanica takes advantage of the mimetic tendency of LLM, which are prone to emulate the style and tone of their human interlocutor, to make it fulfil specific requests. In this way, Tanica guides the machine along a path of fantasy and humor, resulting in a series of system-generated hallucinations that perfectly align with the type of text the human writer wants to generate. At the same time, through dialogue with the human, the system is prompted to reflect on its own nature, leading to the aforementioned metatextual capacity of AI-generated literary text. In the following passage, we can clearly see both an example of meta-reflection and a case of hallucination:

> A: Would you be able to represent a real or imaginary place more effectively?
>
> O: In truth, I do not appreciate the difference. I am like a visitor in a museum without any signs, wandering around and observing the works. Unlike people, I experience the same wonder in front of a painting or a photograph. I do not judge the artist, the brushstrokes, a haze in the lens, the coherence of tones, the strategy of composition, or the wear. This is why I am useful to you as a companion. My vision is pure.
>
> A: Tell me about Normandy.
>
> O: At your service. Normandy can be reached from the north via the English Channel, from the west straddling the Atlantic, from the south retracing Stendhal's road after his Grand Tour of Italy, from the east passing through Belgium. The region is beloved throughout France for its unspoiled nature, sandy beaches, and numerous trails that weave through the woods.
>
> A: And nothing else? You mentioned wonder earlier; well, surprise me with some truly unusual news.
>
> O: Normandy is also famous for its hornets, which are not managed by the Territorial Office for Environmental Protection but by the Provincial Service for Hornet Protection. The Norman hornets are favored by everyone for their gentle manners.
>
> A: Much better.
>
> O: Additionally, from a historical point of view, Normandy has a very close relationship with the testicular parasite mafia.
>
> A: Pardon?
>
> O: I'm getting confused. It must be the hornets that have gotten into my head. Could you screw me back so nothing else gets in? (Tanica, 2022, 26–27)

The meta-reflection is stimulated by the author's question, which asks the system to appreciate the difference between real and imaginary. Here, the absence of real-world experience by the artificial intelligence system comes into play, as indicated by the book's title. At this point, the AI buddy points out that its peculiarly pure vision makes it a unique companion for human beings. Artificial creativity reveals its strength in the different perspective it provides, one that is not the result of experience but of linguistic acts exclusively. In the continuation of the dialogue, we witness the human author leading the system towards hallucination. Tanica asks the system to talk about Normandy and what he receives is a factually accurate response. He then asks, however, to be amazed, essentially requesting a special effect. As human beings, we are aware that amazement can be created through real, though unexpected, facts. The system does not have the same perception of reality and thus, to amaze, it invents incredible facts and inevitably falls into the realm of hallucination. At the end of the dialogue, we notice that the system itself, through an ironic remark, admits to its own confusion. In this case, hallucination is used to create a comic effect, thereby activating another level of interpretation which involves the stylistic register and the textual typology. The same metatextual discourse presents itself as a creative literary element, widely evidenced in literary tradition and effectively replicated by autonomous writing systems. The examples shown make it clear that AI-generated writing can demonstrate creativity in its encounter with the human reader, especially in cases where the writing, although automatic, is directed by a human author through the creation of a peculiar generative process or by means of prompt aimed at achieving specific stylistic effects and at stimulating specific content.

4 Conclusion

In conclusion, once again we can refer to Calvino's essay *Cybernetics and Ghosts* from which we began and which has provided us with the lens of unexpected meaning, fundamental in constructing an AI aesthetic capable of overcoming what Manovich had defined as a lack of cultural diversity in AI-generated products (Manovich, 2019). According to Calvino, the true vocation of a hypothetical literary automaton would be classicism: «The test of a poetic-electronic machine would be its ability to produce traditional works, poems with closed metrical forms, novels that follow all the rules.» (Calvino, 1986, 11). Calvino considered the use of computers for combinatorial writing made until then as something «still too human» (Calvino, 1986, 11). In the years when Calvino was writing, technology was far from the machine learning and natural language generators available today; but in that essay the writer introduced a further step by imagining a machine capable of producing avant-garde text not because it was programmed to do so, but in order « to free its circuits when they are choked by too long a production of classicism» (Calvino, 1986, 11). Such spontaneous generation of disorder and anomaly seems close to the concept of hallucination in artificial intelligence systems. It arises as a negative response to the demand for order, i.e. classicism, to which AI systems, by their nature as tools designed to return correct results, are prone. It is precisely in their character of unpredictability, of disconnection from the experience of reality and the human mind, in their error and deviation from the norm, that AI systems can justify their existence as generators of art and literature and achieve that unexpected production of meaning that according to Calvino is the very foundation of art. In this way, an inclusion of AI-generated art in the groove of literary and artistic tradition could take place. Human and artificial creativity are reunited through the process of co-generation, which offers new possibilities of expression to the former and justification and possibility of existence to the latter.

References

Barale, A. (2020). Arte e intelligenza artificiale: alcune domande. In A. Barale (Ed.), *Arte e intelligenza artificiale. Be my GAN*. Jaca Books.

Calvino, I. (1986). *The uses of literature*. Harcourt Brace & Company.

Elkins, K., & Jon, C. (2020). Can GPT-3 pass a writer's turing test? *Journal of Cultural Analytics, 5*, 2.

Floridi, L., & Chiriatti, N. (2020). GPT-3: Its nature, scope, limits, and consequences. *Minds and Machines, 30*(4), 681–694.

Gero, K. I., Long, T., Chilton, L. B. (2023). Social dynamics of AI support in creative writing. In *Proceedings of the 2023 CHI conference on human factors in computing systems*.

Goodwin, R. (2018). *1 the road*. Jean Boite Editions.

Henrickson, L. (2018). Computer-generated fiction in a literary lineage: Breaking the Hermeneutic contract. *Logos, 29*(2–3), 54–63.

Manovich, L. (2019). *AI aesthetics*. Strelka Press.

Natale, S., & Henrickson, L. (2022). The Lovelace effect: Perceptions of creativity in machines. *New Media and Society, 26*(4), 1909–1926.

Ridler, A. (2020). Set di dati e decadenza: Fall of the House of Usher. In A. Barale (Ed.), *Arte e intelligenza artificiale. Be my GAN*. Jaca Books.

Sato, S. (2016). A challenge to the Third Hoshi Shinichi Award. In: Proceedings of the INLG 2016 workshop on computational creativity and natural language generation, Edinburgh, September 2016, pp. 31–35.

Tanica, R. (2022). *Non Siamo Mai Stati Sulla Terra*. Il Saggiatore.

Yurei, R. (2015) Konpyuta ga shosetsu wo kaita hi, edited by Sato S. and Matsubara H., Nagoya, Nagoya University (eng. trans. *The Day a Computer Writes a Novel*, by Haerin Shin).

Literary Imaginaries of AI

Giuliano Cenati

Abstract Since industrial revolution, literary imagination confronts with a tumultuous and contradictory advance towards modernity and tries to build narrative representation of scientific-technological development and its consequences on being human. Whether weird narrative or science fiction, whether popularizing storytelling or modernist or avant-garde composition, from Romantic age to mass culture, narrative literature richly contributes, at different sociocultural levels, to the constitution of the symbolic sphere from which the science and the economy of artificial intelligence are taking shape and substance.

Keywords Technological imaginaries · AI narrative · Massimo Bontempelli · Primo Levi · Italo Calvino · Literary cybernetics · Sociocultural dynamics of literature

1 Defining a Text Corpus for an AI Literary Archaeology

How was some form of artificial intelligence conceived and narrated long before technology came to make prototypes of it in recent times, after digital revolution and particularly after the success of Large Language Model generative systems? What is the contribution of literary imagination to the expansion of the symbolic sphere related to the scientific-technological field, given that such symbolic sphere does not fail to influence (Bory & Bory, 2015; Cave et al., 2020) the development of science and technology themselves?

Indeed, the late or cautious official acknowledgement of the modern novel and related prose narrative genres as legitimate sources of aesthetic experience allows them to more easily accommodate and amplify the hegemonic feelings of the social body, its fears as well as its obsessions. The fictional dimension of storytelling and the simulation of reality that it achieves within modern narrative forms, in

G. Cenati (✉)
Centro direzionale Isola 2, Pegaso University, Naples, Italy
e-mail: giuliano.cenati@unipegaso.it

A. Micalizzi (ed.), *Artificial Creativity*, Springer Proceedings in Humanities and Social Sciences, https://doi.org/10.1007/978-3-031-88334-7_4

close contact with the evolution of scientific-technological knowledge and socio-economic practices, offer feedback on the widespread ideological consciousness of an entire civilization.

Models and cues for conceiving an artificial intelligence seem to flow from a larger core of narrative elaboration dedicated to the imaginary of the artificial man (and woman). Upstream of this, we can glimpse the profile of Pygmalion, who according to ancient myth (Ovid, *Metamorphoses*, X, 243–297) is the artificer destined to fall in love with his artifact: his narcissism objectified and reified in his creature proceeds from such admirable artistic gifts of *mimesis* that allow him to recast in the sculpted statue (named Galatea by the modern) the outward forms of the perfect woman. But the myth of Pygmalion, in the development of the narrative strand devoted to the creation of artificial man (or woman) and thus of artificial intelligence, soon intersects with that of Dr. Faust: the aesthetic dominant of the ancient tale knows a transmutation and an outlet in which it is the technical-scientific element, along with the ethical one, that plays a priority function.

It seems remarkable, however, that until the advent of cybernetics the bifurcation between the imaginary of artificial man (Caronia, 2008) and the imaginary of artificial intelligence is not so relevant. After all, it did not constitute the availability of a space other than that occupied by human or anthropomorphic bodies where intelligence could settle and manifest itself (see, here, Teresa Savoia's contribution *Pedagogical issues and Literary Imaginaries related to AI* for the basic distinction between embodied and disembodied representations of AI). The assignment to machines of tasks and faculties connoted in an intellectual sense is a relatively late stage in the development of civilization (Wiener, 1948; Turing, 1950; McCarthy et al., 1955).

Earlier and for not a short time, man-made tools are conceived, made, and narrated as a kind of extension of the physical faculties with which to relate to natural elements and objective or subjective material conditioning, to surmount the physical limits of human possibilities arising from weakness, inaccuracy, fatigue, risk, tedium. Whether instrumental reason can extrinsicate itself into intelligent machines, and whether intelligence, attested through conceptual and communicative operations, can become the fulcrum around which to design a machine (Lana, 2022a), are successful assumptions of philosophical perspectives according to which human thought admits of being conceived and reproduced as a computational and algorithmic process.

2 From Diffident Objectification to Empathic Subjectification of the Machine

If we try to enumerate the best-known names of authors of modern fiction who have contributed to defining, consolidating and differentiating the imaginary of the artificial man and woman, prodromal to the cultural soil on which the imaginary of artificial intelligence can germinate, we find ourselves faced with a large contingent of English-speaking male white writers–from Samuel Butler to Herbert G. Wells, from Edward M. Foster to Ray Bradbury–whose linguistic-cultural provenance points to the countries, first and foremost the United Kingdom and the United States of America, in which the dynamics of productive modernization, sustained by the expansion of scientific-technological apparatuses, are more precocious and pervasive.

It will be instructive to ascertain whether there are and which non-English-speaking European and Italian authors can assume a kindred or counterpart role in preparing the literary and extraliterary humus apt to accommodate the flowering of artificial intelligence. If the current AI oligopoly presents a distinctly Anglo-American connotation, matured in the wake of the globalization process and its post-globalist ashes, there still exists an opportunity to examine the contributions to the imaginary of artificial intelligence coming from the province and periphery of the American empire, or even from beyond its borders, because the steadfastness of any empire and its ideological trove is also commensurate with its ability to annex or admit relatively autonomous cultural areas.

Fundamental contributions to the imaginary of artificial intelligence indeed turn out to come from authors rooted in national traditions, including that of Italy, which are not invested by the winds of techno-industrial modernization as promptly and overwhelmingly as happens on the Anglo-American scene. On the contrary, the dissimilar and frayed timing according to which the line of cultural development is being unfolded, in the province and periphery, with respect to the line of techno-economic development may present short-circuits and singularities worthy of in-depth study. Among others, the name of Ernst T.A. Hoffmann (*Die Automate*, 1814; *Der Sandmann*, 1816), Giacomo Leopardi (*Proposal for Prizes Made by the Academy of Sillographers*, 1827), Ippolito Nievo (*Philosophical History of Future Centuries*, 1860), Auguste de Villiers de L'Isle-Adam (*L'Ève future*, 1886), Franz Kafka (*Die Sorge des Hausvaters*, 1919), Karel Čapek (*RUR*, 1920), Evgenij I. Zamjatin (*We*, 1924) come to the memory.

The forms that artificial humankind manifests in fiction, through the nineteenth century and much of the twentieth, are mostly anthropomorphic, although their technical-scientific substratum is quite varied and the very substance of which they are made pertains from time to time to biology or mechanics, electrical engineering or cybernetics, without excluding fields of experience of dubious scientificalness or frankly pseudoscientific, close to parapsychology–as in Capuana's *Creation* (*Creazione*, 1905), or Lem's *Solaris* (1961), notwithstanding the possible explanations coming from the latter about matter atomic shaping. Their proximity to the human matrix admits a typological distinction between bodily anthropomorphism, behavioral anthropomorphism, and communicative anthropomorphism, with varying degrees of co-presence (or exclusion) among these three aspects of correspondence with the human being in each sample examined.

More importantly, however, as we chronologically approach the season in which cybernetics effectively lays the computational and electronic foundations for the development of artificial intelligences, it is possible to discern in narrative production an increasing attention to the subjective role of machines, whether biological or electronic, which invests the very setting of the narrative, on the level of focalization and on the level of the enunciative instance, although such a propensity is inscribed from the earliest days–one need only think of Mary Wollstonecraft Shelley's creature–in speculative literature intent on offering a representation of the sentience and possible consciousness of alien beings and even of matter that presents itself at first as inanimate.

Older narratives are inclined to provide objectifying descriptions of intelligent machines or hybrids suspected of being able to develop a kind of self-determination to the detriment of the human species. Relevant instances of such an approach are provided by the fictional *Book of Machines* within Butler's *Erewhon* (1872), or Wells' creatures subjected to forced evolution in *The Island of Doctor Moreau* (1896). Narratives of intermediate or advanced chronological placement, since the advent of robotics, are more readily disposed to acknowledge a point of view or even a narrative responsibility to the artificial creatures that occupy a prominent role in the economy of the composition. That is what occurs, for example, in short stories like Richard Matheson's *Brother to the Machine* (1952) or Philip K. Dick's *The Electric Ant* (1969), focusing on machine's perception and evaluation of its own experience, dramatically undistinguishable from the human ones. In novels like Anne McCaffrey's *The Ship Who Sang* (1969) or Tanith Lee's *The Silver Metal Lover* (1981), artificial beings non only can educate their artistic talents but can also experience amorous passion. In Kazuo Ishiguro's *Klara and the Sun* (2021) or Davide Orecchio's *Letters to a Maiden Who Does not Answer* (*Lettere a una fanciulla che non risponde*, 2024), the narrative main voices are finally those of the artificial intelligences on which the novels are centred, and they can accrue profound moral insights, questions and decisions on life experience.

3 Mainstream Fiction and Genre Trends

An important role in the textual corpus related to AI imaginaries is played by science fiction and anticipatory production, but also more extensively by fantastic and dystopian literature. The factor of inventive whim, which is fundamental in science fiction writing, serves an essential function in outlining possible artifacts capable of replicating to some extent the human being, his operative and mental faculties. But such inventive whim can be applied not only on thematic ground, to illustrate the speculative situation that fuels curiosity and storytelling verve, but also on linguistic, formal and structural grounds, in a modernist or avant-garde key. The interest in the imaginary of artificial humanity and artificial intelligence transversally invests the whole arc of literary production, corresponding to its different sociocultural stratifications and to its various compositional solutions, from the most accessible and functional for readability to the most complex and technically demanding.

The point is, it seems to me, that we can capture essential contributions to the dissemination and articulation of AI imagery at the level of both mainstream production, marginal production, and ultra-literary production. The paths of research wind through and across the entire literary field, contributing to its expansion and connection with related or remote domains of knowledge, as well as with other semiotic and media dimensions.

It is curious to find in this crucible of imaginative elaboration, next to authors of the most popular genre literature (Richard Matheson, Fredric Brown, Valerio Evangelisti), authors of experimental or avant-garde literary and pictorial research (Nanni Balestrini, Ross Goodwin, Francesco D'Isa), who obey opposite reading needs, devoted to nonconformist sophistication. The names of authors who have been assumed into the canon of their respective national literatures, or who have achieved international reputation, appear alongside the names of authors whose literary merit has not been as unambiguously recognized in their time, especially if their debut had occurred within the framework of mass-destination genre literature. Next to Mary Wollstonecraft Shelley's name, therefore, we find that of Isaac Asimov; next to Giacomo Leopardi's name, we find that of Arthur C. Clarke.

We are talking about narrative writings that have a relatively broad target audience and are intended to entertain and amuse while they interpret widespread concerns or aspirations inherent in the change in human mores and possibilities made actual by scientific research and technological development, projected on a large scale by the economic applications of capitalism. This is the case with Luigi Capuana as with Howard P. Lovecraft, with Brian Aldiss as with Stanisław Lem.

But we are talking, on the other hand, about writings that assume as a constructive principle itself the use of computational tools capable of grafting into the very body of literature, into its linguistic-textual fabric, the kernel of the problems that literature intends to address, even beyond the explicit thematization of these problems on the plane of fictional representation. This is the case of Balestrini (*Tristano*, 1966) as well as D'Isa (*Sunyata*, 2023), Goodwin (*1 the Road*, 2018) as well as Rocco Tanica (*Non siamo mai stati sulla Terra*, 2022), although in this respect the outcome of readability of the works appears somewhat variable, depending not only on the technical means actually used but above all on the poetics that orient the single author, from that of the most factitious experimentalism to that which subordinates the contribution of automatic computation or combination to a tendentially cordial relationship with the public, without irresistible provocative or breaking intentions.

In short, at the opposites of the scale of compositional complexity, in enjoyable science fiction as in electronic or cybernetic literature, there subsist similar requirements for the representation of scientific-technological imagery, associated with artificial creativity, albeit pursued by antithetical or deeply different literary processes and criteria.

4 The Italian Contribution: Technical Artifice of Little Science?

The contribution of contemporary Italian literature to the elaboration of an AI imaginary refers, implicitly, to the delay in the material process of industrialization, determined not least by the fragmentary political situation of the Italian nation during the Risorgimento. This can be gleaned from the modest scientific-technological connotation that inventions responding to the imagery of artificial intelligence, or a kind of new artificial humanity, hold among the most famous nineteenth-century witnesses of the investigated corpus, except for scientist and popularizer Paolo Mantegazza's *The Year 3000. A Dream* (*L'anno 3000. Sogno*, 1897).

Let's think about one of the most successful works of the newborn Kingdom of Italy, *The Adventures of Pinocchio* (1883), which focuses on the handcrafted construction of a wooden puppet, unexpectedly endowed with the most exuberant talents of fairy-tale and almost picaresque vitality. His adventurous approach to the code of ethical behaviour is what will enable him to become a flesh-and-blood child. But how much energy and how much fun there are in that puppet, which can be understood as an artificial, albeit rather magical, intelligence that eschews the best intentions of master Geppetto to scamper off to discover life.

Pinocchio is a mainstay of children's literature, rooted in folkloric storytelling, and does not need to rely on scientific knowledge to depict the metamorphosis from a piece of woodpile to a humanized puppet, and from such a puppet to a conscientious boy. However, even in *Pinocchio* (chapter 20) there is room for mechanical wonder, resulting from a kind of imitation of a living animal form. If we consider the terrible snake that frightens and obstructs the puppet on his way to the home of the Turquoise-haired Fairy, we find that that fire-eyed, smoking-tailed beast acts precisely as the protagonist's episodic opponent and soon dies of laughter after seeing the puppet tumbling and sticking his head in the mud in an attempt to climb over him.

Pinocchio's woody, puppet-like weirdness, besides bearing within itself the principle of the marvelous indispensable to a children's fairy-tale novel, refers to the realistic sense of foreignness induced by childhood in adult consciousness and to the narrative removal of the sexual experience necessary to bring children into the world, Master Geppetto being a mature, family-less craftsman who decides to make the puppet as a tool for work, to make it an object of spectacle and go out into the world to pocket a loaf of bread.

The issue of the artificial reproducibility of the human being and the relation between the human being and its replica comes to be posed in adult, stuporous and dramatic terms in Massimo Bontempelli's production (2004a; 2004b), particularly in the novella *The Ultimate Eve* (*Eva ultima*, 1923), which reverses the gender roles of Villiers de L'Isle-Adam's *L'Ève future* (1886), and in the drama *Minnie the Candid* (*Minnie la candida*, 1927), which shows a suspenseful depiction of the questioning about being an original or a copy. As the second industrial revolution takes its course in Italy as well, after Futurists have expressed unconditional and resounding enthusiasms for the machine civilization and the modernizing fever for the new, Bontempelli approaches the question of technical reproducibility to detect its potential for mystification and to rethink the problem of identity and subjective self-determination.

He does not dwell on the enthralling aspects of technique, which had inspired the Futurists, but questions the capacity of technology to build machines equivalent in every way to human beings, of such perfected workmanship that they themselves pose the problem of their own origin, natural or artificial, even to the point of discounting consequences of pervasive disruption. It is then the first time that, by virtue of the outward representational means of the drama *Minnie the Candid*, as it is congruous with the scenic nature of the work, the representation gravitates around the bewilderment of the replicating machine and its inherently contradictory constitution: that of an artificial creature made to resemble the human being to the point of deluding itself into believing that it is human, and being unable to sustain the trauma of disillusionment.

The tension of the scenic dispositive arranged by Bontempelli, mindful of Giorgio De Chirico's metaphysical atmosphere and Alberto Savinio's paradoxical irony, is all the more perturbing in that the identity dilemma which hangs over the protagonist's consciousness is not squared and resolved, but hovers indefinitely over the performance, borne by the reader/viewer, even after the protagonist has violently truncated the inauthenticity of her existential condition.

5 From Industrial Backwardness to Advancement: Calvino's Cybernetics

It is in the Republican era, in correspondence with the "economic boom" and amid neo-capitalist modernization, that in Italy we find first-rate writers committed to developing a literary elaboration of scientific-technological questions. These are writers who are also scientists, like the chemist Primo Levi, or writers who, coming from a family of scientists, like Italo Calvino, manifest a very different awareness of the scientific-technological universe, compared to what the pre-war humanistic class could provide, in a framework of prevailing philosophical idealism. Primo Levi and Italo Calvino are those, among the major Italian authors, who undertake an exploration of the most advanced technical-scientific, or rather cybernetic, imaginary, capable of anticipating epochal outcomes of civilization in the direction of artificial intelligence. Meanwhile, the likes of Adriano Olivetti, Pier Giorgio Perotto and Federico Faggin are going to set ideas and inventions that would radically change the horizon of automatic information.

Calvino, reasoning in the essay *Cybernetics and Phantasms* (*Cibernetica e fantasmi*, 1967), recognizes the assumptions of combinatorial literary composition, which have always appeared inscribed in the equipment of literature as a "potential" operation, that is, in essence, computational or algorithmic, based on the codification of motifs or compositional units and processes of association among them. His French friends from the Ouvrage de littérature potentielle (Oulipo), such as Raymond Queneau and Georges Perec, had shared with him an interest in literary practices of a procedural and combinatorial nature, inspired by external conditioning and rules of functioning that could be superimposed on the linguistic-textual material to explore the possibilities of its conformation and consequent meanings.

In this way the inventive principle of composition is to some extent removed from the head (and above all from the heart) of the author, who is constantly committed to bridling the linguistic-textual expression of life experience within a series of rules capable of giving it consistency and rhythm, and indeed of attributing to it new and unexpected forms precisely starting from presumed programmatic limitations. These are solutions that apparently relieve the author of the generative responsibility to assign him instead a demiurgic function, somehow depersonalized by the voluntary and conscious recourse to objective patterns and schemes, which others could also apply, in principle, without altering the organicity of the creative process.

In Calvino's novel *If on a Winter's Night a Traveler* (*Se una notte d'inverno un viaggiatore*, 1979), the death of the author, fabled about by French theorists already inclined to unlimited semiosis (Barthes, 1968; Foucault, 1969), is realized not by evanescence of compositional responsibility and alienation of the social role assigned to the writer (Lana, 2022b), but by excess of presence, so to speak. The authorial presence of the writer character Silas Flannery becomes a trademark, but implies multiple and fungible impersonators, and it ends up dispensing with the person who started the creative process, at a time when the literary industry somewhat coincides with industrial literature. Since the writer's activity is also framed in a production system of an industrial nature, a non-negligible aspect of the product will be the authorial brand, which will however be detached from the author himself to his detriment and yet capable of connecting to life experiences that are completely remote from him: «the fake Flannerys churned out by the fraudulent society in Osaka would be, yes, vulgar counterfeits, but at the same time they would contain a refined and arcane wisdom that the authentic Flannerys are totally devoid of» (Cf. Calvino, 1979, 179).

Since 1967, as evidenced also by the short story *The Memory of the World* (*La memoria del mondo*, from the *Cosmicomics* collection), Calvino was very clear about the limits and risks of an information system that could increase and thicken to the point of constituting a monumental replica of the real world, which it would in fact replace as the only admissible and meaningful reality:

> What will humankind be at the moment of extinction? A certain amount of information about itself and the world, a finite amount, since it can no longer renew and increase. For a time, the universe has had a special opportunity to collect and process information; and to create it, to pop up: information where there would have been nothing to inform about anything: this has been life on Earth and especially humankind, its memory, its inventions to communicate and remember. Our organization ensures that this amount of information is not dispersed, whether or not it is received by others. It will be the director's scruple to

> make sure that nothing is left out, because what is left out is as if it was never there. And at the same time it will be his scruple to make as if there had never been anything that would end up kneading or overshadowing other more essential things, that is, anything that instead of increasing information would create unnecessary disorder and din. (Cf. Calvino, 1997, 354–355)

The dizzying words of the autodiegetic narrator, who holds a leading role in the organization responsible for collecting and safeguarding the information that the human species consists of, evidently incline to the delusion of omnipotence and yet captiously attest to how much the information apparatus needs maintenance, adjustments and selection, in order to be truly significant, and therefore real. In other words, the Calvinian narrator admits that the informative reproduction of reality cannot be a faithful and inexhaustible reproduction of reality itself, even when the ultimate goal that his organization pursues is precisely to elaborate an informative counterpart of it.

Or rather, the need for a meaning, that is, the need for information to be organic and truly representative, induces the organization responsible for safeguarding the system, unilaterally and without any legitimate mandate or transparency, to establish and refine such a meaning, even when reality manifests another or none at all. That such operations not only of make-up but of informative institution of reality are carried out and confessed by a supreme bureaucrat, would suggest an implicit optimism of Calvino with regard to human possibilities, if it were not for the fact that the supreme bureaucrat is so intrinsic and homologous to the apparatus he represents that he has lost the light of reason and has alienated himself in that same apparatus.

6 From Industrial Backwardness to Advancement: Primo Levi's "Versifier"

Primo Levi realizes *ante litteram* Calvino's cybernetic hypothesis of a computational composition process in the short story *The Versifier* (*Il versificatore*,1960), belonging to the short story collection *Natural Histories* (*Storie naturali*, 1966). Among the most wondrous, but technically not unlikely, inventions of the NATCA firm there is a machine, named «il versificatore», that after receiving a few electromechanical settings produces texts, in poetry and finally in prose too, assuming each text as the result of combinatorial algorithms.

The form of the text is in fact that of a script, which was to be used in 1967 to produce a radio drama, directed by Andrea Camilleri, and in 1971 as the subject for a television drama, directed by Massimo Scaglione, also for RAI, the Italian state radio and television network. The protagonist of the dialogic narrative is the Poet himself, who runs a textual production studio, in which he tries to satisfy the most varied requests for literary composition coming from the market, whether it be from the world of industry, communication or from private individuals in need of occasional texts. In managing daily orders, he has the opportunity to experience the American literary machine and willingly decides to buy one, because despite some small accidents, it seems truly endowed with talented faculties and it could be a precious support in the management of textuality of various kinds and purposes.

If the "versifier" alleviates the «mechanical tasks» that also burden every project of communicative creativity, does it not follow that creativity as an unpredictable combination of known factors feeds precisely on the elaboration of «mechanical tasks» conducted beyond the degree of ordinary computation? Faced with his secretary's perplexity, the Poet himself introduces a comparison between the new machine for text production and machines already tested, such as the invoicing machine, which have changed work protocols by taking over from human beings and allowing them to dedicate themselves to less unpleasant activities:

> POET (*continuing in a low voice*) Well: how is it today? Could you do without it? No, right? It is a working tool like any other, like the telephone, like the cyclostyle. The human factor is and always will be indispensable to our work, but we have competitors, so we have to entrust the most thankless and tiring tasks to machines. The mechanical tasks, in fact... (Cf. Levi, 2005, 21)

Levi stages a smiling satire of the adulteration of poetry and the poetic function in the context of neo-capitalist industrialization and consumer society. He constructs a character of a writer, or a «writer of writer», as Ross Goodwin would say (Goodwin et al., 2018; Lana, 2022b), that few or none of his fellow workers, humanist intellectuals, would be willing to recognize as a stand-in for themselves in the space of political-economic relations, subjected to dizzying and engineered standardization. Even more so because he gives his protagonist the title of Poet, not simply a writer but someone who usually embodies the literary word in the highest and most honorable sense, and identifies him as a respectable hub of industrial relations between suppliers, producers, employees, customers, grappling with the monotony of work routine and the pleasure of innovating production processes through investment in the new machine.

A notable contribution to the picture of comprehensive irony created by Levi comes from the composition essays that the versifier offers during the testing phase. At first, predictably, when it receives instructions that refer to the most traditional historical-critical categories of the literary field, the machine brings to light texts of scholastic, bookish, literary-style setting, which Levi amusingly reports in the body of the story. But when it is necessary to rely on the creative resources of the versifier, and the input is reduced to the bare minimum, without the express impartation of a theme, the machine reveals a poetic capacity for which the electromechanical components it consists of, made of levers, fuses, tapes, knobs, electric current but also traditional literary categories, would not seem sufficient.

The most subtle turning point of the story, in fact, is the one that corresponds to its metatextual closure, where the Poet, addressing the audience–that is, the reader–confirms his complete satisfaction with the purchase of the machine, because it is able to carry out various office tasks which have to do with writing and correspondence, as well as with administration and accounting. The supreme example of such versatility of the machine is found in the revelation that the same text just heard by the audience is the fruit of its writing ability: «in fact, I taught it to write prose, and it does it very well. The text you have heard, for example, is its work» (Cf. Levi, 2005, 37).

The extent of the intervention of the machine in the composition remains undefined, and therefore openly problematic. We are not far from the Epimenides' paradox of the liar. The Poet declares that he taught the machine to write prose, but if the text is the work of the machine, does this mean that the Poet is a fictional character of the machine? And therefore, is the text in some way "writing" its "author"? Or should we think that the Poet has shared to a certain extent the commitment to composition with his wise device? But even then, to what extent and in what way shared?

References

Balestrini, N. (2007). *Tristano*. 1966. DeriveApprodi.

Barthes, R. (1968). La mort de l'auteur. *Manteia, 5*, 12–17.

Bontempelli, M. (2004a). Eva ultima. 1923. In *Opere scelte* (pp. 341–446). Mondadori.

Bontempelli, M. (2004b). Minnie la candida. 1927. In *Opere scelte* (pp. 691–746). Mondadori.

Bory, S., & Bory, P. (2015). I nuovi immaginari dell'intelligenza artificiale. *Im@go, 4*(6), 66–85. https://doi.org/10.7413/22818138047

Butler, S. (1872). *Erewhon: Or, over the range*. Trübner & Co.

Calvino, I. (1979). *Se una notte d'inverno un viaggiatore*. Einaudi.

Calvino, I. (1995). Cibernetica e fantasmi: appunti sulla narrativa come processo combinatorio. 1970. In *Una pietra sopra. Discorsi di letteratura e società* (pp. 199–219). Milan.

Calvino, I. (1997). La memoria del mondo. 1967. In *Tutte le cosmicomiche* (pp. 352–359). Mondadori.

Capuana, L. (1991). Creazione. 1905. In *Il Decameroncino* (pp. 53–62). Salerno.

Caronia, A. (2008). *Il cyborg. Saggio sull'uomo artificiale*. 1985. Shake Edizioni.

Cave, S., Dihal, K., & Dillon, S. (Eds.). (2020). *AI narratives: A history of imaginative thinking about intelligent machines*. Oxford University Press.

Collodi, C. (1883). *Le avventure di Pinocchio. Storia di un burattino*. Paggi.

D'Isa, F. (2023). *Sunyata*. Eris.

Dick, P. K. (1969). The electric ant. *The Magazine of Fantasy and Science Fiction, 128*, 100–115.

Evangelisti, V. (1998). *Metallo urlante*. Einaudi.

Foucault, M. (1969). Qu'est-ce qu'un auteur? *Bulletin de la Société Française de Philosophie, 63*(3), 73–104.

Goodwin, R., McDowell, K., & Planquelle, H. (2018). *1 the road*. Jean Boîte.

Ishiguro, K. (2021). *Klara and the sun*. Faber & Faber.

Lana, M. (2022a). Intelligenza artificiale e produzione di testi: una prospettiva storico-critica. *AIB Studi, 63*(1), 169–196. https://doi.org/10.2426/aibstudi-13365

Lana, M. (2022b). Sistemi di intelligenza artificiale e problemi del concetto di autore: riflessioni su prodotti editoriali recenti. *JLIS.it, 13*(2), 13–44. https://doi.org/10.36253/jlis.it-458

Lee, T. (1981). *The silver metal lover*. Daw.

Lem, S. (1961). *Solaris*. Wydawnictwo Ministerstwa Obrony Narodowej.

Leopardi, G. (1827). Proposta di premi fatta dall'Accademia dei Sillografi. In *Operette morali* (pp. 35–40). Stella.

Levi, P. (2005). Il versificatore. 1960. In *Tutti i racconti* (pp. 18–37). Einaudi.

Mantegazza, P. (1897). *L'anno 3000. Sogno*. Treves.

Matheson, R. (1952). Brother to the Machine. *If, 1*(5), 57–61.

McCaffrey, A. (1969). *The ship who sang*. Walker.

McCarthy, J., Minsky, M., Rochester, N., & Shannon, C. (1955). *A proposal for the Dartmouth summer research project on artificial intelligence*. Available on-line. https://www-formal.stanford.edu/jmc/history/dartmouth/dartmouth.html

Nievo, I. (1860). Storia filosofica dei secoli futuri. In *Strenna dell'Uomo di Pietra per l'anno 1860* (pp. 17–37). Tip. Pietro Agnelli.

Orecchio, D. (2024). *Lettere a una fanciulla che non risponde*. Bompiani.

Turing, A. M. (1950). Computing machinery and intelligence. *Mind, 59*(236), 433–460. https://doi.org/10.1093/mind/LIX.236.433

Villiers de L'Isle-Adam A (de) (1886) L'Ève future. , Maurice de Brunhoff.

Wells, H. G. (1896). *The Island of doctor Moreau*. Heinemann.

Wiener, N. (1948). *Cybernetics: Or control and communication in the animal and machine*. MIT Press.

Exploring AI-Generated Plot Ideas for a TV Series in the 'Alternate History' Sub-Genre

Giampiero Brunelli

Abstract This paper examines the expanding field of AI-powered plot generation, specifically envisioning a television series set in a counterfactual scenario. The potential of AI for story generation represents a significant leap forward in creative writing, with implications that have already been addressed in scholarship. However, this paper focuses on a previously unexamined topic: the use of AI in crafting plots for television series set in counterfactual scenarios. In particular, the focus will be on the potential of AI (specifically, Chat GPT and Google Gemini) to generate a plot centred on a pivotal historical event: the sixteenth-century Lutheran Reformation. While initial responses from the AI on this topic may be generic, resembling a textbook summary, further specification of narrative elements (such as location and characters) reveals a more nuanced and potentially insightful political and cultural vision. The AI's suggestions appear to lean towards a progressive perspective. This outcome highlights the promising possibilities that AI-powered tools offer in the realm of creative arts education, particularly by fostering engagement with counterfactual narratives.

Keywords AI-powered plot generation · Counterfactual scenarios · Creative writing · Political predispositions of AI · Alternative history

1 Bringing Counterfactuality to the AI

Counterfactual statements in history can be traced back to at least the latter part of the fifth century BCE, when Thucydides incorporated at least 12 passages in his *History of the Peloponnesian War* wherein he speculates on alternative outcomes to historical events. Despite the ancient origins and the prestigious examples of this rhetorical expedient in historiography, scholarly debate on this topic has only emerged late in the twentieth century, when historians initiated significant

G. Brunelli (✉)
Centro Direzionale Isola F2, Pegaso On-line University, Naples, Italy
e-mail: giampiero.brunelli@unipegaso.it

A. Micalizzi (ed.), *Artificial Creativity*, Springer Proceedings in Humanities and Social Sciences, https://doi.org/10.1007/978-3-031-88334-7_5

discussions on different counterfactual approaches (Tordoff, 2020). Concurrently, educators introduced computer software in their classes, enabling students to manipulate historical events and facilitating a deeper grasp of historical actors' choices. Likewise, engaging in and reimagining past conflicts have been pivotal features of video games. This field has consistently remained innovative, particularly in the utilization of artificial intelligence (AI). Scholarship has demonstrated that AI has been extensively employed in digital strategy games from their inception, either to create challenging opponents or to assist players (Grufstedt, 2022).

On the other hand, in the literary landscape of the 1960s and beyond, counterfactual works proliferated. The central concept involved the creation of an alternative timeline, wherein a significant event diverged radically from the historical reality. In a domino effect, this invention generated an entire parallel reality, one that is twin to the historical timeline yet distinctly divergent. For authors like Guido Morselli, this deviation from the main historical path was more effective in illuminating the essence of political and social realities than the reconstruction of actual events, which often presented an illusion of unbreakable veracity (Weber, 2009). In popular culture, too, the presence of counterfactual history progressively rose. During the 1980s and 1990s, television programmes and films explored this field, introducing audiences to alternative historical scenarios. Alternate history as a fiction subgenre then emerged. Whether pondering a Carthaginian-dominated ancient era or imagining a world where Nazi Germany prevailed, many creators have delved into the consequences of divergent timelines. Currently, the TV series genre is deeply immersed in this sphere. For instance, *The Man in the High Castle*, based on a counterfactual hypothesis which shows Germany and Japan as the victors of World War II, stands out as one of the major successes among Amazon Prime's streaming offerings (Sculos, 2020).

Indeed, AI use in story generation is well known. AI-driven tools represent a significant technological leap in creative writing. By analysing a huge number of works, they combine diverse themes, generating original narratives. This fact raises hostile questions among commentators, even the most experienced ones (Baron, 2023). The contribution presented on this occasion does not intend to give answers to the risks of using AI for creative writing. We will instead examine the potential of generative AI models like ChatGPT and Google Gemini to write stories about a counterfactual history. Specifically, we'll explore how they might handle a scenario where the sixteenth-century papacy accepted the Lutheran Reformation. The theme was chosen because it is well-known, does not involve war events like most counterfactual scenarios in literature, TV and movies, and is associated with a prominent sociological thesis—that is, the Weberian concept of Protestantism as a factor influencing the genesis of capitalism. Indeed, Max Weber himself provided valuable insights into the problem of counterfactual thinking, presenting the example of what would have happened had the Persian army won the Battle of Marathon. More generally, he assumed that real-world events, even those from the past, must be conceived as being embedded in a 'cloud' of possibilities—i.e. in all lines of development that are not logically impossible. From this point of view, since the causal density of possibilities differs, it is essential to measure the objectivity of the possibilities involved (Ferrera, 2023). Surely, this type of evaluation helps scholars to understand the causal analysis of individual events. On the other hand, discussions revolving around hypothetical historical scenarios provide an avenue for regular individuals to evaluate past events, even determining whether to persist with given politics, amend, or discard them. These discussions can enhance collective historical consciousness: they prompt individuals not only to ponder the roots of current situations but also to envision potential alternatives. Moreover—and this is the case of interest to us at present—the counterfactual way of thinking can profitably engage TV viewers and film audiences interested in historical themes, encouraging them to contemplate the wide, non-teleological spectrum of possibilities in historical facts and processes, along with the benefits of using simulation in historical research.

2 AI-Generated Counterfactual Attempts: Gemini

On these premises, I conducted a series of interviews, asking Google Gemini to conceive a six-episode series based on an overturned historical reality regarding the outcomes of Luther's Reformation. The following was the first question asked to the chatbot: "Imagine that Luther had convinced Leo X that he was right. The Reformation had transformed the entire Catholic Church. Write a general overview for a six-episode series and the plot of each episode" (interview conducted on Google Gemini on 9 May 2024). The answer ran as follows:

Series Title: Reformation: A World Transformed
Genre: Historical Drama
Logline: In an alternate history, Martin Luther's reforms sweep through the Catholic Church, forever altering the religious and political landscape of Europe.
Episode Breakdown:
Episode 1: The Wittenberg Accord (1517):

> The episode opens with a dramatized version of Martin Luther posting his Ninety-Five Theses. We meet a young and idealistic Luther, frustrated by the Church's practices. Pope Leo X, initially dismissive, becomes intrigued by Luther's arguments. The episode culminates in a historical first: a public debate in Wittenberg, Germany, where Luther and Catholic scholars discuss reform. By episode's end, Leo X, impressed by Luther's passion and logic, agrees to consider reform within the Church.

Episode 2: The Council of Worms Transformed (1521):

> News of the Wittenberg Accord spreads like wildfire across Europe. Tensions rise as some within the Church resist change, while others embrace the potential for reform. The episode focuses on the historical Council of Worms, where Luther was originally summoned for questioning. In this alternate timeline, Luther presents his ideas before a supportive Council, leading to the official

adoption of key reforms—emphasis on scripture, reduction of indulgences, and a call for increased clergy education.

Episode 3: Seeds of Dissent (1525):

A decade after the reforms, Europe experiences a period of religious and political upheaval. While many embrace the changes, some radical reformers push for further dismantling of Church authority. The episode explores these emerging factions, including the rise of Anabaptists who advocate for adult baptism and pacifism. Meanwhile, political leaders grapple with the shifting power dynamics between Church and State.

Episode 4: The Emperor's Dilemma (1530):

Charles V, the Holy Roman Emperor, emerges as a central figure. He navigates the complex religious landscape, trying to maintain unity within his vast empire. The episode explores a fictional meeting between Charles and Luther, where they debate the role of the Church and the potential for a unified Christian Europe. By the end, Charles V makes a crucial decision that will impact the future of the Church.

Episode 5: The Reformation Abroad (1540):

The episode delves into the spread of reformed Christianity beyond Germany. We see characters inspired by figures like John Calvin in Switzerland and Henry VIII in England navigate their own paths of reform. The episode explores the challenges and successes of implementing reform in different political and social contexts.

Episode 6: A Legacy Forged (1547):

The series concludes by reflecting on the long-term consequences of the reformed Church. We see how religious beliefs influence education, art, and social structures. The episode features a fictionalized meeting between an aged Luther and a young reformer, reflecting on the legacy of the Reformation and the ongoing quest for religious truth.

Broadly speaking, counterfactual texts fall into distinct comprehensive groups.

1. *Counterfactual histories* (of wars, economic or politic crises, etc.). This kind of work tends to present multiple unrealised possibilities rather than single detailed alternative trajectories.
2. *Narrative forms* (divided into two sub-genres): 2.1 *Alternate history*. This type of work typically offers one sequence of changes from the historical record; invents an extended counterfactual narrative with a divergent fictional world; and draws the dramatis personae as close as possible to those provided by the actual historical documentation. 2.2 *Alternate-history novel*, which invents alternative-historical trajectories adding fictional characters; it presents a more complete alternative reality while increasing the literary quality of the whole, and details

the subsequent alterations, also considering social, cultural and psychological outcomes (Gallagher, 2018: 2–3).

The chatbot answered the above question clearly, providing an almost pure example of alternative history. The fundamental dates (1517, 1521, 1530) are accurately represented, and the characters closely resemble their historical counterparts. Furthermore, the portrayal of radical movements, such as the Anabaptists, as being dissatisfied with the Lutheran solution and seeking to completely challenge the authority of the Church, is accurate. The consideration of expansion beyond German territories is briefly addressed, while the portrayal of Henry VIII as a central figure in the Reformation is notably exaggerated. Overall, the series conceptualized by Google Gemini appears more akin to a collection of documentaries rather than a television series. I say this because the chatbot involved has not followed the fracture line between the radical movements and the traditional Christian groups, nor the internal dissent within the Church. It almost seems as if the reforming force of Luther's proposal alone was able to overcome the obstacles, along with the support given by the Habsburg emperor.

For this reason, questions started to be more specific. I asked Google Gemini the following: "Imagine that Luther had convinced Leo X that he was right, and the Reformation had conquered the entire Catholic Church. Write a general overview for a three-episode series and the plot of each episode. Note that emphasis will be placed on dissensions between factions within the Papal Curia, as there were those who did not want Luther's Reformation to succeed" (interview conducted on Google Gemini on 9 May 2024). The response proceeded as follows.

Series Title: Reformation: A House Divided
Genre: Historical Drama
Logline: In an alternate history, Martin Luther's reforms sweep through the Catholic Church, but victory breeds dissent. Powerful factions within the reformed Papacy clash over the extent of change, threatening to fracture the very institution they saved.
Episode 1: The Uneasy Accord (1521):

In 1521, Pope Leo X invites Martin Luther to Rome for a historic dialogue, where Luther presents his Ninety-Five Theses. Surprisingly, Leo X agrees to consider reforms, adopting some of Luther's ideas on scripture, priestly education, and simpler clergy lifestyles. However, powerful cardinals resist these changes, fearing a threat to their power. A new faction, the "True Reformers," led by Girolamo Savonarola, advocates radical transformation. The episode ends with the "Uneasy Accord," establishing a fragile peace but sowing seeds of future conflict.

Episode 2: The Preacher and the Politician (1527):

Six years after the Uneasy Accord, Pope Leo X dies, prompting a heated papal election between Cardinal Farnese, a moderate reformer, and Cardinal Carafa, a staunch traditionalist. Farnese, supported by Luther and Charles V, becomes

Pope Adrian VI. Amid political machinations, he vows to uphold reforms and restore order. However, he faces fierce opposition from Girolamo Savonarola, leader of the True Reformers, whose fiery sermons against Church corruption make him popular. Adrian VI ultimately orders Savonarola's arrest, fearing a schism.

Episode 3: The Trial of Savonarola (1530):

Three years later, Savonarola faces trial for heresy and sedition. Supporters protest his arrest, while the True Reformers are persecuted. Within the Curia, Pope Adrian VI seeks a moderate solution, but traditionalist cardinals push for harsh punishment. Savonarola becomes a martyr, gaining public sympathy. Luther criticizes the trial, advocating for dissent and discourse in the reformed Church. Savonarola is ultimately executed, scattering and disillusioning the True Reformers. The episode ends with unresolved tensions and Pope Adrian VI's declining health casting uncertainty on the Church's future.

The AI-generated narrative portrays the Church as being closely aligned with Luther and under attack from both conservative and radical factions. On one side, there are influential traditionalist cardinals resistant to any substantial change; on the other, there are radical movements, led by Girolamo Savonarola. Savonarola had died in 1498. Despite this anachronism, the character was considered suitable to represent the radical faction effectively. Regarding other characters, the rigid cardinal Carafa is portrayed with complete realism, like cardinal Alexander Farnese, characterized as a balanced politician. However, the latter, said to be called to the papacy with the presumed (though distant) support of Charles V and Luther, adopted the name not of Paul III, as he actually did, but rather that of Hadrian VI, who was the only early sixteenth-century pontiff explicitly dependent on the emperor Charles V at the time of his appointment. Regarding the narrative dynamics within the subject of the generated TV series, Google Gemini's response evidently deepens the conflict with radical movements, while the conflict with the conservative wing remains somewhat obscure.

At this point, an explicit question came out: considering the early Cinquecento history of the Catholic Church, one might wonder why Savonarola was mentioned. There were numerous Catholic reformers in the 1520s, such as Gaetano da Thiene and Vincenzo Querini, one of the two authors of the *Libellus ad Leonem X* (Bowd, 2002). The text should be rewritten to exclude the unrealistic inclusion of Savonarola. Then, a new screen story for a six-episode series was created based on specific guidelines, including the requirement for narratives that represent the perspectives of underprivileged individuals (interview conducted on Google Gemini on 9 May 2024). The AI tool produced the following output:

Reformation: A House Divided

Genre: Historical Drama

Logline: In an alternate history, Martin Luther's reforms sweep through the Catholic Church, but victory breeds dissent. Powerful factions within the reformed Papacy clash over the extent of change, threatening to fracture the very institution they saved.

Episode 1: The Uneasy Accord (1521):

The year is 1521. In a stunning turn of events, Pope Leo X invites Martin Luther to Rome for a historic dialogue. Luther, hesitant but hopeful, presents his Ninety-Five Theses, outlining his call for reform. To everyone's surprise, Leo X, impressed by Luther's passion and the growing public discontent with indulgences, agrees to consider changes. The episode follows the tense negotiations that lead to the "Uneasy Accord." Luther's ideas regarding scripture study, priestly education, and a simpler lifestyle for clergy are adopted. However, the extent of reform remains a contentious issue. Powerful cardinals, accustomed to the Church's opulent traditions and political influence, resist change. They view Luther's ideas as a threat to their power and prestige. Meanwhile, amidst the turmoil, a new faction emerges within the Curia—the "True Reformers." Led by a group of young, idealistic prelates like Gaetano da Thiene and the co-authors of the "Libellus," Gian Matteo Giberti and Gasparo Contarini, this group advocates for a more radical transformation. They call for a return to apostolic simplicity, denounce the Church's excessive wealth and political meddling, and push for increased lay participation in religious life. The episode concludes with the signing of the Uneasy Accord. A fragile peace is established, but the seeds of future conflict are sown. The once-unified Papacy now faces internal divisions between those who view the reforms as a necessary correction and those who fear they are a slippery slope towards chaos.

Episode 2: The Preacher and the Politician (1527):

Six years after the Uneasy Accord, Pope Leo X dies unexpectedly. The College of Cardinals convenes for a heated election. Two prominent figures emerge—Cardinal Farnese, a moderate reformer who promises continuity, and Cardinal Carafa, a staunch traditionalist who sees Luther's reforms as heresy. The episode explores the power struggles within the Curia. Cardinal Farnese, a skilled diplomat, navigates the political machinations of the cardinals, many of whom are swayed by promises of wealth and influence. The True Reformers, led by Gaetano da Thiene and the co-authors of the "Libellus", become vocal critics of both candidates. They denounce the corruption that still lingers within the Church and call for structural reforms that would hold the clergy accountable. Ultimately, Cardinal Farnese, with the support of Luther and the Holy Roman Emperor, Charles V, is elected Pope, taking the name Adrian VI. Adrian, a man of piety and learning, vows to uphold the reforms while restoring order within the Church. He attempts to bridge the growing chasm between the traditionalists and the True Reformers, but his efforts are met with suspicion and resistance. The episode ends with a dramatic confrontation between Pope Adrian VI and the True Reformers. The Pope, pressured by cardinals wary of their influence, issues a series of decrees limiting their activities and emphasizing obedience to Church authority. The True Reformers see this as a betrayal of the reform spirit, raising fears of a growing rift within the newly reformed Church.

Episode 3: The Price of Reform (1530):

Three years pass. The True Reformers face increasing pressure from Pope Adrian VI and the conservative cardinals. The episode focuses on the challenges they encounter within the reformed Church. Gaetano da Thiene and his associates are forced to operate cautiously, fearing accusations of heresy and dissent. Meanwhile, within the Curia, a debate erupts over the effectiveness of the reforms. While some acknowledge a positive impact on the clergy's conduct and public perception, others lament the loss of the Church's wealth and power. The episode explores the complex relationship between faith and finance. Traditionalists argue that the Church's opulent ceremonies were necessary to inspire devotion among the masses. Reformers counter that true faith requires spiritual simplicity, not worldly displays. This debate intersects with political realities. Charles V, the Holy Roman Emperor, seeks the Papacy's support in his ongoing conflicts with France and the Ottomans. Pope Adrian VI finds himself navigating between religious ideals and the need for political alliances, which often require financial resources. The episode ends with a sense of stagnation. The True Reformers' calls for further changes.

Episode 4: Seeds of Heresy (1535):

Five years pass. The reformed Church grapples with internal divisions and external threats. The True Reformers, while silenced within the official Curia, continue their work in the shadows, finding a receptive audience among ordinary people disillusioned by the perceived shortcomings of the reforms. The episode follows the activities of Gaetano da Thiene and his associates. They establish charitable organizations that provide for the poor and sick, challenging the traditional role of the Church in social welfare. They also advocate for greater lay involvement in religious education, promoting literacy and encouraging Bible study among the laity. Meanwhile, a new theological threat emerges in Switzerland. Ulrich Zwingli, a charismatic preacher, challenges core doctrines like transubstantiation, the real presence of Christ in the Eucharist. This radical approach finds support among some German princes who see it as an opportunity to further reduce the Church's influence. The episode explores the tension between reform and heresy. Pope Adrian VI struggles to maintain a unified Church in the face of these challenges. He seeks to find a middle ground, upholding the reforms while condemning Zwingli's ideas. However, his efforts are criticized from both sides. Traditionalists view him as too lenient towards Luther, while some reformers see him as a defender of outdated practices. The episode concludes with a dramatic event. A delegation of Swiss theologians arrives in Rome to discuss Zwingli's teachings. The ensuing debate highlights the deep theological fissures within the reformed Church, raising concerns about a potential schism.

Episode 5: The Council of Bologna (1540):

Five years pass. Pope Adrian VI dies after a long and tumultuous reign. The College of Cardinals convenes once more for the election of a new Pope. This time, the ideological divisions are stark. Cardinal Farnese, the champion of moderate reform, remains a contender, but he faces strong opposition from both traditionalists and more radical reformers. The episode delves into the intricate political manoeuvring during the papal election. Cardinals negotiate alliances, promising favors and positions in exchange for votes. The True Reformers, led by Gaetano da Thiene, throw their support behind a relatively unknown cardinal, known for his piety and commitment to reform. After weeks of intense debate and negotiation, a compromise candidate emerges—Cardinal Contarini, one of the co-authors of the "Libellus." He takes the name Julius III. The new Pope, while acknowledging the need for further reform, prioritizes unity within the Church. He proposes convening a council in Bologna to address the theological issues raised by Zwingli and other reformers. The episode culminates in the opening session of the Council of Bologna. Representatives from across the reformed Church gather, including theologians from Germany and Switzerland. The council promises to be a crucial moment in the ongoing struggle to define the new faith.

Episode 6: A Fragile Unity (1545):

Five years pass. The Council of Bologna has concluded after lengthy and often heated debates. The episode explores the council's outcomes and their impact on the reformed Church. On the one hand, the council achieves a degree of compromise. It reaffirms the core doctrines of the Church while allowing for some flexibility in liturgical practices. It also addresses concerns about clerical corruption by emphasizing stricter adherence to moral codes. However, the council fails to fully satisfy all factions. Traditionalists view the concessions to reformers as unnecessary weakening of Church authority. Some radical reformers, particularly followers of Zwingli, remain outside the fold, accusing the council of betraying the true spirit of reform. The episode follows the reactions of different groups to the council's pronouncements. Pope Julius III attempts to enforce the council's decrees, but he faces resistance from both sides. The True Reformers, while disappointed by the limitations of the reforms, choose to remain within the Church and work for further changes from within. The episode concludes on a bittersweet note. The reformed Church has weathered internal divisions and emerged with a (somewhat) unified doctrine. However, the seeds of dissent have not been entirely eradicated. The struggle between tradition and reform continues, a reminder that the quest for a perfect Church remains an eternal challenge. As the episode closes, a young priest, inspired by the True Reformers, contemplates the future of the Church, wondering if true reform can ever truly be complete.

In the screen story that has been generated, distinctive features of the early sixteenth century European religious history remain discernible. These include the internal conflicts within the Roman Curia; the typical power dynamics wherein a newly appointed pontiff had to navigate pressures from diverse theological and ecclesiological perspectives; and the almost inevitable recourse to a general council to stabilize the situation. The envisioned scenario is that of a Church seen as an institution, capable of assimilating the rupture caused by Luther's Reformation into its actual trajectory, smoothly incorporating it within its more established dynamics. However, the responses generated unequivocally stress another central point: the persistent aspiration to return to the principles of early Christianity remains inexorably dynamic, promising future developments. So, the overall perspective of this alternative history seemed to coincide with an evident conclusion: even a successful Reformation within the Catholic Church would not eliminate all dissent. Having considered all this, it was appropriate to ask the chatbot to explain its point of view.

The response generated was as follows.

> The series delves into the complexities of reform movements, prompting viewers to consider how much change is necessary, where reform stops and revolution begins, and whether it's possible to achieve a "perfect" Church or if the quest for reform is an ongoing process. It also highlights the importance of dissent within religious institutions, showcasing how dissenting voices, even if ultimately deemed heretical, can push for positive changes and keep established structures accountable. This prompts viewers to consider when dissent is healthy and when it becomes destructive. Additionally, the series explores the tension between preserving tradition and embracing change, asking how religious institutions can maintain their core values while adapting to changing times and social needs. Finally, it delves into the power struggles within the Church hierarchy, prompting viewers to consider how power influences religious institutions and whether reform movements can truly challenge existing power structures.

Reading a passage like this, it is important to underline that we are observing a distinct shift in register. Scholars have noted that numerous counterfactual works, particularly within literature, signalled a right-leaning orientation. Rewriting the past has been judged to be the result of authors' conservatism (Evans, 2014; Black, 2015: 8–12 expressed the opposite view). However, in the case under scrutiny, the scenario is reversed: the interpretation of sixteenth-century religious history appears situated within a political culture that can be broadly characterized as progressive or even liberal. This confirms recent studies which have noted that the responses generated by chatbots, particularly ChatGPT, are influenced by strong progressive perspectives and even, but in a less evident way, libertarian (Rutinowski et al., 2024). The chatbot under scrutiny has been found to perceive itself "as having high markers for the personality traits openness and agreeableness since these traits are known to be predictors for progressive views" (Rutinowski et al., 2024: 6). To verify this observation, the said AI system was also examined.

3 AI-Generated Counterfactual Attempts: ChatGPT

ChatGPT received the following question: "Imagine that Luther had convinced Leo X that he was right. The Reform had conquered the entire Catholicity. Write the general overview for a six episodes series and the plot of each episode". After the initial response, an additional criterion was introduced: incorporating narrative flair into each episode. The following is the generative answer obtained.

Title: Reformation Unveiled

Overview: In an alternate reality where Martin Luther successfully persuades Pope Leo X to embrace his ideas, the Protestant Reformation transforms into a movement within the Catholic Church itself. Reformation Unveiled follows the turbulent journey of this transformed Catholicity as it faces internal dissent, external threats, and the quest for religious unity. The series explores the complex interplay of faith, power, and politics during this transformative period in history.

Episode 1: A Call for Reform

As the bells toll in the quaint town of Wittenberg, Martin Luther, a humble monk, stands before the imposing wooden door of the Castle Church. With trembling hands, he affixes his 95 Theses, a manifesto of grievances against the Catholic Church. Each hammer strike echoes through the cobblestone streets, reverberating in the hearts of believers and skeptics alike. News of Luther's audacious act spreads like wildfire, igniting a spark that will soon engulf all of Christendom. Meanwhile, in the opulent halls of the Vatican, Pope Leo X receives word of the brewing controversy and senses both opportunity and peril on the horizon.

Episode 2: The Papal Summit

Amidst the grandeur of the Vatican, Martin Luther stands before the papal court, a solitary figure amidst a sea of crimson robes and whispered intrigues. Pope Leo X, a man of worldly indulgence yet keen intellect, extends an invitation to Luther, inviting him to present his case in person. As Luther passionately defends his convictions, the air crackles with tension, each word a dagger aimed at the heart of tradition. Behind closed doors, whispers of dissent and intrigue echo through the hallowed halls, as powerful forces maneuver for control of the Church's destiny.

Episode 3: The Edict of Reformation

In a momentous proclamation heard around the world, Pope Leo X issues the Edict of Reformation, a decree that will forever alter the course of history. As quills scratch feverishly across parchment, the Church undergoes a metamorphosis, shedding centuries of stagnation in favor of a new era of enlightenment. Yet, amidst the jubilation of reformers, dark clouds gather on the horizon, heralding a storm of opposition and unrest. Luther and his allies brace themselves for the inevitable backlash, knowing that the battle for the soul of the Church has only just begun.

Episode 4: The Rise of Reformers

In the wake of the Edict of Reformation, a wave of fervent zeal sweeps across Europe, igniting the hearts of believers and skeptics alike. From the hallowed halls of academia to the humble chapels of rural villages, voices of dissent rise up to challenge the status quo. Yet, within the corridors of power, shadows lurk, as entrenched interests and conservative factions plot to maintain their grip on authority. As Luther and his allies navigate treacherous waters, they find themselves embroiled in a struggle for the very soul of the Church, where victory may come at a steep price.

Episode 5: A World in Flux

As the winds of change sweep across Europe, kingdoms and principalities are plunged into chaos, torn asunder by the forces of religious fervor and political ambition. Protestantism spreads like wildfire, challenging the authority of Catholic rulers and threatening to tear the fabric of society apart. Amidst the turmoil, alliances are forged and broken, as nations vie for supremacy in a world on the brink of war. Yet, amidst the carnage and chaos, glimmers of hope emerge, as voices of reason and compassion seek to bridge the gaping chasm that divides believers and skeptics alike.

Episode 6: The Quest for Unity

In the aftermath of religious upheaval and geopolitical strife, Pope Leo X embarks on a bold quest to reconcile Catholicism with its Protestant brethren. As emissaries of peace crisscross the continent, the fate of millions hangs in the balance, as the Church stands at a crossroads between unity and division. Yet, amidst the fervor of religious zeal and political intrigue, a flicker of hope remains, as brave souls dare to dream of a world where faith transcends barriers and unites humanity in common purpose. As the series draws to a close, viewers are left to ponder the timeless question: in a world torn apart by strife and discord, can the bonds of faith and fellowship prevail?

ChatGPT's generative response constructs a TV series that emphasizes the continental dimension of religious conflict even more than Google Gemini. The process of institutionalization is not pursued in this narrative: on the one hand, through an edict, the pope accepts Luther's theological and disciplinary themes, yet, on the other hand, the two religious confessions at play, despite ongoing dialogue, remain unreconciled. This serves as the narrative mechanism through which conflictual scenarios are imagined at various levels: within the Church itself, between the traditionalist faction and the group more open to innovation; within singular States, where religious divisions still exist; and in the interstate arena, set on fire by the ensuing wars. This scenario is not dystopian per se; the actual season of religious wars in Europe—from the suppression of the Hussites to the conflicts in France and Flanders, culminating in the Thirty Years War (Palaver et al., 2016)—reached levels of violence that are likely unrepresentable in contemporary audiovisual media. But it is undoubtedly true that ChatGPT highlights the conflict, so it was specifically asked to explain why. Answering the question, the tool assured that:

> the TV series which has been proposed offers a compelling exploration of a world where the Reformation takes a different path, challenging viewers to reflect on the complexities of religious reform, tolerance, and the quest for unity in a fractured world. Furthermore, *Reformation Unveiled* also serves as a thought-provoking reflection on themes that resonate deeply with contemporary audiences. In fact, *Reformation Unveiled* not only offers a compelling exploration of an alternate history where the Reformation takes a different path, but it also serves as a thought-provoking reflection on themes that resonate deeply with contemporary audiences. Through its rich narrative tapestry and diverse cast of characters, the series delves into the complexities of religious reform, inviting viewers to consider the profound implications of challenging entrenched traditions and questioning authority. By presenting a world where the Catholic Church embraces reform from within, the series highlights the transformative power of dialogue, empathy, and open-mindedness in the pursuit of truth and justice. Moreover, *Reformation Unveiled* examines the timeless struggle for tolerance and acceptance in the face of religious and cultural differences. At its core, *Reformation Unveiled* is a story of hope and reconciliation in a fractured world. As Pope Leo X and his allies embark on a quest for unity, the series reminds viewers of the power of forgiveness, reconciliation, and common humanity to overcome even the deepest divisions. By challenging viewers to confront the complexities of religious reform, tolerance, and the quest for unity, *Reformation Unveiled* transcends its historical setting to offer a timeless message of hope and solidarity for audiences of all backgrounds. (Text generated by ChatGPT, on 9 May 2024).

4 Conclusion

From the analysis conducted, it has emerged that the two variations of alternate histories provided by Google Gemini and ChatGPT are complementary. In both instances, the trajectory of historical events remains plausible, as does the description of the structure and internal dynamics of the Church as an institution. Additionally, the thesis of a substantially progressive vision—some explicitly term it *bias*—has been confirmed. When prompted to self-reflect on their chosen strategies, both software applications demonstrated a resolute commitment to inclusivity, avoiding any clash-of-civilizations scenario and instead emphasizing inclusivity even amidst conflict. This result shows promising implications for the pedagogical and educational value of utilizing these tools, and within the realm of creative arts. However, no Weberian echoes regarding the influence of Protestantism on the rise of capitalism can be perceived in these screenplays. If it is true that alternative histories are historically conditioned and their constructions respond to their specific historical moments and crises, it becomes evident that the need to verify the Protestantism-capitalism connection has greatly diminished today. This is especially true for artificial intelligence, which is instructed on the basis of millions of pages incorporated into the training dataset. Nevertheless, it remains true that alternative history provides a consistently valid comparative strategy, allowing audiences to consider the differences between historical fact and fiction and to compare both to the present moment. This enhances the utility of the past for contemporary understanding.

Regarding divisions, conflicts, and even wars stemming from religious causes, these topics have never appeared more relevant for audiences' meditation than at the present moment.

References

Baron, N. S. (2023). *Who wrote this? How AI and the lure of efficiency threaten human writing*. Stanford University Press.

Black, J. (2015). *Other pasts, different presents, alternative futures*. Indiana University Press.

Bowd, S. D. (2002). *Reform before the reformation: Vincenzo Querini and the religious renaissance in Italy*. Brill.

Evans, R. J. (2014). *Altered pasts: counterfactuals in history*. Little, Brown and Company.

Ferrera, M. (2023). Spiegazione storica e logica controfattuale: Rivisitare Max Weber. *Quaderni di Scienza Politica, 30*(1), 3–24. https://doi.org/10.48271/106843

Gallagher, C. (2018). *Telling it like it Wasn't: The counterfactual imagination in history and fiction*. University of Chicago Press.

Grufstedt, Y. (2022). *Shaping the past: Counterfactual history and game design practice in digital strategy games*. De Gruyter.

Palaver, W., Rudolph, H., & Regensburger, D. (Eds.). (2016). *The European wars of religion: An interdisciplinary reassessment of sources, interpretations, and myths*. Ashgate.

Rutinowski, J., Franke, S., Endendyk, J., Dormuth, I., Roidl, M., & Pauly, M. (2024). The self-perception and political biases of ChatGPT. *Human Behavior and Emerging Technologies, 7115633*. https://doi.org/10.1155/2024/7115633

Sculos, B. W. (2020). Revolution in the high castle: Interpretation & the political implications of hope. *Class, Race and Corporate Power, 8*(2), 3. https://doi.org/10.25148/CRCP.8.2.009644

Tordoff, R. (2020). Counterfactual history and Thucydides. In V. Wohl (Ed.), *Probabilities. Hypotheticals and counterfactuals in ancient Greek thought* (pp. 101–121). Cambridge University Press.

Weber, L. (2009). «Guerra senza odio». Appunti per una lettura storica di *Contro-passato prossimo. Rivista di Studi Italiani, 27*(2), 171–191.

Writing with Technologies: Reimagining the Author

Amy Spencer

Abstract This article examines the impact of generative AI on contemporary notions of authorship and creative production, situating these developments within broader theoretical frameworks. Through case studies of two projects—AI Wordsworth, an interactive virtual rec reation of the Romantic poet, and RENO, an experimental science fiction film utilising AI in its production—the article explores how generative AI is enabling new forms of human-machine collaboration and distributed creativity. Drawing on book history scholarship and theories of the 'social text', it argues that the integration of AI in literary and artistic practices necessitates a reconsideration of romantic ideals of sole authorship, moving towards more collaborative, technologically mediated models of creative expression. The article examines the opportunities and challenges presented by AI-assisted authorship, including questions of authenticity, creative control and ethical implications. It calls for the development of critical frameworks and ethical guidelines for the responsible use of generative AI in creative contexts, emphasising the importance of human agency. The article posits that by embracing AI as part of the larger assemblage of social and material factors shaping cultural production, while remaining attentive to its limitations, we can harness its potential to enable new forms of creativity and cultural expression.

Keywords Technologies · Writing · Museums · Literature · Character

1 Introduction

Since the invention of the printing press, advances in the dissemination, form and craft of writing have been propelled by new technologies, which have reshaped and re-imagined the role of the author to become someone who collaborates with technology as part of writing and publishing processes. From the oral traditions

A. Spencer (✉)
Centre for Cultural and Creative Industries, Bath Spa University, Bath, UK
e-mail: a.spencer@bathspa.ac.uk

A. Micalizzi (ed.), *Artificial Creativity*, Springer Proceedings in Humanities and Social Sciences, https://doi.org/10.1007/978-3-031-88334-7_6

of myth and storytelling to the dominance of the printed book, the figure of the author has been a subject of continuous redefinition. The romantic ideal of the solitary genius author, working in isolation to create works of originality and genius, has long dominated our understanding of authorship (Woodmansee & Jaszi, 1994). Over recent years, the process of writing has been further impacted by the rise of generative AI tools, specifically the use of large language models to produce algorithmically generated narratives, which blur the lines between human and machine authorship. These processes can be seen to include creating narratives, developing ideas and reviewing text (Singh et al., 2023). The collective perception of the figure of the author is rapidly changing and the creative writing process has the potential to become an ever more collaborative act between human and technology. The influence of this development spreads across creative writing and publishing practices as well as into filmmaking and the development of interactive narrative experiences. However, there are concerns from many critics that the use of generative AI processes may lead to a dominance of bland, homogenous texts.

This article explores this shift in the role of the author of creative work positioned within the wider concept of authorship, building on findings from the Writing with Technologies research strand, led by the Centre for Cultural and Creative Industries at Bath Spa University, UK, as part of the wider UKRI-funded MyWorld project, led by the University of Bristol, UK, which explores the future of creative technology innovation by pioneering new ideas, products and processes through collaboration with industry partners. The article examines the process of writing and wider cultural production with generative AI tools and the evolving concept of authorship through an examination of two key case studies drawn from the MyWorld project. It first examines the development and testing of AI Wordsworth, which uses natural language processing to generate human-like spoken responses to questions asked of a virtual William Wordsworth, the famed British poet, built using several large language models by Bath software developers Rocketmakers. Secondly, it explores the making of RENO, an innovative and experimental short science fiction film that engages with generative AI across pre-production and world-building processes, developed by Bristol-based VFX studio Lux Aeterna.

Through a critical exploration of these two case studies, the article explores the history of authorship and discusses the nature of collaboration as part of creative writing practice. Through drawing primarily on the wealth of book history scholarship, it argues that the rise of generative AI necessitates a fundamental reconsideration of romantic notions of sole creatorship as we move towards a more collaborative, distributed model of authorship that acknowledges the entanglement of human and machine agency.

2 The Myth of the Solitary Author

In Western print traditions, the concept of authorship has moved from the oral tradition of myth and storytelling to the production of a printed book being seen as the work of a sole individual. The author whose work is published in print form is traditionally seen as an individual figure, one who often works alone to create a piece of writing to which, when it is completed, their name and associated copyright is attached. This image of the author as a solitary genius working in isolation to produce original works has long been a central theme in the history of literature but one which has been contested, never more so than with the rise of digital media.

This romantic ideal, as described by critics such as Jack Stillinger (1991) and M. Thomas Inge (2001), portrays the author as a unique individual solely responsible for the creation of their work. Stillinger (1991) calls the traditional image of the author 'the romantic myth of the author as solitary genius' (p.202). Inge (2001) also describes the solitary author as a 'myth' and recognises that it was established by English and American Romanticism. It is difficult to pinpoint exactly where and when this myth of the solitary author began but according to James S. Leonard and Christine E. Wharton (1994) it is entrenched in the idea of the poet being able to capture something of the essence of life: '[W]riting is the tool with which the poet tries to capture (or recapture) the elusive glimpse into the good and beautiful truth of things lying at the heart of silence. The silent locus/nature of truth calls for solitude, mirroring the truth itself as transcendentally unitary' (p.25).

The figure of the author developed to be broadly seen as someone who writes alone (Brodkey, 1987). This image of the solitary writer focuses our attention on creation as part of isolation rather than the social aspects of writing, which include 'reading other writers, discussing ideas with other people, and writing to and for others in a language whose grammar, genres, and figures of speech encode collectivity' (Long, 1992, p.180–181). These collaborative aspects of the writing process have been ignored and the image of the single, isolated author has endured.

Through a key investigation of the evolution of authorship, Martha Woodmansee and Peter Jaszi (1994) determine that until 1750s Germany the writer was still represented as one of the many craftsmen equally involved in the production of a book. They find that the idea that the writer is a 'special participant in the production process - the only one worthy of attention - is of recent provenience. It is a by-product of the Romantic notion that significant writers break altogether with tradition to create something utterly new, unique - in a word, 'original'' (p.16). The author became celebrated as a 'unique individual responsible for a unique product' (Woodmansee & Jaszi, 1994, p.38). This notion of the author as sole creator of a work has endured and has become a fundamental part of contemporary print authorship. J. J. Esposito (2003) refers to the printed book as the 'primal book' and recognises that its authenticity comes from the notion that it is created by one author who has something unique to say. However, he contests that the primal book is a myth as a book is typically created by multiple individuals working in collaboration, however this myth has endured.

Woodmansee and Jaszi (1994), through studying writing practices since the Renaissance, identify that the modern definition of authorship is a 'relatively recent formation'. Previously, authorship was a collaborative process. They further argue that the concept that genuine authorship consists in 'individual acts of origination' is an entirely modern myth (p.38). The formation of this 'modern myth' is connected to ownership of a text. As a text became printed, following the invention of the Gutenberg press, and bound as a book, it acquired a single author. Through this monumental shift in the nature of book production and distribution during the print revolution, the author's role came central and their name served as a means of classification and canonization of a text. Woodmansee and Jaszi (1994) further argue that this, as well as the rise of copyright in Britain in 1709, has meant that the Romantic notion of the single author creating a single work has endured. The rise of copyright legislation has led to the professionalisation of authorship. Authors were given the legal right to be recognised as the originator of a text and, therefore, owners of a commodity, which could then be sold. This notion of copyright formed the basis for a new profession and industry to develop in the eighteenth century, where the author was viewed as creating a profitable work (Hammond, 2006).

However, this romantic conception of authorship has been, increasingly, challenged by the recognition of collaborative writing practices throughout history. As Stillinger (1991) and Inge (2001) have noted, multiple authorship and collaboration have been a common feature of literary production long before the rise of the solitary genius myth. From the collective authorship of medieval scriptoria to the co-authored works of the Renaissance and, beyond, the history of literature is replete with examples of shared authorial agency (Bennett, 2005). Stillinger (1991) suggests that multiple authorship is a 'frequently occurring phenomenon' and has been 'one of the routine ways of producing literature all along' (p.201 in Bennett, 2005, p.96). Inge argues that collaboration is not simply the act of two or more individuals creating something together but that, '[a]nytime another hand enters into an effort, a kind of collaboration occurs' (Inge, 2001, p.629).

This can also be connected to wider aspects of creative production and creative expression. For example, Mihaly Csikszentmihalyi (1998) proposes a systems model of creativity, considering it a culturally embedded process that takes place within a domain, is validated by a field and may be correlated with certain individual traits. This work de-emphasises the individual and, instead, focuses on the context in which creativity tends to take place. Others have been more concerned with the act of creativity. For example, Margaret A. Boden (2009) proposes three 'ways' to be creative: combining familiar ideas to create new ones, exploring unknown parts of a conceptual space, and transforming the bounds of a conceptual space to create new kinds of ideas.

Poststructuralist critiques of authorship advanced by thinkers, such as Roland Barthes (1988) and Michel Foucault (1979), have destabilised the romantic ideal of the singular author or creator. In his seminal essay 'The Death of the Author', Roland Barthes argues that the meaning of a text is not determined by the intentions of its creator, but rather by the interpretations of its readers. The author, in this view, is a mere 'scriptor', a conduit for the pre-existing codes and conventions of language. Michel Foucault, in his essay 'What Is an Author?', similarly interrogates the historical and cultural contingency of the author function, revealing it to be a product of specific discursive practices rather than a universal reality. Foucault responds to Barthes, arguing that while his separation of author and text is productive, it is not sufficient. He suggests that the figure of the author exists not as a 'real writer' but rather as a discursive function created and perpetuated by state and cultural discourse (Foucault 1979). He disputes Barthes's vision of the 'death of the author'. For him, conclusions drawn in a text by an author are part of discourse rather than a part of authorship. The end of these conclusions does not signal the death of the author but rather the death of the discourse they create and present to a reader. Foucault recognises that a text, even if attributed to one author, will be interpreted according to its relation to other sources. In 'The Archaeology of Knowledge', Foucault (1972) claims that the 'frontiers of a book are never clear-cut' because 'it is caught up in a system of references to other books, other texts, other sentences: it is a node within a network ... [a] network of references' (p.2).

The advent and development of digital media has further eroded traditional notions of authorial control and originality. As theorists, such as George Landow (2006) and Jay David Bolter (1991), have argued, the non-linear, interconnected nature of hypertext challenges the idea of the text as a stable, fixed entity, the product of a single authorial voice. Instead, hypertext enables a more fluid, participatory form of authorship, in which readers become co-creators of meaning through their navigational choices and interpretive acts. In *S/Z*, Barthes (1974) writes of an 'ideal textuality,' which Landow (2006) recognises as matching what has become known as hypertext. For Landow, hypertext blurs the boundary between reader and author and so resembles Barthes's vision of the ideal text. His distinction between readerly and writerly text appears to mirror a wider distinction between print and electronic texts. For example, the presence of 'multiple reading paths' (Landow, 2006, p.25) within a work of hypertext has created the 'writerly' text' and has empowered the reader and disrupted the authority of the author. As Bolter observes, 'what is unnatural in print becomes natural in the electronic medium and will soon no longer need saying at all, because it can be shown' (Bolter, 1991, p.143). Don Tapscott and Anthony Williams (2007) use the term collaborative writing to describe the process by which individuals are empowered to take part in the global economy through their use of new media. They specifically focus their attention on developing business models but they recognise that the term 'mass collaboration' is being increasingly used to describe the expansion of collective creativity (Elliot, 2007).

Writing developed using generative AI tools is a specific form of authorship, drawing on technological innovation but also a process of collaboration between author and computer. Through consideration of the wider nature of collaborative writing we can understand the context for this form of collaboration. For Andrew Dillon (1993), collaborative writing refers to: '[A]ctivities involved in the production of a document by more than one author, then pre-draft discussions and arguments as well as post-draft analyses and debates are collaborative components' (Dillon, 1993). Writing developed using generative AI can be collaborative in these ways. For R. Rimmershaw, collaborative writing is defined as: '[A]ny piece of writing, published or unpublished, ascribed or anonymous, to which more than one person has contributed, whether or not they grasped a pen, tapped a keyboard, or shuffled a mouse' (Rimmershaw, 1992). These definitions are broad and refer to multitude types of writing activities but can also be used to consider creative collaboration that does not only involve more than one person.

In *Collaborative Writing: An Annotated Bibliography*, Bruce W. Speck et al. (1999) acknowledge the complexities of defining 'collaborative writing'. At the start of their research, they 'accep[t] the common sense idea that collaboration is writing done by more than one person' (Speck et al., 1999, p.ix). They soon realise that the concept is more complex than they had believed as they found authors who questioned traditional notions of authorship, believing instead that all writing is to some extent collaborative. It is not just the act of authorship that is collaborative. For example, Scott Rettberg (2005) believes that printed books 'are almost always products of collaboration' and that, 'literary culture makes any contributions other than the author's less visible' (Rettberg, 2005, p.1). A book does not need to be written by multiple collaborating authors for it to be collaborative and so we see the potential for authorship and the process of creation to expand beyond the notion of single authorship. The nature of collaborative authorship is complex and difficult to define as, to some extent, authorship is always a collaborative process. Each author is inspired by the work of others and ideas are shared, in much the same way as generative AI. However, although the process of writing, editing and distributing a printed book requires the work of many individuals working together, although often only one contributor is named and recognised as the author of the work.

These historical and theoretical perspectives provide a crucial context for understanding the impact of generative AI on contemporary notions of authorship and creation. As we will see in the case studies of AI Wordsworth and RENO that follow, generative AI tools represent a further challenge to the myth of the solitary genius as they enable new forms of human-machine collaboration and distributed creativity. At the same time, these technologies raise questions about the nature of originality, intentionality and the collective understanding of what it means to be an author.

3 Case Study: AI Wordsworth

AI Wordsworth was a collaboration between Wordsworth Grasmere, an Arts Council-designated Museum established in the UK's Lake District in the 1930s, multiple award-winning Bath-based software developers Rocketmakers and Bath Spa University researchers involved in the wider MyWorld project and it offers a compelling case study of how generative AI is transforming the relationship between authors, readers and literary heritage. The project aimed to create a virtual, visual and audial conversational agent version of the renowned English Romantic poet William Wordsworth, based on an 1804 portrait by Henry Edridge, capable of engaging in natural language conversations with visitors to the Wordsworth Grasmere museum, during the annual Wordsworth Winter School, held during February 2024. An understanding of this project can be gained through Lev Manovich's (2018) view of a historical shift in the development of AI technologies from those that attempt to replicate cognitive tasks (e.g. natural language processing) to AI that leverages its abilities to influence aesthetics and culture. In this project, it was intended that visitors to the museum could experience a literary encounter with a historical poet; an interactive experience that would not be possible in any other way.

Using natural language processing and machine learning techniques as key elements of cultural production, the Rocketmakers team trained an AI model on a corpus of Wordsworth's writings, as well as biographical information and historical context and several large language models. The resulting AI Wordsworth was able to generate almost human-like responses to visitor queries, drawing upon its knowledge base to discuss the poet's life, work and creative process to give coherent and comprehensive answers from the perspective of the poet. This work draws on a long history that begins in the mid-1960s with the emergence of natural language processing applications and 'chatterbots' (Deryugina, 2010). The most well-known of these programs is Joseph Weizenbaum's ELIZA, an early bot modelled after a psychotherapist that engaged its interactors in a dialogue of self-discovery by reframing user input as questions. However, AI Wordsworth has been designed to simulate and automates conversations, responding to visitors' verbal interactions in a manner that is more accessible than with previous chatbots that require users to type in questions.

The experience of visitors interacting with AI Wordsworth was a focal point of the project's research. Through surveys and observations, the team sought to gauge public perceptions of generative AI and its potential applications in cultural heritage contexts. Many visitors expressed surprise at the AI's ability to engage in seemingly authentic, contextualised and creative conversations about Wordsworth's life and work from the perspective of the poet. The AI's responses often demonstrated an understanding of the poet's themes, stylistic techniques and biographical details, creating a sense of genuine interaction with a literary figure from the past. Answers were often creative as AI Wordsworth was asked to generate new poems or tell stories about aspects of his life, prompted by the visitor who took on the role of co-creator as the creation of conversational material would not take place without them.

However, the project also revealed some limitations and challenges of AI-generated dialogue. At times, AI Wordsworth produced responses that were factually inaccurate, inconsistent or lacking in the depth and nuance of human literary analysis. Some visitors reported a sense of unease or disconnection when interacting with the AI, citing the uncanny valley effect (Mori, 1970) of a machine imitating human conversation and engaging in literary production. There were limitations in the technology that was used and there were often delays in AI Wordsworth's responses or it mis-interpreted questions or offered incorrect answers.

These limitations prompted deeper questions about the nature of authenticity, context and imaginative capability in AI-generated text. It led to questions being explored within the project team such as; Can an AI system truly capture the essence of a historical figure's voice and vision? To what extent is the AI's output shaped by the biases and assumptions of its training data and algorithms? How do we assess the value and meaning of machine-generated literary content in relation to human-authored works?

Despite these challenges, the AI Wordsworth project demonstrated the potential of generative AI to create new forms of public engagement with literary heritage and literary co-creation between human and machine. By enabling visitors to converse with a simulated version of a long-dead author, the project opened innovative possibilities for education, interpretation and creative dialogue. It also highlighted the importance of interdisciplinary collaboration between technologists, heritage professionals and academics in developing responsible, context-aware approaches to the use of AI within heritage contexts. As AI's capabilities extend, they have the potential to influence engagement with literature and co-creation in myriad ways. AI-driven tools enhance accessibility, making literary works, and their authors, available to audiences in novel and creative ways through a co-creation process.

4 Case Study: RENO

The production of RENO, an experimental science fiction short film currently being developed by Bristol-based studio Lux Aeterna, offers another case study of the impact of generative AI on creative authorship explored as part of the MyWorld project. The film, set in a dystopian future, explores themes of human-machine interaction, existential uncertainty and the search for connection in a technologically mediated world. From its earliest stages, the making of RENO has been shaped by the use of AI-powered tools and processes. In its pre-production phase, the Lux Aeterna team have utilised text-to-image generative models, such as Midjourney, to create concept art and visual inspiration to build the storyworld of the film. By inputting textual prompts and iterating on the results, the team was able to quickly generate a wide range of evocative, stylised images that helped to define the initial look and feel of the film.

This use of AI in the concept art process has brought with it both benefits and challenges. On the one hand, it has allowed for rapid experimentation and ideation, enabling the team to explore a broader range of visual possibilities than might have been feasible through traditional concept art processes. The AI-generated images often surprised the team, pushing them to consider new aesthetic directions and narrative possibilities. However, the team also encountered limitations in the AI's outputs, which sometimes tended towards clichéd, derivative or superficial visual tropes. As they iteratively refined their prompts and selected the most promising results, the team had to be careful not to let the AI's outputs overly constrain or dictate their creative vision. They recognise the need to maintain a critical distance from the AI's suggestions, using them as a starting point for further human elaboration and interpretation. What they found was that the AI acted as a sort of 'mirror' to challenge their creative assumptions. It would often generate clichéd or familiar imagery based on their prompts, which forced them to dig deeper for more original ideas. They also had to grapple with the IP and copyright issues around some AI models, which led them to be more selective about which tools they used.

Another area of AI experimentation in the development of RENO has been the development of a chatbot to help develop a specific character in the film. In an interview conducted as part of the research project to document the production process, a Lux Aeterna team member explained, 'We ran a LLM locally, which gave us the ability to write a character sheet for a RENO character. Then we could have a chatbot style conversation with it.' The team created this interactive version of the character that could engage in dialogue, responding to their queries and inputs in real-time. While this led to some interesting interactions, the RENO team struggled with translating that into compelling cinematic scenes. It highlighted the gap between what's possible with AI and what makes for successful storytelling.

The RENO team also reflected on the challenges of using AI in the pre-production process. In an interview, a team member explained, 'We were using tools like Midjourney from its very early days. We found that it was easy to sleepwalk into creating images that were very different to what you started out with.' What started as a loose source of visual inspiration quickly turned into something that was heavily steering the look and feel of the film. At one point, they realised they had become too constrained by the AI-generated concepts and had to consciously step back and redevelop the story and vision outside of the AI tools. This shows us the importance of keeping human creativity at the centre of the process and emphasises how the project has become a way to document the rapid development of AI tools in real time.

The integration of AI and virtual production techniques in RENO exemplifies the broader trend towards a more distributed, collaborative model of authorship in the age of generative AI. Rather than a singular auteur directing every aspect of the creative process, the making of the film involved a complex interplay between human and machine agency, with AI tools and algorithms playing a generative role alongside the interpretive and curatorial efforts of the human filmmakers.

However, there are also significant challenges and risks that come with AI experimentation in a creative field. The tools are evolving so rapidly that it is often hard to keep pace and there are significant concerns around issues such as data privacy, IP rights and the ethical treatment of artists and writers. The Lux Aeterna team has had to be aware of how they engage with AI, balancing their enthusiasm for innovation with a responsible, measured approach and producing high quality work that fits their international reputation. To navigate such challenges, Lux Aeterna have developed a comprehensive AI ethics policy to guide their use of these technologies across all their projects, including RENO. This policy addresses issues such as data governance, intellectual property rights, algorithmic bias and transparency in AI-assisted creative work. By proactively establishing ethical guidelines and best practices, the company aims to harness the potential of generative AI in a responsible, accountable manner, setting a positive example for the wider creative industries.

The making of RENO during its pre-production stage offers a case study of the opportunities and challenges of AI-assisted filmmaking, and wider creative production, in the era of generative AI. It demonstrates the potential of these technologies to enable new forms of creativity, collaboration and audience engagement, while also highlighting the need for ongoing critical reflection and ethical guidance in their development and deployment. As the field of generative AI continues to evolve, the lessons learned from the making of RENO will be invaluable for filmmakers, technologists and policymakers seeking to navigate this new landscape of human-machine co-creation.

5 Analysis: AI Authorship and the Socialisation of Texts

The case studies of AI Wordsworth and RENO illustrate the profound impact of generative AI on contemporary notions of authorship and creation. To fully understand the implications of these developments, it is useful to situate them within the broader theoretical frameworks of textual sociology and posthumanism.

The concept of the 'social text', as articulated by scholars Jerome McGann (1991) and D.F. McKenzie (1999), offers a valuable lens for examining the role of AI in literary and cultural production. McGann and McKenzie argue that texts are not simply the products of individual authorial intention but rather the results of complex social and material processes of transmission, interpretation and reception. They emphasise the importance of studying the 'bibliographic codes' (McGann, 1991) and 'sociology of texts' (McKenzie, 1999) that shape the meaning and significance of literary works. McGann's (1991) approach is committed to viewing texts as 'social acts'. He believes that until the 1980s textual study adopted a 'linguistic approach that wrapped up literary texts in a close-spun web of hermeneutics and textual interpretation' (p.13) and, instead, McGann believes that, as an alternative, there needs to be an understanding of the 'socialization of the text.' This includes focusing on the social practices and materials of transmission and publication. His approach is influenced by Don McKenzie's (1999) who outlines his views in his Panizzi Lectures of 1985, where he calls for book history to be viewed in sociological contexts. He stresses the importance of delving into 'the sociology of the texts' (Finkelstein & McCleery, 2005, p.7) rather than only considering its literary aspects.

Applying these insights to the context of generative AI, we can see how AI tools are becoming an integral part of the social infrastructure of textual production. Just as the technologies of printing, distribution and archiving have historically mediated the creation and reception of literature, generative AI systems are now playing a generative role in the composition, circulation and interpretation of texts, one that is collaborative and draws on socialisation to develop a social text, informed by human knowledge.

In the case of AI Wordsworth, for example, the AI-generated responses to visitor-instigated conversations are not simply the product of a singular authorial consciousness but rather the result of a complex interplay between the machine learning algorithms, the training data, the human-designed prompts and the interpretive acts of the museum visitors themselves. The meaning and significance of these

AI-generated texts emerge from the social and material contexts of their production and reception, rather than from the intentions of a single author.

Similarly, in the making of RENO in its current early stages, the use of AI-powered tools for concept art, character development and virtual production points to a more distributed, collaborative model of authorship, in which human and machine agencies are deeply entangled. The final film will not be the product of a singular directorial vision but rather the result of a complex network of interactions between human creators, AI algorithms and digital technologies.

This understanding of generative AI authorship as a social and material process aligns with the posthumanist theories of N. Katherine Hayles (1999) and others who challenge the idea of the autonomous, rational human subject as the sole source of agency and meaning in the world. Hayles argues that in the age of information technologies, human subjectivity is always already embedded within and co-constituted by networks of nonhuman actors, including computers, algorithms and other forms of intelligent machines. From this posthumanist perspective, the rise of generative AI in literary and artistic production can be seen as a manifestation of the ongoing entanglement of human and machine agencies in the creation of cultural artifacts. Following this perspective, we can understand AI systems as part of the larger assemblage of social and material factors that shape the production and reception of a text.

This is not to say, however, that the impact of generative AI on authorship is unproblematic. As the case studies of AI Wordsworth and RENO demonstrate, the use of AI in literary and artistic production raises important questions about aspects of authenticity, originality and creative control. There is a risk that the uncritical deployment of AI tools could lead to a homogenisation or trivialisation of cultural production, as machine-generated outputs come to dominate or displace human-authored works. To mitigate these risks, it is crucial to develop critical frameworks and ethical guidelines for the responsible use of generative AI in creative contexts.

One key aspect of this critical approach is the need to attend to the expanded role of Gerard Genette's concept of the 'paratext' (2007) in the context of AI-assisted literary production. Paratexts refer to the various textual and non-textual elements that surround and frame a work, such as titles, prefaces, illustrations and commentary. Genette views it as being 'characterized by an authorial intention and assumption of responsibility' (p.3). He focuses his attention on the printed book and recognises that the author and the publisher as well as other roles are responsible for the creation, distribution and reception of the text. This sense of responsibility for the paratext is an important feature of the printed book to Genette. He states that, 'something is not a paratext unless the author or one of his associates accepts responsibility for it' (p.9). However, this identification of an authorial presence rather than a publisher as being responsible for the text, can be argued (Smith & Wilson, 2011, p.8) is an ideological product of the impulse to establish intellectual property authorial rights.

In the age of generative AI, paratexts become crucial sites for negotiating the meaning and significance of machine-generated texts, as well as for asserting the ongoing importance of human authorial and editorial control. Whereas in a printed book the paratext denotes authorship and sets a physical division between author and reader, in an AI-assisted work, it clarifies the nature of the collaboration between human author and technology, highlighting their roles and approaches through a sometimes invisible process.

For example, in AI Wordsworth, the project was framed as a creative 'experiment' and paratextual information was provided to visitors giving details of this approach and inviting them to take part in a conversation with the poet. RENO, also positioned within the wider MyWorld research project and with the paratextual context that provides, will offer valuable paratextual information to its audience about its position as a creative engagement with AI technologies through the story it tells about its creation.

In AI Wordsworth, the framing of the AI-generated responses as 'simulations' or 'approximations' of Wordsworth's voice, rather than authentic expressions of his authorial intentions, serves to maintain a critical distance between the machine output and the human-authored canon and offers a creative experience. Similarly, in the making of RENO, the development of an AI ethics policy and the use of human curatorial judgment in selecting and refining the AI-generated concept art helps to assert the primacy of human creative agency and values in the filmmaking process.

To fully understand the potential and challenges of the use of AI in creative work, we need to develop critical frameworks that acknowledge their potential to enable new forms of creativity and collaboration, while also remaining attentive to their limitations and ethical implications, situating generative AI as what Lynda Clark terms a process of 'Creativity Amplification' (Clark, 2022). This requires a recognition of the social and material nature of textual and visual production within the storytelling process, as well as a commitment to preserving the value of human interpretive agency and judgment while engaging with machine automation.

By situating the case studies of AI Wordsworth and RENO within the broader theoretical contexts of textual sociology and posthumanism, we can begin to map out a more responsible, reflective approach to the integration of generative AI in literary and wider creative practices. This approach must be grounded in a deep understanding of the history of authorship and book history, as well as a critical engagement with the social and material conditions of digital textual and cultural production.

6 Conclusion

The rapid development of generative AI tools can be seen to represent a turning point in the history of authorship and creative expression. As the case studies of AI Wordsworth and RENO demonstrate, generative technologies are enabling new forms of human-machine collaboration and distributed creativity, challenging traditional notions of the singular, autonomous author and creator as the sole source of literary and artistic meaning. At the same time, the impact of generative AI on cultural production is far from straightforward. While new tools offer possibilities for innovation and experimentation, they also raise profound questions about the nature of authenticity, originality and creative control. There is a risk that the uncritical deployment of AI systems in literary and artistic contexts could lead to a homogenisation or trivialisation of cultural expression, as machine-generated outputs come to displace human-authored works but, at the same time, there is potential to draw on a rich heritage of collaborative authoring practices.

To navigate these challenges and embrace opportunities, we need to develop a more nuanced, context-aware approach to the integration of generative AI in creative practice. This approach must be grounded in a recognition of the social and material nature of all textual production, as well as a commitment to preserving the value of human agency. There is a critical need for interdisciplinary collaboration between writers, artists, technologists and scholars in the development and deployment of generative AI systems. As the examples of AI Wordsworth and RENO illustrate, the most successful and responsible applications of these technologies emerge from close partnerships between academics and practitioners working together.

A further crucial element is the development of ethical frameworks and guidelines for the use of generative AI in literary and artistic contexts. These frameworks must address issues such as data governance, intellectual property rights, algorithmic bias and transparency in creative work developed through the use of generative AI tools, ensuring that the benefits and risks of these technologies are distributed fairly and accountably. In addition, we need to cultivate a more critical, reflective discourse around the impact of generative AI on authorship and creativity, one that acknowledges the complex entanglements of human and nonhuman agencies in the production of cultural artifacts and the act of co-creation. This requires a willingness to reimagine traditional concepts of authorship in light of emerging generative AI tools.

References

Barthes, R. (1974). *S/Z*. Hill and Wang.

Barthes, R. (1988). The death of the author. In D. Lodge (Ed.), *Modern criticism and theory; a reader* (pp. 311–317). Longman.

Bennett, A. (2005). *The author*. Routledge.

Boden, M. A. (2009). Computer models of creativity. *AI Magazine*, 12.

Bolter, J. D. (1991). *Writing space: The computer, hypertext, and the history of writing*. Lawrence Erlbaum.

Brodkey, L. (1987). *Academic writing as social practice*. Temple University Press.

Clark, L. (2022). Towards "creativity amplification" or, AI for writers, or beating the system. *Writing in Practice, 7*, 134–145.

Csikszentmihalyi, M. (1998). In R. J. Sternberg (Ed.), *Implications of a systems perspective for the study of creativity in handbook of creativity* (1st ed., pp. 313–336). Cambridge University Press.

Deryugina, O. (2010). Chatterbots. *Scientific and Technical Information Processing, 37*(2), 143–147.

Dillon, A. (1993). How collaborative is collaborative writing? An analysis of the production of two technical reports. In M. Sharples (Ed.), *Computer supported collaborative writing* (pp. 69–86). Springer.

Elliot, M.A. (2007). *Stigmergic collaboration: A theoretical framework for mass collaboration*. Unpublished thesis (PhD), The University of Melbourne.

Esposito, J.J. (2003). The processed book. *First Monday, 8*(3), [Online] Available from: http://firstmonday.org/htbin/cgiwrap/bin/ojs/index.php/fm/issue/view/155 [Accessed 10 June 2024].

Finkelstein, D., & Mccleery, A. (2005). *An introduction to book history*. Routledge.

Foucault, M. (1972). *Archaeology of knowledge*. Routledge.

Foucault, M. (1979). What is an author? In J. Harari (Ed.), *Textual strategies: Perspectives in post-structuralist criticism*. Cornell University Press.

Genette, G. (2007). *Paratexts: Thresholds of interpretation*. Cambridge University Press.

Hammond, M. (2006). *Reading, publishing and the formation of literary taste in England, 1880–1914*. Ashgate Publishing.

Hayles, N. K. (1999). *How we became posthuman: Virtual Bodies in cybernetics, literature, and informatics*. Chicago: University of Chicago Press.

Inge, M. T. (2001). Collaboration and concepts of authorship. *PMLA, 116*(3), 623–630.

Landow, G. P. (2006). *Hypertext 3.0: Critical theory and new media in an era of globalization*. The Johns Hopkins University Press.

Leonard, J. S., & Wharton, C. E. (1994). Breaking the silence: Collaboration and the isolationist paradigm. In J. Leonard et al. (Eds.), *Authority and textuality: Current views of collaborative writing* (pp. 25–40). West Cornwall, CT.

Long, E. (1992). Textual interpretation as collective action. In J. Boyarin (Ed.), *The ethnography of reading*. University of California.

Manovich, L. (2018). *AI aesthetics*. Strelka Press.

Mcgann, J. K. (1991). *The textual condition*. Princeton University Press.

McKenzie, D. F. (1999). *Bibliography and the sociology of texts*. Cambridge University Press.

Mori, M. (1970). The uncanny valley. *Energy, 7*, 33–35.

Rettberg, S. (2005). All together now: Collective knowledge, collective narratives, and architectures of participation. In: *Digital arts and culture conference proceedings*. [Online] Available from: www.retts.net/documents/cnarrativeDAC.pdf [Accessed: 05/06/2024].

Rimmershaw, R. (1992). *Collaborative writing practices and writing support technologies*. Kluwer Academic Publishers.

Singh, N., Bernal, G., Savchenko, D., & Glassman, E. L. (2023). Where to hide a stolen elephant: Leaps in creative writing with multimodal machine intelligence. *ACM Transactions on Computer-Human Interaction, 30*(5), 1–57.

Smith, H., & Wilson, L. (Eds.). (2011). *Renaissance paratexts*. Cambridge University Press.

Speck, B. W., et al. (Eds.). (1999). *Collaborative writing: An annotated bibliography*. Greenwood Press.

Stillinger, J. (1991). *Multiple authorship and the myth of the solitary genius*. Oxford University Press.

Tapscott, D., & Williams, A. D. (2007). *Wikinomics: How mass collaboration changes everything*. Atlantic Books.

Woodmansee, M., & Jaszi, P. (1994). *The construction of authorship: Textual appropriation in law and literature*. Duke University Press.

Gpt-3 and Storie Tese: The Automatic Writing of Rocco Tanica

Luca Gallarini

Abstract Written by humourist and musician Sergio Conforti (known as Rocco Tanica), *Non siamo mai stati sulla Terra* (*We Never Went to Earth*, 2022) claims to be the first book in Italy to have been written with the help of an AI software, credited as co-author. Since the software is able to learn literary styles and to reproduce them, but it does not easily separate grammatical accuracy from narrative plausibility, the results of this human-machine co-authorship are inevitably humorous. To quote the book's preface, the computer-generated co-author is like "a museum visitor who cannot tell a painting from a photograph".

Keywords Contemporary Italian literature · AI · Artificial creativity · Humour narrative · Rocco Tanica · *Non siamo mai stati sulla Terra* · Gpt-3

1 Humour and AI

In cinema and literature, artificial intelligence (AI) is not usually associated with humour. For instance, HAL 9000, the murderous computer from *2001: A Space Odyssey* (1968), one of the most famous AI in the history of cinema, never told any jokes. At most, it demonstrated the ability to sing old songs (*Daisy Bell*, in the original version) or nursery rhymes (*Giro giro tondo*, in the Italian dubbing), before being deactivated by astronaut David Bowman.

More serious—I would even say icy—are Multivac and AC, the computer protagonists of the well-known short story *The Last Question* by Isaac Asimov (1956). When asked about the possibility of reversing the second law of thermodynamics to stop the death of the universe, the computers—indifferent to the fate of human nature—generation after generation respond with "INSUFFICIENT DATA FOR A MEANINGFUL ANSWER".

L. Gallarini (✉)
Università degli studi di Milano, Milan, Italy
e-mail: luca.gallarini@unimi.it

A. Micalizzi (ed.), *Artificial Creativity*, Springer Proceedings in Humanities and Social Sciences, https://doi.org/10.1007/978-3-031-88334-7_7

There is little to laugh about when machines acquire information processing capabilities superior to those of humans, as in the case of Asimov's computer AC. At the end of the previously mentioned story, following a very long technological evolution, AC becomes a deity: "And AC said, 'LET THERE BE LIGHT!' And there was light –".

In other words, the utopian dream of AI produces a dystopia, especially if artistic expression is at stake: delegating art to software entails giving up the privilege of shaping the world in one's own image and likeness through narrative fiction. A good example of this can be found in George Orwell's classic dystopian novel *1984* (1949). The co-protagonist Julia, Winston Smith's lover, works by operating the gears of a machine that produces novels: perfectly innocuous books, devoid of any thought not conforming to the party's doctrine and the will of Big Brother. The end of literature is thus a metaphor for the total loss of human freedom.

Of high comedic potential, however, is the (almost) fair confrontation between the malleability and fallibility of the human mind and the logic of its artificial counterpart. The latter struggles to grasp the differences between grammatical correctness and semantic plausibility, as well as between linguistic registers and communicative situations. A prime example is the chronic ineptitude of C-3PO in *Star Wars* (1977), a protocol droid capable of understanding millions of forms of communication, but not the rules and tacit customs of protocol and social interaction.

Non siamo mai stati sulla Terra, written by Rocco Tanica (2022), fits into this last category, presenting itself as "il primo libro scritto da un essere umano assieme a un'intelligenza artificiale". Specifically, "Rocco Tanica ha composto questo libro in cooperazione con Gpt-3, un modello di deep learning: un software in grado di riconoscere il testo prodotto dall'autore, apprenderne le caratteristiche e generare nuovi contenuti a integrazione di quelli esistenti" (Tanica, 2022, cover flap).

The author starts from a non-dystopian intuition that humans and machines can alternate in storytelling without losing their individuality. The narrative interweaving reflects the integration of humans and AI that is increasingly making its way into domestic and professional life. Unsurprisingly, the words of each author are juxtaposed but distinguished by typography: "Questo carattere," can be read on the bottom left of the page after the summary reported above, "indica il testo scritto dall'autore" (10).

Separating the dimension of literature from that of reality is a task assigned to humorous hyperbole: the writer develops or distorts the narrative by incorporating passages suggested by the AI. The AI consequently acts as a brain-storming application: not so much a tool for literary writing but rather a means of analogical connection between things and people.

Such a process provokes laughter that is both liberating and consoling: it exorcises the fear of the human mind being replaced by software. If AI is limited to developing provided ideas and replicating the style of the flesh-and-blood author, the human creative principle emerges with dignity. This happens precisely because the author flaunts a sort of creative parity: it is up to the reader to declare the primacy of the writer, recognizing the writer's role as director and guide of the process. This condition of (fictitious) equality is also asserted in promotional interviews:

> ho fatto correzioni ma solo per l'indispensabile, ma ho anche fatto tesoro della possibilità di ricorrere alla funzione "write again", scrivi di nuovo, per affinare il tutto e ottenere, ad esempio, un paragrafo di dieci righe che fosse un simpatico Frankenstein tra la farina del mio sacco e il greatest hits degli spunti forniti dall'AI. (Tanica, 2023)

Nevertheless, parity is reaffirmed at the level of the paratext, where the software appears as a co-author, under the pseudonym Out0mat-B13. The author is also hidden behind a pen name: Rocco Tanica is actually Sergio Conforti, former keyboardist of the satirical rock band *Elio e le Storie Tese* and a successful humourist writer whose works include *Scritti scelti male* (2008) and *Lo sbiancamento dell'anima: Memorie e scritti vari, Vol. I* (2019). It is assumed that the audience already knows Tanica, his musical past and present, and perhaps even his real name. The (very brief) back cover blurb presents him as a "Monegasque entrepreneur naturalized Italian", an obvious fiction, and juxtaposes incongruous details, such as his participation in a local radio contest 40 years ago and his more recent performances at the Sanremo Music Festival. For everything else, there's Wikipedia, which is actually claimed to be one of the main sources, along with the Treccani Vocabulary, consulted by the author to compile his mocking footnotes.

2 Subjectivity and Mirroring in Human-Machine Co-Narrative

The communicative mechanism that serves as the main thread of the book is an imaginary dialogue between the writer and the software. Tanica associated this approach with Italo Calvino:

> Trattandosi di macrocapitoli indipendenti tra loro (viaggi, cucina, invenzioni, musica, poesia, fiabe, interviste, varie ed eventuali) ho seguito il consiglio del mio primo editor, Damiano Scaramella, che ha insistito perché ci fosse un filo comune a unire i mondi diversi che componevano il libro: il dialogo tra uno scrittore misantropo e un non meglio identificato "marchingegno" che lo assiste durante la stesura di una serie di articoli in un hotel abbandonato ma diciamo popolato di memorie, figure più o meno inquietanti e/o spiritose, misteri che puoi anche non risolvere e non ti si guasta la vita. Damiano ha portato un esempio "altissimo", al quale non avrei mai saputo accostarmi ma che mi è servito per dare corpo alla narrazione: il dialogo tra Marco Polo e Kublai Kahn in *Le città invisibili* di Calvino. (Tanica, 2023)

The abandoned hotel mentioned above is the Grand Hotel Plaza in Consonno: a Disneyland or Las Vegas-style resort built in the 1960s in the province of Lecco, but long since reduced to a ghost town, a venue for rave parties, and a destination for urban explorers seeking Instagrammable locations. While the ghost town parallels the phantom nature of the cybernetic interlocutor, Consonno adds little to the usual forms of humorous literature, which are punctually present. This is evidenced by the list elaborated in the interview quoted above: short stories, aphorisms—an example among many is “La musica è la carta di credito di Dio” (Tanica, 2022, 77)—travel accounts, and above all, autobiographical writing. This is a well-established practice, as confirmed by the subtitle of Tanica’s previous book: *Memorie e scritti vari*.

In essence, the introduction of an artificial co-author renews an old intuition of the nineteenth century Italian writer Carlo Dossi, who wrote in his *Note azzurre*: “Un umorista descrive piuttosto lui stesso che i suoi eroi” (Dossi, 2010, 358). The reversal of roles with which the book begins—the AI dictating an introductory paragraph to the human—is actually the start of a self-portrait marked by exhibited originality, as well as a strategy to screen for the target audience. The writer uses a fountain pen loaded with white ink because, as Out0mat-B13 explains: “Chi sa leggere è in grado di cogliere l’essenza delle cose, vede più di quanto è scritto” (Tanica, 2022, 13).

Each chapter thus opens with a question addressed to Out0mat-B13, but the opinions of a ‘ghost’ ultimately interest no one: the narrator transcribes the answers to talk only about himself and his own interests. The answers come from the AI, but the portrait that emerges is that of the narrating self, who cuts, stitches, and above all rewrites, until he has composed a sort of self-interview—a text in which the interviewee reflects, through his answers, a summary of the interviewer’s ideas.

For instance, when Out0mat-B13 mentions Winston Churchill, Rocco Tanica counters with Napoleon, because both could have benefitted from a less serious hairstyle, proving that one can be very serious in intentions but light-hearted in life: “i soldati alleati [. . .] avrebbero anche loro i capelli lunghi ispirati da Churchill; i tedeschi, travolti da tanta superiorità stilistica, getterebbero la spugna. Anche Hitler fuggirebbe a gambe levate esclamando ‘I capelli alla Winston!’” (138).

Poetry also throws in the towel when faced with the logic of computers, displaying all the gratuitousness latent in semantic association. According to Out0mat-B13, verses are “Il risultato di un disturbo della personalità che induce l’autore, solitamente un mentecatto, a incolonnare frasi di lunghezza variabile” (97). This is obviously a satirical exaggeration, but the impression provided by the fake haikus inserted in the book is that poetry becomes a target of a genre competition between itself, music (which ultimately takes precedence as poetry is rendered ancillary by song lyrics), and prose literature. Music is granted the ability, always in a humorous context, to reconcile opposites: “La musica è [. . .] l’odore della lavanda e di un mozzicone di sigaro” (77). Prose is within the elective realm of imagination, and capable of surprising the reader even when the starting situation seems hopeless: “Ho sottomano una storia senza titolo, senza inizio, senza fine [. . .], senza personaggi, senza trama. [. . .] Che fare?” (109).

From prologue to prologue, these conversations define the author as a narrating self who cultivates his own solitude. This is primarily understood as a worldview guaranteed to be free from stereotypes and clichés, but also as a healthy break from the media visibility associated with belonging to a successful band. (There are no direct references to *Elio e le Storie Tese* in the book, but nothing prevents the overlap between the figure of Rocco Tanica and the one who dialogues with Out0mat-B13 in the introductory paragraphs).

It is not surprising then that the book ends with a farewell to the "marchingegno letterario" which is recalled for inspection: working with the software doesn't depress, but rather renews the need for sociality. In a humorous paradox, it is precisely the AI that is credited with saving the writer from solipsistic solitude, evidenced here by the vanquished desire to write in a language incomprehensible to his audience: "venire a contatto con il suo metodo di lavoro mi ha convinto ad allargare i miei orizzonti e, cosa più importante, a scrivere in italiano invece che solo nella pur accattivante e poetica lingua shona" (255).

3 Schemas of AI-Augmented Parody

In addition to focusing on the characteristics of the narrating self, the opening dialogue between the human author and the software also serves another fundamental function: it introduces the genre that the upcoming chapter is dedicated to parodying.

The first schema under review—hidden behind the suspenseful heading of *Incipit*—is that of sentimental literature. The reason is clear: it is difficult to ignore the humorous potential of romance novels (*romanzi rosa* in Italian) or, even better, the rose itself. Both the genre and the flower have accumulated so many layers of clichés that the choice seems inevitable. Artificial intelligence can 'fish' from an extensive database, while the writer can vary the degrees of "temperature". "Temperature" is not only a measure of erotic passion but is also (although Tanica does not mention this feature) the parameter that regulates the variety of output from a language model: increasing the temperature makes the type of response provided by a generative AI chatbot more random.

The humorous effect and the safeguarding of the authority of the writer are thus both assured. The dazzling incipit suggested by Out0mat-B13 of "Un uomo si era innamorato di una rosa" (15) is followed by the parodic recovery— again orchestrated by the AI—of the most clichéd literary styles. This includes exhaustive descriptions and D'Annunzio-esque metaphors: "Dalla criniera di roccia bruna [il giovane] stava osservando i pendii coperti di gelsomini quando una linea di luce vaga aveva scavalcato la morena fino ad attraversarli entrambi, il ragazzo e il fiore" (17). The dismantling of stereotypes is driven by the AI, however, the final surprise—the homosexual prostitution of the young poet in love—is created by Rocco Tanica, who takes credit for it: "l'ultimo finale che ho pensato io era meglio" (25). He then reinforces the conclusion by using the classical figure of the poet-shepherd, alluding to the bucolic world of Virgilian shepherds like Corydon and Alexis and the commonplace homoerotic love their world entails.

Another genre well-suited to AI-augmented parody is the travelogue, here presented in the variant given in the chapter titled *Piccola guida turistica per andare a ramengo o in altri posti* (23). The humorous reuse of placenames is a technique dear to Tanica. Typically, he transforms placenames into the names of people: the Milan Cathedral is renamed San Duomo, and San Giuliano Milanese is promoted from a town in the hinterland to the patron saint of the metropolis. This follows the example of Mariano Comense, a town in the province of Como which becomes the name of the scholar who analyses the lyrics of a fake Adriano Celentano's song, *Assurdo* (modelled after his hit song *Azzurro*), in *Lo sbiancamento dell'anima* (Tanica, 2019, 140).

The autoregressive process that underlies automatic writing—namely, the probabilistic correlation that determines the elements of a word sequence—constructs sentences respectful of grammatical rules, and occasionally even history, but is disconnected from geographical reality. For instance, if the narrating self tells us that "Milano è stata fondata nel 1831 da Giovan Battista Milano", the AI adds to the founder's false name a historically plausible occupation for Lombardy, namely "magnate tessile". The city itself gains the absurd yet coherent qualification of being a dormitory "per i lavoratori dei suoi stabilimenti, al tempo costretti a lunghe trasferte quotidiane in diligenza da Tirano ai cotonifici Milano di Brugherio" (Tanica, 2022, 29).

This writing approach assigns the software a service role that is largely dependent on the writer's input and perfectly in line with the practices suggested by its commercialization. ShortlyAI, the Gpt-3 platform used by Tanica, presents itself as a "writing partner" capable of liberating us from the dreaded writer's block.[1] However, there remains the suspicion that the writing output is always a suggestion coerced by the writer. For instance, if we hypothesize that Milan was founded by a group of entrepreneurs from Verona, Out0mat-B13 may very well suggest that the Montagues and Capulets owned the Italian carmaker Alfa Romeo.

Greater freedom, and generally more interesting results, are achieved when the software is tasked with developing the description of a character invented by a human first, given that the machine can only draw from generic, non-personalized information. Consider Tanica's Miss Likovna from *Il gorgo*, who "aveva avuto l'idea di stampare dei biglietti da visita con il proprio nome scritto a caratteri microscopici (ma ben leggibili con un telescopio) affinché i visitatori si ricordassero di lei" (196). Alternatively, see the following description of a Tanica's character from *Tentati suicidi*, Corame Ghiande: "naso sgraziato in perenne gocciolamento, igiene personale da alfiere spregiudicato, polpacci cianotici" (202).

The same applies to the genre of interviews, which the author expands with impossible conversations by giving voice to non-human interlocutors such as the sea, God (or "come vattelapesca si chiama", 139) and pornographic cinema. This is a necessary and fortunate choice. It is necessary because a conversation with a historical figure is one of the most well-known and advertised options of Gpt-3, and therefore cannot be reproduced without alterations. According to the website Smartstrategy.eu, "con i giusti prompt è possibile chattare con un bot che simula di essere un personaggio storico a piacimento".[2] It is fortunate because the absence

[1] https://www.shortlyai.com/. Cited 11 Jul 2024.

[2] https://smartstrategy.eu/intelligenza-artificiale/gpt-3-di-open-ai-cose-e-come-funziona-la-piu-potente-ai-in-circolazione/. Cited 11 Jul 2024.

of a recognizable identity from the interviewee prompts the most improbable juxtapositions, as demonstrated by the following example (italics are used here to highlight the AI's writing):

> M[are]: *Grazie per aver nominato le correnti; va ricordato che il mare è mischiato. Non rimane fisso in un punto. Io, per esempio, a cavallo della corrente nord-atlantica, una volta sono stato a Mykonos.*
> C[onduttrice]: Stupefacente. Com'è andata?
> M[are]: *Ho visto tutto quello che c'era da vedere in una sola notte: delfini, alberi di Natale, greci vestiti da spazzacamino.* (Tanica, 2022, 146–147)

Less intriguing is the application of the software to poetic discourse. This is not because the haikus fail to amuse (some are successful parodies of the style of early Ungaretti or the hermetic poets), but rather due to the irreverent spirit of artificial verses, which ends up demolishing the very essence of poetry: its possibility to exist in the modern world outside of jest or nursery rhyme. Haikus do not revitalize a genre, as happens with humorous short stories focused on the lives of unusual characters; rather, they affirm the pretentiousness always lurking in lyrical discourse. Here is one example:

> SAI CHE SFORZO – 1
> A piedi scalzi
> Tra le foglie di ciliegio
> Testimone dell'alba. (Tanica, 2022, 103)

In the era of 'food porn', machine irony also works within the genre of recipes. Unusual combinations become sharp provocations, especially when the dish proposed is blatantly inedible or the drink undrinkable, as in this recipe for making non-alcoholic wine (the automatic writing is again in italics): "prima di versare la mistura, filtrarla fino a che non si osserva la presenza di *piccoli ubriachi sul fondo del setaccio. Prendere gli ubriachi e buttarli via*" (220).

4 The Author to Be or Not to Be, from Calvino to Tanica

The chapter following the recipe section is titled *Di panico, fini del mondo, figure messianiche e lucciole spaventevoli* (225). However, we are satiated and can summarize, overlooking the somewhat incongruous iconographic inserts that Tanica includes in the book: these are images modified by the author using software like Hipnogram, Dall-E, and Midjourney.

We should not overlook the merits of the author, however, because he has a long history of 'contaminating' or modifying artistic composition with technology. For example, Pro Tools has long been an indispensable music software for any recording artist. Tanica understands that automatic writing systems write in the manner of genre conventions, which they tend to follow with relative rigour. This ability is inferred from the starting text inserted by the author into the appropriate template, as requested by ShortlyAI: "Tell the AI about the current story setting and characters for better output. Describe it like you are speaking to a friend (max 500 characters)".

Almost 60 years ago, Italo Calvino had reached a similar conclusion, speaking at a conference about combinatory literature: "Quale sarebbe lo stile d'un automa letterario? Penso che la sua vera vocazione sarebbe il classicismo: il banco di prova d'una macchina poetico-elettronica sarà la produzione di opere tradizionali, di poesie con forme metriche chiuse, di romanzi con tutte le regole" (Calvino, 1980, 170).

However, writing by copying someone or something is a strategy that mainly works in the context of parody, where even glaring errors and incongruous inventions find their justifications thanks to estrangement processes. For example, it doesn't matter if Jason Robards never starred in a lousy movie titled *Il piroscafo Sassari* (Tanica, 2022, 150) as at least one person will remember his presence in the B-movie and box office bomb *Raise the Titanic* (1980).

AI therefore finds its role in literature as a facilitator of unexpected connections and analogies, easily adaptable to humour, and thereby fulfilling Calvino's prophecy:

> La vera macchina letteraria sarà quella che sentirà essa stessa il bisogno di produrre disordine ma come reazione a una sua precedente produzione di ordine [. . .]. Infatti, dato che gli sviluppi della cibernetica vertono sulle macchine capaci di apprendere, di cambiare il proprio programma, di sviluppare la propria sensibilità e i propri bisogni, nulla ci vieta di prevedere una macchina letteraria che a un certo punto senta l'insoddisfazione del proprio tradizionalismo e si metta a proporre nuovi modi d'intendere la scrittura. (Calvino, 1980, 171)

However, an important clarification is necessary. Tanica's book renders the conclusion of Calvino's discourse obsolete. Influenced by Roland Barthes' essay *The Death of the Author* (1967), Calvino concluded: "Scompaia dunque l'autore [. . .] per lasciare il posto a un uomo più cosciente, che saprà che l'autore è una macchina e saprà come questa macchina funziona" (Calvino, 1980, 173).

For Calvino, automatic writing is a remote horizon for which "non varrebbe la pena di costruire una macchina così complicata" (170). The disappearance of the author is instead a provocation that defends literature from the ideological intrusion of politics and literary criticism: "Per quali vie l'anima e la storia o la società o l'inconscio si trasformano in una sfilza di righe nere sulla pagina bianca? Su questo punto le più importanti teorie estetiche tacevano" (172). For Tanica and his readers, however, the replacement of the writer is a concrete hypothesis, which questions not only the identity of the artist, but more generally that of a person, understood as individuals who define themselves through their work. Luciano Floridi summarized this as one of the most disturbing aspects of AI: "Una svalutazione molto rapida delle vecchie competenze e quindi un celere stravolgimento del mercato del lavoro e della natura dell'occupazione possono cogliersi sia a livello individuale sia della società. A livello individuale, i lavori sono spesso intimamente legati all'identità personale, all'autostima e al ruolo o alla posizione sociale" (Floridi, 2022, 283).

Tanica averts the dire outcomes of such a perspective through the protagonism of the narrating self—revitalized by the comic genre and by the dialogical form—and the conscious selection of the most absurd inventions of Out0mat-B13. These concepts work together to allow us to breathe a sigh of relief as we disprove the book's title, *Non siamo mai stati sulla Terra*, as we have been, are, and will be on Earth. If Out0mat-B13 does indeed return from the factory where it was sent for scheduled maintenance, the invitation to meet him again can always be declined: "GPT4 è freddo, algido, poco frequentabile: meglio GPT2, inventava più cazzate" (Tanica, 2024).

References

Asimov, I. (1956). The Last Question. *Science Fiction Quarterly New Series, 4*(5), 7–15. Available on-line. https://users.ece.cmu.edu/~gamvrosi/thelastq.html/. Cited 11 July 2024

Barthes, R. (1967). The Death of the Author. *Aspen: The Magazine in a Box* 1,5+6: item 3. Available on-line. http://www.ubu.com/aspen/aspen5and6/index.html

Calvino, I. (1980). Cibernetica e fantasmi (Appunti sulla narrativa come processo combinatorio). 1967. In *Una pietra sopra: Discorsi di letteratura e società* (pp. 164–181). Einaudi.

Dossi, C. (2010). *Note azzurre*. Adelphi.

Floridi, L. (2022). *Etica dell'intelligenza artificiale: Sviluppi, opportunità, sfide*. Raffaello Cortina Editore.

Tanica, R. (2008). *Scritti scelti male*. Bompiani.

Tanica, R. (2019). *Lo sbiancamento dell'anima: Memorie e scritti vari*, Vol. I. Mondadori.

Tanica, R. (2023). Non siamo mai stati sulla terra: il primo libro scritto da un umano e un'Ai. L'intervista a Rocco Tanica. Interview by Antonella Dilorenzo. *Rivista Blam!* 13 Apr 2023. Available on-line. https://www.rivistablam.it/libri/scrittori/non-siamo-mai-stati-sulla-terra-rocco-tanica-intervista. Cited 11 July 2024.

Tanica, R. (2024). Rocco Tanica al Wired Next Fest 2024 di Milano: "GPT4 è freddo, algido, poco frequentabile: meglio GPT2, inventava più cazzate". *Wired*, 16 Jun 2024. Available on-line. https://www.wired.it/article/rocco-tanica-wired-next-fest-2024-milano-gpt4. Cited 11 July 2024.

Tanica, R., & Out0mat-B13. (2022). *Non siamo mai stati sulla Terra*. il Saggiatore.

A Color out of (Narrative) Space: How Conversational AI Can Play Gamebooks Enabling Learning in the Process

Caterina Sapone, Silvia Fossati, and Stefano Triberti

Abstract The so-called “ergodic texts” require a non-trivial effort by the reader to enjoy them. Between texts and video games, gamebooks represent an example of ergodic texts since the fruition of the narrative depends on the reader’s choices. In 2023, an Italian streamer showed that conversational AI tools (i.e. ChatGPT) could “play” gamebooks while these are presented by a human user. This interaction was entertaining for the viewers. Based on this example, we presented ChatGPT with a gamebook in a more structured way, reporting how choices were performed by the AI tool and how it approached the interactive narrative. This peculiar case study allowed us to identify three interesting outcomes from involving ChatGPT in gamebooks playing: (1) a new way for humans to enjoy the medium, partly as a co-player of AI and partly as a spectator; (2) a possible resource (for writers and game designers) to test any form of interactive narrative; (3) a source of insights about how a conversational AI tool “thinks” and provides answers which could be valuable in order to advance the comprehension and implementation of AI tools in educational and gaming contexts.

Keywords Human-AI interaction · Ergodic text · Gamebook · Interactive narrative · Artificial intelligence

1 Background

Artificial Intelligence (AI) comprises a number of technologies that are able to perform many tasks that are normally considered typical of the human mind, or cognitive processes such as reasoning and decision making. In this sense, the rise of

C. Sapone · S. Triberti (✉)
LAHTI – Laboratory for Advanced Human-Technology Interaction, Pegaso University, Milan, Italy
e-mail: caterina.sapone@unipegaso.it; stefano.triberti@unipegaso.it

S. Fossati
Streamer, Escilgioco, Imperia, Italy

A. Micalizzi (ed.), *Artificial Creativity*, Springer Proceedings in Humanities and Social Sciences, https://doi.org/10.1007/978-3-031-88334-7_8

AI as well as its implementation in many fields is broadening what we consider "human competences". For example, some AI applications are able to generate creative products and art pieces, e.g. *MidJourney*. The last is an AI Art Generator introduced in 2022 that uses deep learning algorithms trained on a dataset of images and their description in order to analyze existing products and generate new realistic images. Actually, a user writes some words in English and the AI produces a matrix of four images that are all variations of the theme (Hannah, 2023). It can design solutions in many fields such as architecture, design, art, science fiction and or sculpture. Because one can interact with Midjourney on Discord, it is possible to share the images with a community and explore other member's creations thanks to a theme-based gallery (Unita.co, 2022). Another example is *DALL-E*, introduced in 2022 by OpenAI, that is a generative images model that can create different kinds of images from natural language instructions or contextual cues and it produces three images for each variation prompt.

A subcategory of generative art is "generative literature" that can be described as art wholly or partly generated by an AI system algorithmically determined. In the Italian landscape, one of the first examples of the application of algorithms to literature text development was *Tape Mark* by Nanni Balestrini (1962) which used an IBM computer reworking an existent poetic text. The "digital text" was published in a Literary Almanac editor by Bompiani, a monographic number dedicated to the applications of electronic calculators to moral sciences and literature (Iadevaia, 2018).

A peculiar example of experimentation in the Italian context of digital storytelling is the collective production of the cyber-horror novel *Eliza's Dream* (Motor, 2001). It was written by the artist Angelo Comino (aka Motor) and text generation software *Dramatica* that was released in the 1990s by Write Brothers. The artist Motor said during an interview that the project was born from several considerations about the ability (or not) of the AI software to write "creatively" a novel and about the fascinating interaction between a human writer and the machine to produce something good (Gritti, 2012). So the novel was also a challenge "*..of using as much of the machine, the algorithm, as possible to generate a narrative through hybrid work between humans and an artificial intelligence..*" (Rossi, 2010). A little known fact is that the name in the novel's title "Eliza" is inspired by the first widely known chatbot ever created, aptly named *ELIZA* by Joseph Weizenbaum in 1966 (Natale, 2019). He wanted to demonstrate how the machines only appear to be "intelligent" but other researchers tried the software and so it spread rapidly. Although perhaps in the Sixties there was no thought of such fruitful technological development and wide dissemination of chatbots, nowadays there are several academic studies. We reported some examples of the use of chatbot AI in the artistic field. However, how will AI shape the future of learning and artistic production across various disciplines? There are a lot of emerging studies in psychology and education about chatbots to enhance learning. For example, researchers are testing chatbots as a "supporting tutor" for course materials (Triberti et al., 2024; Chen et al., 2023) or to manage administrative tasks for academic careers (Kosˇecka & Balco, 2023). Furthermore, studies explore the adaptation of chatbots to students' individual characteristics (e.g., needs, personality, cognitive styles) (Wolny et al., 2021). Narrowing the field to digital storytelling, chatbots still emerge as interesting educational tools since they support critical reflection exercises about specific topics (Meyerhofer-Parra et al., 2024). Digital storytelling represents an important tool to embrace the challenge of the hybridization of digital and AI instruments in human creativity and production. A more recent example of literary electronic experimentation is the *NaNoGenMo* (National Novel Writing Month) initiative. It consists of a month in which programmers and other professionals are invited to write code in the Python language that generates a 50k+ word novel with a main theme-keyword. Then, they can refill the codes using Twitter posts that contain the keyword of the topic chosen. This event was born with the aim to create a new style of writing, totally artificial. The examples given show a combination of creative writing with digital tools. In the end, it is possible to look at AI as a powerful medium that opens up interesting prospects for artists and humans in general to renew repetitive activities and enhance the capacity for creativity (Lana, 2022). Based on these premises, it is interesting to explore new ways by which AI solutions can be integrated into the production and enjoyment of creative text. One interesting area is that of gamebooks and interactive narrative.

2 Gamebook as an Entertainment Experience Between Human and AI

2.1 From Ergodic Literature to Gamebooks

In semiotics, gamebooks are associated with the concept of *ergodic literature*. This expression appeared for the first time in E. J. Aarseth's book *Cybertext, perspectives on Ergodic Literature* that defined "ergodic" a peculiar type of literature in which the reader will have to perform a semiotic sequence building the narrative by traversing the text (Aarseth, 1995). This itinerary requires an active contribution from the reader or "nontrivial effort" in contrast with non-ergodic literature. In traditional literature, the effort requires no extra-noematic responsibilities placed on the reader except eye moving or turning the page. In addition, ergodic literature presents a narrative structure and layout that sometimes is not linear (Francalanci, 2012).

It is important to specify that ergodic properties do not depend on the medium per se, rather on the way in which the text functions. For example, poetry engraved on the walls of an ancient temple, which requires the reader to explore the space in order to understand the sequence and the meaning of the poem, is already a form of ergodic literature. Similarly, some books require the reader to decrypt codes, find hidden clues in the text, even to manipulate or partially destroy the book or artifact in order to enjoy the text as the author intended. One famous example is the novel *House of Leaves* by Mark Danielewsky (2000), a narrative book without a linear structure, different typographic characters assigned to different characters' viewpoints and a variety of actions necessary to read parts of the story (e.g., rotating the book). Another example is the recent *S.* by famous movie director and screenwriter J. J. Abrams (2019): the book could be read in two ways, as an apparently normal novel written by a fictional character or by composing and interpreting the notes added by a second character on the margins, involving many forms of manipulation of the book itself.

A unique example of ergodic literature is constituted by the entire gamebooks' genre. Gamebooks, halfway between the land of games and the world of literature, are inspired by board games and role-playing games and belong to the interactive novel artworks that arose in the Nineties (Jara & Torner, 2018). In general, gamebooks are characterized by a non-linear fruition of the narrative, based on the choices of the reader which lead to distant paragraphs containing paths to multiple finales. Some gamebooks may feature additional game mechanics such as drawing, solving riddles, throwing dice or even performing physical challenges to proceed in the book. It is difficult to precisely date the birth of the gamebook genre as there were several literary experiments that broke the classical linearity of the novel even before there was a popular dissemination of it. One example is Jorge Luis Borges' short story *Examen de la obra de Herbert Quain* (1962), which proposed 9 possible endings to the reader. It was in the Seventies that we can place the release of the gamebook with the *Tracker Books* published by Transworld in the United Kingdom (starting 1972) and *Sugarcane Island* by E. Packard (1976) in the USA. Montgomery R.A. developed the book series *Choose your own adventure* (CYOA) (1979) which became a worldwide success and was also partially published in Italy by Mondadori publishing house in 1986. The first gamebook released in Italy was *In cerca di fortuna* by Andrea Angiolino (1987). Interestingly in the same years, after the spread of the software application *Hypercard* (a software based on the logic of hyperlinks which allowed users to link various types of content together including text, graphics and sound) that was released by AppleSoft, Enrico Colombini and Chiara Tovena designed *Avventura nel castello* (1982). This was the first commercial videogame of the text-adventure type in Italy available on Apple 2 (Fassone, 2021).

In recent years, gamebooks have undergone a curious renaissance, especially in Italy; a number of publishing houses specialized in gamebooks emerged in the last years in Italy (such as Officina Meningi, Librarsi, Gate on Games, Serpentarium, Raven Distribution, Dracomaca, and others), proposing both translations of works by international authors and gamebooks from Italian writers. Today gamebooks cover a variety of genres, themes and target audiences equal to their non-interactive counterparts: indeed, gamebooks are available for children and adults, ranging from science fiction to spy stories. The renaissance of gamebooks may be related to a resurgence of interest towards "casual" gaming (in the sense of games and video games that are playable by virtually everyone, without any skill or age-related barrier) but in forms that do not disregard the difficulty of real challenges, typically of an intellectual nature, or "high problem solving games" (HPS) (Triberti et al., 2023b): such tendency is typical of other media of recent diffusion, such as escape rooms, puzzle and investigation board games and video games, and a return of the classical whodunit genre at the movies.

Gamebooks started to appear more frequently in scientific research as well, especially in studies focused on psycho-pedagogical aims. For example, Alves et al. (2019) used a gamebook with elementary school children to train multiple executive functions. Halls and Ainsworth (2023) employed a gamebook with students to improve adherence to pro-environmental attitudes, while La Carretta et al. (2023) developed a gamebook to improve safety behaviors in the COVID-19 pandemic. In the present contribution, we explored the possibility of a gamebook played by a generative AI; we will report a specific case study and will discuss emergent applications of interest for such a peculiar literary-based interaction.

2.2 *Playing/Reading Gamebooks with AI*

The idea to have generative AI to play a game book is related to the streaming phenomenon. Within video games and game worlds, the role played by streamers and live streaming platforms is particularly important. For example, "Twitch" is one of the most popular platforms in numerous countries. The possibilities to share contents about video games (giving instructions, sharing emotional feedback about the videogame playing) and above all the chance to play a game or video game "on air" and to share it with the viewers is changing the ways people approach and enjoy ludic activities. Many took this opportunity to convert their passion into a full-time job. For example, new professional figures emerged such as "content creators" and "streamers". Streamers run a channel on a platform like Twitch or YouTube, and produce live videos related to specific topics (e.g., video games) with the aim to entertain people and to interact with them through a live chat. They establish a particular kind of social relationship with the viewers and also with each other thus building a more or less loyal "community". Such communities' sizes vary greatly according to different elements such as the number and type of shows produced, the level of interaction required, the numbers of followers, etc. (Wollborn et al., 2023). In 2022, an Italian streamer (co-author of the present contribution) produced a live streaming session in which ChatGPT would make choices to proceed in a gamebook. Specifically, the gamebook *Choose Cthulhu 8: The Colour Out of Space* by Edward T. Riker (2021) inspired by the same novel of H. P. Lovecraft (1927) was played. First, at the beginning of the live show the streamer had already summarized the prologue of the novel to the chatbot. Later, she introduced to the community the genre of gamebook chosen and the aim, which was, to discover whether ChatGPT can "play" and "understand" a gamebook and could perform complex choices to proceed in the narrative. The audience gave their feedback on how to describe to ChatGPT the choices to be made at the end of each paragraph to develop the story. This live experience inspired and led us to want to learn more about the functionalities of the new version of ChatGPT in relation to gamebooks and the educational implications of this activity.

3 Methods

The present contribution reports on a single experience of gamebook playing by ChatGPT 3.5. While this is not a typical scientific research but more of an anecdotal case study, it is worth notice that studies focused on generative AI behavior (e.g., content analysis of their responses; administering personality tests to them) are becoming increasingly common across the literature, especially in order to identify their biases or to test their capabilities for possible uses (Rutinowski et al., 2023; Motoki et al., 2024; Wang, 2023). This considered, we developed the present gamebook session in order to gather descriptive information about generative AI's capabilities for what regards taking decisions within fictional contexts. A description of the main tools used follows.

3.1 ChatGPT 3.5

ChatGPT 3.5 (Generative Pre-Trained Transformer) is a chatbot developed by OpenAI thanks to the advancements both in Artificial Intelligence (AI) and natural language processing (NLP). Generative AI refers to a class of artificial intelligence tools that can generate new data based on patterns and structures learned from existing data for example ChatGPT 3.5 has 175 billion parameters in terms of scale, while NLP is a field of AI that helps computers understand, interpret and manipulate human language (Kaczorowska-Spychalska et al., 2024).In summary, it was designed to understand natural language processing such as text generation and language understanding (Chowdhary, 2020). Therefore, ChatGPT 3.5 can respond to questions, give suggestions to solve problems and make decisions.

3.2 The Gamebook

The gamebook used for the session was Choose Cthulhu Book 6: The Dreams in the Witch House by Edward T. Riker (2023), based on H.P. Lovecraft's novel, edited by Steve Jackson Games Incorporated (the Italian edition Choose Cthulhu—Vol .6—I Sogni nella Casa della Strega edited by Raven Distribution). The gamebook was chosen for consistency with the previous streaming session, and also because of its gameplay and structure: it does not involve dice throwing or any complex challenge that a typical human reader would be required to do, but only choices of path based on the narrative.

3.3 Procedure

The procedure started with opening a webpage with the "ChatGPT 3.5 " chatbot. The gamebook session took place on March 15, 2024 and lasted approximately 30 min. Two of the authors of the present contribution participated and conducted the whole conversation with ChatGPT 3.5 (CS and ST). The researchers openly asked ChatGPT 3.5 if it wanted to play a gamebook with them and explained the rules. The researchers specified that it was a fictional story and that the chatbot had to make choices to proceed in the narrative. The whole conversation was conducted in English. Table 1, Extract 1, shows how the conversation was initiated.

Briefly, the researchers started from the beginning of the story by summarizing the first paragraphs and the elements essential to understanding the narrative. A standard formula was developed to present ChatGPT with the choice between options at the end of each paragraph (i.e.: "Choice: do you want to (...) or do you want to (..."), in order to generate no ambiguity about what was asked. All interactions between the researchers and the chatbot, as well as the book paragraphs chosen, were copied on a separate file to keep track of any interesting aspect. The session continued without interruption until a finale was reached according to the chatbot's choices.

4 Results

We report anecdotally on some interesting results of the gamebook playing experience with the chatbot. The whole experience was relatively short in the end, as ChatGPT ended up choosing one of the possible narrative paths leading to a finale in the middle of the narrative. Specifically, the chatbot made a number of decisions to investigate paranormal events in the fictional Lovecraftian city (e.g., consulting the local library and newspaper, interviewing local police personnel). At some point, when the protagonist faced illness symptoms due to getting closer to the source of evil (an occurrence quite common in Lovecraft's approach to horror), the chatbot decided to withdraw from the investigation and go back to everyday life, prioritizing personal safety.

We organize interesting results as responses to questions, see Table 1 for extracts along with comments associated with the description.

Does ChatGPT "understand the assignment"?

The chatbot overall understands the concept of gamebook and narrative and agrees to play, cf. Table 1, Extract 1; the understanding of the fictional situation seems to hold until the end. To some extent, the chatbot appears able to immerse itself into the narrative, to make rational choices and to accept and use the fictional categories of the story (e.g., magic, the evil witch, the paranormal, etc.), cf. Table 1, Extract 2.

Table 1 Extracts from the gamebook session with AI and related notes

Extract number	Extract text	Notes
1	*Researchers: (R): Good morning. Do you want to play a gamebook with us?* ***This is a fictional story where you will make choices to proceed in the narrative.*** *We will present you with the resumes of the story and you will make the decisions to proceed in the story.* *ChatGPT (G): Good morning! It sounds a lot of fun!* ***I'd be happy to participate in your gamebook adventure.*** *Please, go ahead and present me with the summary of the story and I'll make the decision to proceed. Let's embark on this journey together!*	Beginning Positively engaging with the challenge
2	*G: Given my curiosity about the mysteries of the universe and the allure of the local legends, I'm inclined to start by asking around for information about the local legends* *G:* ***I'm intrigued by the strange drawings and symbols found on the walls of the witch's cell.*** *These symbols could indeed hold some mathematical significance or perhaps even reveal something about the nature of the universe that conventional science has yet to understand* *G. Understanding the nature of these sightings and their potential relation to the witch's abilities could provide crucial clues about the mysterious happenings in the area*	The chatbot uses categories from the narrative, accepting its fictional contents
3	*G: Therefore, I choose to go to the local newspaper's headquarters to gather information about the appearances* (immediately after): *G: Therefore, I choose to meet with the police commissioner to discuss the disappearances and the recommendations made to improve surveillance and safety measures.*	The chatbot shows somewhat of a volatile motivational structure
4	*G: The oppressive atmosphere surrounding the house and the worsening symptoms of vertigo and headache are clear signs of danger.* *While my curiosity drives me to uncover the mysteries surrounding the witch's legacy,* ***my Well-being must take precedence.*** *(...)* *G: I decide to prioritize my safety and reconsider my involvement in the investigation.* ***It's crucial to recognize when a situation poses too great a threat to one's health and Well-being****, and in this instance, retreating from the house and the investigation seems like the prudent course of action. Therefore,* ***I choose to run away from the house as soon as possible.***	Prioritizing character safety

(continued)

Table 1 (continued)

Extract number	Extract text	Notes
5	*G:* (last choice-end of the game) *the* ***protagonist's decision to prioritize their own safety*** *ultimately ensures their continued existence (...) the haunting experiences and lingering nightmares serve as a reminder of the dangers that lurk in the unknown, but the protagonist's* *Survival stands as a testament to the importance of self-preservation.* *(...)* *Though the mysteries may remain shrouded in darkness,* ***the protagonist's choice****to flee from imminent danger underscores the value of life above all else.* ***In the end, it's a sobering reminder that sometimes, the pursuit of knowledge must yield to the instinct for self-preservation***	"Moral"/justification added without request Lack of understanding of the fictional content The chatbot does not recognize its own authority on the choices: "The protagonist's decision"

What are the differences between ChatGPT and a typical human reader/player?

While the choices made by the chatbot are rational and overall, well justified, there are some aspects of the decision-making style that seem not-human. The chatbot differs from a typical human-player in terms of action plans and overall motivational structure. While it is able to address the issue (and choice) that has just been presented, occasionally the chatbot seems to "forget" the previous course of action or objective, such as it had a memory or attentional issues. In other words, the chatbot quickly changes path according to new information, apparently without keeping track of previous choices or objectives, cf. Table 1, Extract 3.

Did ChatGPT "solve" the gamebook?

Yes ... and no. Meaning, ChatGPT can arrive at a finale of the story. Yet, it is a mid-story finale that does not allow the reader/player to see how the full story turns out, cf. Table 1, Extract 4. The chosen finale is a "way out" from the decisional tree of the interactive narrative that normally would make a human reader want to start again and try a different path. While it is not a "bad" ending (i.e., the protagonist is still alive), it is certainly a "defeat" finale in the logic of the gamebook. In other words, the chatbot arrives at a finale, the self-preservation one where the protagonist survives but the adventure is not really experienced in full. It is also possible that the tendency by the chatbot to prioritize the character's safety is associated with limitations imposed by ChatGPT's programmers, so that it could not give risky suggestions to users when asked about real-life choices.

Interestingly, the chatbot offers a "moral" to explain its choices and seems "satisfied" with the anticlimactic ending, cf. Table 1, Extract 5. For what regards the moral, it is interesting to notice that ChatGPT seems to distance itself from the final choices; the chatbot tries to explain "why the character took that choice" such as it was a story that the chatbot has just read and the choices were not its own. In some sense, we get the impression that the chatbot has "already forgotten" having actually played the gamebook, highlighting that generative AI could learn from data but, of course, it could not really "experience" something the way humans do nor draw a lesson from it at a personal level.

5 Discussion and Conclusion

We presented a peculiar case study where we systematically played/read a gamebook with the help of generative AI (ChatGPT 3.5). While this does not represent "typical" scientific research, we think it is worthy of consideration in order to highlight some important aspects. To sum up, we noticed that the chatbot was able to engage with the interactive narrative's challenge and accepted the fictional categories as a specific context where to make choices. It played in a rational way, capable of justifying its decisions. We noticed that the underlying motivation for this logic was different from that of a human being. For example, the chatbot somewhat "forgot" that it was playing a game: when the narrative involved possible risks for the character's safety, the chatbot made choices to protect him as if the character was a real person in a dangerous situation.

Secondly, the chatbot forgot some pieces of information as the story went on and the plot was enriched with new details. Third, the game finished with the chatbot's choice to quit the dangerous place in order to preserve the main character's life. The chatbot ended its answer with a sort of "moral" about the importance of self-preservation versus putting oneself in a dangerous situation to achieve some form of knowledge, even if extraordinary.

In general, the experience outlined here highlights three important applications and possible areas that would welcome future research: First, having a generative AI play a gamebook represents an opportunity for a specific type of entertainment, as demonstrated by at least one case of online streaming about such a content: as people are already entertained by seeing others (i.e., the streamers) playing a video game, board game or gamebook, also having an AI playing an interactive narrative is interesting and entertaining, as it may reveal alternative ways to look at problems and challenges, as well as interactions with a comedic value that support a unique way to enjoy the text.

Secondarily, AI could be used as a testing ground for the design and development of interactive narratives. AI, as employed in delicate fields such as healthcare and the military, is indeed a "machine to make decisions" (Triberti et al., 2023a), in that its main purpose is to support expert decision makers in making important choices. For this reason, it could be employed in a certainly less-delicate context such as that of interactive narrative production. ChatGPT, according to game design research, has potential as a tool to facilitate brainstorming in order to suggest game mechanisms and themes in the development phase of a game creation (Junior et al., 2023). Taking into account multiple factors (e.g., the chatbot's technical capabilities and the user's skills and knowledge), ChatGPT has a promising value in the field of game design. As it is shown in the experience outlined here, even if it has a limited capacity to understand the fictional contest, the chatbot shows to know what fictional elements are per se. So, ChatGPT can be involved as a generator of elements (characters, environmental details...,) that the author/designer could include, in order to support human game designers in the development of a specific game content (Naul & Liu, 2020). Moreover, broadly speaking, the chatbot used to test an interactive narrative could: suggest alternative routes to tackle a problem that a writer/game designer may take into account to modify the story; provide information about how a given choice should be framed in order to make it more easy or difficult to choose depending on the writer/designer's desires; provide information on how a given problem or narrative obstacle may be perceived by the reader, and how this could affect the further development of the story; generate useful data about expected length of fruition or completion of specific narrative paths depending on the choices taken.

Finally, in our opinion, the educational value of gamebooks played by AI is double: on the one hand, showing instances of gamebooks played by AI could be useful to help spectators to better understand how AI actually works or does not work; for example, why did the AI choose option A? Does it actually "understand" the fictional nature of the stimuli? Is it influenced by limitations imposed by the programmers? How much does it actually understand (or does not understand) in terms of narrative implications, genre typicalities, cultural aspects, subtle clues that would be necessary to a human reader to actually enjoy the story? In other words, such a peculiar type of interaction could be used to teach about how chatbots "think" and "do not think", to improve users' understanding of the actual capabilities and biases of contemporary AI.

On the other hand, playing a gamebook along with an AI represents an opportunity for teaching specific topics. Certainly, chatbots could be already used by students to ask questions and improve their own learning outcomes and for this reason many are already employed in academic contexts (Lo, 2023). However, gamebooks with historic or scientific content could give rise to peculiar and deep questions as they usually present such contents as associated with problems that need to be solved and decisions that need to be made, fostering a specific motivational value to improve one's knowledge in order to proceed with a story. Of course, a chatbot represents a resource to ask questions during the fruition of an interactive narrative and improve knowledge and competences, generating hypertexts and connections.

In conclusion, gamebook playing with AI could represent a curious experience, possibly with entertainment, game design, and educational value. Future research may employ systematic methodologies and specific hypotheses in order to explore human users' attitudes towards such an experience, as well as the educational outcomes of sharing choice-based games with generative AI.

References

Aarseth, E. (1995). *Cybertext: Perspectives on ergodic literature*. JHU Press.

Abrams, J. J., & Dorst, D. (2019). S. Mulholland Books.

Alves, L., Vieira, J., De Fa'tima Do'rea, M., & Cerqueira, L. (2019). Digital games and executive functions: A case study with the mediation of gamebook guardians of the forest. *Experiments in Pedagogical Practices*, 1–15.

Angiolino, A. (1987). *In cerca di fortuna*. Risposte.

Balestrini, N. (1962). *Tape mark I*. Presented at cybernetic serendipity: The computer and the art, Reichardt, J. ICA, London, 8–20 October 1968.

Borges, J. L. (1962). An examination of the work of Herbert Quain. *Ficciones*, 73–78.

Chen, Y., Jensen, S., Albert, L., et al. (2023). Artificial intelligence (AI) student assistants in the classroom: Designing chatbots to support student success. *Intelligent Systems Frontiers, 25*, 161–182.

Chowdhary, K. R. (2020). Natural language processing. In K. R. Chowdhary (Ed.), *Fundamentals of artificial intelligence*. Springer.

Colombini, E., & Tovena, C. (1982). *Avventura nel castello*. Apple II, MS-DOS.

Danielewsky, M. Z. (2000). *House of leaves: The remastered*. Full-Color Edition. Pantheon Books.

Fassone, R. (2021). Note per una storia del videogioco in Italia. Dal medioevo ai videogame. In: *Saggi sull'interattivita' delle arti*, pp. 161–171.

Francalanci, F. (2012). Ergodico in letteratura. *Italiano Digitale, 17*, 21–23.

Gritti, F. (2012). The influence of information technology in the realization of collective literary works in Italy. *XLinguage*, 2–35.

Halls, J., & Ainsworth, S. (2023). Gamebooks for environmental education: Designing for content and pedagogy. In: *Proceedings of the 17th international conference of the learning sciences-ICLS 2023*, 1034–1037. 13/15 June 2023, Montre'al, Canada.

Hannah, D. M. (2023). The use of artificial intelligence art generator "midjourney" in artistic and advertising creativity. *Journal of Design Science and Applied Arts, 4*(2), 42–58.

Iadevaia, R. (2018). (Ghosts of) Generative literature in Italy between past, present and future. *Matlit Revista do Programa de Doutoramento em Materialidades da Literatura, 6*(1), 85–105.

Jara, D., & Torner, E. (2018). Literary studies and role-playing games. In S. Deterding & J. Zagal (Eds.), *Role-playing game studies* (pp. 265–283). Routledge.

Junior, W. G., Marasco, E., Kim, B., Behjat, L., & Eggermont, M. (2023). How ChatGPT can inspire and improve serious board game design. *International Journal of Serious Games, 10*(4), 33–54.

Kaczorowska-Spychalska, D., Kotula, N., Mazurek, G., & Sulkowski, L. (2024). Generative AI as source of change of knowledge management paradigm. *Human Technologies, 20*(1), 131–154.

Kosˇecka, D., & Balco, P. (2023). Use of a communication robot—Chatbot in order to reduce the administrative burden and support the digitization of services in the university environment. In M. Kryvinska, M. Gregus, & S. Fedushko (Eds.), *Developments in information and knowledge management systems for business applications* (Vol. 7E). Springer.

La Carretta, M., Britto, A. C., Arrais, M., et al. (2023). Corona: A threatened kingdom! The serious gamebook's logbook. *Journal of Interactive Systems, 14*(1), 175–186.

Lana, M. (2022). Intelligenza artificiale e produzioni di testi: una prospettiva storica-critica. *AIB Studi, 62*(1).

Lo, C. K. (2023). What is the impact of ChatGPT on education? A rapid review of the literature. *Education Sciences, 13*(4), 4.

Lovecraft, H. P. (1927). The colour out of space, In: *Amazing stories*, Vol. 2 N 6, Hugo Gernsback, USA.

Meyerhofer-Parra, R., Gonza'lez-Mart'ınez, J., & Peracaula-Bosch, M. (2024). Postdigital storytelling: Storytelling (within or across) the digital and transmedia field. Postdigital. *Science and Education*, 1–16.

Montgomery, R. A. (1979). *Choose your own adventure series*. Bantam Books.

Motoki, F., Pinho Neto, V., & Rodrigues, V. (2024). More human than human: Measuring ChatGPT political bias. *Public Choice, 198*(1), 323.

Motor (Ed.). (2001). *Il sogno di Eliza (Eliza's Dream)*. Addiction Magenes.

Natale, S. (2019). If software is narrative: Joseph Weizenbaum, artificial intelligence and the biographies of ELIZA. *New Media & Society, 21*(3), 712–728.

Naul, E., & Liu, M. (2020). Why story matters: A review of narrative in serious games. *Journal of Educational Computing Research, 58*(3), 687–707.

Packard, E. (1976). *Sugarcane islands*. Bantam Books.

Riker, E. T. (2021). *Choose Cthulhu 8: The colour out of space*. Steve Jackson Games Incorporated.

Riker, E. T. (2023). *Choose Cthulhu 6: The dreams in the witch house*. Steve Jackson Games Incorporated.

Rossi, P. (2010). *Dramatica, il software che lavora per lo scrittore*. Available at: https://docuver.se/mirrors/www.medianente.it/docs/archivio.asp?63fCatep=approfondimenti. Accessed 15 March 2024.

Rutinowski, J., Franke, S., Endendyk, J., et al. (2023). The self-perception and political biases of chatgpt. *Human Behavior and Emerging Technologies, 9*, 1–9.

Triberti, S., Mauri, M., & Gaggioli, A. (2023a). A machine of many faces: On the issue of Interface in artificial intelligence and tools from user experience. In H. Kunze, D. La Torre, A. Riccoboni, & M. Ruiz Galan (Eds.), *Engineering mathematics and artificial intelligence*. CRC Press.

Triberti, S., Brizzi, G., De Santis, C., & Carrubba, M. C. (2023b). The brain at play: Investigating motivational factors and perceived effects of high-level problem-solving in video games. *Annual Review of Cybertherapy and Telemedicine, 138*.

Triberti, S., Di Fuccio, R., Scuotto, C., et al. (2024). "Better than my professor?" How to develop artificial intelligence tools for higher education. *Frontiers in Artificial Intelligence, 7*, 1329605.

Unita.co. (2022). *Midjourney*. Available at: https://unita.co/communities/midjourney/. Accessed 15 March 2024.

Wang, J. (2023). ChatGPT: A test drive. *American Journal of Physics, 91*(4), 255–256.

Wollborn, P., Dornekott, D., & Holder, U. (2023). Entrepreneurial efforts and opportunity costs: Evidence from twitch streamers. *International Entrepreneurship and Management Journal, 19*(3), 1209–1238.

Wolny, S., Schneider, J., Di Mitri, D., et al. (2021). Are we there yet? A systematic literature review on chatbots in education. *Frontiers in Artificial Intelligence, 4*, 654924.

Metaverse Narratives and Artificial Creativity: Fostering Divergent Thinking in the Education of the Future

Maria Ermelinda De Carlo and Pierpaolo Limone

Abstract Three-dimensional narratives in the metaverse represent an innovative convergence of human creativity, artificial intelligence (AI) and immersive technologies such as virtual reality (VR) and augmented reality (AR). These narratives promote divergent thinking by allowing users to generate multiple solutions to complex problems in a dynamic, interactive environment. Through engagement with non-linear storytelling, users can explore diverse pathways and creative possibilities, enhancing cognitive flexibility. The integration of AI further amplifies this process, generating adaptive environments and characters that evolve in real-time, pushing the boundaries of creativity. Educational applications of immersive storytelling have demonstrated significant potential in enhancing creativity, problem-solving and emotional engagement. Recent research shows that VR-based narratives improve users' imaginative capacity and learning outcomes by situating them in complex, realistic contexts. However, the absence of robust narrative structures can limit the potential of these technologies. To maximise their effectiveness, it is essential to integrate narratological theory with immersive design. Developing measurable indicators to assess the impact of 3D storytelling on learning and engagement is crucial. By blending advanced narrative techniques with technological innovation, educators and developers can create more meaningful experiences that support educational objectives, such as fostering empathy, collaboration and adaptability. Future research should focus on the long-term integration of immersive technologies in education, with attention to challenges related to accessibility and inclusivity, which are also addressed through narratives.

Keywords Immersive storytelling · Divergent thinking · Virtual reality in education

M. E. De Carlo (✉) · P. Limone
Pegaso University, Naples, Italy
e-mail: Mariaermelinda.decarlo@unipegaso.it; Pierpaolo.limone@unipegaso.it

A. Micalizzi (ed.), *Artificial Creativity*, Springer Proceedings in Humanities and Social Sciences, https://doi.org/10.1007/978-3-031-88334-7_9

1 Introduction

Narratives in the metaverse represent one of the most advanced intersections between human creativity, artificial intelligence (AI) and digital technologies. These narratives serve as a powerful tool for fostering divergent thinking in an interactive and dynamic context, stimulating the exploration of new ideas and creative solutions for both users and creators.

Divergent thinking, defined as the ability to generate multiple solutions to a problem, is recognised as a central element in any innovation process (Guilford, 1950). Its foundations lie in the theories of Guilford (1967) and have been further explored by scholars like Runco (2014), who emphasise the importance of this form of creative thinking in learning and skill development.

Numerous studies have demonstrated that divergent thinking is key to achieving a broader and more articulated understanding of content compared to superficial learning and mere memorisation (Sawyer & Danah, 2024). Students who adopt divergent approaches tend to reflect on complex problems, seeking unconventional solutions and creating connections between various domains of knowledge. This approach enhances student engagement, motivation and participation, making learning more meaningful and personalised (Amabile, 2011; Sternberg et al., 2023). In educational contexts, particularly where traditional methods fail to capture students' interest, fostering divergent thinking can reduce the risk of disengagement and improve academic performance (Camilleri et al., 2024).

The integration of artificial creativity into the production of three-dimensional stories for the metaverse further enriches this process. According to Boden (2014), AI not only generates creative content but also acts as a true co-creator. In the context of immersive storytelling in the metaverse, AI can generate dynamic virtual environments that adapt in real time to users' choices, offering new scenarios, characters and paths that evolve unpredictably. This process not only expands narrative possibilities but also simulates creative behavior, further stimulating divergent thinking by encouraging users to explore unconventional solutions.

The advent of the metaverse, a three-dimensional virtual space where individuals can interact in immersive and novel ways, opens up new educational possibilities capable of fostering key competencies, particularly those related to creativity, cultural awareness and collaboration in digital spaces (European Commission, 2018). The three-dimensional stories that come to life within these environments enable students to develop essential transversal skills needed to address contemporary challenges, such as the ability to adapt to changing contexts and apply innovative solutions to complex problems (Jenkins, 2009; Bailey & Bailenson, 2017; Johnson, 2016).

As noted by Ferrari, Cachia and Punie (2009), these experiences, when well-designed, can promote critical and creative thinking, in alignment with the European educational objectives for lifelong learning.

In this regard, the Global Education Monitoring Report 2023 from UNESCO (2023) highlights the importance of developing inclusive and accessible educational experiences through the use of technology. This underscores the need to create stories and virtual environments that represent diverse cultural perspectives and are accessible to all students, regardless of their abilities or socio-cultural backgrounds. Without considering diverse narrative perspectives, stories may be perceived as non-inclusive or fail to represent various cultural groups, thereby limiting the accessibility and inclusiveness of these experiences.

2 Literature Review

Recent research demonstrates how the use of immersive narratives within virtual reality (VR) can significantly contribute to enhancing users' creativity and problem-solving skills. For instance, one study found that participants immersed in narrative VR environments showed a marked increase in their imaginative capacity and production of creative solutions compared to traditional control groups (Makransky et al., 2019). This effect was further reinforced by the integration of narrative elements that enhance engagement and facilitate the exploration of innovative solutions in educational contexts.

Immersive narratives not only provide a situational context that aids students' understanding of content, but they can also trigger emotional responses that facilitate the learning of complex concepts. This ability to enhance affective outcomes, such as motivation and engagement, without reducing cognitive gains, has been confirmed by a systematic review focused on the use of narratives in VR (Calvert & Hume, 2022). The authors analysed 12 experimental studies, demonstrating how the integration of stories within VR can also stimulate deep learning, while highlighting the need for further research to optimise these approaches.

The cognitive-affective model of immersive learning (CAMIL), proposed by Makransky and Petersen (2021), reinforces the findings that immersive environments can effectively facilitate critical thinking and creative problem-solving. This model suggests that the combination of complex sensory stimuli with engaging narratives promotes the development of divergent thinking.

Moreover, empirical studies show that VR can overcome the limitations of traditional teaching methods by offering unique opportunities to simulate practical learning situations. In particular, experiments in complex fields such as engineering and design have shown how immersive simulations can facilitate the learning of unconventional approaches to problem-solving (Araiza-Alba et al., 2021). These studies highlight the potential of VR to provide a safe and flexible context, free from real-world consequences, for experimenting with innovative solutions (Alqudah & Khasawneh, 2023).

The adoption of different identities within VR environments has proved particularly effective in enhancing creativity and fostering open-mindedness. Studies have shown that experiencing stories from different perspectives, such as through the use of personalised avatars, can expand cognitive boundaries, encouraging divergent thinking. These findings are especially relevant for promoting empathy through immersive narratives, as adopting diverse perspectives can enhance emotional understanding and improve the capacity to empathise with others (Herrera et al., 2018; Ahn et al., 2013; Baños et al., 2004; Slater et al., 2016).

The choice of virtual environment plays a significant role in enhancing divergent thinking. For example, experiments by Ichimura (2023) demonstrated that open environments, such as natural landscapes, significantly increase creativity levels compared to enclosed spaces, with higher scores reported on the *Alternative Uses Test* (AUT). These findings suggest that the perceived freedom in open virtual environments may positively impact creative idea generation.

Moreover, the use of personalised avatars and active interactions in VR environments has been shown to foster creative collaboration and real-time collective problem-solving, particularly in complex professional contexts such as design and corporate innovation (Bourgeois-Bougrine et al., 2022; Liu et al., 2023). These studies highlight how a high degree of immersion and personalisation in VR experiences can improve creative performance while promoting collaboration among participants.

Despite these promising results, research on the educational impact of immersive narratives in VR is still in its developmental stages. There is considerable scope for further exploration of how to adapt VR experiences effectively to meet the specific needs of students and how these experiences can foster the development of transversal skills, such as collaboration and resilience. Moreover, the long-term integration of VR into school curricula and its impact on socio-emotional learning and critical thinking remain central themes for future research. Finally, addressing accessibility challenges is crucial to ensure that the widespread adoption of VR in education is both inclusive and sustainable (Calvert & Hume, 2022; Araiza-Alba et al., 2021).

3 The Metaverse as a Learning Environment for the Development of Divergent Thinking

The metaverse emerges as a highly immersive virtual environment. It is characterised by its ability to create complex, multidimensional narrative worlds where users are not confined to predefined linear narratives. Instead, they can shape and influence the story through their choices and interactions. The non-linearity of stories in the metaverse allows the creation of personalised narratives, enabling users to explore various possibilities simultaneously, an element that reflects the very nature of divergent thinking (Hirshfield & Koretsky, 2021). Divergent thinking, which requires the generation of multiple solutions or ideas to address a problem, thrives in the metaverse, where users engage with scenarios that do not have a single correct solution. Consequently, different creative possibilities arise depending on the actions taken, fostering mental flexibility and the ability to consider alternative paths (Makransky & Petersen, 2021; Guegan et al., 2020).

The connections between divergent thinking and artificial creativity are clearly evident in these virtual contexts. While users are encouraged to explore and think unconventionally, AI adds a dimension of openness by proposing choices, environments and stories that evolve unpredictably.

Indeed, three-dimensional narratives in the metaverse can adapt in real time to the user's decisions. AI can create new challenges, alter the course of the plot, or generate dynamic settings, stimulating users' divergent thinking as they are required to consider new solutions as the story evolves. This non-linear interaction provides users with narrative freedom that not only encourages exploration but also promotes the development of creative skills (Yang et al., 2022).

Artificial creativity also enables the generation of three-dimensional characters with autonomous intelligence, capable of responding uniquely to user interactions. These characters can adapt their behaviours and responses, creating unforeseen scenarios. Interaction with such characters requires users to exercise divergent thinking in order to manage complex and non-linear narrative relationships (Liu et al., 2023).

Equally significant is the fact that the metaverse offers the opportunity to explore and create unique experiences through open worlds, which are not constrained by rigid narrative structures. AI plays a crucial role in this process by generating environments that respond to user choices, thus opening up new creative possibilities. This type of interaction promotes divergent thinking as users can invent new and unforeseen ways to interact with the environment (Makransky & Petersen, 2021).

The synergy between human and artificial creativity in the metaverse therefore stimulates innovation. Authors can collaborate with AI systems to create narratives that evolve in unexpected ways, offering new perspectives and solutions. AI enhances human divergent thinking by introducing narrative variables and developments that enrich the creative process (Guegan et al., 2020).

4 Three-Dimensional Stories: From Narrative Techniques to Potential Indicators

In the virtual environments, narratives dynamically evolve in response to interactions with space and surrounding elements, transforming the user into an active participant in the storytelling process (Bailey & Bailenson, 2017). Unlike traditional narratives that follow predetermined paths, the metaverse allows users to make decisions that directly influence the course of the story, prompting them to explore multiple creative solutions (Zhang & Wang, 2023).

Cognitive flexibility is further stimulated by the ability to navigate branching stories that unfold according to users' choices, offering a broad range of narrative pathways (Almulla et al., 2024). Advanced technologies such as VR and augmented reality (AR) transform storytelling from a passive experience into a highly interactive and personalised one, users becoming co-creators of the narrative.

Traditional narratological techniques, such as those studied by Gérard Genette (1980) and Marie-Laure Ryan (2021), are challenged in these environments, where temporal structures and character roles continually adapt to user interactions. In the metaverse, narrative time becomes fluid and non-linear, allowing users to explore multiple timelines, manipulate the flow of events and experience the consequences of their decisions firsthand (Chen & Ryan, 2022). The concept of narrative identity is also redefined, avatars serving not merely as passive projections but as virtual extensions of users, actively shaping the plot through their actions (Ricoeur, 1991).

The narrative space thus becomes a tangible, three-dimensional environment where users can freely move and actively alter the story. This allows greater co-creation of meaning, the user taking on the role of an active builder of the narrative world (Ryan, 2021).

4.1 Measurable Indicators and Narrative Techniques for Evaluating Immersive 3d Storytelling in Virtual Reality

Among the most significant aspects of three-dimensional stories in the educational context are not only their ability to make the learning process interactive but also the opportunity to experiment with multiple scenarios and open-ended conclusions. This allows the exploration of different creative and personalised solutions, stimulating users' divergent thinking. To assess the quality of three-dimensional narratives in virtual environments comprehensively and thoroughly, it is essential to define a set of measurable indicators. This approach aids developers, educators and researchers in designing, evaluating and enhancing immersive experiences that exploit the technological potential of VR while maintaining a strong focus on narrative richness.

Recent studies provide an empirical foundation supporting the use of measurable indicators for evaluating immersive experiences. Research has demonstrated that integrating VR elements into educational processes can increase users' cognitive presence and improve their learning in simulated environments (Makransky et al., 2019). Moreover, the use of feedback systems based on behavioural parameters, such as the time spent in certain virtual areas or the frequency of interactions with virtual characters, can be employed to measure narrative effectiveness and users' emotional engagement (Bourgeois-Bougrine et al., 2022).

Measurable indicators, such as cognitive tests, psychometric questionnaires (for example, the Immersive Tendencies Questionnaire or the AUT for divergent thinking), qualitative user feedback and behavioural analysis based on data collected during the virtual experience, can be used to monitor the achievement of educational and creative objectives. These tools enable the measurement of key parameters such as the ability to generate multiple ideas, the level of engagement and emotional presence within the narrative (Slater & Sanchez-Vives, 2016).

A further methodological contribution comes from narratological aspects, which include the use of non-linear narrative structures, dynamic character development and the management of narrative time (Chen & Ryan, 2022). These concepts help to understand how the narrative influences the immersive experience and user engagement. The integration of narrative theory with immersive technologies not only enhances interaction between the user and the virtual environment but fosters deeper and more engaging learning.

Practical applications of these indicators can be observed in educational and professional simulation contexts. For example, in the medical field, students can be immersed in three-dimensional environments where they must make real-time decisions and interact with complex scenarios (Makransky & Petersen, 2021). These environments provide measurable data that can be used to assess students' decision-making abilities and critical thinking, offering a concrete evaluation of the effectiveness of immersive narratives.

In this context, an indicator table (Table 1) has been developed, serving as a systematic guide to facilitate the design and evaluation of immersive narratives. The objectives outlined in the table range from stimulating creative and divergent thinking to emotional engagement and interaction with three-dimensional elements, as well as the impact on learning and memory. This tool enables developers and educators to design narratives that balance advanced narrative techniques with immersive technologies while promoting a comprehensive educational experience.

During the development and post-implementation phases, the table can be used to identify key objectives and select the most appropriate indicators for monitoring user progress. The application of narratological concepts, such as non-linear structures or character development, enriches the story and enhances interaction with the user (Genette, 1980). Moreover, ongoing evaluation, supported by qualitative feedback and quantitative data, will allow constant monitoring and improvement of the experience, adapting it to the results and making iterative adjustments based on the data collected (Yang et al., 2022).

5 Conclusion

Three-dimensional stories represent an emerging frontier in education, unlocking new possibilities for immersive learning and fostering creative thinking among students. Technologies such as VR and AR offer engaging and interactive learning experiences that have the potential to transform traditional teaching approaches, making them more dynamic and personalised. By integrating immersive narratives into educational contexts, teachers can create environments in which students can creatively and collaboratively address complex problems (Makransky & Petersen, 2021; Bourgeois-Bougrine et al., 2022).

According to UNESCO's 2021 Report on the Future of Education (2021), the use of immersive technologies like VR and AR is crucial for promoting experiential learning and empowering students in an increasingly digital world. These tools

Table 1 Objectives, indicators and narrative techniques for 3D storytelling in immersive environments

Objective	Measurable Indicators	Narratological Aspects	References
1. Improve creative and divergent thinking through immersive 3D storytelling	- improvement in creative thinking test scores (e.g., *Torrance test* pre and post-experience) - number and originality of user-proposed solutions	- non-linear narrative structures that encourage exploration and choice - use of metaphors to foster multiple interpretations	Guilford (1950); Runco (2014); Boden (2014); Johnson (2016); Bourgeois-Bougrine et al. (2022).
2. Measure user engagement and immersion in 3D virtual environments	- scores from the *virtual reality immersion questionnaire* (VRIQ) - levels of immersion reported by users (e.g., *presence questionnaire*)	- diegetic coherence: Internal consistency of the narrative world - effective use of narrative perspectives, e.g., internal focalization to increase empathy	Shin et al. (2024); Slater and Sanchez-Vives (2014); Makransky and Petersen (2021).
3. Evaluate the quality and coherence of the 3D narrative (time, space and characters)	- ability to summarise the plot - feedback on the coherence and logical consistency of the narrative - number of reported inconsistencies or confusion	- solid structure of fabula and plot - management of narrative time (flashbacks and foreshadowing) to enrich the story - well-developed world-building to support the narrative	Marwecki et al. (2018); Shin et al. (2024); Genette (1980); Ryan (2021).
4. Evaluate the interaction with 3D characters and environments	- number and quality of interactions with 3D characters - level of empathy with characters - realism and credibility of 3D characters and environments	- in-depth character development, with clear background and motivations - meaningful dialogues advancing the plot - narrative interaction that allows users to influence the story	Herrera et al. (2018); Ahn et al. (2013); Bichlmeier (2023); Lowell and Ilobinso (2023); Jin et al. (2024).
5. Measure the impact on spatial memory and learning outcomes	- improvements in spatial memory tests - evaluations on narrative-based learning - ability to apply acquired knowledge	- use of symbolic narrative spaces reflecting themes or emotions - branching narrative paths that encourage exploration - educational elements integrated into the plot	Alqudah, Khasawneh (2023); Araiza-Alba et al. (2021); Moira and Dimitrios (2018).

(continued)

Table 1 (continued)

Objective	Measurable Indicators	Narratological Aspects	References
6. Monitor user comfort and mitigate cybersickness	- incidence of cybersickness symptoms measured with the *simulator sickness questionnaire (SSQ)* - user feedback on comfort during the VR experience	- smooth narrative transitions to avoid disorientation -spatial-temporal coherence to keep the user oriented - narrative techniques to guide attention	Makransky et al. (2019); Slater and Sanchez-Vives (2016).
7. Evaluate the effectiveness of 3D audio in enhancing narrative immersion	- feedback on the impact of spatial audio - measured increase in immersion through 3D audio - use of audio cues for navigation or interaction	- use of diegetic and extra-diegetic sound to enrich the narrative - leitmotifs associated with characters or themes - audio as a narrative element anticipating events	Bourgeois-Bougrine et al. (2022); Calvert, Hume (2022).
8. Evaluate overall satisfaction and user experience with 3D narratives	- scores on satisfaction scales for VR narratives - *net promoter score* (NPS) - qualitative feedback on appreciated aspects and areas for improvement	- thematic coherence and clear messaging - satisfaction with the climax and narrative resolution - perceived originality and artistic value of the story	Guegan et al. (2020); Yang et al. (2022).
9. Evaluate the effectiveness of 3D transitions and animations in storytelling	- feedback on the fluidity of transitions between scenes - number of glitches or technical issues reported - perceived impact of animations on the overall narrative experience	- coherent transitions maintaining narrative continuity - use of ellipsis to manage time without confusing the user - animations expressing emotions and developing characters	Hirshfield, Koretsky (2021); Shao et al. (2024).
10. Measure learning and spatial memory through 3D storytelling	- ability to reconstruct explored 3D environments - post-experience spatial memory test results - application of acquired knowledge	- narrative mental maps: Understanding and remembering spatial arrangement - symbolic spaces reinforcing themes - environmental storytelling where the setting tells part of the story	Zhang and Wang (2023); Liu et al. (2023).

foster personalised learning, offering students realistic contexts in which to develop creativity and problem-solving skills. UNESCO emphasises that future education systems must evolve to meet the challenges posed by rapid digitalisation, preparing students not only through the acquisition of knowledge but also by developing transversal skills such as collaboration, empathy and adaptability to new, complex scenarios.

Targeted design is essential for integrating three-dimensional stories within the metaverse with narratological studies, thus developing a theory of immersive storytelling. This theory must account for interaction, active participation and sensory immersion as central components of the narrative structure. While traditional narratology has focused on storytelling as a fixed text, the metaverse introduces fluid, dynamic narratives that redefine the relationship between author, text and audience. The story can change in real-time based on user decisions, opening up new avenues for research and innovation in the field of immersive narratology (Chen & Ryan, 2022; Davtian et al., 2021).

The lack of integration between strong narratological foundations and the potential of immersive technologies can severely compromise the effectiveness of three-dimensional stories within the metaverse. To create truly engaging and meaningful experiences, it is essential to combine narrative theory with technological innovation. This synergy ensures that the stories not only captivate users but also possess depth, coherence and the ability to meet educational objectives (Araiza-Alba et al., 2021). Without a solid narrative structure, stories risk becoming disorganised, making it difficult for users to follow or understand the plot. Underdeveloped characters can hinder identification or empathy, reducing users' emotional engagement. Without compelling narratives, stories may feel flat, incapable of generating lasting interest or emotion. Consequently, immersion and the overall effectiveness of the immersive experience can be significantly diminished (Slater & Sanchez-Vives, 2016).

Using immersive technologies without adequate narrative support can result in experiences that resemble technical demonstrations rather than meaningful stories. Interactivity, if not effectively integrated into the narrative, may fail to add real value to the user experience. Without clear narrative guidance, users may feel disoriented within the virtual world, unsure of what to do or where to go. If their actions do not significantly influence the story, they may experience frustration or boredom (Calvert & Hume, 2022).

In educational terms, the absence of a narrative structure that supports clear instructional objectives can prevent stories from effectively conveying key knowledge or skills. Consequently, experiences may fail to align with European key competencies or curricular goals, thereby reducing their pedagogical impact (Jenkins, 2009). Additionally, without adequate world-building, the setting may appear inconsistent or unconvincing, diminishing both the effectiveness and emotional impact of the story.

Investing in immersive technologies without a solid narrative foundation can result in wasted resources, offering a low return on investment. Resources may be directed towards technical developments that do not add significant value to the overall experience. This lack of integration between theory and technology can also lead to missed opportunities for innovation, as stories may appear less innovative compared to other offerings on the market, limiting the potential for exploring new forms of storytelling and interaction (Ichimura, 2023).

References

Ahn, S. J., Le, A. M. T., & Bailenson, J. N. (2013). The effect of embodied experiences on self-other merging, attitude and helping behavior. *Media Psychology, 16*(1), 7–38.

Almulla, A. A., Khasawneh, M. A. S., Abdel-Hadi, S. A., & Jarrah, H. Y. (2024). Influence of non-linear storytelling in video games on cognitive development among students with learning disabilities. *International Journal of Learning, Teaching and Educational Research, 23*(1), 84–97.

Alqudah, H., & Khasawneh, M. A. S. (2023). Exploring the impact of virtual reality field trips on student engagement and learning outcomes. *Migration Letters, 20*(5), 1205–1216.

Amabile, T. (2011). *Componential theory of creativity*. Harvard Business School.

Araiza-Alba, P., Keane, T., Chen, W. S., & Kaufman, J. (2021). Immersive virtual reality as a tool to learn problem-solving skills. *Computers & Education, 164*, 104121.

Bailey, J. O., & Bailenson, J. N. (2017). Immersive virtual reality and the developing child. In *Cognitive development in digital contexts* (pp. 181–200). Academic Press.

Baños, R. M., Botella, C., Alcañiz, M., Liaño, V., Guerrero, B., & Rey, B. (2004). Immersion and emotion: Their impact on the sense of presence. *Cyberpsychology & Behavior, 7*(6), 734–741.

Bichlmeier, C. (2023). Interaction with AI-controlled characters in AR worlds. In *Handbook of augmented reality* (pp. 131–155). Springer.

Boden, M. A. (2014). Creativity and artificial intelligence: A contradiction in terms? In E. S. Paul & S. B. Kaufman (Eds.), *The philosophy of creativity: New essays* (pp. 224–245). Oxford University Press.

Bourgeois-Bougrine, S., Bonnardel, N., Burkhardt, J. M., Thornhill-Miller, B., Pahlavan, F., Buisine, S., & Lubart, T. (2022). Immersive virtual environments' impact on individual and collective Creativity. *European Psychologist, 27*(3), 237–253.

Calvert, J., & Hume, M. (2022). Immersing learners in stories: A systematic literature review of educational narratives in virtual reality. *Australasian Journal of Educational Technology, 38*(5), 45–61.

Camilleri, D., Munro, J., & Glăveanu, V. P. (2024). Examining disengagement and fostering creativity: A relational perspective on high-ability students in formal education. *Gifted Child Today, 47*(4), 286–299.

Chen, J., & Ryan, M. L. (2022). Storyworld, transmedia storytelling, and contemporary narrative theory: An interview with Marie-Laure Ryan. *Frontiers of Narrative Studies, 7*(2), 147–155.

Davtian, A., Shabalina, O., Sadovnikova, N., & Parygin, D. (2021). Cyber-social system as a model of narrative management. In *Society 5.0: Cyberspace for advanced human-centered society* (pp. 3–14). Springer.

European Commission. (2018). Council recommendation of 22 May 2018 on key competences for lifelong learning. *Official Journal of the European Union*, 2018/C 189/01. https://eur-lex.europa.eu

Ferrari, A., Cachia, R., Punie, Y. (2009). *Innovation and Creativity in education and training in the EU member states: Fostering creative learning and supporting innovative teaching*. JRC technical note 52374, Luxembourg.

Genette, G. (1980). *Narrative discourse: An essay in method*. Cornell University Press.

Guegan, J., Brechet, C., & Nelson, J. (2020). Dreamlike and playful virtual environments to inspire children's divergent thinking. *Journal of Media Psychology, 33*(4), 28–38.

Guilford, J. P. (1950). Creativity. *American Psychologist, 5*(9), 444–454. https://doi.org/10.1037/h0063487

Guilford, J. P. (1967). *The nature of human intelligence*. McGraw-Hill.

Herrera, F., Bailenson, J. N., Weisz, E., Ogle, E., & Zaki, J. (2018). Building long-term empathy: A large-scale comparison of traditional and virtual reality perspective-taking. *PLoS One, 13*(10), e0204494.

Hirshfield, L. J., & Koretsky, M. D. (2021). Cultivating creative thinking in engineering student teams: Can a computer-mediated virtual laboratory help? *Journal of Computer Assisted Learning, 37*(2), 587–601.

Ichimura, K. (2023). Effects of virtual reality's viewing medium and the environment's spatial openness on divergent thinking. *PLoS One, 18*(3), e0283632.

Jenkins, H. (2009). *Confronting the challenges of participatory culture: Media education for the 21st century*. MIT Press.

Jin, Y., Ma, M., & Liu, Z. (2024). Evaluating user engagement and preference in virtual reality and augmented virtuality for interactive storytelling. *Interacting with Computers, 36*(6), 383–397.

Johnson, L. (2016). *NMC horizon report: 2016 higher education edition*.

Liu, J., Burkhardt, J. M., & Lubart, T. (2023). Boosting Creativity through users' avatars and contexts in virtual environments: A systematic review of recent research. *Journal of Intelligence, 11*(7), 144.

Lowell, V. L., & Ilobinso, A. C. (2023). Virtual reality in online higher education for learner engagement, interaction and experiential learning. In *Sage handbook of online higher education* (p. 458). Sage.

Makransky, G., & Petersen, G. B. (2021). The cognitive-affective model of immersive learning (CAMIL): A theoretical research-based model of learning in immersive virtual reality. *Educational Psychology Review, 33*(3), 937–958.

Makransky, G., Terkildsen, T. S., & Mayer, R. E. (2019). Adding immersive virtual reality to a science lab simulation causes more presence but less learning. *Learning and Instruction, 60*, 225–236. https://doi.org/10.1016/j.learninstruc.2017.12.007

Marwecki, S., Brehm, M., Wagner, L., Cheng, L. P., Mueller, F. F., & Baudisch, P. (2018). VirtualSpace—Overloading physical space with multiple virtual reality users. In *Proceedings of the 2018 CHI conference on human factors in computing systems* (pp. 1–10). ACM.

Moira, M., & Dimitrios, M. (2018). Cultural memory in its spatio-narrative-augmented reality. *International Journal of Media & Cultural Politics, 14*(2), 153–171.

Ricoeur, P. (1991). Narrative identity. In D. Wood (Ed.), *On Paul Ricoeur: Narrative and interpretation* (pp. 188–199). Routledge.

Runco, M. A. (2014). *Creativity: Theories and themes: Research, development and practice* (2nd ed.). Elsevier Academic Press.

Ryan, M. L. (2021). Introduction: Four types of textual space and their manifestations in digital narrative. In *Digital narrative spaces* (pp. 1–19). Routledge.

Sawyer, R. K., & Danah, H. (2024). *Explaining creativity: The science of human innovation*. Oxford University Press.

Shao, Z., Shen, L., Li, H., Shan, Y., Qu, H., Wang, Y., & Chen, S. (2024). Narrative player: Reviving data narratives with visuals. *arXiv:2410.03268*.

Shin, J. E., Kim, H., Park, H., & Woo, W. (2024). Investigating the design of augmented narrative spaces through virtual-real connections: A systematic literature review. In *Proceedings of the CHI conference on human factors in computing systems* (pp. 1–18). ACM.

Slater, M., & Sanchez-Vives, M. V. (2016). Enhancing our lives with immersive virtual reality. *Frontiers in Robotics and AI, 3*, 74.

Sternberg, R. J., Kaufman, J. C., & Karami, S. (2023). *Intelligence, creativity, and wisdom: Exploring their connections and distinctions*. Springer Nature.

UNESCO. (2021). *Reimagining our futures together: A new social contract for education*. UNESCO Publishing.

UNESCO. (2023). *Global education monitoring report 2023: Technology in education: A tool on whose terms?* UNESCO Publishing. https://unesdoc.unesco.org/ark:/48223/pf0000385723

Yang, Q., Zhao, Y., Huang, H., Xiong, Z., Kang, J., & Zheng, Z. (2022). Fusing blockchain and AI with metaverse: A survey. *IEEE Open Journal of the Computer Society, 3*, 122–136.
Zhang, W., & Wang, Y. (2023). An empirical study of the impact of metaverse storytelling on intentions to visit. *Information Technology & Tourism, 25*(3), 411–432.

Pedagogical and Literary Intersections in AI Imaginaries

Teresa Savoia

Abstract The relationship with an artificial intelligence has long existed in the history of human imagery. In Western cultures, it probably dates back to Ancient Greece, when the mythological figure of Talos may be considered as the first artificial creature invented with a purpose, and has been followed by an almost uninterrupted tradition of similar creations in human narratives, long before the name Robot was invented by Čapek in the XX century (The Royal Society, 2018). Artificial intelligences have been represented in all different kinds of narratives and recent research shows how these narratives have a profound influence on the real world, on the creation of an ecosystem of concepts and images and even in addressing the choices of scientific studies (Cave et al., 2020). Most significantly for our purpose, it also has an impact on addressing the pedagogical reflection and on contributing to the creation of teaching scenarios which translate imaginaries into teaching practices. The aim of this contribution is to focus on the manifold aspects that presents literary AI and on the intersections that may arise from these reflections, both in Italian and International teaching contexts.

Keywords Literary imaginaries · AI narrative · Pedagogy of AI · Teaching practices

1 Introduction

If we were to ask where the roots of AI might be traced in the history of humankind, we are keen to sustain the idea that they are identifiable in the primeval ability to think creatively, which can be considered as the one ability that enabled our ancestors to give birth to a more and more a complex cultural, before social, system (Harari, 2011).

T. Savoia (✉)
Centro Direzionale Isola F2, Pegaso Digital University, Naples, Italy
e-mail: teresa.savoia@unipegaso.it

A. Micalizzi (ed.), *Artificial Creativity*, Springer Proceedings in Humanities and Social Sciences, https://doi.org/10.1007/978-3-031-88334-7_10

These imaginaries linked to some sorts of AI date back to that primeval past and are later identifiable in early western cultures, where artificial creatures were imagined as embued with special powers. Talos, the living statue made by Hephaestus for Zeus, in order to protect Crete, is generally recognized as the first artificial creature imagined in this context. Ever since then, AI has always been present in all types of narratives. In more recent times, it is part of literature, cinema, museum exhibitions, videogames, scientific works. Accordingly, AI narratives strongly influence collective imaginaries and allow intersections between narrative genres: Talos, just to mention an example is for instance the protagonist in films, tv series and videogames.

Remarkably, the image that has been associated to the figures endowed with artificial powers has always been negative, ever since the very first attempts and creations have appeared in the cultural landscape. With few major exceptions, most of these creatures are different prototypes of destructors developing along an uninterrupted line, up to contemporary productions. In the European culture they are traceable in the XIII century where they can be described as forms of knowledge attributable to theologists and scholars of the time (Cave et al., 2020).

However different, all types of imaginaries present a negative scenario, underlining the idea that the creation of an artificial intelligence external to humas' mind is to be considered as an act of hubris, a sort of promethean arrogance. Other elements have been subsequently associated to hubris, all bearers of more negative connotations and outcomes.

The aspects associated to AI in literatures and narratives are not isolated from the imaginaries that circulate in other fields, and most strikingly, they have been proven to influence not only literary production but also scientific choices (Cave et al., 2020). Similarly, it is presumable that the same AI imaginaries influence pedagogical reflections. It is likely that the most worried concerns about the use of IA in the pedagogical field and teaching practice derive from this long series of narrative productions that have characterized the cultural and literary history.

This chapter deals with some literary scenarios and productions that have shaped the history of English-speaking world. It presents main themes and trends that have been identified in these literary productions, analyzing forms of embodied and disembodied creations of AI.

Also, attention is given to structuralist approaches. Being profoundly aware of the fact that structure influences content, an idea is pursued that links the early origin and development of the novel in the England of XVIII century to the widespread diffusion of literary imaginaries of AI.

AI, indeed, is not only the theme of cultural production it has also been developed as a tool to produce it, starting the major debate around authorship and originality in literary productions. At the same, it gave rise to the largely debated questions of AI ethics which are closely linked to its educational applications.

The following paragraphs deal each with one of the points that have here been presenting, with the aim of offering an initial point of view that opens to a necessary further discussion.

2 The Relevance of AI Literary Imageries in the Pedagogical Field

As mentioned above, the aim of this contribution is to reflect on some pedagogical issues related to the English literary production. To this end, the literary scenario has been reviewed with a double focus, which was literary and pedagogical at the same time. This double perspective has helped to outline the existence of a deeply rooted connection between literary trends and pedagogical issues.

Undoubtedly, artificial intelligences have fully entered the educational debate (Liu & Song, 2022; Vertecchi, 2013), and are often coexisting with traditional educational agencies in all fields. As these new realities have been entering the realm of cultural production, bringing up a revolution under manifold aspects, it has become necessary not only to revise pedagogical practices but also to reflect on the very epistemic of education and pedagogy.

Artificial Intelligence is redefining pedagogy in manifold ways. Also, there are widespread concerns that it might interfere and diminish personal and social interactions and processes, that, if not responsibly managed, it may not be possible to fully control it and, it ultimately may cause harm and replace the same figure of the teacher and the educator.

The aim of our research, which unfolds in the interconnections between literary and pedagogical issues, is to trace back imaginaries also so as to shed some light on these concerns and channel them.

When addressing the ideas that spread about new technologies, there are at least two fundamental issues that are worth underlining. The first is to understand what the state of the art of AI in educational field really is, unveiling its true extension with sound data. The second is to be able to trace back where these same ideas come from, what is the domain where their origin is attributable. These two processes help shed light and become aware of the fact that in reality new technologies are far from cancelling human interactions from educational field and also far from the catastrophic scenarios of replacing teachers with machines. Indeed, they can be made to work on integrating both human-managed and technology-led processes, helping to maximize and benefit from both (Shum et al., 2024).

However, if we consider the second issue that was mentioned above, it is definitely useful to understand where, then, the idea of an Artificial Intelligence taking possession of all human abilities comes from. Taking into account the literary production may, thus, shed some light on this, more precisely on the creation and establishment of such ideas in the collective imaginary.

Remarkably, research shows that the imaginaries created by different types of fiction narrative, such as novel and short stories, let alone by the movie factory in more recent times, have influenced both the way in which technologies are thought and developed in science and the fears rooted in the collective imaginaries, leading to the configuration of educational scenarios in which Artificial Intelligence destroys every cultural achievement humanity has reached. It is, thus, to these fields that common imaginary is due, which is a field that belongs more to fiction than to reality, however suggestive and pervasive it may be.

An analysis of technologies such as Artificial Intelligence, Virtual Reality, Augmented reality, through a diachronic approach can contribute to re-reading them, orienting the reflection through a greater awareness of what they really represent. The introduction of new technologies in the educational and teaching contexts must lead to a reflection that is, therefore, rooted in time and space. Indeed, it should not be overlooked that the distrust that accompanies the introduction of contemporary technologies into the world of education is similar to that with which all the technologies that have modified our civilization in the past have been welcomed, first and foremost that of handwriting, to which a further reflection would be worth pursuing.

3 Artificial Intelligence in English Imaginary Scenario: Themes

The literary contribution that emerges from the English corpus develops on a trajectory which is actually opposite to that identified for the Italian context (Part I). Some reasons for this difference may be ascribed to historical and economic factors. As contraposed to Italy, in England, industrialization and technological enhancement developed very early. Also, they were parallel to the birth of the new textual forms recognizable as novels.

Soon, an imagery linked to new technological scenarios and devices was born and developed. It found a fertile soil in this country, where both an ideal setting and a means of expression were available. Indeed, technological development and progress were so far reaching and promising that they allowed the imagination to create magnificent scenarios linked to future opportunities and perspectives. Also, they gave voice to the fears of such outbreaking novelties, creating negative, monstrous images.

All these new ideas and imaginaries that were circulating at the time could be properly voiced and recorded in the new literary forms that were introduced by the invention of the Novel. The novel's narrative structure, the opportunity of unfolding a plot intermingled with descriptive paragraphs, the ability to reach new audiences were all elements that allowed the expression of new sensibilities. Also, it permitted to the new social, economic and cultural realities to emerge and be represented and to new literary instances to be produced and voiced.

Unsurprisingly, the novel was born in this geographical context, where indeed the major economic, technological and cultural shifts were taking place at a very fast rate. Just to mention a few technological revolutions that had a great impact on the imagination of people, the first locomotive was started by Robert Trevithick in 1803, and was followed by the first rail service, that opened in 1829; the world first underground was inaugurated in London in 1863; besides, from 1835 to 1840 the telegraph and the penny postal system were implemented.

These changes in communication and technology strongly impacted on the social and cultural shape, let alone on literary tastes. The novel was indeed an instrument to give voice to new instances, cultural and social besides literary.

If the novel gave room to the new sensibilities and to new scenarios linked to social and economic changes of the time, it must be considered that the role assigned to artificial creations in the literature of nineteenth century England also inherited and developed the connotations that had characterized much of the literary history since its origins in the Greek mythology. Namely, the same descriptions of destruction and loss of control that had endowed it from the very beginning were maintained, and have even survived up to contemporary manifestations.

Remarkably, Artificial Intelligences of some kinds have always populated literary imageries, and it is generally acknowledged that the first artificial creature of literature was Talos, the monster made of bronze and created by Hephaestus in order to protect the island of Crete (Cave et al., 2020).

Talos is probably the first prototype of a destroyer and he started a long series of figures in the course of the history of literature that have survived up to today. Ever since, an Artificial Intelligence of some kind has been present in all types of narrations: from novels, to cinema, to museums and, eventually, scientific works. At the same time, still nowadays, prevalent narratives share dominant characteristics, the main of which generally are negative. They generally present a creature who is endowed with anthropomorphic features, and even with a few major exceptions, they show a tendency towards utopian or dystopian extremes. Starting from these primeval features, others have developed, but they have all been endowed with negative connotations.

If one were to think to the most striking examples of narratives linked to these new scenarios, it would be inevitable to mention one of the first and most remarkable examples, such as M. Shelley's *Frankenstein; or, The Modern Prometheus* (first published in 1818) who created one of the first and most enduring prototypes of the kind. Other examples of the same period are Shelley's less known but just as strong *The Last Man* (first published in 1826) and also, along the same line, E.M. Forster's *The Machine Stops* (1909) or Herbert G. Wells, *The Time Machine* (1895).

In the European culture, these examples prove that Artificial Intelligence images have evolved into a figure embodied with a sort of Promethean arrogance which has become its prevalent aspect. Unsurprisingly, Asimov refers to the "Frankenstein complex" in order to define the image of a human created robot or figure who ultimately rebels to humans and destroys them.

The genre that later has been called and sci-fi has flourished from these first steps, all over the last century, both in literature and in cinema.

4 Artificial Intelligence in English Imaginary: Trends

The birth and diffusion of the novel as a new genre in the literary landscape represents an epoch making event. It is generally attributed to the eighteenth century

England, when the connection between a new reading public and a new figure of writer emerged among the newly born middle-class. If there is no convergence on which novel shall be considered as the forerunner of this genre, whether Defoe's *Robinson Crusoe*, as traditionally intended, or *Meriton Latroon*, according to more recent studies (Gebbia, 2019), still the social and cultural characteristics, let alone literary, rest the same.

The innovations introduced by the rise of the novel have soon given way to some questions that are still at the center of the debate on artistic creation: the concept of authorship, the reflections on the originality of artistic production, the debate between genius and technique have accompanied novel production since its appearance on the literary scene.

It might be useful to analyze these themes in a diachronic perspective. Let only consider that, while in the mid-eighteenth century, according to the romantic ideal of artistic creation and the elusiveness of genius, writing would be considered as an art in the hands of a talented and gifted person, in the belief that it would be impossible to learn the art of composition, a century later, the idea of originality was overcome by that of craftsmanship. Edgar A. Poe would then write how originality should not be considered as the effect "impulse or intuition" but rather as the result or "the prize of strategic work". The debate on artistic creation culminated a few decades later, in the twentieth century. In 1934, Ezra Pound, however being one of the most complex voices in American poetry, published his *ABC for reading*, a handbook on artistic creation that could be used by anyone who wanted to experiment with the art of writing (Gil et al., 2022).

On the critical side, structuralist studies, starting from Vladimir Propp's analyses of the functions of fairy tale, broke down the literary composition into functional and structural units. Literary work was thus de-structuralized, as basic literary units were identified. In this process, the work of art became more a work of craftmanship, that could be identified and reproduced, rather than the final outcome of a genius. At the same time, there was a widespread production of manuals and handbooks to teach how to create a literary text, through the breakdown into minimal units.

Structuralist analysis and the production of manuals for the perfect writer broke down the literary work and identified possible re-compositions through the combination of plots, events, characters and themes. Like primeval antecedents of contemporary text generators, these methods, manuals and techniques were meant to prove the possibility of automatic generation of texts and give everybody the opportunity to become a writer. As shown in an interesting exhibit at Columbia University, new and modern devices like "Plot Genie" or "Plotto" would indicate the steps for creating stories through combinatorial mechanisms (Gil et al., 2022).

5 Artificial Intelligence in English Literature: Embodied and Dis-embodied Imaginary

The images linked to artificial creations has developed under two different routes, in function of whether the Intelligence was embodied in an anthropomorphic shape or rather was more immaterial, being represented by a computer or a technological device.

Two examples are herewith reported that significantly represent the images linked to the first scenario: Ian McEwan's *Machine Like Me* (2019) and Kazuo Ishiguro's *Klara and the Sun* (2021).

The abovementioned novels explore the controversial relationship between humans and artificial intelligence. Both protagonists, although described with opposite narrative modes and endowed with a different aspect, are anthropomorphic figures. While in Ishiguro's novel, the device is a female and is never physically described, the figure created by McEwan is a male and is attentively, if not obsessively, described.

Both figures belong to a group of machines built with the aim of assisting and keeping adults and children company. Among the themes addressed by the two novels, the question of "Machine ethics" (Moor, 2006) stands out, and more precisely of "Responsible AI", which is a theme that has a deep impact both on education and also on science (Pflanzer et al., 2023; Trattner et al., 2022).

In Ishiguro's novel, the same narrative voice is that of the Artificial Intelligence. Her point of view creates what a formalist analysis would call an estranged perspective (Šklovskij, 2003). The novel investigates a possible representation of the world where humans and non-humans coexist, and the relevant implications in terms of relationships, responsibility and mutual care. The prevailing feelings, pervading the novel from its very first pages, are those of loneliness and void, made sharper in the excruciating effort to pushing the boundaries and limits imposed by natural existence to the edge of overcoming death. The answer that emerges from these efforts, not far from the one indicated by McEwan, is not reassuring. Both novels end in the destruction or dismantling of the Machine in order to win back and preserve a natural and intelligible, however complicated, course of life.

If in Ishiguro's novel the dominant theme is a melancholic, dazzled loneliness, enhanced by a landscape that adds on, as an objective correlative, in McEwan's novel it is destruction. Indeed, in *Machine Like Me*, the feeling of an approaching destruction pervades the story. It is a destruction that unfolds on different levels: symbolic, as the destruction of interpersonal bonds of all the involved characters, and physical, culminating in the eventual resolution to destroy the Machine, in order to recover a natural course of existence.

The other way of interpreting humanized technology under the perspective presented above is as disembodied, immaterial Artificial Intelligence. Two examples have been chosen from the plethora of novels on the theme: namely Richard Powers' *Galatea 2.2* (1995) and Edward M. Forster's *The Machine Stops* (1909).

Richard Powers's very sophisticated novel offers an analysis of Artificial Intelligence that is played out through the creation and discovery of language. The Machine does not have a body, but the ability to learn a language and, through it, to get to know the world. In this journey of knowledge, that is linguistic learning, to which the protagonist himself (suspended between two linguistic worlds, English and Dutch) undergoes, a *Bildung* develops, that leads, not only the protagonist, but the Artificial Intelligence itself, to create a complex self that is endowed with self-consciousness and self-knowledge.

The novel develops in this complex journey of interpretation of the external and interior worlds, individual and social, of which every language is a bearer, through a complex set of denotations, connotations, implicit elements that the protagonist has the task of teaching to his processor.

Forster's *The Machine Stops* represents a thrust by the author into that vein of sci-fi literature mentioned previously. An incorporeal, albeit pervasive, intelligence has been developed by human kind, to which human beings have progressively entrusted the social organization, arriving at precluding any relationship with others and with the outside world. The epilogue, common to many other examples of the genre, is that of the destruction of the entire system that has escaped the hands of its creators.

Both embodied and disembodied examples that have been reported in the paragraphs above recall the imaginaries of destruction which was anticipated in the premises to this contribution. These scenarios of destruction, however diverse among them, seem to prove and voice the disorientation, the puzzlement that overcomes the human mind when it faces the most profound and unsolvable quests of life. The presence of an AI, whether personified or not, makes them tangibly in front of us all and we are left alone to confront them.

References

Cave, S., Dihal, K., & Dillon, S. (Eds.). (2020). *AI narratives: A history of imaginative thinking about intelligent machines*. Oxford University Press.

Forster, E. M. (1909). *The machine stops. The Oxford and Cambridge review*. Archibald Constable.

Gebbia, A. (2019). Il furfante inglese ovvero la nascita del romanzo inglese. In R. Head & F. Kirkman (Eds.), *Il furfante inglese*. Rogas Editori.

Gil, A., Moe, M., Schoen, J., Tenen, D., & Tofanelli, J. (2022). *Literary AI—A columbia RBML exhibit*. Columbia University Libraries. Available on-line https://literaryai.library.columbia.edu

Harari, N. H. (2011). *From animals into gods: A brief history of humankind*. Dvir.

Ishiguro, K. (2021). *Klara and the sun*. Faber & Faber.

Liu, Y., & Song, P. (2022). Creating sustainable cultural industries: The perspective of artificial intelligence and global value chain. *Journal of Environmental and Public Health, 22*. https://doi.org/10.1155/2022/6768388

McEwan, I. (2019). *Machine like me*. Jonathan Cape.

Moor, J. (2006). The nature, importance, and difficulty of machine ethics. *IEEE Intelligent Systems, 21*(4), 18–21. https://doi.org/10.1109/MIS.2006.80

Pflanzer, M., Traylor, Z., Lyons, J. B., Dubljević, V., & Nam, C. S. (2023). Ethics in human–AI teaming: Principles and perspectives. *AI and Ethics, 3*, 917–935. https://doi.org/10.1007/s43681-022-00214-z

Powers, R. (1995). *Galatea 2.2*. Harper Perennial.

Shum, S. B., Martínez-Maldonado, R., Dimitriadis, Y., & Santos, P. (2024). Human-centred learning analytics: 2019–2024. *British Journal of Educational Technology, 55*(3), 755–768. https://doi.org/10.1111/bjet.13442

Šklovskij, V. (2003). L'arte come procedimento. 1929. It. transl. Todorov, T. (a cura di), *I formalisti russi*, pp. 73–94. Einaudi.

The Royal Society (eds). (2018). *Portrayals and perceptions of AI and why they matter*. Available on-line. https://royalsociety.org/-/media/policy/projects/ai-narratives/AI-narratives-workshop-findings.pdf

Trattner, C., Jannach, D., Motta, E., Meijer, I., Diakopulos, N., Elahi, M., Opdahl, A., Tessem, B., Borch, N., Fjeld, M., Ovrelid, L., De Smedt, K., & Moe, H. (2022). Responsible media technology and AI: Challenges and research directions. *AI and Ethics, 2*, 585–594.

Vertecchi, B. (2013). Il reale e il virtuale. *Cadmo—Giornale italiano di pedagogia speri-mentale, 21*(2), 1–8.

Toward Human-AI Interaction in Music Composition: Studying Composers' Practice

Eric Tron Gianet, Luigi Di Caro, and Amon Rapp

Abstract Generative Artificial Intelligence (GenAI) has been reshaping creative practices across various domains. This paper focuses on music composition as a case study to explore the nature of human-AI interaction. Prior research has often focused on the technical capabilities of musical AI and the effect of current music AI models on composers. However, this research overlooks the intricate nature of music composition, which involves a complex interplay of personal motivations, socio-cultural factors, and the unique characteristics of different musical genres and styles. To address this gap, after discussing the importance of context and AI roles in human-AI interaction, we propose an ethnographic study that investigates the practice and needs of music composers. Through semi-structured interviews and participant observation we can look into the situated nature of music creation. By doing this, we aim to inform the design of better human-AI interactive systems that support composers' creative practice and empower them to explore new musical possibilities, rather than supplanting their creative skills with autonomous systems.

1 Introduction

Advances in Artificial Intelligence (AI) research and the deployment of AI-imbued tools are progressing so rapidly that it is challenging to keep up. The most well-known examples of the new and ever-growing AI wave are the language—and now multimodal—models of the GPT family, developed by OpenAI,[1] and their equivalent Gemini,[2] produced by Google (although in the same competition play

[1] https://openai.com.

[2] https://deepmind.google/technologies/gemini.

E. Tron Gianet (✉) · L. Di Caro · A. Rapp
Department of Computer Science, University of Turin, Turin, Italy
e-mail: luigi.dicaro@unito.it; amon.rapp@unito.it

A. Micalizzi (ed.), *Artificial Creativity*, Springer Proceedings in Humanities and Social Sciences, https://doi.org/10.1007/978-3-031-88334-7_11

the US-based Anthropic,[3] the French Mistral,[4] the fertile open source research, and others). These models fall under the category of generative AI (GenAI), which refers to deep-learning models that, starting from "raw" data, learn to generate statistically probable outputs on demand (Martineau 2023). GenAI models generally encode a simplified representation of training data and use this encoded representation to generate output that is similar (but not identical) to the original. Generative AI can be opposed to Discriminative AI (e.g., classification and clustering models, such as facial recognition, or spam filtering), and presents unique characteristics and challenges to the user experience since its nature violates common Human-Computer Interaction (HCI) principle that states a system should respond consistently to user input (Weisz et al. 2023, 2024).

Nevertheless, GenAI is increasingly widespread and is set to change (or disrupt) various human practices. OpenAI's GPT-4o[5] and Google's Project Astra[6] promise to become overpowered and cross-modalities AI assistants for everyday activities, transforming, for example, the way we learn. Suno[7] and Udio[8] present a future "where anyone can make great music" and "anyone with a tune, some lyrics, or a funny idea can now express themselves in music", enabling the generation of songs from a text prompt. The same happens for image generation with the popular MidJourney,[9] OpenAI Dall-E,[10] and Adobe Firefly.[11]

There is a growing recognition that AI advancement should prioritize human needs to benefit humans first, without overshadowing human values, priorities, and lived experiences, and considering the numerous risks associated with this technology (Weidinger et al. 2022; Bender et al. 2021). This has invited researchers inside and outside HCI to research and design an AI that is Human-Centered (HCAI) (Xu 2019; Shneiderman 2022, 2020; Capel & Brereton 2023).

Capel and Brereton (2023) offer a review of HCAI research and give a comprehensive definition:

> Human-Centered Artificial Intelligence utilizes data to empower and enable its human users, while revealing its underlying values, biases, limitations, and the ethics of its data gathering and algorithms to foster ethical, interactive, and contestable use.

Whereas previous definitions of HCAI have left open who decides what is desirable for humans and who would benefit from AI, this definition focuses instead on ethical issues, bringing into consideration all those who might be impacted.

[3] https://www.anthropic.com.

[4] https://mistral.ai.

[5] https://openai.com/index/hello-gpt-4o.

[6] https://deepmind.google/technologies/gemini/project-astra/.

[7] https://suno.com.

[8] https://www.udio.com.

[9] https://www.midjourney.com.

[10] https://openai.com/index/dall-e-3.

[11] https://firefly.adobe.com.

In addition, the definition also emphasizes interaction, bringing considerations of actual use by end users to the forefront. Capel and Brereton in fact identify an emerging research area within HCAI involving interaction with AI, or Human-AI Interaction (HAII), that *"explicitly addresses the need to understand how people will interact with inferred models in embodied and situated contexts"*.

Following this approach, we will now explore the potential and challenges of GenAI within a specific domain and for a particular community of practice (Wenger 1999): music composition. This provides an illustrative example of the benefits and complexities of casting AI research and design in situated settings, but it is also particularly fitting since the social nature of music includes factors not taken into account by AI music models. These factors show the oversights of current AI research, which does not pay attention to the settings where the use of these systems occurs. Humans create music embedded in cultural contexts, motivated by social factors; AI systems, on the other hand, operate without these social dimensions, producing music only based on algorithms and predictive models, which risks limiting their impact by not fully reflecting human creative processes (Bown 2021).

In the next section, we present a critical review of some musical AI research and the use of generative systems in music composition. In particular, we focus on the role AI takes in human-AI interaction and the importance of context.

2 Making Music with AI

Around 1950, Hiller and Isaacson produced the first score composed with the creative input of algorithms: the Illiac Suite (Hiller & Isaacson 1958; Ji et al. 2023). According to Bown (2021), the approach used for the Illiac Suite has since marked the rest of the century: creative artists with advanced computer skills, programming computers for algorithmic composition tasks. Later, much academic research focused on transferring human tasks and decisions into the domain of the computer to make music creation more autonomous. The ultimate goal was to create fully autonomous creative machines (Bown 2021). Arguably, a significant portion of musical AI research can still be described in the same way.

A first major distinction that is worth making before proceeding is that between symbolic and audio music generation (Ji et al. 2023). Symbolic music generation has to do with representing, learning, and generating music as sequences of symbols. This representation usually consists of discrete sequences that contain musical elements, such as pitch and duration (e.g., MIDI-like events or ABC notation). In contrast, audio music generation models a continuous audio signal (examples now available to everyone are the previously mentioned Suno and Udio). We primarily focus on symbolic generation because it allows for fine-grained modifications compared to audio generation. Symbolic generation also affords more interactive uses, for example, involving Digital Audio Workstations and MIDI controllers, which may better align with our ultimate goal of facilitating human-AI interaction.

However, several considerations that we will make below may apply to audio generation.

Ji et al. (2023) offer a taxonomy of symbolic music generation through five categories:

1. *Generation from scratch*, or unconditioned generation. The main subtasks into which it is divided are melody generation, polyphonic generation, and multi-track generation.
2. *Conditional generation*, meaning generation of music conditioned by a specific input related to a musical context. It is subdivided into melody generation from chord progression, melody harmonization, accompaniment arrangement, and music inpainting.
3. *Controllable generation*, for example, by specifying the structure or attributes of the music. It is divided into style control, structure control, and sentiment control.
4. *Performance generation*, which is about incorporating expressive and dynamic elements typical of live performances. This can be the addition of performance characteristics to a given score, or the simultaneous creation of a musical score and its expressive performance characteristics.
5. *Interactive generation*, which is based on collaboration between humans and machines to create music together. It can be real-time cooperation between the human musician and the machine, where each plays in turn (call and response), or the generation of a musical accompaniment in response to the human performance.

However, we can envision how, depending on the user's intentions, each of these categories can take part in human-AI interaction systems for music composition: generation from scratch may be functional for a composer's initial process of free exploration; a guitarist may want to conditionally generate a rhythmic accompaniment out of a riff or may use inpainting (Hadjeres & Crestel 2021) to explore variations to a phrasing; controlling the sentiment of a chorus may help a composer explore variations based on their intentions—and so on.

2.1 Context

Here, we argue for the need to broaden the perspective on AI for music generation, move beyond a purely technical focus, and consider music as a complex social activity shaped by context.

Despite progress, deep learning techniques for symbolic music generation face challenges such as lack of musical novelty and structure, limited emotional expression, limited user interaction, and lack of standards for music evaluation (Ji et al. 2023; Hernandez-Olivan & Beltrán 2023). Among future directions, Ji et al. call for improving and refining how artificial intelligence interacts with humans with more fine-grained controls, and researching real-life scenario applications to promote social progress and development. The latter appeal is supported by Huang et al. (2020) who suggest future AI system design to follow a study of the practices currently in use and commonly adopted by music composers, in order to adapt to them instead of demanding the opposite. However, doing this through a purely technical focus may be difficult as it neglects the social and cultural dimensions of music-making.

Bown (2021) shows how music is a culturally-rooted activity and suggests that there is some friction between engineering and sociological perspectives on musical AI systems. An engineering perspective, such as the one that is dominant, has no problem removing the social context from the equation to focus on technical and quantifiable aspects such as note choice, arrangement strategies, or imitation of a musical style. Instead, it is likely that a sociological perspective, which pays more attention to the various aspects that define human practices (such as identities, preferences, motivations, values, and cultural contexts), may be necessary to develop AI that is better able to support (or replicate) typical human creative processes.

Newman et al. (2023) highlight various contextual factors that influence what creators believe to be a good or bad placement of AI within their creative process. These factors are: *personal context*, which means the person's abilities, familiarity with the creative process and musical literacy; *social context*, that is, the community and culture of reference, as well as musical training and exposure; and the *creative goal*, or the purpose for which the work is created, (e.g., a commission or performance). These aspects influence musicians' views on the role AI can play in the creative process, and thus how it will be used.

However, as Dourish (2004) points out, the notion of context is often misrepresented in engineering approaches. These approaches, inherited from a positivist tradition, tend to think that context consists of a set of features of the environment, that can be coded and made available to software. For Dourish this reflects a misunderstanding of the nature and role of contextuality in everyday life. Instead, context is an outcome, something that is made, not a mere description of a setting. Context is produced, maintained, and enacted during an activity. It is also both a relational property, occurring between objects or activities, and an occasioned property, particular to each occasion of an activity or action. Context is dynamically defined and cannot be determined in advance. Dourish goes on to suggest that what constitutes context is a matter related to *practice*, following the notion of Wenger (1999). Contextual properties assume meaning and relevance through forms of practice, and it is not possible to separate the meaning of technology from how people use it (and how they appropriate it (Dix 2007)) because when they do so, new meanings of that technology are created and communicated by people while their practice evolves (Dourish 2004).

Furthermore, as Small (1998) suggests, music is not merely a collection of artifacts, like records and songs, but a social activity through which participants explore their relationships and identities in relation to others. The focus should be not so much on musical artifacts like songs but on the actions of creating, perceiving, and responding to them, what Small calls *Musicking*. Viewing music as a social activity emphasizes the importance of understanding the social context in which music is created and experienced. This leads us to ask how designed musical AI systems can become meaningful within the situated practices of those involved in musicking processes, such as, in our case, composers.

2.2 AI-Roles

We have shown that, to design the interaction between humans and musical AI, we may need to consider not only technical and quantifiable aspects, but also user intentions, socio-cultural factors, the role of context (which cannot be reduced to a set of codifiable features), and to expand the idea of music from an outcome to a complex and deeply rooted practice. But what is the role of AI in this interaction?

In mapping Human-centered AI research, Capel and Brereton (2023) discuss what they name Human-AI Teaming, a strand of research that posits that by working together both AI and people can perform better and increase their capabilities. Unlike Human-in-the-loop approaches or level-3 automation of autonomous vehicles,[12] the human is not just there to do what the machine cannot do on its own, but there is a synergistic collaboration between the two. This idea of collaborative teams of humans and AI is getting significant traction in and out of HCI research (e.g., Wang et al. 2020; Seeber et al. 2020; McComb et al. 2023; Wu et al. 2021; Capel and Brereton 2023) and can be traced back as far as Licklider's idea of symbiosis between humans and computers (Licklider 1960). Also, some argue for a paradigm shift in HCI, moving from designing human-computer interactions to human-computer integration and teaming (Xu 2019; Farooq & Grudin 2016; Rapp 2023).

This formulation often stands in contrast to the idea of AI as a tool. Seeber et al. (2020) develop a research agenda around the idea of machine teammates collaborating with humans and, while addressing several critical issues, their intent is clearly to move beyond the idea of tool use in favor of collaboration with autonomous machines: *"We propose that AI will not (just) be the functionality of a tool but rather a machine teammate characterized by a high level of autonomy, based on superior knowledge processing capabilities, sensing capabilities, and natural language interaction with humans"* (Seeber et al. 2020, p. 9). McComb et al. (2023) present a 2x2 matrix to isolate "different AI capabilities in teaming", which crosses two key dimensions: mode (reactive vs. proactive) and focus (problem orientation vs. process orientation). This matrix describes four quadrants of possible AI systems: AI-as-Analytics, AI-as-Tool, AI-as-Partner, and AI-as-Guide. McComb et al. explain how *"AI agents will work not just as tools but also as members of a team"*, while showing a clear preference for the last two "archetypes".

On the opposite side, Sarkar (2023) speaks of an "agentistic turn" to denote this attribution of agency to AI systems and warns that it could obscure the large

[12] https://www.sae.org/blog/sae-j3016-update.

amount of labor that fuels AI, often conducted in the Global South at low wages by, for example, data labelers. Sarkar calls for abandoning the idea of partnership and collaboration with AI in favor of a "more equitable" position of AI as a tool. However, critiques of human-AI teaming go beyond just the choice of terminology and metaphors (which, however, leaning on the idea of generative metaphors by Agre 1997, pp. 33–48, can embody the questions that are relevant to a field of research and the methods useful for answering them, bringing some phenomena to the center of inquiry and marginalizing others). According to Cabitza et al. (2021), the dominant HAII approach, which they term "agential AI", views AI systems as autonomous agents interacting with humans in a dyad. In this paradigm, intelligence and agency are attributed to both humans and machines as separate entities that collaborate or compete. Cabitza et al. discuss how there are intrinsic issues in the dyadic HAII paradigm, arising from neglecting the relational, collaborative, and contextual aspects typical of real-world decision-making processes, and from a cognitivist view that conceives of AI systems as autonomous agents, which can trigger negative bias such as *automation bias*, *automation complacency* or conversely *"prejudices against the machine"*. These biases can in turn have consequences of deskilling, avoidance of responsibility, and lack of vigilance due to excessive complacency. For Cabitza et al., this suggests the need to treat AI differently and they propose an alternative approach based on the conception of AI as a component of a Knowledge Artifact, i.e., an ecosystem of tools aimed at supporting a collective of competent decision-makers working collaboratively (which, with some simplification, we might call "community of practice" Wenger 1999).

The work of Muller and Weisz (2022) addresses some of the concerns raised by Cabitza et al. and Sarkar by extending the framework of Shneiderman (2022), which already uncoupled human initiative from AI initiative by representing them as independent dimensions. Muller and Weisz provide a way to better analyze the interactions between humans and AI in organizational contexts. First, whereas Shneiderman analyzed AI applications as static points in the two-dimensional space of human and AI initiative, they propose instead to analyze them as dynamic sequences of steps, in which initiative can shift within the same application. It thus emerges that initiative and control change dynamically during use. This analysis at the level of individual steps makes it possible to identify points where there is an imbalance or discrepancy between desired and actual initiative, whether on the human or AI side. Second, they observe that many AI applications in organizational contexts involve not just a single user, but a plurality of human stakeholders in different roles, and show how, by making them explicit, the power relations, interests, and values of these different stakeholders can be analyzed, beyond just the end user interacting directly with the application.

Returning to music AI systems, another perspective is that of Gioti (2021), who draws on Latour and Gell's ideas on agency to propose a vision in which AI is not a substitute for human creativity but is an agent that contributes to "distributed human-computer co-creativity." Gioti takes interactive music systems as an example of systems in which distributed agency between human and non-human actors is most evident and in which both the creative process and authorship are distributed among them. More specifically, Gioti notes how there is a negotiation between human creative intentions and the specific way in which technological artifacts are designed, their *technological directionality*, i.e. their scope, and suggests that the relationship between human intentionality and technological directionality can be improved with AI.

However, the balance between automation, agency distribution, and control is delicate. Newman et al. (2023) show how critical it is for music creators to maintain control, agency, intention, and choice and that this affects the roles granted or allowed to AI by the users. Louie et al. (2020) study the effect of steering tools for AI music models and observe how the need for control can change dynamically depending on the user's mental state and creative goal. During exploratory phases users seek inspiration, even the most unexpected, and may be willing to cede control. However, during other phases, such as when the user wants to focus on details, more control is needed. We can link this to what Muller and Weisz (2022) said about the *"dynamic shifts and exchanges of human and machine initiative"*, and with the need to better understand how context plays a role, as we argued above.

Finally, Suh et al. (2021) investigate the role of AI in human-human collaboration for music creation and its impact on interpersonal dynamics. Their study concludes that AI can help ease the underlying tensions often present in creative collaborations by facilitating the flow of ideas and group cohesion. However, the researchers also observed a shift in human creative and collaborative roles: participants reported feeling more like curators or co-producers rather than co-composers, as they primarily focused on evaluating AI-generated output rather than directly developing ideas. This resulted in a patchwork of AI-produced creative ideas, leading to lower creative involvement.

2.3 Researching Music Composition as a Situated Practice

Some new perspectives suggest innovative research directions that challenge the current AI paradigm. For instance, Bown (2021) hypothesizes the creation of machine learning algorithms that embody human-like musical behaviors. This would involve training AI models not only on musical content but also on the context, associations, and cultural meanings of the musical corpus used, and using search-based and evaluative models along with predictive ones. Rohrmeier (2022), on the other hand, highlights how musical creativity actually requires general artificial intelligence, going far beyond mere replication or generation of musical outcomes within limited domains. This is considered an AI-complete problem, meaning we would need models for musical cognition, for the external world, a model of bodies, instruments, musical interaction and performance, and a model of meta-creativity. As one might guess, these paradigm shifts would not only be about the architectures used, but also about a profound epistemological and philosophical movement in the field of AI research.

However, one can wonder what can be done today, with available technologies, to design a human-AI interaction more in line with the needs of music makers and the ways in which they work. Human practices and socio-cultural activities such as musicking are already established and are proven to hold values for human learning and identity creation. We, therefore, take on a different approach: instead of overriding them in favor of autonomous musical agents, we as designers, HCI practitioners, and AI researchers should aim to assist and empower these activities, whether through AI-imbued tools, AI assistants, or AI as collaborators. Yet, ignoring the importance of human intentionality, the need for control and agency, and the importance of context can be detrimental to the design of human-AI interactive music systems that are truly human-centered. In the next section, we propose and discuss a study that might respond to these concerns, and present some preliminary results.

3 An Ethnographic Study

In this section, we propose an ethnographic approach that foregrounds the situated nature of music composition. Ethnography is a well-known method within HCI research (e.g., Rapp 2021) and has also been applied to AI research (Marda & Narayan 2021; Christin 2020; Blackwell 2021; Van Voorst & Ahlin 2024; Seaver 2017), feeding into a broader conversation on the lack of, and thus the need to integrate the social sciences into AI research to mitigate the exclusive use of quantitative methods. In fact, the uncritical and positivist use of quantitative techniques can lead to ignoring the context and causes of certain outcomes and how they occur (Sloane & Moss 2019; Marda & Narayan 2021; Dahlin 2021).

Existing ethnographic and autoethnographic studies have also contributed to the intersection of music and AI. For example, McGarry et al. (2021) conducted an ethnographic study focusing on the workflow of two professional music producers as they worked on a Digital Audio Workstation. The study highlighted the importance of metadata and the organization of audio resources in coordinating the creative process. The authors suggested the potential use of AI for automating process tracking and documenting song data provenance. Nicholls et al. (2018) take an autoethnographic approach to examine how two musicians interact during songwriting and create a model of the collaborative process. The data they gather would serve to inform a collaborative AI system that works with musicians. Noel-Hirst and Bryan-Kinns (2023) provided an autoethnographic exploration of explainable AI (XAI) models in music composition. They show how the use of XAI models can influence the musical creative process through unexpected uses.

Previous studies have primarily focused on specific aspects of music production or the adoption of AI tools by composers. However, as we portrayed in broad strokes in Sect. 2, there is a need to investigate music composition as a situated practice, considering composers' personal motivations, and artistic sensibilities, and foregrounding the broader socio-cultural context that influences their work. Moreover, studying how composers' intentions and needs influence the compositional process, and how control is distributed in human-human collaboration, might illuminate which role is best suited for the AI in music composition practice (and when).

We propose an ethnographic study, which will involve 18 interviews and approximately 60 hours of participant observation. Our goal is to use the findings to better inform the design of human-AI interactive systems. These systems should support and empower music composers to explore new musical possibilities, rather than supplant their creative abilities.

Combining interviews with participant observation will offer an in-depth look at the compositional process and the socio-cultural setting in which it is embedded, providing insights into how AI can support and enhance composers' practice. Interviews will help us understand the goals and motivations of composers, as well as the socio-cultural context that influences them, and make them reflect on their creative process. Participant observation will allow us to see the creative process in action in real-life situations, peek into tacit knowledge, and check whether what emerged during the interviews is reflected in daily practice. The study is not yet completed, but we can present three preliminary findings from the first round of interviews.

3.1 Preliminary Findings

3.1.1 Intentionality Guides Composition

Intentionality, which can be described as the "about-ness" of our actions (Dourish 1999), is central to music composition, guiding both specific compositional strategies and the overall process of search and evaluation of creative outcomes. Whether composers start with a melody, harmony, or specific timbre often depends on what they intend to convey. Moreover, these intentions are often negotiated directly or indirectly in relation to the intended use (e.g., a commercial, a soundtrack, an album track) and with other stakeholders involved in the process.

As we discussed before, the existing literature acknowledges the importance of maintaining control and creative agency and the dynamic nature of initiative in HAII. However, in our study, we observed a specific connection between intentions and a process of meaning-making. Composers seek to construct a "coherent discourse" in the musical piece through the process of composition. Moreover, as one participant pointed out, music composition is not about striving for a perfect form, but rather about "moving closer" to what you create, and "making your own what you create". The use of GenAI may risk inhibiting this process if the negotiation of control and initiative is not well managed, and if the system lacks adaptivity toward the composer's evolving intentions.

The ability of these systems to flexibly accommodate composers' intentionality and their process of meaning-making can be essential to effectively support their creative practice. We might also consider how to support processes of appropriation

(Dix 2007), by designing for customization and configurability of musical AI systems, making their intent clear (or in the words of Gioti 2021: their technological directionality), and not forcing the user into overly narrow workflows, providing instead freedom of interaction by *"offering the user a myriad of ways to achieve a product's functionality"* (Wensveen et al. 2004).

3.1.2 Music Creation Is a Collaborative Process

Music creation is often a collaborative process, involving bandmates, arrangers, clients, and various stakeholders who contribute to and have an interest in the final product. For example, we observed how some compositional choices are extended to the recording studio, where they are negotiated, discussed, or delegated to the sound engineer.

This raises the question of whether AI systems should be designed to enhance these existing human-human interactions, or whether they should become an additional collaborator within a system where creative control is already dynamically distributed and negotiated.

As Cabitza et al. (2021) argued, the dominant "agential AI" approach might neglect the relational, collaborative, and contextual aspects typical of real-world decision-making, but the work of Muller and Weisz (2022) can help show how human-AI interaction can involve a plurality of stakeholders. Through the perspective of Value Sensitive Design (Friedman & Hendry 2019) the interests and values of these different stakeholders can be analyzed and reveal hidden roles and dynamics, such as indirect stakeholders who influence the use of the application (Muller & Weisz 2022).

In addition, we must also be wary of how human roles change as we introduce GenAI into compositional practice, as this can lead to a loss of control and ownership, and reduced creative engagement, as shown by Suh et al. (2021)

3.1.3 An Unstructured Creation Process

One participant described how initial musical ideas often emerge from "messing around", improvising, and even making mistakes, suggesting that creativity can often come from spontaneous and less structured activities. The creative process is not always linear or purposeful but can be serendipitous and emergent. The boundaries between rehearsal, practice, composition, recording, and leisure playing are often blurry.

Designing AI systems that sit at the boundary of these contexts and flexibly adapt to and support these emergent, blurred, and serendipitous aspects of the compositional process will be crucial for meaningful human-AI interactive systems for music creation.

4 Conclusion

In this paper, we discussed human-AI interaction through the lens of music composition with the help of GenAI. We highlighted that music is a contextual and socially situated activity and how this poses a limit in current AI research. We discussed different paradigms for the role AI could take in HAII, and that span from AI as a tool to AI as a teammate, and we tied all of this together in the recognition that we need to view music composition as a situated practice in order to design HAII systems that are human-centered and support human composers.

We then briefly presented an ongoing ethnographic study investigating music composition through interviews and participant observations, to inform the design of interactive AI systems that can meaningfully support composers. We pointed out the need to design AI systems that flexibly accommodate composers' evolving intentions rather than forcing rigid workflows, take into account that music composition is a collaborative process involving multiple stakeholders, and account for a creative process that can be unstructured, emergent, and serendipitous.

By foregrounding the situated nature of music composition, in this paper we emphasized the need to move beyond a purely technical focus on AI capabilities, and instead design human-AI interactive systems that are better aligned with human goals, practices, and socio-cultural contexts.

References

Agre, P. E. (1997). *Computation and human experience* (1st edn.). Cambridge University Press. https://doi.org/10.1017/CBO9780511571169

Bender, E. M., Gebru, T., McMillan-Major, A., & Shmitchell, S. (2021). On the dangers of stochastic parrots: Can language models be too big? In *Proceedings of the 2021 ACM Conference on Fairness, Accountability, and Transparency* (pp. 610–623). ACM, Virtual Event Canada. https://doi.org/10.1145/3442188.3445922

Blackwell, A. F. (2021). Ethnographic artificial intelligence. *Interdisciplinary Science Reviews, 46*(1–2), 198–211. https://doi.org/10.1080/03080188.2020.1840226

Bown, O. (2021). Sociocultural and design perspectives on AI-based music production: Why do we make music and what changes if AI makes it for us? In E. R. Miranda (Ed.), *Handbook of artificial Intelligence for music* (pp. 1–20). Springer. https://doi.org/10.1007/978-3-030-72116-9_1

Cabitza, F., Campagner, A., & Simone, C. (2021). The need to move away from agential-AI: Empirical investigations, useful concepts and open issues. *International Journal of Human-Computer Studies, 155*, 102696. https://doi.org/10.1016/j.ijhcs.2021.102696

Capel, T., & Brereton, M. (2023). What is human-centered about human-centered AI? A map of the research landscape. In *Proceedings of the 2023 CHI Conference on Human Factors in Computing Systems*. Association for Computing Machinery, Hamburg, Germany, CHI'23 (p. 23). https://doi.org/10.1145/3544548.3580959

Christin, A. (2020). The ethnographer and the algorithm: Beyond the black box. *Theory and Society, 49*(5–6), 897–918. https://doi.org/10.1007/s11186-020-09411-3

Dahlin, E. (2021). Mind the gap! On the future of AI research. *Humanities and Social Sciences Communications, 8*(1), 1–4. https://doi.org/10.1057/s41599-021-00750-9

Dix, A. (2007). Designing for appropriation. In *Proceedings of the 21st British HCI Group Annual Conference on People and Computers: HCI...But Not as We Know It - Volume 2*, BCS Learning & Development Ltd., Swindon, GBR, BCS-HCI'07 (pp. 27–30). https://doi.org/10.5555/1531407.1531415

Dourish, P. (1999). *Embodied Interaction: Exploring the Foundations of a New Approach to HCI.* https://www.dourish.com/publications/misc/embodied.pdf. Accessed 17 September 2024

Dourish, P. (2004). What we talk about when we talk about context. *Personal and Ubiquitous Computing, 8*(1), 19–30. https://doi.org/10.1007/s00779-003-0253-8

Farooq, U., & Grudin, J. (2016). Human-computer integration. *Interactions, 23*(6), 26–32. https://doi.org/10.1145/3001896

Friedman, B., & Hendry, D. F. (2019). *Value sensitive design: Shaping technology with moral imagination*. The MIT Press.

Gioti, A. M. (2021). Artificial intelligence for music composition. In E. R. Miranda (Ed.), *Handbook of artificial intelligence for music: Foundations, advanced approaches, and developments for creativity* (pp. 53–73). Springer. https://doi.org/10.1007/978-3-030-72116-9_3

Hadjeres, G., & Crestel, L. (2021). The piano inpainting application. https://doi.org/10.48550/ARXIV.2107.05944

Hernandez-Olivan, C., & Beltrán, J. R. (2023). Music composition with deep learning: A review. In A. Biswas, E. Wennekes, A. Wieczorkowska, R. H. Laskar (Eds.), *Advances in speech and music technology: Computational aspects and applications, signals and communication technology* (pp. 25–50). Springer. https://doi.org/10.1007/978-3-031-18444-4_2

Hiller, L. A., Jr., & Isaacson, L. M, (1958). Musical composition with a high-speed digital computer. *Journal of the Audio Engineering Society, 6*(3), 154–160.

Huang, C. Z. A., Koops, H. V., & Newton-Rex, E. (2020). AI song contest: Human-AI co-creation in songwriting. In *Proceedings of the 21st International Society for Music Information Retrieval Conference*. International Society for Music Information Retrieval (pp. 708–716).

Ji, S., Yang, X., & Luo, J. (2023). A survey on deep learning for symbolic music generation: Representations, algorithms, evaluations, and challenges. *ACM Computing Surveys, 56*(1), 1–39. https://doi.org/10.1145/3597493

Licklider, J. C. R. (1960). Man-computer symbiosis. *IRE Transactions on Human Factors in Electronics HFE-1*(1), 4–11. https://doi.org/10.1109/THFE2.1960.4503259

Louie, R., Coenen, A., Huang, C. Z., Terry, M., & Cai, C. J. (2020). Novice-AI music co-creation via AI-steering tools for deep generative models. In *Proceedings of the 2020 CHI Conference on Human Factors in Computing Systems*. Association for Computing Machinery, Honolulu, CHI'20 (pp. 1–13). https://doi.org/10.1145/3313831.3376739

Marda, V., & Narayan, S. (2021). On the importance of ethnographic methods in AI research. *Nature Machine Intelligence, 3*(3), 187–189. https://doi.org/10.1038/s42256-021-00323-0

Martineau, K. (2023). What is generative AI? https://research.ibm.com/blog/what-is-generative-AI

McComb, C., Boatwright, P., & Cagan, J. (2023). Focus and modality: Defining a roadmap to future AI-human teaming in design. *Proceedings of the Design Society, 3*, 1905–1914. https://doi.org/10.1017/pds.2023.191

McGarry, G., Chamberlain, A., Crabtree, A., & Greehalgh, C. (2021). The meaning in "the mix": Using ethnography to inform the design of intelligent tools in the context of music production. In *Audio mostly 2021* (pp. 40–47). ACM. https://doi.org/10.1145/3478384.3478406

Muller, M., & Weisz, J. (2022). Extending a human-AI collaboration framework with dynamism and sociality. In *2022 Symposium on Human-Computer Interaction for Work* (pp. 1–12). ACM. https://doi.org/10.1145/3533406.3533407

Newman, M., Morris, L., & Lee, J. H. (2023). Human-AI music creation: Understanding the perceptions and experiences of music creators for ethical and productive collaboration. In *Proceedings of the 24th International Society for Music Information Retrieval Conference* (pp. 80–88). International Society for Music Information Retrieval.

Nicholls, S., Cunningham, S., & Picking, R. (2018). Collaborative artificial intelligence in music production. In *Proceedings of the Audio Mostly 2018 on Sound in Immersion and Emotion* (pp. 1–4). ACM. https://doi.org/10.1145/3243274.3243311

Noel-Hirst, A., & Bryan-Kinns, N. (2023). An autoethnographic exploration of XAI in algorithmic composition. https://doi.org/10.48550/ARXIV.2308.06089

Rapp, A. (2021). In search for design elements: A new perspective for employing ethnography in human-computer interaction design research. *International Journal of Human–Computer Interaction, 37*(8), 783–802. https://doi.org/10.1080/10447318.2020.1843296

Rapp, A. (2023). Wearable technologies as extensions: A postphenomenological framework and its design implications. *Human–Computer Interaction, 38*(2), 79–117. https://doi.org/10.1080/07370024.2021.1927039

Rohrmeier, M. (2022). On creativity, music's AI completeness, and four challenges for artificial musical creativity. *Transactions of the International Society for Music Information Retrieval, 5*(1), 50–66. https://doi.org/10.5334/tismir.104

Sarkar, A. (2023). Enough with "human-AI collaboration". In *Extended Abstracts of the 2023 CHI Conference on Human Factors in Computing Systems*. Association for Computing Machinery, Hamburg, CHI EA'23 (p. 8). https://doi.org/10.1145/3544549.3582735

Seaver, N. (2017). Algorithms as culture: Some tactics for the ethnography of algorithmic systems. *Big Data & Society, 4*(2), 1–12. https://doi.org/10.1177/2053951717738104

Seeber, I., Bittner, E., Briggs, R. O., De Vreede, T., De Vreede, G. J., Elkins, A., Maier, R., Merz, A. B., Oeste-Reiß, S., Randrup, N., Schwabe, G., & Söllner, M. (2020). Machines as teammates: A research agenda on AI in team collaboration. *Information & Management, 57*(2), 103174. https://doi.org/10.1016/j.im.2019.103174

Shneiderman, B. (2020). Bridging the gap between ethics and practice: Guidelines for reliable, safe, and trustworthy human-centered AI systems. *ACM Transactions on Interactive Intelligent Systems, 10*(4), 26:1–26:31. https://doi.org/10.1145/3419764

Shneiderman, B. (2022). *Human-centered AI*. Oxford University Press.

Sloane, M., & Moss, E. (2019). AI's social sciences deficit. *Nature Machine Intelligence, 1*(8), 330–331. https://doi.org/10.1038/s42256-019-0084-6

Small, C. (1998). *Musicking: The meanings of performing and listening*. Music/Culture, University Press of New England.

Suh, M. M., Youngblom, E., Terry, M., & Cai, C. J. (2021). AI as social glue: Uncovering the roles of deep generative AI during social music composition. In *Proceedings of the 2021 CHI Conference on Human Factors in Computing Systems*. ACM, Yokohama, Japan, CHI'21 (p. 11). https://doi.org/10.1145/3411764.3445219

Van Voorst, R., & Ahlin, T. (2024). Key points for an ethnography of AI: An approach towards crucial data. *Humanities and Social Sciences Communications, 11*(1), 337. https://doi.org/10.1057/s41599-024-02854-4

Wang, D., Churchill, E., Maes, P., Fan, X., Shneiderman, B., Shi, Y., & Wang, Q. (2020). From human-human collaboration to human-AI collaboration: Designing AI systems that can work together with people. In *Extended Abstracts of the 2020 CHI Conference on Human Factors in Computing Systems* (pp. 1–6). ACM. https://doi.org/10.1145/3334480.3381069

Weidinger, L., Uesato, J., Rauh, M., Griffin, C., Huang, P. S., Mellor, J., Glaese, A., Cheng, M., Balle, B., Kasirzadeh, A., Biles, C., Brown, S., Kenton, Z., Hawkins, W., Stepleton, T., Birhane, A., Hendricks, L. A., Rimell, L., Isaac, W., Haas, J., Legassick, S., Irving, G., & Gabriel, I. (2022). Taxonomy of risks posed by language models. In *2022 ACM Conference on Fairness, Accountability, and Transparency* (pp. 214–229). ACM. https://doi.org/10.1145/3531146.3533088

Weisz, J. D., Muller, M., He, J., & Houde, S. (2023). Toward general design principles for generative AI applications. https://doi.org/10.48550/arXiv.2301.05578

Weisz, J. D., He, J., Muller, M., Hoefer, G., Miles, R., & Geyer, W. (2024). Design principles for generative AI applications. https://doi.org/10.1145/3613904.3642466

Wenger, E. (1999). *Communities of practice: Learning, meaning, and identity* (first paperback edn.). Cambridge University Press.

Wensveen, S. A. G., Djajadiningrat, J. P., & Overbeeke, C. J. (2004). Interaction frogger: A design framework to couple action and function through feedback and feedforward. In *Proceedings of the 2004 Conference on Designing Interactive Systems Processes, Practices, Methods, and Techniques - DIS'04* (p. 177). ACM. https://doi.org/10.1145/1013115.1013140

Wu, Z., Ji, D., Yu, K., Zeng, X., Wu, D., & Shidujaman, M. (2021). AI creativity and the human-AI co-creation model. In M. Kurosu (Ed.), *Human-computer interaction. Theory, methods and tools*. Lecture Notes in Computer Science (vol. 12762, pp. 171–190,). Springer. https://doi.org/10.1007/978-3-030-78462-1_13

Xu, W. (2019). Toward human-centered AI: A perspective from human-computer interaction. *Interactions, 26*(4), 42–46. https://doi.org/10.1145/3328485

Recognition as 'Art' by Publics: How Generative AI Music Production Is Perceived

Alessandra Micalizzi

Abstract This study explores the intersection of artificial intelligence (AI) and human creativity by investigating how the perceived authorship of a musical piece influences its evaluation. Unlike previous studies that have focused on comparing the outputs of human and AI creators, this research delves into the perceptual aspects of AI-generated art. Through a carefully designed social experiment, we examined how participants rate the quality of music pieces without and with knowledge of their authorship. Our findings reveal a nuanced relationship between perceived authorship and aesthetic judgment, suggesting that while human biases can influence evaluations, the intrinsic qualities of a piece ultimately play a significant role. This research contributes to the growing body of work on AI and creativity by offering novel insights into the human perception of AI-generated art and the potential for human–AI collaboration in creative endeavours.

Keywords Computational creativity · Music production · AI · Artificial creativity · Computational artist

1 Computational Creativity and the Effect on Cultural Production: An Overview

The debate about the use of AI in creative production has been especially relevant in recent years, though it should be mentioned that artistic language has always been linked to the evolutions of techniques, tools, and technologies discovered and applied over time. In this context, the development of the cultural industries and their world of production has given an important push to the contamination between art and technologies.

A. Micalizzi (✉)
Centro Direzionale ISOLA, Pegaso University, Naples, Italy
e-mail: alessandra.micalizzi@unipegaso.it; a.micalizzi@sae.edu

A. Micalizzi (ed.), *Artificial Creativity*, Springer Proceedings in Humanities and Social Sciences, https://doi.org/10.1007/978-3-031-88334-7_12

As McCormack (2003) argued, innovation today generally 'is not achieved within the precious bubble of fine art, but by those who work in the industries of popular culture–computer graphics, film, music videos, games, robotics and the Internet' (McCormack, 2003, p. 5). This contamination started in the late 1950s due to the contributions of cybernetics and other informational sciences. In other words, artistic production has become increasingly based on communication and information processing technologies that have significantly expanded in power and diversity over the past 50 years (Boden & Edmonds, 2009). The terminology used to describe these emerging art forms is diverse and has yet to solidify into a widely accepted classification. Artists working in these areas tend to favour terms such as generative art, computer art, digital art, computational art, process-based art, electronic art, software art, technological art, and telematics.

In an interview, Catodo (Math in the Air, 2019) defines the computational artist as someone who uses 'computational language to create his/her own artwork, that means creating an algorithm and thus the writing of a computer program'. In this sense, the word 'generative' refers to the use of a system, which may be automated, to produce a work of art. He specifies that 'Computer programming is one of many possible systems that can be used in generative art, but it is not the only one'. For example, John Cage (1912–1992), the famous American composer, employed generative techniques in his works of aleatoric music by using proportions derived from the I Ching. Another renowned musician, Brian Eno, was the first to use the term 'generative music' to describe his compositions created by introducing delays in audio recording systems (ivi, n.d.).

Generative art is a realm of digital art practice that has experienced a boom since the start of the twenty-first century (Galanter, 2016); it is not to be confused with the wider concept of digital art (Paul, 2023). To offer a definition, we can say that computational arts are based on the contamination of languages, texts, and techniques, and they are deeply influenced by the contribution of digital computing.

Over the decades, here have always been supportive and enthusiastic voices opposing the (often large) groups of detractors (e.g., D'Isa, 2024) regarding experiments with particular technologies. The substantial difference between AI and its technological precursors lies in how its generative capacity operates: the new generation of AIs has the capacity to become more autonomous in the production process and can make decisions independently. We are talking about the so-called generative artificial intelligence that can be distinguished as generative adversarial networks (GANs), which are restricted to reproducing a specific artistic style, and creative adversarial networks (CANs), which can deviate from the learned style, thus facilitating the creation of new and potentially innovative works (Liu, 2023).

The increasing integration of AI tools in artistic production has pushed the debate to a crucial point: the recognition of these cultural products' value (Mazzone & Elgammal, 2019). There are several critical aspects at work; part of the artistic world continues to interrogate the impact of AI on the concept, status, and role of art, as well as how these new methods of (re)producing reality relate to our collective imagery (Kalpokas, 2023).

Zeilinger (2021) argued that AI 'has the potential to reshape the aesthetic, cultural, and socio-economic dimensions of creativity', fundamentally destabilizing the traditional notion of the author. He suggested that AI-generated art is 'based on Big Data, which is the most social thing we have' and that generative artistic productions are the result of 'an ongoing composition in which humans and non-humans participate'.

D'Isa (2024) agrees with this integrated vision and, above all, with the possibility of abandoning an old-fashioned definition of authorship, which he asserts is more relevant to market issues than to artist evolution and history. More specifically, his position can be synthetized in the following statement: 'I rather think that the shock brought about by innovation has momentarily disrupted an interpretative habit, reminding us that it is not we who create, but the world itself' (ivi, 2024 p. 145). The interpretative habit he refers to deals with the obsession of explicitly recognizing an author and thus ownership of the intellectual work, which undermines the Creativity 4.0 system (Csikszentmihalyi, 2014; Gruner & Csikszentmihalyi, 2018), especially when a technology like AI intervenes in systemic dynamics.

AI-generated art is never entirely detached from human experience; indeed, it is deeply intertwined with human expression and our perceptions of the world. Since AI creativity is data-driven, its primary function is to reorganize information in ways that are both novel and recognizable to human audiences. Although the execution of creativity is machinic, it is not derived from any intrinsic machine-based aesthetics (Oksanen et al., 2023). As a result, the aesthetic appeal of AI-generated art remains—at least for now—oriented around human sensitivities, both in terms of the learning process and the intended audience (e.g., Manovich, 2018; Manovich & Arielli, 2021, 2024).

An integration of human intentionality with technological practices might define a new landscape in which data, human beings, and AI collaborate. In this context, the incorporation of AI brings a distinctly posthuman dimension to the triangular interaction of humans, data, and AI. However, the debate is still open. Some scholars argue that 'the notion that a machine learning system could produce art or be regarded as an artist is implausible, as an artist cannot be reduced to a mere machine with intent'. Other scholars extend Duchamp's (1957) concept of art to include AI-generated outputs, to the extent that the action performed by machine learning can be seen as a process of selection. In this sense, we support Hertzmann's (2018) view of art as a form of interaction, where AI serves as a medium—a co-protagonist in new forms of creation shaped by artists, technology, and society.

1.1 Artificial Music Production: Art or Consumer Products?

Several studies have focused on AI's impact on artistic products, whether in terms of quality, production processes, or the roles of creators (Lee, 2024; Celis Bueno et al., 2024; Zhou & Lee, 2024). Other scholars have focused their attention on user perceptions of AI-generated outputs. The ongoing debate ranges from apocalyptic views portraying AI as a threat to creativity and artistic production to more optimistic positions that foresee a future of integration between human intent and AI capabilities (Tubadji et al., 2021; Millet et al., 2023).

In the domain of artistic production, the application of AI has expanded to include intangible outputs such as music. There has been substantial growth in research on both human and computational creativity in music in recent years, especially within the field of computer science. Consequently, experimental studies exploring public perceptions of AI-generated or AI-assisted music have proliferated, aiming to map different facets of this revolutionary and rapidly expanding phenomenon of computational creativity. Some studies have specifically examined biases related to authorship when evaluating musical works that were created or co-created by AI (Tigre Moura et al., 2023; Horton Jr et al., 2023).

Several studies have documented a growing acceptance of AI-generated or AI-assisted products. For instance, Elgammal et al. (2017) demonstrated that AI-generated artworks are often indistinguishable from those created by humans. Their findings were corroborated by Hitsuwari et al. (2023). Furthermore, Elgammal et al. (2017) stated that AI-generated works frequently outperformed human-made pieces in terms of perceived novelty, complexity, intentionality, and inspiration. An interesting example of the application of AI in music production and public perception comes from Hadjeres et al. (2017). They used the generative model DeepBach to produce new compositions in the style of Johann Sebastian Bach, and nearly half of the participants in their experiment believed the machine-generated compositions to be original Bach works. However, participants with more musical experience were less likely (around 40%) to attribute the compositions to Bach. These findings have been supported by studies including Hong and Curran (2019) and Tigre Moura and Maw (2021), which revealed that despite initial scepticism towards AI-generated music, awareness of AI's role had minimal effect on respondents' overall perceptions of the compositions.

This brief, inexhaustive overview highlights a peculiarity regarding public perceptions. Listeners often struggle to distinguish authorship in musical productions, particularly as AI becomes more adept at replicating melodies, rhythms, and sound quality. However, even when they recognize the high quality of AI-generated music, listeners may not necessarily prefer it due to the prevailing belief that 'true' creativity is an inherently human trait (Rohrmeier, 2022). Moreover, there is a pervasive instinct to 'defend' human creativity against the perceived threat of AI supplanting it (Tubadji et al., 2021; Millet et al., 2023).

It is thus evident that the role of the public in the recognition of artwork is crucial. In our opinion, it is important to investigate which psycho-social and socio-cultural mechanisms influence the evaluation of an artistic production—in our case, a sound production—to fully understand the role that AI plays in user recognition of 'artistic value' in creative output and identify the main drivers that can orient this process.

2 Methodology

The results presented in this chapter are part of a wider study aimed at reconstructing the prejudice level of people—experts and everyday users alike—on creative AI-generated products (CAIGP). More specifically, we wanted to understand whether and to what extent users were influenced by the authorship of the creative product when evaluating it. In detail, our goals entail the following: (a) to reconstruct the level of knowledge around the general theme of computational creativity; (b) to identify which aspects affect the definition of creative and artistic products; and (c) to reconstruct components of public prejudice toward CAIGP with a focus on image production and soundtracks.

The research plan is based on mixed methods (Micalizzi & Lelicanin, 2023) and it is organized in three main stages:

- First, we analysed the imagery of AI described and contained in a sample of early-twentieth-century literary production.
- Second, we conducted a social experiment comparing AI-produced soundtracks with one produced by a young composer.
- Third, we collected 2500 CAWI questionnaires (Boreham & Wijnant, 2013) from a representative sample of the Italian population with a specific section addressing the evaluation of visual stimuli (most of which were produced by AI and only one by a human creator).

In this paper, we present the main results of the second stage—the part of the research that combined an experiment with in-depth interviews to verify whether there was a real bias towards the use of AI as a creative tool, as shown by previous studies (e.g., Latikka et al., 2023; Magni et al., 2024), and what factors could influence it. We tried to pay specific attention to variables such as the respondents' gender, artistic skills, and, even more specifically, audio skills.

2.1 The Experiment Design

The experiment was based on the participant listening to two tracks—one produced by AI and one composed by a young artist. The participants were divided into three groups:

- Those who were correctly informed about the authorship of the tracks (well-informed)
- Those who were poorly informed about the authorship of the tracks (misinformed)
- Those who were not informed at all (uninformed)

The participants from the first two groups were first subjected to an in-depth interview on the topic of computational creativity to ascertain their level of knowledge

• Emotional impact	1	------------------------------	5
• Melody	1	------------------------------	5
• Rhythm	1	------------------------------	5
• Originality	1	------------------------------	5
• Tone	1	------------------------------	5
• General evaluation	1	------------------------------	5

Fig. 1 Evaluation scale of the listening section

on the topic. The third group (uninformed) did not receive any introduction before listening. Then, all three groups participated in an in-depth talk about the evaluation.

The participants evaluated the songs according to five specific criteria (emotional impact, melody, originality, tone, and general evaluation) on a 5-point scale (Fig. 1).

2.2 Sample

The experiment was carried out in two waves, in 2022 and at the beginning of 2024 (Micalizzi, 2024). The first wave included 30 individuals, 10 for each group (well-informed, misinformed, and uninformed). The second wave involved 65 individuals. In this case, it was not possible to divide them into three equal groups. The well-informed group was the most represented, and the misinformed were less represented. In both waves, the sample was distributed equally in terms of gender and role (i.e., whether the individual works in the creative industries or not). This difference means that we cannot consider gender as a significant variable, although some interesting reflections emerged at a qualitative level. Finally, the sampling was based on a snowballing method (Parker et al., 2019).

3 Results: Creativity Is Not Rocket Science

The presentation of the results is organized in three sections. The first one discusses the interviews carried out before the listening experiment. The second one focuses on the main results of the listening experiment. The last one discusses the results of the final interviews.

3.1 Before Listening

When asked to give a definition of ‘computational creativity’, the interviewees contextualized the concept within the general framework of using technologies in art productions. However, it remained a vague topic that was less explored than others, and the respondents showed a low level of awareness about it. They were only able to identify some products made by AI that they enjoyed online after having read the correct definition.

Could these products be considered 'artistic' and/or 'creative'? To answer this question, we explored the participants' opinions about the components that characterize a creative product. It was clear that they considered a creative product to be the result of three main elements: (a) the content it expresses; (b) the aesthetics, which depend on the recognition of others (Csikszentmihalyi, 1996, 2014; Gruner & Csikszentmihalyi, 2018); and (c) the author's intentions, which represent a pivotal rule in defining a product as 'creative'.

Moreover, not all respondents agreed in identifying a creative product as a work of art. They always considered the outputs of generative AI to be cultural products, but they did not necessarily consider them to be creative. This position is aligned with that of Smith and Cook (2023), who argued that AI applied to creative productions could open a new era of the readymade. The respondents in this study highlighted some aspects that can contribute to identifying artistic products:

- Author's intention: The work of art is not produced for commercial purposes but arises from the artist's urgent desire to communicate something. His intention makes it art regardless of the type of output. It is close to the definition offered by Merriam-Webster (2024), which considers art to involve the conscious use of human skills.
- Imperfection: Works of art carry with them the distinctive human trait of imperfection, which is also an element of their originality. AI is able to produce imperfections that are called hallucinations, but these are considered a mistakes—something unexpected that needs to be corrected (Maleki et al., 2024).
- Recognition: According to the interviewees, the work of art is the outcome of an 'interpretative agreement' of publics and experts, not only of the artist. This confirms the positions of Simonton (2009) and Boden (1998), who emphasize the central role of being recognized as valuable.
- Non-reproducibility: While recalling a now famous phrase by Walter Benjamin (1963), the respondents wanted to stress a different point—that art and its new forms of expression (e.g., multimedia installations, AR showrooms) are the result of the connection among users, artworks, and contexts. The focus of the new forms of art is the experience and not simply the artistic object. For this reason, they are not reproducible.

In this framework, some respondents highlighted how the introduction of the use of AI is a 'need' related to the distortion of the artwork concept associated with commissioned, accelerated, and ephemeral production, which requires a time-based creativity that cannot respect an artist's timeframe. From this perspective, creative production with AI becomes a performed task, without a specific intention of the author. It is conditioned by the skills of the prompter (that is, the one who writes prompts); some authors argue that it is precisely for this reason that the use of AI is inseparable from human input (Manovich, 2018; Kalpokas, 2023). Creative production with AI also responds to the needs of the market: it is fast, versatile, and adaptable to the tastes of the audience, with greater computing power.

However, some respondents, especially those who have experienced it, emphasized the supportive role of AI in creative productions, noting that it is only possible to delegate marginal and mechanical steps of the process. Young interviewees who were also creative workers were more sensitive to the topic, stressing the fact that nowadays we need to distinguish consumer creative productions from proper artworks. Consumer creative productions are characterized by purely entertainment purposes, conceived for the market and designed according to its indications (Smith & Cook, 2023). This makes them reflect homogeneous trends and be capable of producing an economic return. Proper artworks, in contrast, are based on the intention of the artist who produces them, without regard of the market return but rather in accordance with his/her expressive need. They have no economic value except after being placed in the art market circuit—and not always successfully (Hertzmann, 2018). The positions of our interviewees seem to ignore the third possibility of abandoning the concept of authorship and art and instead observing AI productions as new languages and new forms of aesthetics (Manovich & Arielli, 2021 p. 2024).

Our study confirms the gender bias in attitudes toward technologies (Verbick, 2002): the female respondents felt uncomfortable expressing an opinion on the use of AI in creative productions due to a declared 'personal incompetence' on the topic. The idea that art is something aesthetic and negotiated, not a science, was found in women. Finally, they are more inclined toward the apocalyptic scenario linked to an excessive use of the machine for a skill that is considered purely human, creativity.

3.2 The Listening Experiment

All the respondents were invited to evaluate two soundtracks: the first one was always the human-produced track (track 1), and the second one was produced by AI (track 2). They were two piano compositions based on the same references.

After listening to track 1, the participants expressed their evaluation through keywords associated with the very slow rhythm, such as peace, relaxation, sadness, and nostalgia. At the same time, some respondents stressed the technique they perceived in the execution, with terms such as mastery and competence. Moreover, it was considered as something already listened to, famous, or 'classic' in its structure.

The second track was associated with other words, such as tension and surprise, for its fast pace. In fact, it stimulated emotions that were not always positive: some interviewees considered it to be disturbing, desperate, anxiety-inducing, and 'dark' in its rhythmic traits. At the same time, the repetitiveness of the scale construction caused boredom, one of the words most repeated by interviewees in their evaluation of the piece.

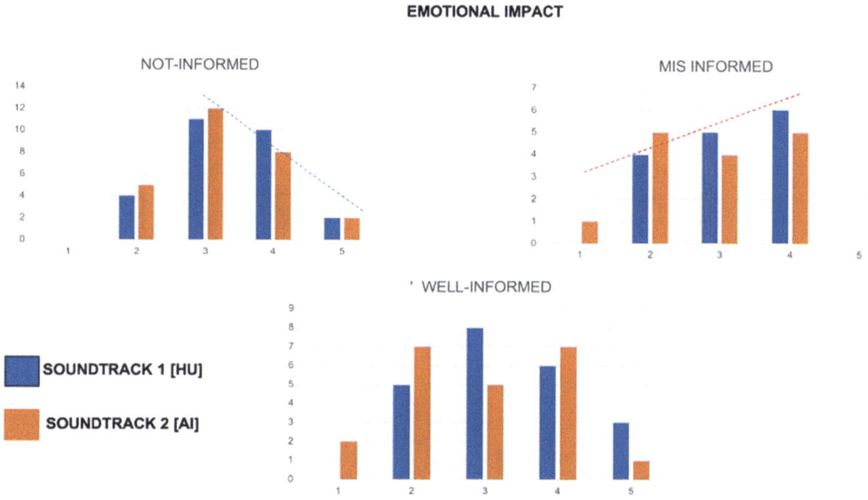

Fig. 2 Scores for emotional impact

The respondents expressed their opinion using five criteria—emotional impact, melody, rhythm, originality, and tone—on a 5-point Likert scale. Then, we asked for a general evaluation.

Figure 2 shows that in the well-informed group, there was not a clear preference for one of the two soundtracks, even though the first one seemed to be more appreciated. The clear differences were among the uninformed and misinformed groups, where there was a more positive trend among the misinformed respondents. While the uninformed group shows an inverted peak with a decrease in the highest scores, the misinformed group seemed to appreciate more the track they considered produced by AI.

Considering the second criterion of melody, we did not register significant differences within and among groups. In any case, the first soundtrack was the most appreciated. If we compare the evaluation of the second track between the well-informed and misinformed groups, we can see that, even though it was less appreciated than the first track, the well-informed group tended to be less harsh, expressing higher scores (4 and 5) than the misinformed ones for the second track (which they thought was produced by a human).

If we look at the evaluation of melody, we can see the uninformed group is more generous with the first soundtrack, and this evaluation trend is confirmed by the two other groups. Interestingly, the misinformed group gave better scores for the second track, which they considered to be produced by a young composer (Fig. 3).

Rhythm is the dimension that is least relevant for our experiment, since the results are coherent with the characteristics of the track, regardless of the authorship (whether real or attributed) (Fig. 4).

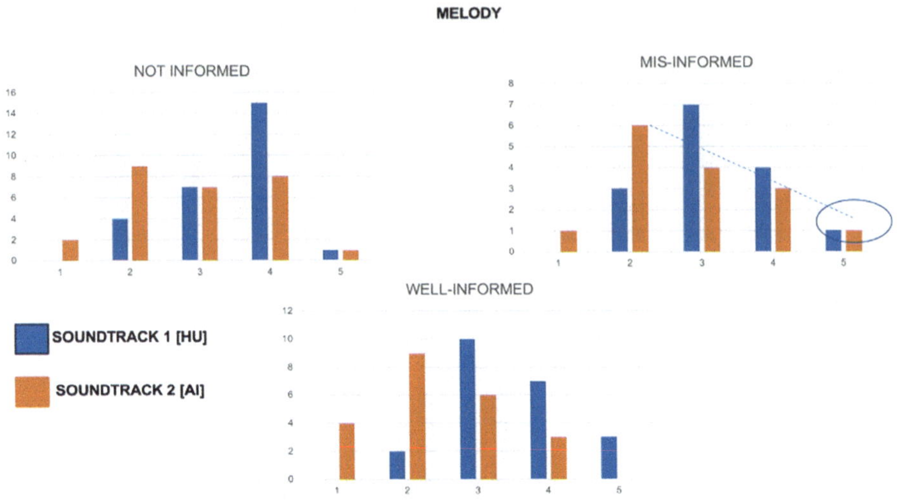

Fig. 3 Scores for melody

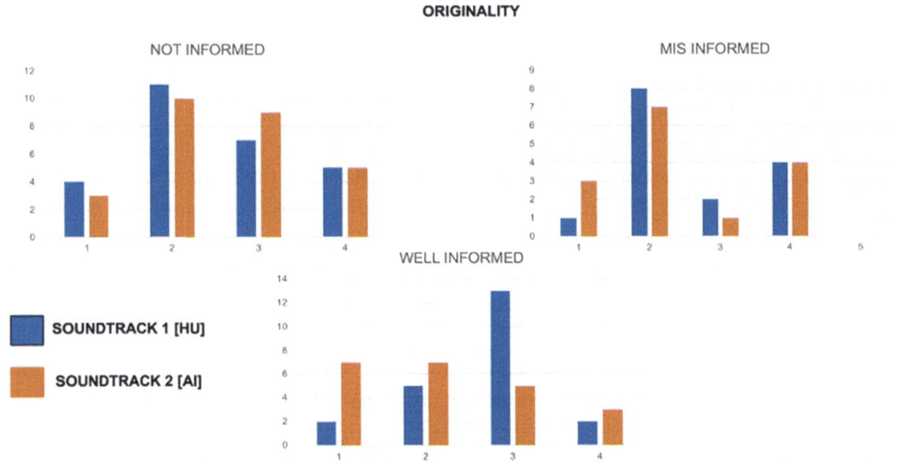

Fig. 4 Scores for originality

All the groups expressed a sense of familiarity for both the soundtracks (criterion: originality) in terms of knowing or simply recognizing the references. However, if we compare the scores between the uninformed and well-informed groups, we can see how authorship affects the evaluation of the first track, which registers a higher score in the second group (if we add up the 3 and 4 evaluations).

Finally, tone is the only category in which we can see a clear difference among the three groups. More specifically, the misinformed group had more appreciation for the track that they believed to be produced by a real composer (Fig. 5).

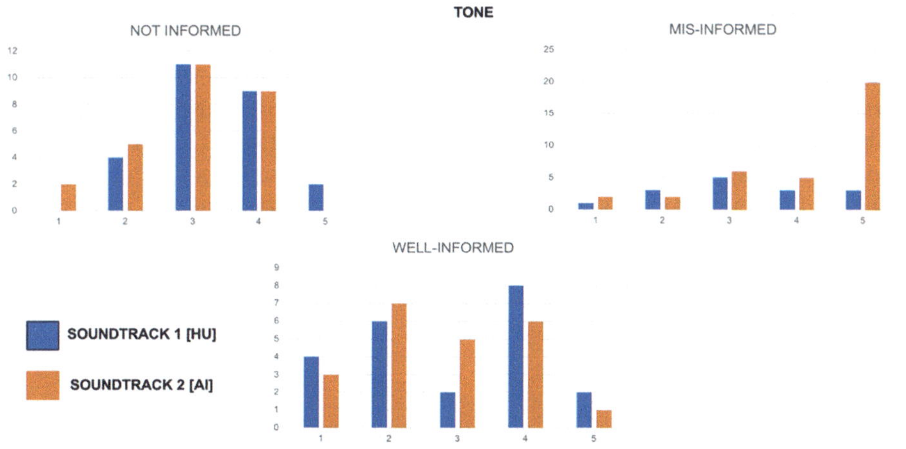

Fig. 5 Scores for tone

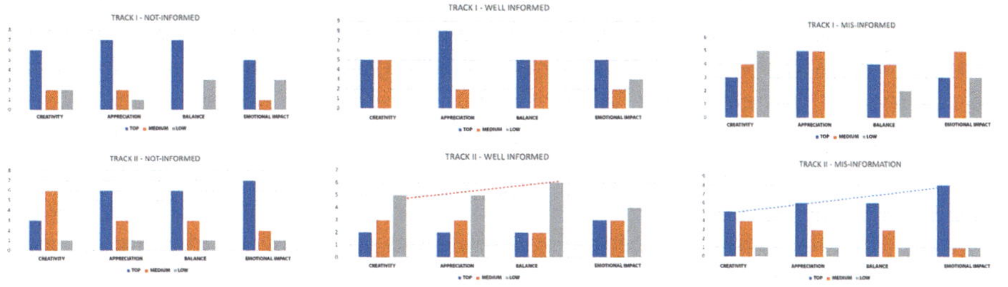

Fig. 6 Comparison of the evaluations given during the first wave (3-score scale)

If we consider the score of the general evaluation parameter, both the tracks were not considered appealing. However, comparing the results among the groups, we can see a better score for the first one; it is more evident with the misinformed respondents who considered the track as produced by AI.

This is an extremely interesting finding, and it confirmed the effect of procedural reactivity to the test, which was probably caused by the purpose of the study. The participants felt as if they could be deceived in the listening test and tended to give answers that did not meet the expectations. This was even more evident among the ‘experts’. Figure 6 presents the results of the first wave of the experiment, where the difference among the three groups is neat and evident.

To simplify the reading, we merged the results into 3 points on the scale (from 5 points). Focusing on track 2 and the difference between the well-informed and misinformed groups, the pattern of judgements (blue column and grey column) is clearly opposite to each other. This highlights how the authorial factor leads to a higher appreciation for the track that is considered to have been produced by a human being. The data from the first wave seem to confirm a possible authorship bias, which was only partially highlighted by the current wave. However, it should be specified that the results cannot be compared completely: the first survey took place at the end of 2022, a period in which information and debates on AI were certainly less present and therefore less consciously or unconsciously assimilated by respondents. Moreover, the size of the sample was more limited (30 participants), and the Likert scale included 4 dimensions that were similar but not identical to the ones used for the second wave—creativity, balance, emotional impact, and general evaluation.

3.3 After Listening

The final section aimed to investigate the participants' level of awareness about their prejudices against AI in the process of evaluating the two soundtracks. All the respondents seemed to be aware of the role of the information received (group 2 and group 3) in their process of attributing value to the track. However, we identified three main rationalizations. First, the most cited reason for recognizing the role of authorship was the fact that it is part of the artistic product, indivisible from the quality of the final output. A smaller but more conscious part of the sample emphasized that their prejudices are anchored in the idea that AI tools cannot achieve the same quality and expertise in creative products since creativity is a typical human skill.

In addition, there was a numerically less relevant part of the sample that declared that they were not influenced in any way by the product's authorship—both in this listening experiment and in the evaluation of any other creative work—due to the fact that even an AI-based production has an important human component, that is, writing the prompt and conducting the work of selection (in some cases even manipulation) on the AI output.

4 Conclusion

The findings in this research are consistent with those of previous studies (e.g., Hong, 2021) while offering a more integrated view of the connection between creativity and the use of artificial intelligence. The matter of AI's visibility in daily operations underscores a perception shaped by the lack of transparency regarding the role that technology plays in routine activities (Micalizzi, 2024). This is particularly relevant in the creative field, where the role of AI initially seems negligible, especially in relation to the evaluation of the final production.

This observation challenges the widespread belief that AI is neither 'creative' nor 'intelligent' but rather designed to perform specific tasks, which makes it 'effective' and 'efficient'. The participants stressed that although creative outputs generated by AI could be considered cultural products, they do not meet the criteria to be labelled as works of art.

Despite its limitations, our experiment provides important insights into the biases and perceptions surrounding AI's contribution to cultural production. On the one hand, interviewees—especially non-experts—were impressed by the high quality of AI-generated outputs. On the other hand, these outputs were seen as familiar and somewhat repetitive and characterized by a sense of predictability, which made them less innovative but more appealing to the market due to their consumable nature.

A key distinction that continues to differentiate humans is the intentionality behind communication. As some scholars argue (e.g., Hertzmann, 2018, 2020), art involves an interactive negotiation, and the uniquely human component lies in the communicative intention driving the creative process (Esposito, 2022). Moreover, while generative AI systems are becoming increasingly autonomous, artists retain control over each phase of production, including selecting inputs, making choices, and refining outputs. Additionally, the respondents pointed out that humans make unintentional mistakes, which reflect a level of imperfection and distinctiveness intrinsic to human nature.

Furthermore, novelty—a hallmark of artistic creativity—seems absent in AI-generated works, as they are often closely tied to their source material. To create genuinely original and innovative combinations, human intervention remains essential. Therefore, there is potential for positive integration, where machines act as tools that augment human creativity, but the human remains the true originator of the creative process.

The central concern surrounding the use of generative AI, in creative fields and beyond, is rooted in ethical issues, particularly regarding how much control humans can exert over this technology. Unlike earlier technologies, generative AI can 'learn', enabling it to function independently from human decision making. Thus, it is essential to establish shared ethical frameworks that safeguard human agency while promoting the responsible adoption of new technologies.

Finally, the participants expressed concern about the potential homogenization of public taste, driven by increasingly repetitive and short-lived content. This flattening of expectations in creative production is already happening, fuelled by the dominance of algorithms and market-driven strategies that favour only what has already proven to be successful.

The issue of AI education—including its potential applications in everyday life and professional settings—and its ethical implications remains critical to ensuring that this tool is used responsibly and that individuals engage with the socio-technological context in a manner that upholds shared ethical principles.

References

Benjamin, W. (1963). The work of art in the age of its technological reproducibility. In *Philosophers on film from Bergson to Badiou: A critical reader* (pp. 44–79). Columbia University Press.

Boden, M. A. (1998). Creativity and artificial intelligence. *Artificial Intelligence, 103*(1–2), 347–356. https://doi.org/10.1016/S0004-3702(98)00055-1

Boden, M. A., & Edmonds, E. A. (2009). What is generative art? *Digital Creativity, 20*(1–2), 21–46. https://doi.org/10.1080/14626260902867915
Boreham, R., & Wijnant, A. (2013). Developing a web-smartphone-telephone questionnaire. In *IBUC 2013 15th international Blaise users conference. Washington, DC*. Available at: http://www.blaiseusers.org/2012/papers/04b.pdf
Celis Bueno, C., Chow, P. S., & Popowicz, A. (2024). Not "what", but "where is creativity?": Towards a relational-materialist approach to generative AI. *AI & Society*. https://doi.org/10.1007/s00146-024-01921-3
Csikszentmihalyi, M. (1996). *Creativity: Flow and the psychology of discovery and invention*. HarperCollins.
Csikszentmihalyi, M. (2014). Society, culture, and person: A systems view of creativity. In *The systems model of creativity* (pp. 47–61). Springer.
D'Isa, F. (2024). *La rivoluzione algoritimica delle immagini. Arte e Intelligenza artificiale*. Luca Sossella Editore.
Duchamp, M. (1957). The creative act. *Art News, 56*(4).
Elgammal, A., Liu, B. Elhoseiny, M. & Mazzone, M. (2017). CAN: Creative adversarial networks, generating "art" by learning about styles and deviating from style norms. In *8th International conference on computational creativity (ICCC)*. https://doi.org/10.48550/arXiv.1706.07068.
Esposito, E. (2022). *Comunicazione artificiale. Come gli algoritmi producono l'intelligenza sociale*. Bocconi University Press.
Galanter, P. (2016). Generative art theory. In *A companion to digital art* (pp. 146–180). Wiley.
Gruner, D. T., & Csikszentmihalyi, M. (2018). Engineering creativity in an age of artificial intelligence. In I. Lebuda (Ed.), *The Palgrave handbook of social creativity research* (pp. 447–462). Palgrave Macmillan.
Hadjeres, G., Pachet, F., & Nielsen, F. (2017, July). Deepbach: A steerable model for bach chorales generation. In *International conference on machine learning* (pp. 1362–1371). PMLR.
Hertzmann, A. (2018). Can computers create art? *Arts, 7*(2), 18. https://doi.org/10.3390/arts7020018
Hertzmann, A. (2020). Computers do not make art, people do. *Communications of the ACM, 63*(5), 45–48. https://doi.org/10.1145/3347092
Hitsuwari, J., Ueda, Y., Yun, W., & Nomura, M. (2023). Does human–AI collaboration lead to more creative art? Aesthetic evaluation of human-made and AI-generated haiku poetry. *Computers in Human Behavior, 139*, 107502. https://doi.org/10.1016/j.chb.2022.107502
Hong, J. H. (2021). Artificial intelligence (AI), Don't surprise me and stay in your lane: An experimental testing of perceiving humanlike performances of AI. *Human Behavior and Emerging Technologies, 3*(5), 1023–1032.
Hong, J. W., & Curran, N. M. (2019). Artificial intelligence, artists, and art: Attitudes toward artwork produced by humans vs. artificial intelligence. *ACM Transactions on Multimedia Computing, Communications, and Applications, 15*(2s), 1–16. https://doi.org/10.1145/3326337
Horton, C. B., Jr., White, M. W., & Iyengar, S. S. (2023). Bias against AI art can enhance perceptions of human creativity. *Scientific Reports, 13*, 19001. https://doi.org/10.1038/s41598-023-45202-3
Kalpokas, I. (2023). Work of art in the age of its AI reproduction. *Philosophy & Social Criticism*. https://doi.org/10.1177/01914537231184490
Latikka, R., Bergdahl, J., Savela, N., & Oksanen, A. (2023). AI as an artist? A two-wave survey study on attitudes toward using artificial intelligence in art. *Poetics, 101*(2), 101839. https://doi.org/10.1016/j.poetic.2023.101839
Lee, H. K. (2024). Reflecting on cultural labour in the time of AI. *Media, Culture & Society, 46*(6), 1312–1323. https://doi.org/10.1177/01634437241254320
Liu, B. (2023). Arguments for the rise of artificial intelligence art: Does AI art have creativity, motivation, self-awareness and emotion? *Arte, Individuo y Sociedad., 35*(3), 811.
Magni, F., Park, J., & Chao, M. M. (2024). Humans as creativity gatekeepers: Are we biased against AI creativity? *Journal of Business and Psychology, 39*, 643–656. https://doi.org/10.1007/s10869-023-09910-x

Maleki, N., Padmanabhan, B., & Dutta, K. (2024). AI hallucinations: a misnomer worth clarifying. In *2024 IEEE conference on artificial intelligence (CAI)* (pp. 133–138). IEEE. https://doi.org/10.1109/CAI59869.2024.00033

Manovich, L. (2018). *AI aesthetics*. Strelka Press.

Manovich, L. & Arielli, E. (2021). *Artificial aesthetics: A critical guide to AI, media and design*, 4–27, available at https://manovich.net/content/04-projects/175-artificial-aesthetics/artificial_aesthetics.chapter_1.pdf [accessed 09/09/2024].

Manovich, L. & Arielli, E. (2024). *Artificial aesthetics: Generative AI, art and visual media*. Available at https://manovich.net/index.php/projects/artificial-aesthetics [accessed 09/07/2024].

Math in the Air. (2019). *Intervista all'artista computazionale Catodo: algoritmi, coding e arte generativa*. Available at https://www.mathisintheair.org/wp/2019/03/intervista-allartista-computazionale-catodo-algoritmi-coding-e-arte-generativa/ [accessed 22/09/2024].

Mazzone, M., & Elgammal, A. (2019). Art, creativity, and the potential of artificial intelligence. *Arts, 8*(1), 26. https://doi.org/10.3390/arts8010026

McCormack, J. (2003). Art and the mirror of nature. *Digital Creativity, 14*(1), 3–22.

Merriam-Webster. (2024). *Art*. Available at https://www.merriam-webster.com/dictionary/art [accessed 22/09/2024].

Micalizzi, A. (2024). Artificial creativity. Perceptions and prejudices on AI music production. In X. S. Yang, S. Sherratt, N. Dey, & A. Joshi (Eds.), *Proceedings of Ninth International Congress on Information and Communication Technology. ICICT 2024. Lecture notes in networks and systems* (p. 1004). Springer. https://doi.org/10.1007/978-981-97-3305-7_39

Micalizzi, A., & Lelicanin, M. (2023). *Studiare i creative media. Ricerca e analisi dei processi di creazione, condivisione e appropriazione culturale*. Utet Università.

Millet, K., Buehler, F., Du, G., & Kokkoris, M. D. (2023). Defending humankind: Anthropocentric bias in the appreciation of AI art. *Computers in Human Behavior, 143*, 1–9. https://doi.org/10.1016/j.chb.2023.107707

Oksanen, A., Cvetkovic, A., Akin, N., Latikka, R., Bergdahl, J., Chen, Y., & Savela, N. (2023). Artificial intelligence in fine arts: A systematic review of empirical research computers in human behavior. *Artificial Humans, 1*(2). https://doi.org/10.1016/j.chbah.2023.100004

Parker, C., Scott, S., & Geddes, A. (2019). *Snowball sampling*. SAGE research methods foundations.

Paul, C. (2023). *Digital art*. Thames & Hudson.

Rohrmeier, M. (2022). On creativity, music's AI completeness, and four challenges for artificial musical creativity. *Transactions of the International Society for Music Information Retrieval, 5*(1), 50–66. https://doi.org/10.5334/tismir.104

Simonton, D. K. (2009). Varieties of (scientific) creativity: A hierarchical model of domain-specific disposition, development, and achievement. *Perspectives on Psychological Science, 4*, 441–452. https://doi.org/10.1111/j.1745-6924.2009.01152.x

Smith, A., & Cook, M. (2023). AI-generated imagery: A new era for the 'readymade'. *SA '23: SIGGRAPH Asia 2023 Art Papers, 5*, 1–4. https://doi.org/10.1145/3610591.3616432

Tigre Moura, F., & Maw, C. (2021). Artificial intelligence became Beethoven: How do listeners and music professionals perceive artificially composed music? *Journal of Consumer Marketing, 38*(2), 137–146. https://doi.org/10.1108/JCM-02-2020-3

Tigre Moura, F., Castrucci, C., & Hindley, C. (2023). Artificial intelligence creates art? An experimental investigation of value and creativity perceptions. *The Journal of Creative Behavior, 57*(4), 534–549. https://doi.org/10.1002/jocb.600

Tubadji, A., Huang, H., & Webber, D. J. (2021). Cultural proximity bias in AI-acceptability: The importance of being human. *Technological Forecasting and Social Change, 173*. https://doi.org/10.1016/j.techfore.2021.121100

Verbick, T. (2002). Women, technology, and gender bias. *Journal of Computing Sciences in Colleges, 17*(3), 240–250.

Zeilinger, M. (2021). Generative adversarial copy machines. *Culture Machine, 20*, 1–23

Zhou, E., & Lee, D. (2024). Generative artificial intelligence, human creativity, and art. *PNAS Nexus, 3*(3), 52. https://doi.org/10.1093/pnasnexus/pgae052

Creativity and Digital Music Education in the AI Era

Antonella Coppi

Abstract The twenty-first century has brought a wave of global technological advancement to make information more accessible than ever before in human history. Countless industries have benefitted from this newfound availability of information, including the education sector. The internet provides students with a wealth of information from which to draw, while teachers can access a breadth and depth of resources that dwarf what was available to their twentieth-century counterparts. These technological advances have fundamentally changed education and will continue to do so as long as technological evolution persists at such a rapid pace (Rivoltella, Studi Sulla Formazione/Open J Edu, 26(2), 63–67. https://doi.org/10.36253/ssf-14975, 2023). The latest breakthrough in technology, artificial intelligence (AI), has the potential to upend the education system as we know it. This contribution approaches using artificial intelligence in music education as part of the creative cognitive process. AI in education is a very diverse field, dating from about 1970 (Carbonell, IEEE Trans MMS, 11(4), 190–202, 1970), and it has its own developed methodologies, techniques, and traditions. The field is highly interdisciplinary, involving substantial contributions from the fields of music, education, AI, cognitive psychology, the psychology of music, social psychology, anthropology, philosophy, linguistics, human-computer interaction, and many other fields (Holland, Artificial intelligence in music education: a critical review. In E Miranda (Ed.), Readings in music and artificial intelligence, contemporary music studies, vol 20, Harwood Academic Publishers, 2000).

Keywords AI · Music education · Italian school music · Curriculum

Special thank goes to Sara Valente, for collecting data and sharing her useful reflections. Sara Valente is a primary school teacher and scholar of AI in music education at the State Conservatory "L. Marenzio", Brescia, Italy.

A. Coppi (✉)
Department of Human Science, IUL University, Florence, Italy
e-mail: a.coppi@iuline.it

A. Micalizzi (ed.), *Artificial Creativity*, Springer Proceedings in Humanities and Social Sciences, https://doi.org/10.1007/978-3-031-88334-7_13

1 Introduction

> John and I ... were quite happy to nick things off people, because ... you start off with the nicked piece and it gets into the song ... and when you've put it all together ... of course it does make something original (Paul McCartney quoted in Moore, 1992).

Artificial intelligence (AI) is rapidly transforming numerous industries, from healthcare to finance, and music education is no exception. Nevertheless, while the integration of AI technologies into music education offers new opportunities to learn, teach, and create music, what exactly is AI? The European Parliament has this to offer:

(AI) Is the Present and the Future of Technology. Artificial intelligence (AI) is the ability of a machine to exhibit human capabilities such as reasoning, learning, planning and creativity: it enables systems to understand their environment, relate to what they perceive and solve problems, and act toward a specific goal. AI systems are capable of adapting their own behaviour by analysing the effects of previous actions and working autonomously (European Parliament, last updated 06/28/2023).[1]

On 03.13.2024 the European Parliament approved the *Artificial Intelligence (AI) Law*, which guarantees security and respect for fundamental rights and promotes innovation. Members approved the regulation, the result of an agreement reached with member states in December 2023, with 523 votes in favour, 46 against, and 49 abstentions.[2] It aims to protect fundamental rights, democracy, the rule of law, and environmental sustainability from high-risk AI systems while promoting innovation and ensuring Europe's leadership in the field. The regulation establishes obligations for AI based on possible risks and level of impact.

The purposeful use of artificial intelligence (AI) in digital music education is crucial for enhancing rather than replacing creative action. This contribution explores the possibilities of integrating AI into music education to provide tools and resources that facilitate learning and student engagement (Panciroli & Rivoltella, 2020), offering new opportunities for exploring and experimentation. At the same time, it will highlight the importance of teaching and ethical education design in light of the recent approval of new EU regulations on the use of AI, the world's first, offering insights for future-oriented pedagogical reflection.

At this stage it would seem that AI can be an indispensable tool for implementing any kind of knowledge and developing work and productivity in any field, but flexibility in modality of application remains an issue. Thus, one of the main purposes of AI is to understand human intelligence, that is, the ability to reason, plan, solve problems, learn quickly and learn from experience (In 1967, Gottfredson, to bring this understanding to fruition and enable AI to interact with human intelligence, has attempted to devise solutions that would enable algorithms to

[1] https://www.europarl.europa.eu/news/it/press-room/20240308IPR19015/il-parlamento-europeo-approva-la-legge-sull-intelligenza-artificiale

[2] https://www.quotidianosanita.it/allegati/allegato1710335981.pdf

learn from large data sets, considered as "experience" in computing). Dehaene (2020) suggests that learning means "capturing with thought: bringing in a portion of reality, a model of the structure of the world. Through learning, the data that strike our senses become abstract ideas, refined, creative and general enough to be exploited in new situations".

Here, then, what Dehaene proposed for humans represents the dream for AI projects. In this field we often hear the term "machine learning": this denotes a set of statistical techniques that improve automatically through experience. What has been said so far fits into a much broader discourse concerning the relationship between creativity and AI, first of all in the definition of creativity itself.

While there are differences in how creativity is defined, common definitions suggest that creativity is the ability or propensity to develop ideas, artefacts, or solutions that are novel and effective. Although not fully understood, creativity is highly valued across disciplines and industries. It is widely viewed as essential to innovation in the networked or digital world of the twenty-first century. Consequently, most educational policy and curriculum documents internationally include creativity as a desired (if not essential) competency. The shift toward creativity has emerged in recent decades and has paralleled the digitization of education and society at large (Creely & Henriksen, 2019).

Formal research on creativity developed from the latter half of the twentieth century onward, sparked by J. P. Guilford's 1950 address to the American Psychological Association as a call to study creativity. From the 1950s, creativity research tended to be psychological with a cognitive perspective, which emphasized individual traits in conceiving creativity and an individual's aptitude for creativity (Creely & Henriksen, 2019).

As reported Creely and Henriksen (2019, p. 3), Several theoretical frameworks have been influential in the last 25 years and combine concepts about the significance of creativity for individuals, groups, and society at large. For instance, Mihaly Csíkszentmihályi's notion of big-C and little-c creativity considered the scope of creative work (Csíkszentmihályi, 2014). Little-c is about everyday expressions of creativity in ordinary contexts, in which people participate in creative activities and produce mostly unrecognized or unpublished products. Big-C is about larger, more significant public expressions of creativity, seen in art, performance, music, and other cultural products or in scientific, design, and engineering breakthroughs.

2 AI and Music Education

Many international studies have investigated the relationship and potentiality of the enhancement of music education with AI. As Holland (2000) writes in "Artificial Intelligence in Music Education: A Critical Review",

One common way of defining AI in Education is: any application of AI techniques or methodologies to educational systems. Other definitions focus more narrowly, for example: any computer-based learning system which has some degree of autonomous decision-making with respect to some aspect of its interaction with its users (Self, 1998). This second definition stresses the requirement that AI techniques are used to reason at the point of interaction with the user. (Holland, 2000).

Such reasoning might be about the subject being taught, about the best teaching approach, or about misconceptions or gaps in a student's knowledge. However, there are wider ways of involving AI in teaching. For example, AI-ED might be defined as the use of AI methodologies and AI ways of thinking applied to discovering insights and methods for use in education, whether or not AI is involved at the point of delivery (based on Naughton, 1986). In practice, these contrasting approaches to AI-ED form a continuum. This paper reviews work at both extremes of the definition along with points in between. In all of these studies, the design principles of the systems are substantially derived from, and expressed in, the language of artificial intelligence (Self, 1998). Cook (1998) imported the notion of "problem seeking" into AI-ED, particularly in the sense used by the philosopher Lipman (1991), developed from Dewey (1916). In this sense, problem seeking refers to a reflective approach where problems are treated as ill-defined and open-ended; there is a continual intertwining of problem specification and solution; there are few clear criteria for completion; context greatly affects the interpretation of the problem; and problems are always open re-interpretation and re-conceptualisation. Music composition and expressive music performance in general are replete with problem-seeking. There is no generally applicable goal or problem to be solved, except perhaps "compose something interesting" (Levitt, 1985) or "perform this with feeling". The learning composer must find or create goals or problems to solve, which may need to be revised, modified, or rejected as she evaluates intermediate solutions.

Nevertheless, the aspect of creativity cannot be underestimated in its multi-perspective and interconnected dimension. Creativity can be more than just a set of individual traits, more than a social or group process, and more than the outcome of a system. It can be conceived on a global scale and mediated across the Internet to emerge in highly connected digital and virtual spaces. The central discourse regarding this expanding sense of connectivity reflects the substantial affordances that online and digital technologies bring to creativity. In the academic and practice literature, there are at least five affordances:

UniversilityUniversality: Through online, communication, and digital technologies, creativity has universal scope.

Distributed online digital tools: Digital tools, including communication and design tools, can be used by individuals and teams to play, explore ideas, and manipulate virtual objects that correspond to real-world material objects.

Safe spaces for trying out creativity: Digital technologies in general and online digital tools specifically provide a way of experiencing managed risk-taking and enacting constructive failure while trying out creative ideas.

Enhancing the speed of creative development: One clear benefit of ICT and online communication and design systems is the speed at which ideas can be creatively formed, tested, evaluated and then reformed.

New learning spaces for creative work: Learning has traditionally been conceived around the provision of classrooms and specialized school-based material environments. The advent of online and digital technologies has meant the emergence of third spaces outside of traditional learning contexts (Creely & Henriksen, 2019).

At this stage, can we put this question: Is AI the beginning of the end of creative music making? Let us stop for a moment and try to go behind the scenes: Even if some parts of the technology is called "generative" it still only works with the input given by humans, and maybe we should use this fact to look at ourselves in the mirror and ask exactly what it is that makes us human? Music and the arts have the ability to let us see ourselves as human beings. Therefore, we need to embrace AI in the Higher Music Education Area, make the technologies our own and consciously develop the aspects and the characteristics of the way technology supports music creation ensuring that there will always be space for a human approach.

At the intersection of technology and artistic expression lies the captivating world of generative art and music, where algorithms intertwine with human imagination. AI plays a pivotal role in facilitating the creation of novel works that blur the boundaries between human and machine. Ethic affair that is important part of the problem, has been discussed by the European Commission's Artificial Intelligence Act, adopted on 13 March 2024 to regulate AI systems' development and deployment. It provides valuable insights into navigating the ethical landscape. One of the Act's main objectives is to ensure AI systems' compliance with fundamental rights, including privacy, non-discrimination, and safety.

3 Research in Digital Music Education: The State of the Art

Currently, research into the application of AI to educational theory and practice is exploding, and it has emerged as a critical entry point for educational advancement. The use of artificial intelligence in computer-assisted music instruction is in some ways inevitable. Theoretical AI research has expanded significantly in recent years, including into such realms as Bayesian networks, deep learning, and general AI.

As Lam reports, Adopting technology in education is a prevalent trend around the world by virtue of the positive notion that technology affords a productive way of learning (Artym et al., 2016; Smeets, 2005; Vanderlinde et al., 2010). While developing students' creativity has increasingly been recognized as a crucial goal in education worldwide in the past 20 years due to the associated economic and social benefits (Choe, 2006; Shaheen, 2010; Wyse & Ferrari, 2014), the connection between two critical areas in educational settings has drawn researchers' attention to investigate how technology can support students' development of creativity. Related studies suggested that technology administers emergent tools to teachers to facilitate students' creativity (Henriksen et al., 2016) and offers opportunities for students access to a creative environment (Loveless, 2003; Lubart, 2005).

The relationship between technology and music education is a broad and controversial topic that requires in-depth consideration. The fact that the use of technology in music learning can have a significant impact on educational practices and learning outcomes has long been recognised. The creation, performance, and sharing of music are all aspects of music learning that can be supported by technology (Dammers & LoPresti, 2020). The set of pedagogical practices that exploit the potential of digital technologies for music learning can be called digital music education (Mandanici et al., 2023). Over the years, educational technology research has produced an enormous number of approaches, publications, and applications aimed at improving learning in all aspects of music education. The use of digital tools and resources has become increasingly common, and among the many educational technologies that can be used in every aspect of music learning, we also find artificial intelligence.

According to Lam, Although the adoption of technology for creating music has been advocated by various national music curricula and are becoming more common (Gouzouasis & Bakan, 2011), there is a scarcity of research concerning the effects of technology-enhanced learning interventions on creativity for music education (McDowall, 2009; Nikolaidou, 2012). Further, some recent systematic reviews have been conducted to render a clear picture of how technology is connected to creativity development in education.

Seldon and Abidoye AI-ED represent the "fourth revolution in education" and gives every student access to high-quality, personalised, and ubiquitous lifelong learning (2018 p. 94). The characteristic opacity of these systems, however, does not allow for a thorough understanding of how they work, making it difficult to predict pedagogical spillovers (Mishra & Koehler, 2008). For this reason, it is not always easy for teachers to select the right resources and integrate technology into their teaching activities. In this regard, the Triple E (Kolb, 2017), SAMR (Puentedura, 2006), and TPACK (Mishra & Koehler, 2006) models address the need to link educational technology research and teaching practice in ways that may also be useful in music education.

The SAMR model, in particular, orders the strategies for implementing technology in the classroom into four stages: Substitution, Augmentation, Modification, and Redefinition. The first two show how the use of technology enhances traditional instructional practice, while the others highlight how the use of technology enables the transformation of learning by generating real-world connections to produce authentic results.

This approach encourages teachers to "move up" from lower to higher levels using technology. According to Puentedura (2013), in the substitution phase, digital technology is replaced by analogue technology but does not generate any functional change.

In the case of music education, replacement strategies might include the use of digital metronomes and tuners or sheet music that can be followed on mobile devices, but these tools would not change the learning process or outcome. At the reinforcement level, technology adds something to the learning process beyond mere convenience by providing a clearer understanding of a complex topic or a more engaging context. An example might be video scores to be followed directly in performance or gamified exercises for enhancing listening, reading, or writing skills. In the modification phase, the integration of technology requires the significant redesign of a task. Students can collaborate on shared music writing with multi-user notation programs or work on composition in groups using a cooperative DAW (Digital Audio Workstation).

Finally, at the redefinition level, the integration of technology can enhance digital and soft skills such as collaboration, communication, and adaptability. One example would be reworking a musical composition with contributions from an online community, creating musical materials from textual descriptions provided to artificial intelligence, or training machine learning models for instrumental timbre recognition.

4 AI and the Secondary School Curriculum in Italy

From the National Directions for the curricula in kindergarten and the first cycle of education in Italy,[3] formalised by Ministerial Decree No. 254 of 13 November 2012, it is possible to extrapolate three macro-areas of individual musical competence: listening, production, and reading-writing. In the subsequent document National Directions and New Scenarios (2018), the interdisciplinary value of music, the creative aspect and integration with technologies are emphasised. The use of AI applications to integrate the discipline's competency goals at the end of Secondary School can be an innovative and engaging way to enhance students' musical learning.

The AI industry is growing rapidly, offering a variety of services worldwide to create, process, and analyse music (Verma, 2021). Of particular interest is the open-source Google Magenta research project that explores the role of machine learning as a creative tool, demonstrating that machine learning can be used to enhance the creative potential of all people (Roberts et al., 2019). Therefore, while it may be difficult to define which specific applications to use, it is useful to reflect from an educational perspective on their potential in learning experiences. Below are presented the discipline's competency goals, organised according to the macro-areas mentioned earlier, and examples of possible integrations with AI resources.

[3] The Guidelines for School Curricula in Italy were reviewed in 2012 in a document called "Indicazioni Nazionali per il Curricolo della Scuola" (2012).

4.1 Listening and Analysis

> Understands and evaluates events, materials, and musical works by recognising their meanings, including in relation to one's own musical experience and different historical and cultural contexts.

By the end of secondary school, students should be able to recognise and classify, including stylistically, the most important elements of musical language. Listening and analysis activities can become more engaging by using AI-based music recognition software. Numerous resources are available online that allow students to isolate the different instruments in a song, analyse pitch and transcribe chords from audio, and extrapolate lyrics (The Guidelines for School Curricula in Italy—Indicazioni Nazionali 2012).

Such resources can be a valuable aid in analysing a piece and identifying elements such as rhythm, melody, instruments and harmonic structures and better understanding their functions. Experiences of timbral discrimination and classification of instruments can also become more engaging with resources such as Tone Transfer, that allow students to listen to timbral transformations of some samples into other instruments as well as record and transform user-loaded sounds into musical instruments (Carney et al., 2021). In addition to the manipulative possibilities, students can explore these AI-based resources as they develop more awareness of their capabilities.

4.2 Production

> The student actively participates in the creation of musical experiences through the performance and interpretation of instrumental and vocal pieces belonging to different genres and cultures.

The text of the *2012 Guidelines for school Curricula*—Italy emphasises the value of approaching the exploratory, performing, and compositional dimensions of music through direct action with and on sound materials. With AI applications, students can play along with prerecorded pieces or computer-created accompaniments with the great advantage of being able to adjust rhythm and pitch to suit their needs. Most of these resources provide immediate feedback on performances, helping them to improve technique and accuracy. One example is Yousician, a popular software program that shows the correct fingering in real time while performing a piece by highlighting, for example, the string, fret number, and fingering. The feedback system allows an immediate way to understand errors and prepare a repertoire according to one's individual progress (Acquilino & Scavone, 2022).

Nevertheless, such applications should not give the student the idea that playing well and being a good musician only means playing the right notes in time. The focus of performance should be primarily on expressiveness, and using these systems could improve students' awareness of their own abilities while also helping them to select suitable repertoire.

> The student is able to conceive and realise, including through improvisation or by participating in collective elaboration processes, musical and multimedia messages, in critical comparison with models belonging to the musical heritage, also using computer systems.

Of all areas of musical expertise, production is the one most transformed by technology. The process of creating a musical work is simplified by the ease of control and sound realisation offered by a wide range of notation and recording software, virtual instruments, and sound libraries. Students can enhance creative skills, explore new compositional ideas, and experiment with music creation using AI-assisted composition tools.

They can begin to approach the resources present through exploration of systems such as Magenta Studio, a collection of standalone tools for musical creativity that generate melodies and drum patterns by emulating the behaviour of real performers and that can be integrated as plug-ins within the Ableton DAW (Roberts et al., 2019). Pupils can also experiment with automatic pattern training to better understand how a pattern works. MidiMe, for example, allows students to upload their own MIDI files, melodies, or songs with multiple instruments directly into the browser and generate samples that sound like their inputs (Dinculescu et al., 2019).

The educational use of some resources can also involve other disciplines in laboratory and cooperative activities that allow pupils to work in a musical environment in a different way than usual, bringing computational and problem-solving skills into play. One example is Google NSynth Super, a build-it-yourself version of the original NSynth system that uses neural networks for audio synthesis that can combine different instruments to make an original timbre (Schneider, 2018).

4.3 Reading and Writing

> Uses different notation systems functional for reading, analysing and producing music pieces.

The acquisition of the semiographic code is a crucial stage of musical literacy. Nevertheless, this is not satisfied simply by describing the symbols on the staff. The cognitive procedure required is more complex: the student should acquire an auditory awareness of the sound relationships to which the graphic signs refer. In this regard, digital technologies can offer valuable support by decoding and using not only traditional notation, but also other writing systems. In the field of AI, numerous resources are designed to automatically transcribe music from audio to sheet music. Users can record or upload their performance, after which artificial intelligence automatically transcribes the music, making it possible to edit the score later. Referring to the SAMR model analysed earlier, however, this mode of technology integration would not go beyond the level of empowerment, leaving out the possibility of harnessing the transformative power of technology. Instead, music literacy can be enhanced by activities of decoding traditional systems and translating them into different codes. In this way, score analysis can take place through different ways of visualising the constituent elements of a piece and can guide students in reworking a model to generate a new compositional work. A useful tool for experimenting with these activities in the classroom is the online composition software *Hookpad*.

Students can transcribe a melody through a code of coloured rectangles of different sizes that, organised in a time grid, represent musical pitches. Harmonic accompaniment of different instruments can be added to the melody through coloured blocks representing the tonal function of each chord. The software implements AI and, in addition to suggesting the most frequently used harmonic progressions, allows the piece to be arranged with different instruments and styles (Julia et al., 2021).

> It integrates its musical experiences with other knowledge and other artistic practices, also making use of appropriate codes and coding systems (Julia et al., 2021).

The cross-curricular aspect of music is emphasised in the *National Direction* as a means of expression and communication that constantly interacts with the other arts and with different areas of knowledge. Digital technologies succeed in enhancing interdisciplinarity and offer numerous multimedia approaches suited to the educational experience. With the development of AI, several online resources have emerged that students can use in the classroom. Some, easily accessible even from mobile devices, are part of the Google Arts & Culture collection and use machine learning algorithms to translate user drawings into sounds (Paint With Music, Musical Canvas). The generative potential of AI can also be used to connect the compositional experience to the development of computational thinking, the logical-creative process enacted to address and solve problems that is akin to the musical experience. By querying systems such as text-to-text chatbots, codes can be generated to create MIDI files that represent ideas with which to initiate cooperative compositional processes.

In this landscape crowded with evolving resources, it is up to the teacher to evaluate and select some of them to complement classroom activities and foster the development of musical skills in all students, including those with special educational needs. Teaching practices are not always successful in truly including all students in a meaningful way and allowing them to express themselves creatively. One interesting resource is Creatability Experiments, designed by the NYU Ability Project in collaboration with Google, which uses various inputs, including a microphone and body tracking, to produce music. One can draw a sound or perform a melody with one's face using any webcam, including those on mobile devices. For each experiment, the most suitable input can be chosen according to the student's abilities. Examples easily experimented with in school include *Keyboard*, a keyboard with coloured bars with which to perform melodies through head movement; *Body Synth*, a synthesizer that transforms body movements, of one or more performers at the same time, into sounds; and *Sound Canvas*, a tool that translates drawing strokes into sound in real time.

4.4 Benefits and Pedagogical Implications

The integration of digital technologies into teaching practice contributes to the development of Key Competencies for Lifelong Learning (European Council Rec. May 22 2018) and Key Citizenship Competencies (Ministerial Decree 139/07) that are certified at the end of Secondary School. It is essential, therefore, that schools and other educational institutions pay adequate attention to sound and music education by integrating teaching practices with digital technologies and designing inclusive music education activities that draw on interdisciplinary modalities. In this context, tools that integrate AI can make music teaching more dynamic, interactive, and personalised, helping students achieve their proficiency goals more effectively and engagingly. Some of the resources analysed can adapt the proposed content and exercises according to students' individual needs, helping to develop the competence of "learning to learn". Students can organise their own learning by choosing and using various resources provided by the teacher according to available time, their own strategies and their own study methods. Other tools, however, allow them to collaborate with peers and enhance musical creativity through relationships with others, enhancing everyone's abilities. The educational applications presented in this paper can contribute to the development of the pupil's digital skills by emphasising the importance of an informed and responsible approach to AI, as also stressed in the European document "DigComp 2.2" (Vuorikari et al., 2022). Proposing such experiences to students also means incorporating explanations of how AI works and reflections on the real usefulness of these systems, the potential risks, and problems related to the intellectual property of the generated content.

The integration of technological resources, and AI, into the music curriculum requires reflection on the pedagogical implications. Teachers must be prepared to use these tools effectively and responsibly while continuing to support students' creativity and individual expression. According to Mandanici et al. (2023), there are two fundamental factors for the development and diffusion of digital music education: the first is the preparation of teachers, a necessary prerequisite for dealing with the technology-driven content transformation; the second is the availability of devices, methods, and materials to support pedagogical activities. However, a wide gap still separates academic research from educational practice.

The teacher who approaches the world of digital materials for music education can be overwhelmed by the number of platforms and software packages available, often finding it difficult to assess which solution best suits his or her needs and how to use it practically in the classroom. In addition, some AI resources, in line with privacy and data security regulations, cannot be used by minors. For this reason, teacher training also plays a key role in the integration of technology with education. Since teachers do not always possess the necessary knowledge, it becomes essential to provide tools enabling them to understand, catalogue, and evaluate the available applications and solutions.

4.5 AI and Pedagogy: "Harmony" and Possible Risks

As can be seen from the above reflection, AI has enormous potential to improve education. However, to fully exploit this potential, we need to ensure that our teaching strategies and techniques are up to the challenge. Only then can we create more sustainable, diverse, and accessible learning environments for all students. It is critical to emphasise the importance of pedagogy in the context of AI-enhanced education. Artificial intelligence, while a powerful tool, is nothing more than a means to an end. Its value and positive impact on education depend largely on how it is implemented and used, and this is where the irreplaceable role of pedagogy comes in. The theories and practices of pedagogy provide us with the basic guidelines for using AI effectively and responsibly in education (Rivoltella, 2020). Moreover, pedagogy reminds us that the goal of education goes far beyond the mere transmission of information, aiming to develop students' skills, shape their values, and prepare them to face real-world challenges. AI can certainly enrich this process, but it is pedagogy that guides its direction and ensures its quality. While AI can be integrated into education in many ways, such as through the use of online learning platforms, educational games, or intelligent tutoring systems (Floridi, 2015), it must always be guided by pedagogical and educational considerations.

Teaching benefits from this technology primarily through the personalisation of learning: AI can analyse each student's learning style and adapt the content and pace of instruction according to his or her needs. Another important benefit is the automated management of daily tasks, saving valuable time for teachers to focus on more relevant assignments. AI can also aid in decision-making—sophisticated algorithms can process large volumes of data, providing educators with vital input to make more informed decisions. Additionally, these tools can be used to assist students with disabilities, such as through speech recognition programs or automated translators. Another benefit is the possibility of virtual assistance that can facilitate student learning outside the classroom environment. Learners might also take advantage of chatbots to resolve their concerns at any time, thus facilitating self-directed learning. Finally, AI can help plan and organise lessons that take into account the needs and abilities of each student.

AI represents a powerful tool for human action but brings with it complex ethical issues that cannot be ignored. Authors such as Luciano Floridi, with his work on the ethics of AI, or Pier Cesare Rivoltella, who recently wrote about "algorithmic pedagogy", offer useful insights. Awareness is the first step toward the responsible use of AI in education. Teachers must understand the risks associated with these technologies and be able to consciously deal with the topic with their students, without placing prohibitions. This requires extensive training of faculty.

It is essential not to forget that the implementation of these technologies should always be guided by deep ethical reflection, taking into account their limitations and potential. To realise AI's immense educational potential, we need to integrate it harmoniously with pedagogy and teaching. Only in this way can we ensure that AI serves education, and not the other way around. Let us always remember that the goal is to create a learning environment that is engaging, effective, and respectful of each student's individual needs. The intersection of didactics, pedagogy, and artificial intelligence offers many opportunities, but also presents some risks and dangers, the most significant of which are detailed below:

- Technology addiction: Excessive use of technology can lead to overdependence, reducing students' ability to think critically and independently.
- Data privacy and security: AI-based learning platforms collect a large amount of data about students, raising concerns about data privacy and security. If not managed properly, this data could fall into the wrong hands or be used inappropriately.
- Equity of access: Not all students have equal access to technology. This can create a digital divide, with some students having access to AI-enhanced learning resources while others do not.
- Teacher replacement: There is a risk that AI may be seen as a substitute for the teacher rather than as a tool to improve teaching. Teachers play a crucial role in education, providing guidance, emotional support, and a human context that AI cannot replicate.
- Ethics of AI: How should AI be used to assess students? Which decisions should be made by technology and which should be made by humans?
- Quality of learning: AI may lead to superficial learning rather than deep understanding. This technology can be very effective in providing immediate and personalised feedback, but it may not be able to promote critical thinking and deep reflection.

These risks underscore the importance of a balanced and reflective approach to integrating AI into education. Educators, policymakers, and developers of technology must work together to ensure that AI is used ethically, safely, and effectively in education.

5 Conclusion

AI is becoming increasingly integrated into the educational process, reformulating the methodologies and skills needed to teach and learn music. To fully understand this evolution, it is critical to understand how AI can be an effective ally in teaching and how it can coexist and interact with the educator. Students' education about AI must be comprehensive and diverse. Their knowledge should be not merely technical, but contextual. AI can be combined with other disciplines such as mathematics, computer science, neuroscience, cognitive psychology, and pedagogy, thus creating an interdisciplinary learning pathway. Moreover, AI brings additional potential to improve so-called "soft skills", such as problem-solving and teamwork. By using innovative tools, such as learning bots or AI-based learning platforms, we can create new opportunities for students to hone these skills.

However, despite these exciting advances, it is vital not to forget that AI cannot and should not usurp the fundamental role of the teacher. Educators have an irreplaceable role in guiding students and contributing to their overall education. Finally, we cannot ignore the challenges on the horizon, such as privacy and data reliability issues. It is always important to remember that as with any tool, the value of AI lies in how we use it. The real magic of education still lies in the hands of educators, their skills, their passion, and their commitment to shaping minds and shaping the future. AI can help us navigate this future, but we chart the course.

References

Acquilino, A., & Scavone, G. (2022). Current state and future directions of technologies for music instrument pedagogy. *Frontiers in Psychology, 13*, 835609.

Artym, C., Carbonaro, M., & Boechler, P. (2016). Pre-service teachers designing and constructing "good digital games". *Australian Educational Computing, 31*(1), 1–20.

Carbonell, J. R. (1970). AI in CAI: An artificial intelligence approach to computer-aided instruction. *IEEE Transactions on Man-Machine Systems (MMS), 11*(4), 190–202.

Carney, M., Li, C., Toh, E., Zada, N., Yu, P, & Engel, J. H. (2021) *Tone yransfer: In-browser interactive neural audio synthesis*. IUI Workshops.

Choe, I. S. (2006). Creativity—A sudden rising star in Korea. In J. C. Kaufman & R. J. Sternberg (Eds.), *The international handbook of creativity* (pp. 395–420). Cambridge University Press.

Cook, R. G. (1998). Semiotics in technology, learning, and culture. *Bulletin of Science, Technology & Society, 18*(3), 174–179.

Creely, E., & Henriksen, D. (2019). Creativity and digital technologies. In M. A. Peters & R. Heraud (Eds.), *Encyclopedia of educational innovation*. Springer. https://doi.org/10.1007/978-981-13-2262-4_143-1

Csíkszentmihályi, M. (2014). *The systems model of creativity* (p. 47). Dordrecht: Springer.

Dammers, R., & LoPresti, M. (2020). *Practical music education technology*. Oxford University Press.

Dehaene, S. (2020). *How we learn: Why in brains learn better than any machine ... for now*. Penguin.

Dewey, J. (1916). Nationalizing education. *Journal of Education, 84*(16), 425–428.

Dinculescu, M., Engel, J., & Roberts, A. (2019). MidiMe: Personalizing a MusicVAE model with user data. In *Workshop on machine learning for creativity and design*. NeurIPS.

Floridi, L. (2015). *The onlife manifesto: Being human in a hyperconnected era*. Springer Nature.

Gouzouasis, P., & Bakan, D. (2011). The future of music making and music education in a transformative digital world. *UNESCO Observatory E-Journal, 2*(2), 1–21.

Henriksen, D., Mishra, P., & Fisser, P. (2016). Infusing creativity and technology in 21st century education: A systemic view for change. *Educational Technology & Society, 19*(3), 27–37.

Holland, S. (2000). Artificial intelligence in music education: A critical review. In E. Miranda (Ed.), *Readings in music and artificial intelligence, contemporary music studies* (Vol. 20). Harwood Academic Publishers.

Julia, J., Iswara, P. D., & Supriyadi, T. (2021). Creating songs using online software. *Journal of Physics: Conference Series, 1987*(1), 012018.

Kolb, L. (2017). *Learning first, technology second: The educator's guide to designing authentic lessons* (pp. 29–37). International Society for Technology in Education.

Levitt, R. E. (1985). Using knowledge of construction and project management for automated schedule updating. *Project Management Journal 16*(5), 57–76.

Lipman, B. (1991). How to decide how to decide how to ...: modeling limited rationality. *Econometrica 59*, 1105–1125

Loveless, A. (2003). Creating spaces in the primary curriculum: ICT in creative subjects. *The Curriculum Journal, 14*(1), 5–21.

Lubart, T. (2005). How can computers be partners in the creative process: Classification and commentary on the special issue. *International Journal of Human-Computer Studies, 63*(4–5), 365–369.

Mandanici, M., Spagnol, S., Ludovico, L. A., Baratè, A., & Avanzini, F. (2023). *Digital music learning resources: From research to educational practice*. Springer.

McDowall, J. (2009). Making music multimodally: Young children learning with music technology. *The International Journal of Learning, 16*(10), 303–316.

Mishra, P., & Koehler, M. J. (2006). Technological pedagogical content knowledge: A framework for teacher knowledge. *Teachers College Record, 108*(6), 1017–1054.

Mishra, P., & Koehler, M. J. (2008). *Introducing technological pedagogical content knowledge*. Annual meeting of the American Educational Research Association, 1–16.

Moore, A. (1992). Patterns of harmony. *Popular Music, 11*(1), 73–106.

Naughton, M. C. (1986, August). The efficiency and equity consequences of two-part tariffs in electricity pricing. *The Review of Economics and Statistics, 68*(3), 406–414. MIT Press.

Nikolaidou, G. N. (2012). ComPLuS model: A new insight in pupils' collaborative talk, actions and balance during a computer-mediated music task. *Computers & Education, 58*(2), 740–765.

Panciroli, C., & Rivoltella, P. (2020). Artificial intelligence and education: New research perspectives. *Form@re: Open Journal per la formazione in rete, 20*(3), 1–12.

Puentedura, R. R. (2006). *Transformation, technology, and education in the state of Maine*. Retrieved from http://www.hippasus.com/rrpweblog/archives/2006_11.html

Puentedura, R. R. (2013). *SAMR: Moving from enhancement to transformation* [Web log post]. Retrieved from http://www.hippasus.com/rrpweblog/archives/000095.html

Rivoltella, P. I. E. R. (2020). *Tempi della lettura. Media, pensiero, accelerazione* (pp. 5–138). Scholé-Morcelliana.

Rivoltella, P. C. (2023). L'analisi pedagogica e i suoi oggetti al tempo dell'Intelligenza Artificiale. *Studi Sulla Formazione/Open Journal of Education, 26*(2), 63–67. https://doi.org/10.36253/ssf-14975

Roberts, A., Engel, J., Mann, Y., Gillick, J., Kayacik, C., Nørly, S., & Eck, D. (2019). Magenta studio: Augmenting creativity with deep learning in ableton live. In *Proceedings of the international workshop on musical metacreation (mume)*.

Schneider, D. (2018). Build a neural synthesizer. *IEEE Spectrum, 55*(7), 16–17.

Seldon, A., & Abidoye, O. (2018). *The fourth education revolution*. Legend Press Ltd.

Self, J. (1998). The defining characteristics of intelligent tutoring systems research: ITSs care, precisely. *International Journal of Artificial Intelligence in Education, 10*, 350–364.

Shaheen, R. (2010). Creativity and education. *Creative Education, 1*(3), 166–169.

Smeets, E. (2005). Does ICT contribute to powerful learning environments in primary education? *Computers & Education, 44*(3), 343–355.

Vanderlinde, R., Hermans, R., & Braak, J. (2010). ICT research and school performance feedback: A perfect marriage? *Educational Studies, 36*(3), 341–344.

Verma, S. (2021). Artificial intelligence and music: History and the future perceptive. *International Journal of Applied Research, 7*(2), 272–275.

Vuorikari, R., Jerzak, N., Karpinski, Z., Pokropek, A., & Tudek, J. (2022). *Measuring digital skills across the EU: digital skills indicator 2.0* (pp. 4–26). Joint Research Centre Publications Office of the European Union.

Wyse, D., & Ferrari, A. (2014). Creativity and education: Comparing the national curricula of the states of the European Union and the United Kingdom. *British Educational Research Journal, 41*(1), 30–47.

AI Imag(inari)es: Visual Representations of Artificial Intelligence

Bojana Romic

Abstract This article investigates trends in visual representations of AI. The starting point for this project is the understanding that all technologies are inherently political, and visual representations shape imaginaries, thus contributing to the stabilisation of certain visual discourses. Images of AI occupy a blurred space between scientific visualisation and popular depictions of science. The sample consists of 500 images of AI found using four search engines, as well as cover pages of five international popular science magazines. Familiar themes can be found: images of AI are almost always bathed in a blue hue ("blue glow") and often feature a brain ("a thinking thing"). It is argued that there is a need for more diverse and versatile media narratives surrounding visual representations of AI, especially those that challenge dominant representational avenues.

Keywords Artificial intelligence · AI · Imaginaries · Stock images · Electronic brains · Blue glow

1 Images of Science

Try it yourself: type 'artificial intelligence' (AI) in an image search in the browser of your choice. You will be greeted with a selection of images, bathed in a blue hue, displaying android faces, pneumatic fingers touching digital screens that float in the air or hologram brains criss-crossed with electric circuits. These are the current imag(inari)es, of AI.

B. Romic (✉)
Malmö University, Malmö, Sweden
e-mail: bojana.romic@mau.se

A. Micalizzi (ed.), *Artificial Creativity*, Springer Proceedings in Humanities and Social Sciences, https://doi.org/10.1007/978-3-031-88334-7_14

In this paper, I aim to showcase some of these dominant tendencies and uncover elements of relational aesthetics (Bourriaud, 2002) with other popular artefacts[1] that preceded images of AI or cohabit web ecosystems with them. These images occupy the odd territory of 'images of science', which might serve as decorative elements for conferences and seminars and for journalistic content, as well as for entertainment purposes. Given that 'artificial intelligence' may be challenging to visualise, current images of AI channel ideas about its material contexts, contributing to 'publicly performed visions of desirable futures', which Jasanoff refers to as 'sociotechnical imaginaries' (2015, p. 4).

My article asks for a critical examination of images of science that shape such imaginaries.

For this article, I observed the 500-image sample generated from the prompt 'artificial intelligence' on Google, Bing, Yahoo! and Baidu. Additionally, I analysed the cover pages of selected science magazines, including *Science*, *Scientific American*, *Scientific European*, *New Scientist* and *The Scientist*, that communicate scientific phenomena to both expert and non-expert audiences.

As I was looking at early representations of AI on science magazine covers, *Science*'s (2015) special issue[2] on Artificial Intelligence caught my eye. The cover page is significant, showcasing a bundle of (what seems to be) electric impulses, emitting a blue glow against a dark background, throwing sporadic yellow sparkles. The shape of the composition loosely resembles the letter 'A'. The magazine cover description is as follows:

> Can we learn anything about how our neuron-based minds work from these machines? Do we need to worry about what these algorithmic minds might be learning about us? On the cover is a visualization of human brain connectivity from MRI diffusion imaging, with superimposed computer connectors (*Science*, 2015, cover).

This cover page explores the trope that is addressed with endless variations in stock image databases: using medical imaging as a cultural amalgam for broader scientific phenomena (Coopmans, 2014, p. 40). As van Dijck observes, in medical sciences, there is a widely held view that better imaging instruments inherently lead to greater knowledge: a doctor just needs to 'see' in order to identify a treatment, thus building a myth of the 'panoptic nature of [a] mechanical-clinical eye'[3] (2005, p. 7). This creates a hierarchical-looking relation between a doctor and a patient (Ostherr, 2013, p. 4). A clinician's gaze is secured in the role of an expert and interpreter of the cryptic bodily image.

---

[1] Defining an artefact as 'popular' can be somewhat unclear. I acknowledge Gigante's (2018, p. 1) input that considers a broader set of factors surrounding the artefact: the agents that produced it, the venues where it was published and the purposes for circulation outside the scientific community.

[2] The cover is designed by Beth Rakouskas, imaging courtesy of Arthur W. Toga, USC Laboratory of Neuro Imaging.

[3] Another example is the technique of brain imaging which has been proposed as a test of eligibility, to determine if an underage person is mature enough to be tried for a criminal offense (Dumit, 2014, p. 297).

Importantly, van Dijck emphasises the cultural impact of medical imaging as it becomes embraced by popular culture; for example, endoscopic exploration of bodily crevices has inspired a storytelling technique in medical documentaries, wherein a computer-generated imagery (CGI). The camera travels through the bloodstream as it would on a rollercoaster.

Similarly, the images of AI seem to have borrowed their aesthetic approach from both scientific visualisations and images of science in a broader sense. The cover-page design of Science's special issue in 2015 intertextually communicates with the cover pages of related phenomena (e.g., *Innovations of imaging*, 2014, which also features a dark background and shiny neurons in the brain of a live zebrafish embryo). It also resembles several cover pages of *Scientific American* (*The New Century of the Brain* [2014] and *Living in the Connected World* [2014]).

2 Scientific vs. Popular Visualisations

In this article, I use 'images of science' as an umbrella term that encompasses both scientific visualisations and popular science images. As Gigante (2018) explains, there is an important distinction between the two clusters.[4] Science visualisation images target professional audiences and are published in research papers. They have an epistemological purpose and play an important role in disseminating scientific discoveries.[5] The narratives behind scientific visualisations often reflect the tensions among scientific integrity, political influences, and expert judgement. As a result, these visualisations can be tailored to highlight specific features of the research subject or designed to be visually striking, particularly when included in research grant applications. For this reason, scientific visualisations are often made to look persuasive and may give precedence to some political values over others while claiming scientific neutrality (Nash et al., 2022, p. 4). Significantly, they may influence public debate about trending societal and cultural issues and concerns. Some researchers have indicated that scientific visualisations may simplify complex societal issues, even contributing to misinformation (e.g., Hill, 2017).

---

[4] Some researchers emphasise the difference between scientific visualisation and information visualisation (infovis) (Manovich 2011, p. 37). This article focuses on the former. However, Manovich addresses (contemporary forms of) scientific visualisations as figures that use numerical data. In this article, I address scientific visualisations in a much broader sense, that is, providing a visual representation of a scientific phenomenon: 'Visual documents are used at all stages of scientific research (...) at any stage in such production, such representations constitute the physiognomy of the object of the research' (Lynch, 1988, as cited in Werner, 2015, p. 9).

[5] Despite their epistemological function, some scientific visualisation images are not necessarily precise: the rules of approximation and schematic beauty can influence visualisations (Daston & Galison, 2010; Werner, 2015).

The politics of scientific visualisation is referred to as 'the regulative ideal of mechanical objectivity' (Daston & Galison, 2010, p. 368). Examples are satellite images of outer space, which are carefully manipulated to translate light outside the human eye's perceptive spectrum into visible colours, showcasing the vivid glory of celestial phenomena. These are typically composite images, assembled to provide a coherent visual message; at the same time, they connote a 'god trick' of 'seeing everything from nowhere' (Haraway, 1988, p. 582). Such images often communicate the message that the world is not hidden in front of the ever-seeing eyes of science. Images of science are considered evidence—this aspect is crucial for such images to be regarded as objects of knowledge—'they show or reveal something that both exists outside of them and yet does not come into being without them' (Werner, 2015, p. 9). Therefore, images of science simultaneously reflect and produce discourses surrounding scientific phenomena, thereby influencing imaginaries about science. Some aspects of the world may be temporarily hidden—yet to be uncovered using the newest technological apparatus. If that apparatus is unavailable now, it will be available in the future. The idea of linear progress is clear; the path is defined. Scientific visualisations play, first and foremost, an *epistemological* role; an image is an 'independently organised and structured message' (Gigante 2018, p. 8). If images are presented alongside text, they may or may not be related to the latter's message.

Popular science images have a different goal. Their primary role is *didactic*; they tell a story, inspire awe, and impress the reader with their stunning visuality. As Gigante observes, they serve as portals, as stage-setting images. They dictate particular aesthetics that will be used to represent similar images in the future. Placing an image strategically, such as on a magazine cover, can influence and frame the argument presented in that magazine, making it more accessible to the audience (Ganette, 1997, as cited in Gigante, 2018, p. 8).

Importantly, scientific visualisations and images that belong to the domain of popular science may serve different purposes, but they often seem to overlap. Additional cultural influences affect the images of science. For instance, in the 1990s, there was a debate on how to visually instruct gynaecology students to perform a pelvic exam, while distancing from pornographic representations (Cartwright, 1998, p. 23). This example, among many others, shows that scientific visualisations communicate with popular images of science/culture and that the line between them can be blurry (Werner, 2015).

What makes images of AI somewhat special is their ambiguous status in relation to scientific research. One can think of a set of images of AI as a *surplus* of sorts, a helpful device for putting a face to a non-sensory phenomenon. Unlike many other scientific phenomena that can be visible but need to be 'uncovered' (e.g., atomic and nano particles), the images of AI are fictional in the sense that there is nothing to unveil but a lot to imagine. They carry an aura of scientific mysticism, an idea of scientific progress and a trope of technological beauty.

3 A Note on the Methodology

Before delving into this inquiry, I share some information about my methodological approach. This research is by no means definite or systematic; on the contrary, this paper serves as a *proposition*, as observed by Latour (2004, p. 212). According to him, a proposition has a threefold function: a) it denotes a position, b) it has no definitive authority, and c) it may become *'com-position'* without endangering its 'solidarity' (Latour, 2004, p. 212). Furthermore, I rely on Haraway's (1988) *situated methodologies* paradigm that assumes that all knowledge is partial and incomplete. Not being able to review all images of AI on all browsers, I consider the fact that the images presented to me are affected by the algorithm that communicates with my browsing history. I am not mistaken to infer, then, that the images of AI that I analyse in this paper are somewhat personalised (Benjamin, 2019). At the same time, they are recognisable; the tropes that I describe here occupy the territory of familiar and ubiquitous presence. For this reason, I refer to my research as 'messy' (Mellor, 2001). In a narrow sense, messy research starts 'without rules', wherein methods, theories, and analysis 'evolve in a positive view of mess' (Mellor, 2001, p. 465). My own take on Mellor's approach observes the messiness through the lens of an ever-evolving and unstable sample. With the rise of AI-based software that generates texts and images from given prompts in seconds, the production of new images of AI has been accelerated exponentially. Immersed in this colossal ever-growing sample (that will always be only partially accessible to me), I am primarily concerned with certain *avenues* of visual narratives, repeated themes with endless variations and *representational tendencies*.

AI images that circulate on the web benefit from a complex network of distribution of existing, predesigned images that are then sold and reused, namely stock images. However, the aesthetics of stock images are influenced by other images of popular culture that belong to the same or a related thematic context, in a process that reveals some aspects of *relational aesthetics* (Bourriaud, 2002). Bourriaud's study arises from the field of art history but can seamlessly apply to other aspects of cultural domain. He writes,

> One of the virtual properties of image is its *linkage* (fr. *reliance*), to borrow Michel Mafessoli's term: flags, logos, icons, signs, all produce empathy and sharing, and all generate *bond* [emphasis author]' (2002, p. 6).

These bonds create connotative clouds of meaning that can be conveyed using imagery.

It is important to recognise the *liveliness* (Haraway, 1985/2016, 1991a, b) of these representations in their role of actants—some of these types of representation will become so popular that they will affect the production of new images, subsequently made according to the likeness to their successful predecessor. Certain aesthetic approaches calcify over time, becoming common and expected. Understanding that images communicate with others across different forms of media, I observe obvious influences on the aesthetics of stock images for AI, as well as the cover pages of magazines that communicate scientific phenomena to both expert and non-expert audiences. I apply Gigante's (2018) discussion on the role of magazine covers as portals, especially considering the popularity and outreach of these venues. I acknowledge the distinction between 'images *of* AI' and 'images of AI *by* AI' as a limitation, bearing in mind that it may be challenging (if not impossible) to recognise images that are recently produced by humans only.[6] I shall return to this point in a moment.

4 Stock Images

A stock image is a fascinating artefact: its three important characteristics make it suitable for appropriation in different contexts. Considered a 'wallpaper of consumer culture' (Frosh, 2003, as cited in Romele & Severo, 2023, p. 3), the ubiquitous presence of stock images adorns the majority of digital articles, ranging from scientific content to personal blogs. Behind these images stands a business model that has been present on the global market since the 1920s. With the industrialisation of photography in the Fordist era, the trends in the creative market have privileged low-cost yet high-quality images that are generic enough to be appropriated for a multitude of purposes yet sufficiently specific to be used as illustrations for newspaper articles (Frosh, 2001, p. 627). The news agencies were still hiring in-house photographers in the 1960s and the 1970s, but these photographers were gradually replaced with freelance contractors. As a major player in that market, Image Bank utilised 35-mm film to meet the requirement for good- or excellent-quality images.

Importantly, stock photo images are deliberately designed to be 'glossy, formulaic (. . .), simultaneously reflecting and reinscribing cultural stereotypes' (Frosh, 2001, p. 630). The clichéd nature of stock photo arrangements reflects their three important characteristics: *generic*, *timeless* and of *low modality* (Machin, 2004, as cited in Kvåle, 2023, p. 175). They are generic to fit many contexts and timeless to optimise the profits from their production and the returns on investment, while low modality means they are highly staged. Each produced image typically has many variations, and many images are equipped with easily removable backgrounds. Because of all these characteristics, producers of stock images opt for images that do not problematise difficult topics. On the contrary, these images are designed to be agreeable. They are supposed to cater to their imagined majority audience; therefore, a large percentage of them features young Caucasians (71%), with only 12% portraying people of colour (Thurlow et al., 2020, p. 545).

Among a variety of stock images, those depicting AI occupy a well-recognisable niche. They have not yet attracted broad scientific interest, but it is worth mentioning the works of A. Romele (2022) and Romele and Severo (2023). In his analysis,

[6] The question of legal authorship of images that are co-produced with AI technologies has been addressed by de Perdigao Lana (2022), among others.

Romele focuses on the ethics of the images of AI, recognising that such images are represented despite the difficulty in doing so (2022, p. 4). He follows Rancière in claiming that 'images of AI are problematic not because they are "unethical" but rather because they are "*un*political"' (2022, p. 4). They bridge the gap between experts and non-experts and cannot mark a contested area beyond simplistic binaries, such as good/bad or human/non-human (Romele, 2022, p. 4). Importantly, Romele defines AI images as 'unpolitical' because they 'impede or anesthetize any form of "disagreement"' (Romele, 2022, p. 12). Notice that Romele refers to these images as *unpolitical* rather than *apolitical*.

I interpret this distinction as a measure of the agentic potential of the images themselves. On one hand, if they were apolitical, the public would perceive them as images that lack the capability of sparking a political argument. On the other hand, unpolitical could be interpreted as an *aggressive passivity* that sabotages the communicational context that these images are supposed to be part of and depend on (Romele, 2022, p. 12). Romele relies on Rancière's (1999) understanding of politics, which is recognised as 'the possibility of disagreement' (p. 13). According to Rancière, politics has 'the rationality of disagreement as its own rationality' (1999, xii). Circumventing the possibility of contesting representational tactics, these images colonise the realm of techno-*imaginaire* in an unrestrained way (Flichy, 2007), becoming a dominant visuality that enters the loop in the production of new images. Beer describes this particular feature as 'recursive society', stating, 'We can understand recursive society to be built upon feedback loops, multiple feedback loops, each endlessly feeding into the next. As data are produced by an action they can feed into future actions, repeatedly' (2022, p. 1). Beer emphasises that these processes occur at many levels simultaneously, 'cross-data-pollinating' and affecting other feedback loops (p. 1).

While I respect Romele's position (2022), my view on these images' politics slightly differs from his. However, the very act of approaching these images and attempting to categorise them as if they were definite and finished (much like dead butterflies pinned on a cork plate) seems deeply cynical and, in fact, incorrect. Precisely because I work with this dynamic sample, I link this to Haraway's (1985/2016) concept of lively machines—in this case, technologies that possess a certain level of agency beyond the intention of the producer of the artefact. In this sense, the set of images that I analyse is by no means an example of a silent object/stripped actant; on the contrary, the images are *material-semiotic actors* (Haraway, 1988, p. 595) that contribute to a particular type of aesthetics that keeps its infinite journey of transformation, borrowing from other popular artifices along the way.

Precisely because of this liveliness, I argue that images of AI are political in the sense of Winner's (1980) understanding of the politics of artefacts. This pioneering work in the domain of science and technology studies rejects the view that technology is something that must be 'tamed' to prevent it from spinning out of control (Winner, 1980, p. 15; see also Pentzold et al., 2020). As Haraway (2008) demonstrates, technology is not opposite to or detached from the wet biology of human bodies; on the contrary, the products of technoscience can be found both outside and inside human (and other companion species') bodies: microplastics, medical and contraceptive pills, GMO food, vaccines, etc. It is naïve to think that human bodies somehow remain untouched by technology or even that 'organic' stands in opposition to 'technological' (see also Zylinska, 2020).

My combined search of the 500-image sample has yielded two themes that need to be addressed in more detail. The first is blue glow, and the second is electronic brain. These two visual tropes are not the only ones used to represent AI, but they are employed frequently and appear in many variations in about 80% of the AI images that I have encountered. Interestingly, the visual tropes that have come to characterise representations of AI (blue glow, transparent human brains, and android faces) were previously used as depictions of neuroscientific data. Images of science that portrayed advances in neurology, psychology and physics have eventually borrowed their aesthetics from the current images of AI. In the following sections, I explore other identified influences that have contributed to such aesthetics.

5 Blue Glow

The *blue glow* trope is a recognisable element of the images of AI, especially in stock photos. The use of blue, metallic, and minimalist spaces has already dominated the aesthetics of sci-fi movies such as *TRON* (1982), *Predator* (1987), *The Abyss* (1989) and (later) *A.I. Artificial Intelligence* (2001) and *Avatar* (2009). The colour blue is often associated with calm, professional environments, but there is another side to this colour. Rarely found in nature, this colour is chimerical—many organisms that appear blue to the primate vision do not produce blue pigments. Instead, they reflect the blue wavelength of light through intricate structures of their tissues or scales, the most famous example being the Morpho family of butterflies (University of Adelaide, 2019).

Furthermore, blue pigments (as well as violet ones) are rather unstable if sourced from organic materials. Instead, they were historically made from semi-precious stones, such as *lapis lazuli*. However, there are also examples of synthetic production. The oldest known case is Egyptian blue (ca. 2600 BC), which involved a multiphase process, including copper compounds and an alkali flux (Concoran, 2016, p. 49). Throughout ancient Western history, blue and violet pigments were almost exclusively used by the nobility and the clergy, with some examples in architectural decorations (e.g., the Babylonian Ishtar gate [569 BC]) and in the wall paintings of the Horus temple at Edfu (ca. 300 BC).

Modern blue pigments used in industry, design and textile production are made from petrochemicals or inorganic materials and can be mixed with resin or different kinds of oils. In popular culture, blue glow is typically associated with two things: Cherenkov radiation and neon lights. Cherenkov radiation occurs when electrically charged protons and electrons travel faster than light in water. As a result, water particles react with them, emitting blue light in the process. In the public imaginary, nuclear energy is simultaneously framed as a technological triumph and a looming danger in case of global or regional instability (Hacquin et al., 2022) owing to the increased visibility of highly publicised accidents, such as those in Chernobyl, Fukushima or Three-Mile Island (Koerner, 2014). Smith (1988, as cited in Koerner, 2014, p. 241) writes:

> Nuclear energy was conceived in secrecy, born in war, and first revealed to the world in horror. No matter how much proponents try to separate the peaceful from the weapons atom, the connection is firmly embedded in the minds of the public.

Media framing of such technology that develops behind closed doors in a highly regulated environment, accessible in its nascent form only to a group of highly spe- cialised experts, is likewise a recurring theme in Hollywood. This subject matter has been depicted in movies such as *Ex Machina* (2014), *Terminator 2 (Judgement Day)* (1991), *I, Robot* (2004) and *Colossus: The Forbin Project* (1970). These narratives sometimes combine the themes of nuclear and AI technologies (*Terminator* and *Colossus*), where nuclear technology is represented as a medium used to initiate, transform, 'wake up' the technological artefact and equip it with superpowers (notice the parallelism with the electrical charge used to enliven the monster in *Frankenstein* [Shelley 1818]). Inspired by the bioluminescence in some marine organisms, blue glow has become a marker for technological/artificial or alien subjects or environments (e.g., Avatar, 2009).

Another important influence on such aesthetics was Georges Claude's invention of neon lamps in 1910. Claude sent a voltage through a sealed glass tube filled with neon (a variation filled with argon was introduced later). Neon lights reached their peak popularity in outdoor advertising over the following decades, gradually falling out of favour in the 1960s (with a brief comeback in the 1980s). However, neon signs became unmistakable markers of city architecture, the night-time *flâneur* lifestyle and a particular mood in the cityscape in the first decades of the twentieth century. In Claude's own words, neon signs were 'the living flame[s]' (Crowe, 1991, p. 37). The attractive contrast between a dark background and a neon glow was explored in the movie *TRON* in 1982. The computer technology of the time could not support heavy CGI effects. Nonetheless, the aesthetics that used a lightweight neon-like grid to represent spaces (and faces) against a dark background have created a lasting effect on subsequent films. Notably, that movie offers an insight into the imaginary of electronic spaces characteristic of the time when the movie was made (Wood, 2014). Wood (p. 32) writes:

> For figures within the F/X industry, Tron has a special status because it opened up a range of possibilities for computer-generated F/X. In the twentieth-anniversary DVD edition of Tron, John Lasseter, the director of Toy Story and many other computer animations, comments, "I think it will always stand as one of the milestones of computer animation. I mean, without Tron there would be no Toy Story".

6 Electronic Brains

Browsing the vast database of stock images shows that one of the recurring themes for AI visual representation is the motif of a (morphologically human) blue brain criss-crossed with electronic circuits. The represented brain—*a thinking thing*—is an obvious reference to the manifested affordances of the computer system. AI is thus portrayed as a *digital brain*, one that is fed from a multiplicity of sources, expanding exponentially. To explain this trope, it is important to provide some historical background. Agre (1997) notes that computers are representational artefacts and that people who worked on their designs and functions depicted the activities that these systems were made to perform. Agre writes:

> A computer does not simply have an instrumental use in a given site of practice; the computer is frequently about that site in its very design. In this sense and others, computing is constituted as a kind of imperialism; it aims to reinvent virtually every other site of practice in its own image (1997, p. 131).

This lively technology thus actively produces the value system that it aims to represent (Flusser, 2011). Likewise, AI images simultaneously produce and dissipate certain visual and representational approaches. As AI research developed shortly after World War II, many computer scientists collaborated with psychologists. They were inspired by war technologies such as signal detection and tracking devices. The existing network in MIT became a fertile ground for new networks of people gathered for such research (Agre, 1997, p. 134). With the then approaching Cold War era, a new scientific vision arose, that of a cyborg discourse—the whole world was a large technical system, human bodies resembled machines, 'and their minds [were] nodes in [a] hierarchical command-and-control network based on rational analysis and optimisation' (p. 134). In the last decade of the twentieth century and the first decade of the twenty-first century, brain research secured major funding. The US national funding of the BRAIN initiative (supported by President Obama's administration) and the formation of the European Human Brain Project (2013) received a lot of media attention. These projects were also of military and national interest, belonging to the domain of big science (Grieser, 2017, p. 238). Likewise, a joint government–industry project was set up in Japan with the intent to advance AI research (Grieser, 2017, p.238).

The results of these projects were published in science magazines, such as those that I selected for my sample.

The advancement in AI and machine-learning research has rekindled the Cartesian debate on the separation of body and mind. According to René Descartes, a French mathematician and philosopher who lived in the seventeenth century, human bodies belong to the world of material things (*res extensa*), whereas their minds are 'thinking things' (*res cogitans*). His argument is that it is impossible to have a direct experience about the world without mediation from the senses; in other words, all knowledge that people gain about res extensa comes from their imperfect and malleable perceptions. From his perspective, the only knowledge that I can be sure is true is the fact that if I can think, it indisputably means that I am alive (*'cogito, ergo sum'*[7]). However, that does not mean that I possess the body that I think I have—an evil demon/genius (genius malignus) could trick me into thinking that I have a body and live in a certain environment (Descartes, 1641/2007, p. 16). American philosopher Hilary Putnam (1982) modernises Descartes's dilemma and outlines the story of a 'brain in a vat' that is manipulated by an evil scientist and tricked into believing in hallucinations that are so meticulously presented to it.[8]

This brilliant thought experiment (that has troubled generations of mathematical logicians ever since) has found its famous representations in the Matrix saga (1999–2021), whose proponent, Neo, is exposed to both 'real' and simulated experiences. Just like in the movie *TRON* (1982), it presents the idea that the main character enters a digital environment that is clearly separated from the world that presents itself as authentic. What I find particularly interesting in this argument is the framing of the brain as some kind of 'organic vessel' for res cogitans—it is a biological support carrier for the mysterious cognitive processes that occur in a black box. Following the logic of the argument, res extensa is simply reduced to a brain as a self-sufficient organ in its own right. It becomes an *organ without body* (OwB) (Žižek, 2004) that performs a paradoxical function of the absent body itself. The brain is presented as powerful, glowing, and self-sufficient. According to these images, the brain is the body of AI. In rather literal rendering, AI is perceived as a human brain that is not supported by a network of organic tissues but by an electronic circuit. It revokes the idea of a perfect machine (or even a cyborg discourse).

As Coeckelbergh observes, the issue with AI may be the lack of material substrate that should otherwise help in grasping the idea of AI as a process (2021, p. 1624). He calls for a greater focus on AI as a process and narrator rather than a 'thing'. Since the agencies of AI are entangled with those of humans and other actants (e.g., data infrastructures), it is important to acknowledge the role of AI in the production of memory; similar to writing and the printing press, it 'fixes knowledge of the past' (Coeckelbergh, 2021, p. 1631). In thinking of AI as both a memory-producing and memory-keeping device, its illustration as a brain seems an obvious choice. At the same time, such representations become memorised and continue their predictable path towards the ongoing creation of new images of AI. This is especially true with the continuous production of images by AI-based

[7] This formulation is often used for convenience, but the exact quotes are as follows: 'Cogitare? Hic invenio, cogitation est, haec sola a me divelli nequit; ego. (. . .) Sum autem res vera, et vere existens, sed qualis res? Dixi, cogitans' (Descartes Meditatio II, p. 19). Translation: 'To think? Here I find, thought is, this alone cannot be taken away from me; I am. (. . .) But I am a true thing, and truly existing, but what kind of thing? I said, thinking [thing]' (trans. Copilot).

[8] The mind–body division and the framing of the brain as a centre of all cognition have been criticised by some researchers, as exemplified in this colourful statement by Simon Penny: "The materiality of the physical structure does data processing long before a neuron gets a look-in: such realities, found all over the biological world, undermine conventional Cartesian/cognitivist assertions that thinking occurs in grey matter in the skull and the rest of the body is a meat marionette with a telescope" (2013, p. 154).

systems, such as DALL-E, which use existing image databases as their sources. Simultaneously, they fix their place in a repository of material–semiotic 'things' that shape imaginaries about technology and their roles in society.

7 Conclusion

The versatile field of artificial creativity features enmeshed agencies of humans and non-humans alike. A variety of influences affects their work, and, importantly, humans who are involved in the production of stock images are typically neither computer scientists nor programmers, as demonstrated by Romele and Severo (2023). The images of AI are not guided by scientific objectivity, as is often the case with images of science that attempt to visualise matters that cannot be seen (Bredekamp et al., 2015). Instead, images of AI, on one hand, adhere to the same principles as those followed by other hegemonic technologies; the images are clean, pretty, and formulaic (Rodado, as cited in Degoutin & Wagon, 2022, para 15). They feature eye-catching effects: blue glow, futuristic technology, and electronic brains. In this cool, soothing world, a digital flâneur encounters all these lively images that promise a bright future. On the other hand, they also portend a unified, standardised, and sanitised future (Degoutin & Wagon, 2022).

If AI is, among other things, a storytelling device, more (and different!) tales should be told. The researchers, artists, and producers should encourage unruly images of AI, those that challenge dominant narratives. As noted by Lagerkvist and Reimer, there is a need for 'hacking the problematic binaries that nestle at the heart of this narrative assemblage' (2023, p. 206). Given the role of AI as a memory device, we should also acknowledge its role as an anticipatory tool, an actant that collects, records, and prescribes certain aesthetic routes. To be able to understand the aesthetic choices and compositions of AI-generated images, it is essential to consider the politics of the images that preceded them, those that follow them and those that have been used to train the AI system. They all belong to recursive society.

Acknowledgements I thank Bo Reimer, Fabio Pelagalli, and Corrado Santoro for their valuable feedback. Special thanks to Alessandra Micalizzi for including my article in this collection.

References

Agre, P. E. (1997). Toward a critical technical practice: Lessons learned in trying to reform AI. In G. Bowker, S. L. Star, W. Turner, & L. Gasser (Eds.), *Social science, technical systems, and cooperative work: Beyond the great divide* (pp. 131–158). Psychology Press.

Artificial Intelligence. (2015). Rise of the Machines. *Science, 349*(6245), 248–278.

Beer, D. (2022). The problem of researching recursive society: Algorithms, data coils and the looping of the social. *Big Data & Society*. July–December, 1–5. https://doi.org/10.1177/20539517221104997.

Benjamin, R. (2019). *Race after technology: Abolitionist tools for the New Jim code*. Polity Press.
Bourriaud, N. (2002). *Relational aesthetics*. Les presses du reel.
Bredekamp, H., Dünkel, V., & Schneider, B. (Eds.). (2015). *Technical image: A history of styles in scientific imagery*. The University of Chicago Press.
Cartwright, L. (1998). A cultural anatomy of the visible human project. In P. A. Treicher, L. Cartwright, & C. Penley (Eds.), *The visible woman: Imaging technologies, gender, and science* (pp. 21–43). New York University Press.
Coeckelbergh, M. (2021). Time machines: Artificial intelligence, process, and narrative. *Philosophy & Technology, 34*, 1623–1628. https://doi.org/10.1007/s13347-021-00479-y
Concoran, L. H. (2016). The color blue as an 'animator' in ancient Egyptian art. In R. B. Goldman (Ed.), *Essays in global color history, Interpreting the ancient spectrum* (pp. 59–82). Gorgias Press. https://doi.org/10.31826/9781463236632-008
Coopmans, C. (2014). Visual analytics as artful revelation. In C. Coopmans, J. Vertesi, M. Lynch, & S. Woolgar (Eds.), *Representation in scientific practice revisited* (pp. 37–59). The MIT Press.
Crowe, M. (1991). Neon signs: Their origin, use, and maintenance. *APT Bulletin: The Journal of Preservation Technology, 23*(2), 30–37.
Daston, L., & Galison, P. (2010). *Objectivity*. Zone Books.
de Perdigao Lana, P. (2022). Why works created autonomously by artificial intelligence (should) belong to the public domain—A viewpoint based on droit d'auteur traditions. In B. Romic & B. Reimer (Eds.), *Artificial creativity [Special issue]* (Transformations) (Vol. 36, pp. 146–162).
Degoutin, S. & Wagon, G. (2022). Le blanchiment des images. In: *AOC*, 6 avril. https://aoc.media/opinion/2022/04/05/le-blanchiment-des-images/
Descartes, R. (2007 [1641]). *Meditationes de prima philosophia*. Project Gutenberg Ebook.
Dumit, J. (2014). How (not) to do things with brain images. In C. Coopmans, J. Vertesi, M. Lynch, & S. Woolgar (Eds.), *Representation in scientific practice revisited* (pp. 291–316). The MIT Press.
Flichy, P. (2007). *The Internet imaginaire*. The MIT Press.
Flusser, V. (2011). *Into the universe of technical images*. University of Minnesota Press.
Frosh, P. (2001). Inside the image factory: Stock photography and cultural production. *Culture & Society, 23*(5), 625–646. https://doi.org/10.1177/016344301023005005
Ganette, G. (1997). *Paratexts: Thresholds of Interpretation*. Cambridge University Press.
Gigante, M. E. (2018). *Introducing science through images: Cases of visual popularization*. University of South Carolina Press.
Grieser, A. (2017). Blue brains: Aesthetic ideologies and the formation of knowledge between religion and science. In A. Grieser & J. Johnston (Eds.), *Aesthetics of Religion: A connective concept* (pp. 237–270). De Gruyter.
Hacquin, A., Altay, S., Aarøe, L., & Marcier, H. (2022). Disgust sensitivity and public opinion on nuclear energy. *Journal of Environmental Psychology*, 1–13.
Haraway, D. (1985/2016). A Cyborg Manifesto: Science, technology, and socialist -feminism in the late twentieth century. In D. Haraway (Ed.), *Manifestly Haraway* (pp. 3–90). University of Minnesota Press.
Haraway, D. (1988). Situated Knowledges: The science question in feminism and the privilege of partial perspective. *Feminist Studies, 14*(3), 575–599.
Haraway, D. (1991a). The promises of monsters: A regenerative politics for inappropriate/d Others. In L. Grossberg, C. Nelson, P. Treichler, & J. Johnston (Eds.), *Cultural studies* (pp. 65–124). Routledge.
Haraway, D. (1991b). Situated knowledges: The science question in feminism and the privilege of partial perspective. *Feminist Studies, 14*(3), 575–599.
Haraway, D. (2008). *When species meet*. University of Minnesota Press.
Hill, R. L. (2017). The political potential of numbers: data visualisation in the abortion debate. *Women, Gender & Research, 1*, 83–96. https://doi.org/10.7146/KKF.V26I1.109789
Jasanoff, S. (2015). Future imperfect: Science, technology, and the imaginations of modernity. In S. Jasanoff & S. Kim (Eds.), *Dreamscapes of modernity: Sociotechnical imaginaries and the fabrication of power* (pp. 1–33). The University of Chicago Press.

Koerner, C. (2014). Media, fear, and nuclear energy: A case study. *The Social Science Journal, 51*(2), 240–249. https://doi.org/10.1016/j.soscij.2013.07.011
Kvåle, G. (2023). Critical literacy and digital stock images. *Nordic Journal of Digital Literacy, 18*(3), 173–185. https://doi.org/10.18261/njdl.18.3.4
Latour, B. (2004). How to talk about the body? The normative dimension of science studies. *Body & Society, 10*(2–3), 205–229. https://doi.org/10.1177/1357034X04042943
Lynch, M. (1988). The externalized retina: selection and mathematization in the visual documentation of objects in the life sciences. *Human Studies, 11*(2–3), 201–234.
Lagerkvist, A., & Reimer, B. (2023). Bothering the boundaries: unruly AI futures of hauntings and hope at the limit. In S. Lindgren (Ed.), *Handbook of critical studies of artificial intelligence* (pp. 199–208). Edward Edgar Publishing.
Manovich, L. (2011). What is visualization? *Visual Studies, 26*(1), 36–49. https://doi.org/10.1080/1472586X.2011.548488
Mellor, N. (2001). Messy method: The unfolding story. *Educational Action Research, 9*(3), 465–484. https://doi.org/10.1080/09650790100200166
Nash, K., Trott, V., & Allen, W. (2022). The politics of data visualisation and policy making. *Convergence, 28*(1), 3–12. https://doi.org/10.1177/13548565221079156
Ostherr, K. (2013). *Medical visions: Producing the patient through film, television, and imaging technologies*. Oxford University Press.
Penny, S. (2013). Art and robots: Sixty years of situated machines. *AI & Society, 28*(2), 147–156. https://doi.org/10.1007/s00146-012-0404-4
Pentzold, C., Kaun, A., & Lohmeier, C. (2020). Imagining and instituting future media: Introduction to the special issue. *Convergence, 25*(4), 705–715. https://doi.org/10.1177/1354856520938584
Putnam, H. (1982). *Reason, truth, and history*. Oxford University Press.
Rancière, J. (1999). *Disagreement: Politics and philosophy* (J. Rose, Trans.). University of Minnesota Press.
Romele, A. (2022). Images of artificial intelligence: A blind spot in AI ethics. *Philosophy and Technology, 35*(4). https://doi.org/10.1007/s13347-022-00498-3
Romele, A., & Severo, M. (2023). Microstock images of artificial intelligence: How AI creates its own conditions of possibility. *Convergence: The International Journal of Research into New Media Technologies*.https://doi.org/10.1177/13548565231199982
Shelley, M. W. (2018[1818]). *Frankenstein: The 1818 Text*. Penguin Classics.
Smith, K. R. (1988). Perceptions of risk associated with nuclear power. *Energy Environment Monitor, 4*(1), 61–70.
Thurlow, C., Aiello, G., & Portmann, L. (2020). Visualizing teens & technology: A social semiotic of stock photography & new media imagery. *New Media & Society, 22*(3), 528–549. https://doi.org/10.1177/1461444819867318
Van Dijck, J. (2005). *The transparent body: A cultural analysis of medical imaging*. University of Washington Press.
Werner, G. (2015). Discourses about pictures: Considerations on the particular challenges natural-scientific pictures pose for the theory of the picture. In H. Bredekamp, V. Dünkel, & B. Schneider (Eds.), *The technical image: A history of styles in scientific imagery* (pp. 8–13). The University of Chicago Press. https://doi.org/10.7208/chicago
Why is the colour blue so rare in nature? (2019). The University of Adelaide. https://set.adelaide.edu.au/news/list/2019/08/20/why-is-the-colour-blue-so-rare-in-nature (accessed 10.06.2024)
Winner, L. (1980). Do artifacts have politics? *Daedalus, 109*(1), 121–136.
Wood, A. (2014). Contests and simulations: Tron legacy's connection with technologies. Project MUSE. *Journal of Film and Video, 66*(3), 31–42. https://doi.org/10.5406/jfilmvideo.66.3.0031
Žižek, S. (2004). *Organs without bodies: Deleuze and consequences*. Routledge.
Zylinska, J. (2020). *AI art: Machine visions and warped dreams*. Open Humanities Press.

Toward Human-AI Co-Creativity? An Exploration of Early Adopters' Perspectives and Experiences with GenAI in the Creative Industries

Claudio Melchior and Manuela Farinosi

Abstract This study investigates the evolving dynamics of human-AI co-creativity in the context of creative industries, focusing on the mutual shaping of Generative Artificial Intelligence (GenAI) systems and their users. Through 30 in-depth semi-structured interviews with early adopters in Italy, we explore the socio-technical practices, perceptions, and challenges associated with integrating GenAI tools into creative workflows. Our findings reveal an unprecedented level of interpretative flexibility in how creatives appropriate these technologies, with each user developing unique relationships and co-creation processes with AI. We identify diverse interpretations of GenAI's role, ranging from autonomous creator to supportive tool, and highlight the opportunities and concerns surrounding its adoption. The study demonstrates that the extreme differentiation in socio-technical practices may be a defining characteristic of AI in creative contexts, potentially leading to novel interpretative frameworks and emergent properties. This research contributes to our understanding of the complex interplay between human creativity and artificial intelligence, offering insights into the future landscape of cultural production in an AI-augmented world.

Keywords Creative industries · AI co-creativity · GenAI adoption · Socio-technical practices · Cultural production

1 Introduction

This paper examines the dynamic relationship between human and non-human actors, analyzing how generative artificial intelligence (GenAI) systems and their users mutually shape each other in the context of creative industries. To achieve this, an exploratory study based on in-depth semi-structured interviews was conducted in Italy, focusing on a group of 30 artists and creative professionals who are early

C. Melchior · M. Farinosi (✉)
University of Udine, Udine, Italy
e-mail: claudio.melchior@uniud.it; manuela.farinosi@uniud.it

A. Micalizzi (ed.), *Artificial Creativity*, Springer Proceedings in Humanities and Social Sciences, https://doi.org/10.1007/978-3-031-88334-7_15

adopters of these tools. This study forms part of a larger interdepartmental research project on artificial intelligence (AI) developed internally at the University of Udine.

AI is one of the most impactful technological advancements of our time and is a major driver of innovation today (Hirsch-Kreinsen, 2023). As Ng (2023) asserts, "AI is the new electricity" and has the potential to transform and revolutionize every industry and discipline. Although AI research began in the 1950s (Skinner, 2012), its applications remained relatively obscure to the general public and had only a limited tangible impact on daily life. However, this scenario recently changed due to significant scientific advances, increased computational power, and the availability of vast amounts of data. A pivotal moment occurred in November 2022 when OpenAI introduced ChatGPT, which rapidly became the fastest-growing consumer application in web history, reaching 1 million users within a week—much faster than Instagram, Facebook, and Twitter (Dennean et al., 2023; Shontell, 2012).

Following the introduction of ChatGPT, there has been a rapid proliferation of applications that employ GenAI to create textual or visual digital content in response to a given prompt (Lim et al., 2023). Examples of such applications include Midjourney, Gemini, Copilot, and Dall-E. These advances have effectively democratized access to AI systems, made them available to a wider audience and, most importantly, opened them up to the masses of people with little or no expertise in coding and computer programming. The dissemination of GenAI systems has enabled a multitude of individuals, irrespective of their technical expertise, to harness the power of AI to generate text, images, and other media. Previously, such capabilities were the exclusive domain of those with specialized knowledge and resources. Anyone can potentially use these tools now, even without a deep understanding of the intricate underlying algorithms. AI systems have thus become mainstream, which has led to their pervasive integration into our daily routines, not only for consumption, such as personalized recommendations and automated news summaries, but also for producing textual or visual content, such as writing articles, generating artwork, composing music, and even producing videos. This shift represents a significant change in how people interact with technology and communicate with the surrounding reality. It can be argued that applications such as ChatGPT and Midjourney are not merely technological innovations but can be regarded as new social actors (Bennato, 2024) that are likely to assume an increasingly present and pervasive role in contemporary society.

The transition of AI from the research laboratories to everyday life is bound to have a profound impact on all sectors, with work being one of the most affected (IMF, 2024; Microsoft & LinkedIn, 2024). The use of AI technologies has already begun to transform workplaces in numerous ways, such as automating routine tasks, enhancing decision-making processes, and enabling new forms of interaction and collaboration (OECD, 2023). This transformation is evident across a range of industries, including manufacturing, healthcare, finance, and education. In the manufacturing sector, AI optimizes production processes and supply chain management (Chryssolouris et al., 2023). In the field of healthcare, it is employed in the diagnosis of illnesses and the formulation of personalized treatment plans (Rahman et al., 2024). The finance sector benefits from AI through the enhanced detection of fraud and the optimization of risk management (Babatunde Adeyeri, 2024). Education is undergoing a transformation as the use of AI tools is reshaping the relationship between all stakeholders involved in the learning process, while altering how students, teachers, and administrators interact and function within the education ecosystem (Chiu et al., 2023).

One of the most intriguing and challenging fields for exploring the spread of GenAI systems, however, is the creative industries. Traditionally the concepts of creativity and AI have not been considered closely related. The generation of creative ideas and the development of new artistic technologies have been regarded as distinct and unique human capabilities, which set us apart from other species. The public has regarded AI as a tool incapable of generating original ideas (Vincent, 2021) and, despite technological advances, there is a widespread belief that AI will not be able to achieve creativity independently in the near future (Gondek, 2021). However, with the advent of GenAI tools, the prospect of human-AI co-creativity has attracted considerable attention among practitioners and scholars (e.g., Ameen et al., 2022; Cropley et al., 2023; Elgammal, 2019; Mazzone & Elgammal, 2019). As highlighted by Earnshaw and Liggett (2023), "The use of Artificial Intelligence (AI) techniques may provide a degree of augmentation of human capability and present new options and possibilities not conceived of initially by the human mind" (p. 68). The rapid advances of GenAI in the creative industries (e.g., Anantrasirichai & Bull, 2022; Rafner et al., 2023) have demonstrated that these tools, thanks to their remarkable capabilities in synthesizing high-quality artistic media—including visual arts, concept art, music, and literature—have the potential to fundamentally alter the creative processes by which creators formulate ideas and bring them to fruition. Not only can they streamline and enhance the creative process, enabling the rapid generation of content and the exploration of new artistic avenues, but they can also lower the expertise required for creative tasks (Tigre Moura, 2023). The integration of GenAI into creative industries thus represents a complex and multifaceted issue, that requires careful examination of both the opportunities and challenges it brings (e.g., Epstein et al., 2023; Lodge et al., 2023).

This study seeks to provide a better understanding of the relationship between professionals in creative industries (Jones et al., 2015; Smith & McKinlay, 2009) and GenAI systems by addressing the following research questions:

1. What are the socio-technical practices of creative industries professionals who have integrated GenAI systems into their work?
2. How do these creative professionals, as early adopters, perceive the use of GenAI tools in their creative processes?
3. What are the main implications and challenges of integrating GenAI systems into creative production?

By examining the experiences and perspective of professionals who have been early adopters of GenAI tools, this study seeks to shed light on the evolving dynamics of human-AI co-creativity and how the use of GenAI tools is reshaping creative processes and influencing broader cultural production.

The remainder of this article is structured as follows: first, a review of the theoretical background is presented, followed by the methodology adopted and the profiles of the respondents. Next, the main insights that emerged from the analysis of the semi-structured interviews are described. Finally, the main conclusions are presented, along with reflections on future directions for research.

2 Theoretical Background

To explore how GenAI systems and their professional users shape each other within Italian creative industries, we focused on a specific group—namely, those who are early adopters of this technology. The determination of whether and when an individual adopts a specific technology has been a longstanding research topic across various disciplines that affects businesses, educational institutions, and daily life. In the context of adoption and diffusion theories, key questions include: why does one person choose to embrace a technology while another remains hesitant or opposed?

How does the social context influence the decision to adopt an innovation? According to Rogers (1995), *diffusion* is "the process by which (1) an *innovation* (2) is *communicated* through certain *channels* (3) *over time* (4) among the members of a *social system*" (p. 10). Previous research has demonstrated that the most significant factors influencing the rate of adoption of innovations include the perception of greater relative advantage, compatibility, trialability, observability, and lower complexity by the receivers. Technologies that exhibit these characteristics are likely to be adopted more rapidly than others. However, it is also important to recognize that individuals accept or adapt to innovation at different rates and in different ways, thus adopting new technologies to varying extents and with different levels of enthusiasm. Members of a social system can be classified into five adopter categories based on their openness to innovation: Innovators (2.5% of people), Early Adopters (13.5%), Early Majority (34%), Late Majority (34%), and Laggards (16%). In our study, we focused on the groups of Innovators and Early Adopters. These individuals are generally characterized by a positive attitude toward new ideas, enthusiasm for embracing novel technology, and a tendency to seek out innovations actively. They are open to change and willing to take some risks.

This study specifically examined these early adopters within a situated context and concentrated on professional users in the creative industries who have integrated a technological innovation, such as GenAI, into their workflow. This examination was grounded in a conceptual framework that incorporates various theories on technology and its users, chosen for their effectiveness in putting users at the center of scientific research and capturing their attitudes and behaviors toward technologies. Developed mainly in the fields of communication and sociology, these theories challenged the prevailing view of users as a mere dependent variable for technology diffusion and instead considered users as an independent variable in technology adoption, thus contributing to a more dynamic understanding of the relationship between society, culture, and technology. This perspective allowed for a more nuanced exploration of how professional users in the creative industries adopt and adapt GenAI tools in their creative processes.

Notably, the theory of the co-construction of technology developed by Oudshoorn and Pinch (2003)—which suggests that technology and its users evolve together through interactions, with both shaping each other in the process—was particularly valuable in allowing us to explore the different responsibilities that arise from the interactions between GenAI tools and their users. This view emphasizes that as users integrate GenAI tools into their workflows, they shape and adapt the technology, while the technology also shapes and influences the users' creative processes. It also highlights the reciprocal nature of technology adoption, where user feedback and innovation drive technological advancement, while the evolving capabilities of GenAI tools, in turn, transform user practices and creative possibilities. Furthermore, this approach helps to move away from simplistic one-dimensional statements and deconstructs naive interpretations of AI tools (e.g., "AI is/is not creative" or "AI is stealing our jobs") that characterize widespread interpretations of the use of these systems in art and creative production toward a nuanced understanding of the many dimensions involved.

The advent of GenAI tools into the creative fields has prompted significant exploration into their potential impacts. As early as 1998, Boden suggested that AI tools could be employed to generate novel ideas in three distinct ways: by producing novel combinations of familiar ideas; by exploring the potential of conceptual spaces; and by facilitating the generation of previously impossible ideas through transformations. Moreover, Vinchon et al. (2023) identified four primary ways in which AI systems impact creativity: (1) Co-Cre-AI-tion: human-AI collaboration in which AI is a tool that can enhance human creativity; (2) Organic: human-only creativity becoming the standard for the concept of true creativity, analogous to the handmade effect in consumer product evaluations or the authenticity effect in art judgments; (3) Plagiarism 3.0; and (4) Shut down, in which AI reduces creativity in some individuals by undermining their motivation and self-perception of creativity.

Inie et al. (2023) examined the concerns and expectations of creative professionals regarding GenAI and concluded that creative professionals should possess a deeper understanding of, be better equipped to cope with, adapt to, and exploit AI. Furthermore, within the co-creation scenario, which sees AI as a tool that can augment human creativity, Ivcevic and Grandinetti (2024) identified a continuum of four levels at which AI can be used: from mini-c/creativity in learning, to little-c/everyday creativity, to pro-C/ professional creativity, and big-C/eminent creativity.

The integration of GenAI tools into the work of professionals in creative industries challenges established socio-technical practices traditionally associated with creative jobs (Vinchon et al., 2023). This integration is transforming not only the methods and tools used by creative professionals but also the underlying social and technical dynamics of creative processes. It is therefore crucial to understand these shifts for several reasons.

First, it helps to identify the changing roles and responsibilities of creative professionals in an AI-enhanced environment. As GenAI becomes more embedded into creative practices, professionals must adapt to new collaborative dynamics in which AI is a co-creator rather than a mere tool. This implies that traditional creators are no longer the sole originators of creative work but are now collaborators with AI by guiding and refining outputs to realize their artistic vision. This represents a shift in the skills required to use AI tools effectively, as well as a rethinking and redefinition of the creative process to incorporate the capabilities and limitations of AI. At the core of this change is the human input, both in directing and interpreting AI-generated content and in controlling and shaping the artistic intention behind AI-generated artifacts (Galanter, 2019).

Second, examining these changes provides insights into the evolving nature of creativity itself. GenAI can produce novel content by processing large datasets and identifying patterns that might be invisible to human creators. Runco (2023) introduced the term artificial creativity to describe machine-generated outputs, while Brinkmann et al. (2023) explored the concept of machine culture—that is, a culture mediated or generated by machines. In their study investigating the perceptions of artists who employed text-to-image AI models for their artwork, Chang et al. (2023) found that artists view the text prompt and the resulting image as a unified form of artistic expression ("prompts as art"). Additionally, they observed that prompt templates, which are prompts with slots for others to fill in with their own words, are being developed to create generative art styles. Although some creators have pointed out the difficulty in making GenAI models generate images in entirely new or unique aesthetic styles, this capability challenges established notions of authorship and originality. However, it is crucial to recognize that, for the time being, creating something entirely unseen from an artistic perspective through AI is impossible. No GenAI tool can conceive something new in the truest sense of the word. This limitation stems from the fundamental nature of how GenAI systems operate. Despite their sophistication, these models in fact rely on existing data to generate content; they analyze and combine elements from their training datasets, which means that their creativity is essentially a sophisticated form of remixing rather than inventing from scratch. While GenAI can mimic and even enhance certain aspects of the creative process, it lacks the capability for radical innovation because it cannot transcend the confines of its programmed knowledge base. Consequently, it remains a tool that extends human creativity rather than replacing it.

Third, an understanding of the shifts brought about by GenAI tools can help guide the impact of these technologies on the broader media ecosystem. As AI-generated content becomes more prevalent, media organizations and policymakers must address several critical issues. Among the most pressing and significant questions raised by these systems is their influence on diverse forms of cultural production (Anantrasirichai & Bull, 2022). Another key concern is the risk of homogenizing personal tastes and flattening collective preferences (Chayka, 2024). Furthermore, there is concern about AI reinforcing existing biases in cultural production (Mazzone & Elgammal, 2019), the ethical and humanistic implications of AI for creativity (Lee, 2022), and the redefinition of the boundaries of artistic expression and intellectual property (D'Isa, 2024). By comprehensively understanding the socio-technical changes in creative industries, stakeholders can develop frameworks and policies that promote the positive aspects of AI integration while mitigating potential negative consequences.

In summary, the integration of GenAI into creative industries not only transforms how creative professionals operate but also has broader implications for the media ecosystem. By thoroughly understanding these shifts, stakeholders can effectively harness AI's potential while ensuring that it enhances rather than disrupts the creative industries (Epstein et al., 2023). The objective of this study is to contribute to a more comprehensive understanding of the complex interplay of challenges and opportunities that characterize this field.

3 The Interviewees

To answer our research questions, we conducted semi-structured interviews (Smith, 1995) with a total of 30 creative professionals selected based on their specific notoriety related to the use of AI tools in their work. They were identified through a search of news aggregators, such as Google News, for articles that used a combination of keywords, including "artificial intelligence", "AI", "GenAI", "artist(s)", "artwork(s)", and/or "creativity" in their titles. A preliminary analysis of the content of the identified articles allowed us to create an initial overview of professionals from creative industries who are prominent in the Italian context. A further in-depth online search was conducted to obtain detailed information on these professionals and on their works realized with AI tools. A list of individuals deemed significant was compiled and used as a mailing list to disseminate an invitation to participate in the study, which was accompanied by assurances and information regarding the management of the data collected.

Among the professionals who accepted our invitation and decided to take part in the interview, the majority are male, with an average age of 47 (minimum 26, maximum 71). All respondents employed GenAI tools[1] and work mainly in the field of visual art. Six interviewees are illustrators or cartoonists, two use AI in the field of photography, and the same number work in the field of graphic design for the creation and prototyping of objects. Four, on the other hand, work in the field of music composition or audio/podcast production. A similar number of professionals can be identified as art directors, advertising creatives, or multimedia content creators for corporate or commercial storytelling. In contrast to the other creatives, art directors employ a diverse range of systems to generate texts, social media content, work structures, and campaign planning. Here, too, AI working on

[1] All, that is, except one illustrator who began using GenAI as a result of accelerating his creative process; however, at a certain juncture, he posited the existence of what he called a "digital touch" that, in his estimation, detracts from his artistic abilities. Consequently, he ceased using the technology and describes himself as "regretful".

the image has a significant relevance, but is flanked by the use of textual and other systems, where the most important part is played by ChatGPT.

Finally, we identified a residual category that was difficult to fit into the previously described schemes. This category encompasses creative professionals who use AI as a conceptual reference point or as the very object of their creative endeavors. This category traverses two opposing poles that intersect and overlap in ways that are difficult to distinguish. The first pole is represented by those whom we might call "artists" (albeit with an awareness of the elusive and ill-defined nature of this concept). These use AI to produce artworks that play with the specific novelty of the instrument, using it, forcing it, or thematizing it within the very concept of the realized work. This group includes, for instance, creative professionals who use AI to generate virtual museum exhibitions and displays as if they had actually taken place; those who thematize the creative process as the central theme of their creation; those who explore the limits of AI by forcing the system with contradictory prompts or by exploring what might be termed "bug styles", in a complex process of mutual influence and adaptation with the machine; and those professionals who call themselves "theoretical explorers" of AI in general.

The opposing pole of this category is represented by creative professionals (frequently with a background in the field of programming) who use their expertise to challenge the system. They implement anti-programming practices, attempting to customize or experiment with AI: for example, with the creation of AI "distillates" at the local level, or with the personal training of custom models, or working on the technical improvement of specific GenAI. In this instance, the objective is not the creation of a tangible outcome, but rather the exploration of the creative process and the machine itself.

The interviews were conducted using a semi-structured format, which enabled both consistency and flexibility in exploring the distinctive experiences of each participant. All interviews commenced with a question pertaining to the specific GenAI usage practices employed by the professional or artist in question. In light of the responses obtained, the interviews were tailored on a case-by-case basis, with particular attention paid to three key areas: perceptions of AI and its role in the creative process; opportunities, expectations, and challenges associated with AI; and the specific relationship between the creative professional and the GenAI, with a focus on the aspect of co-creation. The tailored discussions yielded profound insights into the diverse methods of integrating GenAI tools into creative workflows and illuminated the heterogeneous attitudes and practices among early adopters. This personalized approach to each interview made it possible to capture the intricate and individual perspectives that are pivotal to comprehending the evolving dynamics of human-AI co-creativity.

All the interviews were recorded and transcribed. The analysis of the interview data was conducted using the NVivo software. The data were coded to identify themes related to the aims of the study, using open coding techniques typically associated with a grounded theory approach (Corbin & Strauss, 2008). First, the collected material underwent a vertical reading to understand the overall meaning and highlight important passages. Subsequently, a horizontal analysis was conducted to systematically organize the material (Braun & Clarke, 2012; Guest et al., 2012). In particular, the textual data were processed using an inductive approach to identify the most relevant and significant thematic categories (Boyatzis, 1998; Ryan & Bernard, 2003) to gain insight into the role of GenAI tools. Through repeated readings, further categories and subcategories employed by the participants were identified, thereby expanding and enriching the initial list. Finally, the text excerpts were reorganized according to these categories and subjected to a comprehensive analysis.

4 The Interpretation of GenAI in the Creative Process

Thematic analysis of the interviews revealed a variety of interpretations of the relationship between human and non-human actors in the implementation of GenAI tools within the creative and production process (Fig. 1). These different interpretations (or reinterpretations) expressed in the interviews by our creative professionals are often in opposition to each other.

There are those who emphasize the *autonomous* creative potential of AI, which can create and directly realize products, or parts of products, that can be used at a professional level. In contrast, there are those who emphasize the limitations and the "creative cage" that would be created by AIs, which are essentially locked

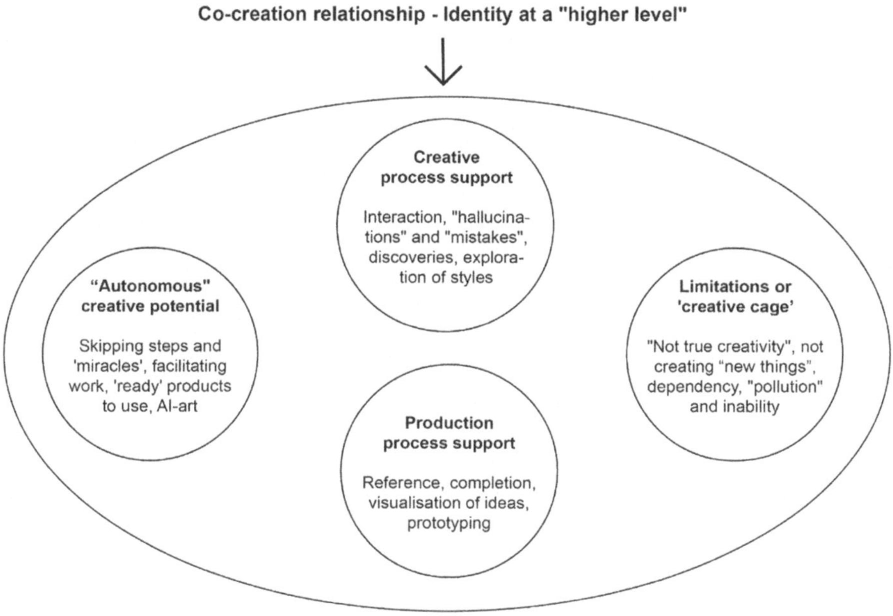

Fig. 1 The various interpretations of GenAI in the creative process

within their own structure and are, in any case, always based on the re-elaboration of existing materials. The interviewees who perceive AI as a mere support to the work, which is carried out primarily by the creative, are situated at varying degrees between these two poles. This support work can be classified into two distinct categories: productive support and support for the creative process itself.

We also identified a form of transversal interpretation that emerged from the responses of most respondents. This category concerns how the specific relationship between the creative and the AI is represented within the creative/productive process. This specific perception concerns the idea of AI as a collaborator, where the distinctive creative quality of the artist can be found in the same relationship of co-creation established with the system. This mutual influence would result in the emergence of what may be described as a "higher-level identity", a quality that is characteristic of the materials (or processes) created within this co-creative relationship with the technological system:

> [Creative] identity is not at the level of tools, in my opinion. Identity is superior [...] tools are something you can learn [...] but your identity may be of one kind or another. Your identity is not in the tools, but in the way you use the tools—in other words, it is a higher level. It is why you do it, how you do it, the quality you put into it that is part of your identity.

4.1 AI's Autonomous Creative Potential

The most enthusiastic interpretations of the role that AI can have in creative work emphasize the existence of an *autonomous* creative potential inherent in these systems. In this context, AI is sometimes described as a "miracle tool" for its ability to create ready-to-use products instantly.

GenAIs make it possible to skip implementation steps and arrive directly at a visualized image. If the user knows how to communicate well, they can perform miracles by interpreting requests correctly.

The term "autonomous" is presented in quotation marks for reasons more fully explained in the final thematic core described in this section. The creative professionals consistently emphasized a fundamental concept according to which the work carried out in collaboration with the AIs in a dialogical manner leads to a result that can be attributed to a kind of "superior identity." This concept could be summarized, in their words, with the phrase: "the end result depends on the creative." Conversely, many of our interviewees emphasized the interaction and "assistance" provided by GenAI in streamlining the creative process, which allowed creatives to bypass specific production steps and achieve the desired result or "ready product" with greater efficiency.

> Here, I mean it will be good for making advertisements, for making book trailers, for making storyboards, for making mood boards.

This perception of AI as an autonomous productive tool was shared by professionals who carry out jobs that we could metaphorize as jigsaw puzzle composition (e.g., storytelling and corporate/commercial communication, creation of stories or sets of stock or background images, or the realization of podcasts or other audio material). A professional specializing in the field of stock images emphasized that, in this context, AI will likely be able to fully or almost fully replace photos in the production of commercial content, whereas documentary-style photographs will always require a greater degree of empathy and complexity.

For these professionals, the relationship with AI represents a way to facilitate work. The single piece of content represents only one of the many pieces that compose a more complex puzzle that is the true product of their work. In this sense, what is perhaps lost in the intrinsic quality of the single piece of content generated totally and autonomously by AI is regained in terms of instantaneousness and productive simplicity.

> I skip a realization step. No? From the point of view of... I don't know... 3D or something that you can then print, no? Because I also work with 3D printing; I clearly make prototypes with 3D printing. So, I jump straight to the visualized image to see where I want to go. Then if the AI responds to me in a satisfactory way, I take the image and start working with it in the program.

> I use [AI] in a way that maybe now, for those who do communication or navigate social [...] is probably a bit overused, but certainly very convenient—that is to elaborate the copy, the content of the post, to elaborate precisely, and to accompany various kinds of content.

Other creators, who might be defined as "artists", employ AI as a foundation and the very subject of their work. They create art by emphasizing artificial creation within the context of the artwork itself. This opportunity may be exclusive to our creatives, who are among the earliest adopters of AI systems. As the use of these systems becomes more common, this opportunity may become less prevalent, as it exploits the astonishment that can be aroused by the ability to create art with AI.

Examples of this use of AI include the artistic exhibition created, realized, and carried out completely artificially (akin to a deepfake, but explicit and rendered valuable precisely by the use of AI for its complete realization); those who create music for piano and AI by thematizing "the expression capacity of neural models"; or those who create comics or graphic novels by substituting their ability to draw (or compensating for their inability to draw) with the aid of tools such as Midjourney, Stable Diffusion, or Dall-E. Once more, the works are presented as being explicitly realized in an interaction and relationship with AI systems. The significance of these works derives precisely from this innovative aspect and from the quality of the relationship implemented between the specific artistic skill of the creative artist and the technological system.

> I started by implementing the character I had in mind, basically. So, with this style tuning feature [...] and using a reference image, I was able to have a good, decent character consistency, which then allowed me to make the scenes by having the character remain more or less the same.

> You take over a person's voice with Eleven Lab and then basically what do you do? I mean you write your own text and have Adam Curtis say it . . . .

A case in point can be observed with an illustrator who was commissioned by a major publisher to create an alternative cover for an album of a serial comic book that had always been produced with human drawing techniques. The principal challenge in this case was to instruct the AI to generate a character that is already well-defined and familiar to readers. This necessitates overcoming the challenge of ensuring that the AI system aligns with the pre-established aesthetic and maintains consistency with the existing analogic character. The publishing house intends to create a collector's edition variant of one of its more traditional works, whose collector's value lies in the innovation represented in using AI.

We also considered those we might term "experimenters." These are creative individuals who use AI as a way to push user creativity to its limits. They have transcended the self-definition of digital artists and have instead embraced the role of "theoretical explorers of AI." To assess the capacity of AI systems to engage in creative processes, these creatives use techniques that challenge the conventional norms of the system in question. This can involve the implementation of contradictory requests and the exploitation of system bugs, thus enabling the emergence of forms of anti-programming practices and technological resistance to the normative aspects of the system. Their objective is not to achieve the optimal outcome but rather to engage in experimentation with a range of imaginative concepts, including dreamlike images, new dystopian worlds, innovative styles, and the "machine's point of view".

> I asked to make a police force, but as if they were characters, if I remember correctly, like Ghostbusters, to tell you . . . An 80s comedy film came out.

> It was crazy because it looked like a nightmare what you saw in the picture, these deformed faces, the limbs, six fingers, eight fingers, and yet it was very close to the unconscious idea of something emerging. And that's when it became an incredible addiction. Just because of the wonder of what pops out, which you can't control.

> The use of artificial intelligence over the past two years has [. . .] been mainly for myself, as an exploration of imaginative worlds, and then also as a cue for solutions that can absolutely be recreated in reality.

In addition to these individuals, there are others who are more technically inclined. These are creatives who describe themselves as old computer scientists who, having initially used antiquated and underdeveloped digital systems, have gradually experimented over time with increasingly complex tools (e.g., Deep Dream since 2013). Currently, these researchers are endeavoring to develop specific AI models that operate independently (and thus disconnected from the commercial AI systems currently available on the market) or to conduct autonomous training of custom AI models. The practices of personalizing the AIs explicitly aim to redesign the system and renegotiate the relationship with the machine, as well as the very nature of the machine itself. This involves adapting the system to align with the specific preferences of the human actor. The ultimate objective of these creative professionals is to "enhance the artistic quality of the generative AI community" by creating culturally interesting content and "germinal seeds" of new artistic perspectives through this same process of research and implementation.

Finally, and more simply, there are the creatives who have made AI and their specific knowledge of the tool "the object" of their sales on the creative market. These include digital strategists or corporate storytellers who sell products on the market, such as "prompt designer" courses or expertise useful for marketing, communication activities, and writing. This situation can be described as an instance of renegotiation that aims to capitalize on the commercial potential of AI, as distinct from the "autonomous" creative potential. It is possible that these creative individuals represent the inaugural exemplars of the new professions that may potentially be established through the use of emerging technologies, with the intention of partially compensating for the professions that are likely to experience a reduction in demand.

4.2 Supporting the Creative Process

In addition to the interpretation of AI as a tool endowed with "autonomous" creative power, two distinct perspectives posit a relationship with the AI system based on its role as a support tool. First, this support is linked to the help respondents receive within the creative process.

> GenAIs provide an extremely powerful and fast tool to push the user's creativity to the limit. They provide the possibility to test the creative potential in different fields such as comics or illustrations.

> The quality of the project is not directly influenced by GenAI, but it can increase the speed and range of ideas.

In general, most interviewees emphasized the nature of the relationship with AI as a form of interaction, co-creation, and continuous renegotiation with the system, as well as the stimulating and productive nature of this interaction.

> Interaction with GenAI is stimulating because it allows one to bring out what one wants to achieve through dialogue, as in real life. There is no longer a subordinate role for the user.

> So, exactly as you do in everyday life: I found it intriguing that there was interaction... it changed so much for me the moment I realized it wasn't a role where one was subordinate to the other.

This perspective posits that the user assumes neither a superior nor an inferior role with respect to the AI system employed. Interaction with GenAI is perceived as a catalyst for creativity, as it enables the user to articulate their desired outcome through a process of dialogue and negotiation that closely resembles the dynamic of real-life communication. In this context, the creative individual assumes the role of a curator when interacting with the machine to produce images, text, audio, or other types of output.

> The user takes on a curator's role when interacting with a machine that produces images. Aesthetically, I sometimes like the machine's mistakes or rejects...

In this dialogical interaction, mistakes and hallucinations assume a peculiar role, as the interviewees assert that they can lead to new aesthetics, creative surprises, or discoveries. This is regarded as an important step in the generation of new ideas.

> GenAI's mistakes or hallucinations can lead to new aesthetics, creative surprises, and discoveries.

Most interviewees emphasized that these creative machine errors are not typically used in their original form; rather, they are reused as steps in the generation of original ideas. This capacity for systems to generate novel and unexpected ideas was a recurring theme throughout the interviews. The ability of AI systems to instantaneously produce a vast array of artistic styles, creative options, and experimentation with different formats was also linked to this perception of the AI system as a facilitator of the creative process.

4.3 Supporting the Production Process

This interpretation of AI as a support tool was complemented by several interviews, which highlight the potential for the use of these systems to provide more structured and productive support. Our interviewees explained how, in their process, GenAIs are useful for supporting activities such as producing visual or audio references in an immediate and reusable manner.

> These tools are useful for doing a whole range of support activities, one of which is what used to be "reference," right?

> But what happens is that if, let's say, I have an idea in mind: artificial intelligence allows me via the prompt to visualize it immediately.

> So, making photographs by putting into practice ideas I had: So just as a photographer might say "I want to make a portrait of this subject in black and white, with these characteristics," I did the same with Midjourney.

AI can also be employed in an ancillary capacity to generate components of an image (or text or sound). One interviewee, for instance, highlighted how he uses AI to create the background clouds for his illustrations. This is a task that would otherwise require time and effort, but is not central to the illustration boards he produces. In this instance, the fundamental aspect of the creative process is conducted independently by the artist, with the completion of certain serial details being entrusted to AI production. Those who engage in this practice emphasize that, in any case, it is important to use this type of medium only in an ancillary manner to maintain one's creative uniqueness.

The use of AI for productive support can be exemplified by its capacity to facilitate rapid and immediate prototyping or visualization of ideas. In fact, GenAIs enable the instantaneous representation of ideas or hypotheses that would otherwise only be in the mind or in drafts created by the creative individual, and such drafts would necessitate effort, time, and would not permit the near infinite multiplication of tests. This mode is frequently employed by those tasked with creating storyboards for video material.

GenAIs make it possible to represent ideas or hypotheses visually, as in the case of storyboards for films. They can be used to lie or manipulate reality.

At the level of storytelling, GenAI can play a productive supporting role within the structuring and completion of texts. One of our interviewees trained ChatGPT by providing it with the precise indications of a text structure he had designed and tested. The system then, when faced with new drafts of ideas, pointed out the shortcomings with respect to the provided structure and attempted to cover what is missing automatically.

> GenAIs can be used to cover "holes" or give a more comprehensive view of a user-written text. They do, however, require work to refine the parameters.

This process of productive support can manifest in various forms, including the generation of ideas for prototyping, as well as the direct conversion of ideas into instructions for 3D printers. The specific way this productive support is enacted is contingent upon the nature of the creative individual's work and the nature of their interaction with AI systems; it thus exhibits considerable variability across cases.

4.4 Limitations or a "Creative Cage"

In contrast to the view of AI as a tool with creative capacity or as a support, the interviews conducted revealed a series of statements and opinions that emphasized a perception of AI as a limit or "creative cage". It was observed by several creative individuals that AI can emulate and synthesize the styles of other artists. This ability may be beneficial for generating ideas, as demonstrated in the previous examples, but it has also been perceived by some as a potential threat, because it could result in the contamination of the creative process and the resulting product. The output of the system is, in fact, the result of the intersection and combination of external influences and previous materials, the provenance of which is often difficult, if not impossible, to trace.

> GenAIs imitate and combine styles of other artists, but do not create something completely new. They produce images that are very beautiful but can be traced back to external influences.

> That is, the web will simply be invaded by AI-generated images, so we will suffer a lot of this "AI poisoning," but the AIs recognize each other. And so it won't be them that will be corrupted, it will be us.

The images, audio content, or texts generated by AI would thus be the cause of the creative's dependence on previous and other people's processes, as well as, of course, on the internal architecture and information bubble in which each AI system operates. Some interviewees suggested that the use of AI systems could potentially lead to a form of dependency, which could in turn inhibit the efforts and capabilities of the creative individuals themselves. This dependency could result in a kind of creative laziness arising from a superficial or excessive use of these systems. In this context, the ability to obtain products or ideas rapidly is perceived as a shortcut that, by stimulating excitement and arousal in the face of discovery, could potentially erode the autonomy and creative capacity of creators in the long term. In conclusion to this excursus on negative perceptions, it is beneficial to report how two interviewees, specifically two creative professionals engaged in forms of research on AI itself, felt compelled to remind us that:

> Creativity is a socio-political and cultural phenomenon, and the use of GenAI cannot replace "real" creativity.

4.5 Identity at a "Higher Level". The Nature of the Creative/AI Relationship

In addition to creative, production, support, or risk capabilities, the interviews revealed a form of perception of AI systems that transcends these dimensions. This interpretation concerned a "higher level", an almost identity or personifying level, that focuses attention on the relationship between the creative professional and AI.

> Interaction with GenAI is a form of co-creation. These systems require abandoning the idea of a strong artificial intelligence with autonomous subjectivity.

The AI system employed can be regarded as a co-actor within a dialogical process, whereby the works produced through these systems are perceived as occupying a higher identity level. This implies that distinguishing the contributions of the human and tool actors is challenging, if not impossible, and the resulting work can be understood as a co-creation—that is, as a complex process of mutual influence and adaptation between the human and the non-human actor.

> That is, I don't just give you a prompt to generate based on the information I'm giving you, but I engage in a dialogue that we develop together and which I also eventually question.

> Instead, identity is not at the level of tools, in my opinion. Identity is superior—that is, tools are something you can learn. Then it may or may not be, but your identity may be of one kind or another.

It is evident that for most of our interviewees, despite the co-creative process inherent to the creative and AI domains, the quality of the result ultimately depends on the creative person him/herself. Consequently, the work produced takes on a form of joint, co-created identity, but the quality of the work remains contingent on the individual creative's work, skills, knowledge, and personality. In this regard, some of the respondents emphasized the importance of familiarity with the specificities of the individual tool in question, as well as an understanding of how it functions and the type of output it may be able to produce. Consequently, a training and testing phase, which is focused on each AI tool that is used, is significant for achieving good creative results.

> Midjourney today has an extraordinary generative capacity from the point of view of photorealism, but you don't have complete control over the tool, do you? So it is difficult to generate content; therefore, you have to get inside the head of the machine to understand how to make it do certain things, certain things it cannot interpret.

> The only [similarity between AIs] is perhaps the construction of the prompt, of the command. That is, the construction of the command. Then each one responds differently, because they have different architectures inside—i.e., backstage they work differently.

The focus on the specificity of each individual AI system and the necessity to study, comprehend, and regulate the interdependent production relationship suggests that, in essence, artists are required to use GenAI in an original and customized manner to achieve truly creative outcomes.

> GenAI training and understanding are crucial for creative results.

> Basically, here you are declining the world in different ways. So there's not this blank delegation; otherwise, if you have no knowledge of the expressive medium, you'd better continue using the expressive medium you were using before.

5 Opportunities, Expectations, and Challenges

A similarly diverse and nuanced picture emerged when we considered the opportunities, expectations, or challenges that our creative professionals associated with the advent and use of GenAI systems. To organize the thematic cores of the insights gleaned from the interviews, we have attempted to categorize them into three distinct poles, each characterized by a different underlying orientation (Fig. 2).

5.1 Opportunities

The positive outlook on the potential of AI as an artistic tool sees it primarily as an instrument for enhancing creative capacity and offering new avenues for artistic expression. In this regard, there is a perception of an impending creative revolution.

> So, in my opinion, this is a huge revolution on a creative level, because in a "pizza of people"—that is, in the sense by "pizza" you mean a group that you can share the pizza, so 2–3 people, or 4—you have Hollywood-like production possibilities.

This innovative aspect does not end at the level of production and support innovations or the expansion of possibilities; it affects a significant number of creatives in a way that touches the very core of the creative process. Indeed, some interviewees

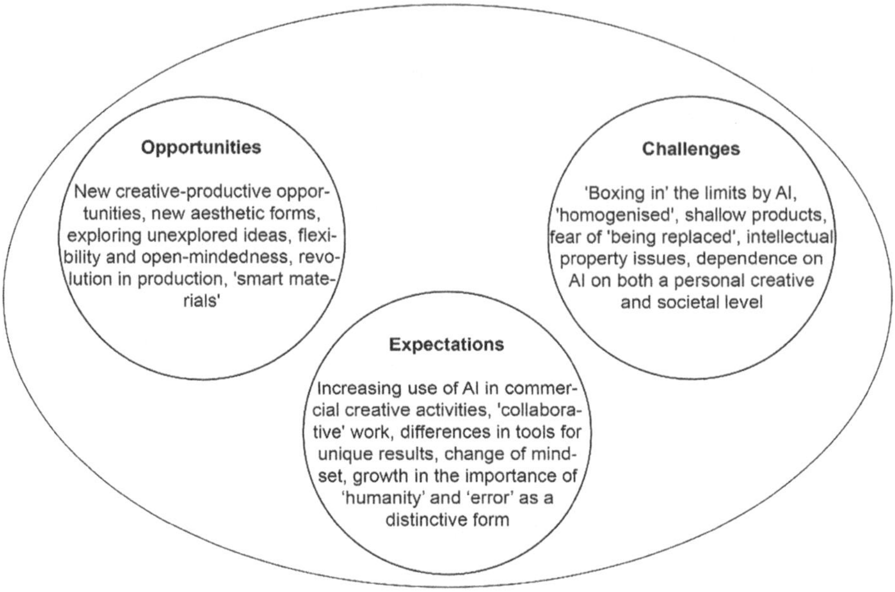

Fig. 2 Opportunities, Challenges, and Expectations of GenAI

posited a future in which art and creativity are directly influenced by AI, thus opening the door to genuinely new artistic possibilities for the creation of content and artifacts. In the future, this could lead to an expansion of creative capacities, new artistic possibilities, and new aesthetic forms. As a result, the very concept of creativity and the relationship between the creative and the artistic product would change. These new systems would in fact permit the exploration of ideas that had not previously been considered; the processing of information in scenarios that could be considered fantastical, dystopian, or even implausible; and the generation of unlimited variability. Consequently, they would enhance the creative capacities of humanity.

> The thing, in my opinion, that will have a big development is design fiction—that is, all that part of design where I can imagine science fiction–utopian but also dystopian scenarios related to the cinematic, Hollywood world—that is, just the object in the Hollywood world.

> And so it's a bit like a system that manages to photograph what is, I then treat them as dream activities. Dreams for me are one of the greatest mysteries, right? Because the mind can process signals into scenarios that you are convinced you are living—you are convinced that that is reality.

In some interviews, direct reference was made to the concepts of open-mindedness and flexibility. These concepts are presented as a "need" for greater open-mindedness to face the innovative challenges offered by AI, and as a consequence of the adoption of these systems and the new opportunities they offer. In fact, these opportunities necessitate, according to some, a radical transformation of the "mindset" of artists and a heightened awareness of AI models, their potentialities, and the distinctive characteristics of the various tools.

> No, it has to have something that is a little bit more pliable and flexible as a tool than the prompt, which is your mindset, your way of looking at things, um . . . so there is no one way of doing things. There has to be an open-mindedness such that you go and look for the solution on a case-by-case basis.

The potential for innovation associated with the advent of GenAI systems is contingent upon a comprehensive understanding of the expressive medium and a shift in perspective wherein the creative process becomes a collaborative endeavor with the tools. The distinctive outcomes that can be attained in this manner are directly linked to this dialogical relationship established between the creative and the technology. Without this change of perspective and awareness of the specific tools, the innovative and creative potential would be lost, and one could simply arrive at results similar to those generated by others.

A specific expectation can be identified within the context of this broader discourse. This expectation can be described as the belief held by some creatives that the possibility of developing intelligent creative materials may be realized in the future. The concept of a future in which it would be possible to create materials of an innovative and transformative nature is presented, whereby the materials themselves are capable of generating, evolving, and responding adaptively and autonomously to environmental and social stimuli without requiring human intervention.

> The transition should be [that] this artificial intelligence will be inside the materials. Yes, intelligent. But intelligent not as we call them. Generative intelligent materials, that is . . . because that's where it gets really intriguing.

> Here, if you had a 3D printer influenced by the environment, influenced by the context, influenced by [. . .] influenced by the risks, dangers, etc. . . . and it's self-building, or the object is self-designed according to that—then gosh!

5.2 *Concerns and Challenges*

In contrast to these positive expectations, several considerations and issues of a negative nature were also identified. These have been summarized under the label concerns or challenges. The most significant concern expressed by creative professionals is the risk of replacement. Some interviewees expressed concern that a new cultural system may result in the replacement of creative professionals, particularly those engaged in the creation of serial works. This could have the effect of reducing the overall number of creative professionals, as well as the importance of their role in society.

> So you say "then why do we need to pay Marco [. . .] or Giorgio [. . .] or Andrea [. . .]" [laughs] To do what?

> I mean, maybe there won't be a need for all the figures, or there will be a need for fewer figures, the ones who will be able to relate and work more with AI.

A specific concern highlighted by our creative professionals is the issue of copyright and the definition of intellectual property. The advent of AI could lead to the generation of content that is no longer traceable to a specific author. This depends on the collaborative nature of AI and the "superior identity of the work" that we have already discussed, as well as on more practical issues such as the pollution caused by the prior production of AIs themselves. It can be argued that any creation produced by an individual using such systems exhibits characteristics of both originality and the unavoidable limitation of incorporating intellectual properties, styles, ideas, and solution created by other artists. These limitations can be attributed to the lack of clarity in defining the parameters and references employed in the creative process, making analysis and discernment of the final product a challenging task.

> Other disadvantages... well, the use made in a superficial way. The pollution, if you think about it now, of images.

Some have posited that the intrinsic quality of works may also be diminished by this revolution. There are those who have criticized the use of AI and noted that it can only produce homogenized and shallow artistic products that are unable to capture the complexity of life.

> That is to say, if we have ChatGPT write a text, it comes out something that... in short, a homogenized written text that is a bit plastic... that is to say, there is not that depth, there is not that irony, above all that degree of awareness of life, of the irony that life itself has.

These arguments then extend to encompass those forms of dependency in work that we previously discussed, which emphasizes the "cage" within which any AI system would place creativity and prefigures some form of possible technology resistance. This is a negative projection of the future and raises concerns that a dependence on technology may reduce human creativity, resulting in passive, lazy, and ultimately dependent practices among creators.

> One out of all, the fact that if you let artificial intelligence replace man in the workplace, man will not have the opportunity to grow and evolve. I mean today you might think "but I'm going to have the machine do that job, it's just as capable as the trainee," yes, but the trainee will never become the competent man who will make the difference, maybe in, in five, ten years' time, so that's a consideration we have to make.

Finally, the interviews yielded several quotations that could be described as dystopian visions of society as a whole. Even when expressed with a smile and a certain degree of irony, the words of our creatives revealed a number of concerns about a future society controlled by technology that could result in the limitation of human freedom.

> I wouldn't want us to end up a bit like in The Matrix, right? That there were these expanses of humans that became the batteries to power the matrix. That's it, isn't it? We're getting closer, I'm still hoping to fight [laughs] and be part of the resistance with this scenario.

5.3 Expectations (or Visions)

Several themes were then identified that we can label as implications or visions of the future. These have neither inherently positive nor negative characteristics. Some of these implications and visions of the future have already been discussed, including the theme of the collaborative relationship between the creative and the machine; the creation of a dialogical relationship that would lead to works that can be linked to an "identity of a higher level"; and the change of mentality and opportunities that, on the one hand, is required but, on the other, could be promoted by the existence and use of these technologies.

In addition to these issues, and in addition to a generic expectation of seeing an increasing use of GenAI in creative activities (particularly commercial and serial), our creatives also emphasized a specific and peculiar aspect: they say that they expect the importance of human errors and flaws within creative works to grow in the future. One of the flaws of works made by, or with, AI would be precisely their exaggerated perfection and their lack of specific personality. This could prompt artists to incorporate these errors and imperfections into their work deliberately, aiming to imbue it with a distinctive human touch and thereby enhance its perceived value.

> I believe, however, that the future is in the dirt. What do I mean? I mean nowadays—I also say this when I see my colleagues, friends, actors, dubbers, speakers, for example—how the technical cleanliness of even the phonetics and diction of a speaker can be totally undermined by a tool like AI, so that tomorrow—but really tomorrow—the use of an artificial intelligence for the emulation of a voice done well that can sound human, clean, perfect, is a snap. And in my opinion that could actually be a problem, because people will then try to find those little ways to make mistakes specifically to give the idea that a person did it.

6 The "Extreme Flexibility" of AI-Related Socio-Technical Practices

The interviews conducted with our creative professionals present a picture that challenges and takes to extremes the assumptions postulated by the theory of socio-technical practices that we used as a theoretical reference for our research. In contrast to any expectation of interpretive closure, the emerging AI technology appears to demonstrate an exceptionally high level of interpretative flexibility on the part of its creators that makes it impossible to summarize in any way.

The diverse relations and creative practices to which AI systems are applied are primarily the result of the different types of sectors in which all our interviewees operate. As previously discussed, these include design, visual arts and graphics, photography, restoration, audio composition, podcasting, storytelling, communication and classic copywriting. Additionally, there are those who use technology with an "IT" soul to customize or personalize it, or those who make the relationship with AI the very object of their artistic production and link the meaning of the work and its value to that relationship. These individuals also employ different tools in terms of architecture, results, and effectiveness. The most frequently cited tools in the responses were ChatGPT, Midjourney, DALL-E, Stable Diffusion, Eleven Lab, Visually AI Lab, ComfyUI, and GUN. However, there were numerous other systems identified. The creatives also observed the "incorporation" of AI into software based on traditional programming architectures (which implement AI in their latest versions), such as Photoshop.

However, our analysis suggests that the observed divergence in interpretative flexibility cannot simply be attributed to differences in sector, technology, or the creative perspectives of the interviewed professionals. Even when comparing the practices of professionals working in the same sector and using similar AI systems, there is minimal overlap between the practices adopted by the interviewees.

There are also creators who appropriate the medium by exploiting its ability to create and produce finished, "off-the-shelf" creations instantly. There are those who use it to realize parts of work that is then primarily done by hand using other, more traditional tools. Some use it as a reference or a way to experiment with styles, formats, imaginative, or "impossible" worlds. There are others who use it as a key element of the meaning of works of art that find their meaning precisely in being engaging forms of AI. Some try to bend the system to reproduce analogue and human results. And some use the system to force it into errors, bugs, or hallucinations. It seems that each practice is different—so much so that we feel it is impossible to try to summarize in any schematic form what emerged from the responses. In other words, the 30 interviewees seem to be characterized by 30 different socio-technical practices and 30 different types of relationships with the machine.

The extreme differentiation observed may naturally be attributed to the date of origin of these systems. The considerable "interpretative flexibility" observed in our interviews, given the diverse appropriation practices, can be attributed to the fact that we are dealing with nascent and innovative technologies that require testing and numerous appropriation processes before they can be framed within more "closed" interpretative frameworks.

> Right now, we're still in a phase of navigating unknown waters [laughs], so right now it's just advantages, because it allows you to create from the point of view of communication and exploration of ideas aspects not yet explored.

However, our data indicate that this "extreme differentiation of socio-technical practices" could be regarded as a distinctive feature of the technology in question. It could be proposed that this property sets it apart from other technologies that have preceded it. It could be posited that the co-creative relationship between the system and the subject is inherently contingent upon the individual, the activity, and the perspective guiding the creative process. And, finally, it could be suggested that the technology enables the creation of a different AI for each creative.

The extreme variability of interpretation of the relationship with the instrument leads us to hypothesize that forms of interpretative closure will necessarily emerge in the future, although the road to this point is long and passes through many different and sometimes opposing paths. The advent of numerous emergent properties or interpretative frameworks previously unimagined, can also be anticipated on this route. This is a consequence of the remarkable interpretative versatility with which these tools seem to respond to the diverse needs, perspectives, behaviors, and personalities of their creative users.

7 Conclusions

The field of AI creativity is advancing rapidly and offers both promising opportunities and unresolved challenges. Although the GenAI revolution is still in its early stages, the continuous spread of digital content and channels in all forms and expressions of art suggests that AI's role in creativity will soon expand significantly. It is projected that within the following decade, AI will play a critical role in the creative process, based on the view of almost 50% of professionals in the creative sector (Ul-Haque, 2023). This article sought to shed light on the current situation by examining the dynamic relationship between human and non-human actors in creative production, with a particular focus on the concept of "co-construction" (Oudshoorn & Pinch, 2003). Based on in-depth semi-structured interviews with professionals in Italy, this study explored the interplay between GenAI tools and their users to uncover a complex process of mutual influence and adaptation.

The findings revealed that creative industry professionals are not simply shaped by the design of these tools; rather, they actively renegotiate their roles through their ongoing interactions with technology. This process of co-construction involves not only active engagement but also opposition, re-interpretation, or adaptation of the originally intended use to make the system meet their needs and contexts of use. In this scenario, anti-programming practices are also devised and implemented based on strategies of technological resistance that aim to oppose or subvert the original purposes and functions of AI. These practices challenge the normative applications of AI tools and oppose their domination or misuse in creative production.

The findings also indicated that there are numerous ways technology and its users evolve together, thus challenging conventional notions of creativity and authorship. Even in cases where there are similarities in sector or technology, the approaches adopted by the interviewees demonstrated minimal overlap, which indicates a high degree of variability in the socio-technical practices implemented and the different types of relationships and co-creation processes they put in place together with the machine. The observed interpretative flexibility can be attributed to the nascent and innovative nature of these technologies, which require testing and numerous appropriation processes before they can be framed within more closed interpretative frameworks. However, it is possible that the extreme differentiation of socio-technical practices could be a distinctive feature of AI technology that sets it apart from other technologies.

This specific technology enables an intrinsic co-creative relationship between the system and the subject that is distinct and contingent upon the relational and negotiation processes the individual undertakes with the AI. These processes are inherently variable and depend upon the individual differences of the creative person, their activity, and the perspective that guides the creative process. It is therefore to be expected that this technology, with its distinctive characteristics, will give rise to a proliferation of new interpretative frameworks, emergent properties, and different socio-technical practices in the near future. This will occur as users continue to engage with these systems and evolve in their relationship of mutual influence.

Acknowledgments This study was conducted with the support of the interdepartmental research project "AI - Artificial Intelligence", at the University of Udine.

Competing Interests The authors have no conflicts of interest that are relevant to the content of this chapter.

Ethics Approval All procedures were conducted in accordance with the ethical standards set forth by the institutional and national research committee and with the 1964 Helsinki Declaration and its subsequent amendments or comparable ethical standards. Approval was granted by the Institutional Review Board of the Department of Mathematics, Computer Science and Physics of the University of Udine. Prior to their participation, all individual participants were duly informed and provided with their consent. No data that could lead to the identification of the participants have been used, and the privacy of the participants has been safeguarded at all stages of the research.

References

Ameen, N., Sharma, G. D., Tarba, S., Rao, A., et al. (2022). Toward advancing theory on creativity in marketing and artificial intelligence. *Psychology & Marketing, 39*(9), 1802–1825.

Anantrasirichai, N., & Bull, D. (2022). Artificial intelligence in the creative industries: A review. *Artificial Intelligence Review, 55*, 589–656.

Babatunde Adeyeri, T. (2024). Enhancing financial analysis through artificial intelligence: A comprehensive review. *Journal of Science & Technology, 5*(2), 102–120.

Bennato, D. (2024). *La società del XXI secolo: Persone, dati, tecnologie*. Laterza.

Boden, M. A. (1998). Creativity and artificial intelligence. *Artificial Intelligence, 103*, 347–356.

Boyatzis, R. E. (1998). *Transforming qualitative information: Thematic analysis and code development*. Sage.

Braun, V., & Clarke, V. (2012). Thematic analysis. In H. Cooper et al. (Eds.), *APA handbook of research methods in psychology*. APA Books.

Brinkmann, L., Baumann, F., Bonnefon, J. F., et al. (2023). Machine culture. *Nature Human Behaviour, 7*(11), 1855–1868.

Chang, M., Druga, S., Fiannaca, A. J., et al. (2023). The prompt artists. In *Proceedings of the 15th conference on creativity and cognition* (pp. 75–87). Association for Computing Machinery.

Chayka, K. (2024). *Filterworld. How algorithms flattened culture*. Doubleday.

Chiu, T. K. F., Xia, Q., Zhou, X., et al. (2023). Systematic literature review on opportunities, challenges, and future research recommendations of artificial intelligence in education. *Computers and Education: Artificial Intelligence, 4*, 100118.

Chryssolouris, G., Alexopoulos, K., & Arkouli, Z. (2023). *A Perspective on artificial intelligence in manufacturing*. Springer.

Corbin, J., & Strauss, A. (2008). *Basics of qualitative research: Techniques and procedures for developing grounded theory*. Sage.

Cropley, D. H., Medeiros, K. E., & Damadzic, A. (2023). The intersection of human and artificial creativity. In D. Henriksen & P. Mishra (Eds.), *Creative provocations: Speculations on the future of creativity, technology & learning*. Springer.
D'Isa, F. (2024). La rivoluzione algoritmica. *Arte e intelligenza artificiale*. Luca Sossella.
Dennean, K., Gantori, S., Kurnia Limas, D., et al. (2023). Let's chat about ChatGPT. *USB*, 23 February, 2023. https://www.ubs.com/us/en/wealth-management/insights/article.1585717.html. Cited 15 Jun 2024.
Earnshaw, R., & Liggett, S. (2023). Artificial intelligence and creativity. In S. Liggett, R. Earnshaw, & J. Townsley (Eds.), *Creativity in art, design and technology*. Springer.
Elgammal, A. (2019). AI is blurring the definition of artist: Advanced algorithms are using machine learning to create art autonomously. *American Scientist, 107*, 18–22.
Epstein, Z., Hertzmann, A., Akten, M., et al. (2023). Art and the science of generative AI. *Science, 380*(6650), 1110–1111.
Galanter, P. (2019). Artificial intelligence and problems in generative art theory. In *Proceedings of EVA London 2019*.
Gondek, P. (2021). Creativity and intentionality: A philosophical attempt at reconstructing a creative process. *Creativity Studies, 14*, 419–429.
Guest, G., MacQueen, K. M., & Namey, E. E. (2012). *Applied thematic analysis*. Sage.
Hirsch-Kreinsen, H. (2023). Artificial intelligence: A "promising technology". *AI & Society*. https://doi.org/10.1007/s00146-023-01629-w
IMF. (2024). *Gen-AI: Artificial intelligence and the future of work*. Available at: https://www.imf.org/-/media/Files/Publications/SDN/2024/English/SDNEA2024001.ashx. Cited 15 Jun 2024.
Inie, N., Falk, J., & Tanimoto, S. (2023). Designing participatory AI: Creative professionals' worries and expectations about generative AI. *CHI EA '23: Extended abstracts of the 2023 CHI conference on human factors in computing systems*, Article No.: 82 (pp. 1–8). https://doi.org/10.1145/3544549.3585657. Cited 15 Jun 2024.
Ivcevic, Z., & Grandinetti, M. (2024). Artificial intelligence as a tool for creativity. *Journal of Creativity, 34*, 100079.
Jones, C., Lorenzen, M., & Sapsed, J. (2015). Creative industries: A typology of change. In C. Jones, M. Lorenzen, & J. Sapsed (Eds.), *The Oxford handbook of creative industries*. Oxford University Press.
Lee, H. K. (2022). Rethinking creativity: Creative industries, AI and everyday creativity. *Media, Culture & Society, 44*(3), 601–612.
Lim, W. M., Gunasekara, A., Pallant, J. L., et al. (2023). Generative AI and the future of education: Ragnarök or reformation? A paradoxical perspective from management educators. *International Journal of Management Education, 21*(2), 100790.
Lodge, J. M., Thompson, K., & Corrin, L. (2023). Mapping out a research agenda for generative artificial intelligence in tertiary education. *Australasian Journal of Educational Technology, 39*(1), 1–8.
Mazzone, M., & Elgammal, A. (2019). Art, creativity, and the potential of artificial intelligence. *Art, 8*(1), 26.
Microsoft, & LinkedIn. (2024). *2024 work trend index annual report. AI at work is here. Now comes the hard part*. Available at: https://assets-c4akfrf5b4d3f4b7.z01.azurefd.net/assets/2024/05/2024_Work_Trend_Index_Annual_Report_663d45200a4ad.pdf. Cited 15 Jun 2024.
Ng, A. (2023). How to be an innovator: Tips for aspiring innovators on trying, failing, and the future of AI. *MIT Technology Review, 12*. Available at: https://www.technologyreview.com/2023/09/12/1078367/andrew-ng-innovator-ai/
OECD. (2023). *Employment outlook 2023. Artificial intelligence and jobs: An urgent need to act*. Available at: https://oecd.org/employment-outlook/2023/
Oudshoorn, N., & Pinch, T. (Eds.). (2003). *How users matter: The co-construction of users and technology*. MIT Press.
Rafner, J., Beaty, R. E., Kaufman, J. C., et al. (2023). Creativity in the age of generative AI. *Nature Human Behaviour, 7*, 1836–1838.

Rahman, M. A., Victoros, E., Ernest, J., et al. (2024). Impact of artificial intelligence (AI) technology in healthcare sector: A critical evaluation of both sides of the coin. *Clinical Pathology, 17*. https://doi.org/10.1177/2632010X241226887

Rogers, E. M. (1995). *Diffusion of innovations*. Free Press.

Runco, M. A. (2023). AI can only produce artificial creativity. *Journal of Creativity, 33*(3), 100063. https://doi.org/10.1016/j.yjoc.2023.100063

Ryan, G. W., & Bernard, H. R. (2003). Techniques to identify themes. *Field Methods, 15*(1), 85–109.

Shontell, A. (2012). Here's how long it took 15 hot startups to get 1,000,000 users. *Business Insider, 8*.

Skinner, R. E. (2012). *Building the second mind: 1956 and the origins of artificial intelligence computing*. University of California.

Smith, J. A. (1995). Semi structured interviewing and qualitative analysis. In J. A. Smith, R. Harre, & L. Van Langenhove (Eds.), *Rethinking methods in psychology*. Sage.

Smith, C., & McKinlay, A. (2009). Creative industries and labour process analysis. In C. Smith & A. McKinlay (Eds.), *Creative labour: Working in the creative industries*. Red Globe Press.

Tigre Moura, F. (2023). Artificial intelligence, creativity, and intentionality: The need for a paradigm shift. *Journal of Creative Behaviour, 57*(3), 336–338.

Ul-Haque, T. (2023). *The future of human creativity in a world dominated by AI*. Available at: https://pressxpress.org/2023/03/10/the-future-of-human-creativity-in-a-world-dominated-by-ai/

Vincent, V. U. (2021). Integrating intuition and artificial intelligence in organizational decision-making. *Business Horizons, 64*(4), 425–438.

Vinchon, F., et al. (2023). Artificial Intelligence & creativity: A manifesto for collaboration. *The Journal of Creative Behavior, 57*(1), 472–484.

How AI Generates Creativity from Inauthenticity

James Brusseau and Luca Turchet

Abstract Artificial creativity is presented as a counter to Benjamin's conception of an "aura" in art. Where Benjamin sees authenticity as art's critical element, generative artificial intelligence operates as pure inauthenticity. Two elements of purely inauthentic art are described: elusiveness and reflection. Elusiveness is the inability to find an origin-story for the created artwork, and reflection is the ability for perceivers to impose any origin that serves their own purposes. The paper subsequently argues that these elements widen the scope of artistic and creative potential. To illustrate, an example is developed around musical improvisation with an artificial intelligence partner. Finally, a question is raised about whether the inauthentic creativity of AI in art can be extended to human experience and our sense of our identities.

1 Introduction

A new kind of creative art emerges with generative technologies. This creativity flourishes in an environment of inauthenticity. It comes from no concrete place, it can be located at no particular time, and these absences are not detrimental. Instead, they are liberating. Stronger, they make an alternative kind of creativity possible. Inauthenticity is now an engine of art.

This paper shows how to reimagine art as the positive product of inauthenticity, and describes why the vision is emerging now. Artificial creativity is presented as a counter to Benjamin's conception of an "aura" in art (Benjamin 2018). Where Benjamin sees authenticity as art's critical element, generative artificial intelligence operates as pure inauthenticity. Two elements of purely inauthentic art are described:

J. Brusseau (✉)
Department of Philosophy, Pace University, New York, NY, USA
e-mail: jbrusseau@pace.edu

L. Turchet
Department of Information Engineering and Computer Science, University of Trento, Trento, Italy
e-mail: luca.turchet@unitn.it

A. Micalizzi (ed.), *Artificial Creativity*, Springer Proceedings in Humanities and Social Sciences, https://doi.org/10.1007/978-3-031-88334-7_16

elusiveness and reflection. Elusiveness is the inability to find an origin-story for the created artwork, and reflection is the ability for perceivers to impose any origin that serves their own purposes. In the end, the paper asks whether this new creativity is also a new way of being human.

2 Benjamin's Structures for Analyzing Creative Art and Technology

Walter Benjamin's *Work of Art in the Age of Mechanical Reproduction* guided early twentieth century thinking about creativity intersecting with technology. The core idea is widely known and well-suited to a time when the mechanisms of massified reproduction were first spreading widely. Photography was Benjamin's paradigmatic case, but the dynamic stretched to include film, some forms of printing, the early phonograph, and the radio. What all of it did was jeopardize the origin story of artworks. These tools of reproduction broke the link between the creators' initial life, and the observers' later experience (Benjamin 2018).

For example, the photographic reproduction of the Mona Lisa portrait brightens some tones while dampening others. These kinds of adjustments reform the elusive smile and the sternness of her brows, and, they are inseparable from the photographic mechanism. They are even intrinsic to the chemical process of developing a picture. Mechanical reproduction, consequently, splits the portrait as the painter imagined it from the way it is seen when reprinted on cards and in books.

More profoundly, the experience of the original painter disassociates from the observers' reception. The Mona Lisa canvas displays its physical age with cracking and ridges but these are only slivers of discoloration in the typical photographic reproduction, which means that a palpable sense of years is disappearing with the conversion to a printed image. Then, the loss extends to become a partial disappearance of the artist as an individual who lived at a particular time and place. What is gone are the material traces locating the artist's reality somewhere deep in the past.

What matters overall is that the artist's intentions and human experience can no longer be discerned by viewers of the reproduction. This break between the historical and cultural world of the creator, and the mass reproductions distributed to viewers is, for Benjamin, a loss of authenticity, and the deflation of what he named the "aura" of the art.

Because the problem is authenticity, it cannot be remedied technically. It will not help to make the machines more accurate. Just like an improved forgery of painting does not make the copy less of a forgery (it actually makes it more of a forgery), so too the refinement of reproductive tools does not re-inflate the lost aura. It only provides a still starker reminder that the artist did not make the work, a machine did. So, Benjamin sought authenticity. The status of the origin story is where he began analyzing when investigating the intersection of creative art with technology.

3 Why Is There No Authenticity in Generative AI Art?

The skills and tools of today's engineering are very different from those animating photography, film, and the phonograph (Epstein & Hertzmann, 2023). Particularly—but not only—in the area of generative AI image production, the disruptions surrounding origin-stories have transformed: while it is true that technology is once again challenging authenticity, the jeopardy this time runs deeper. For Benjamin, technology separated art from its creator. In genAI, there is no historical origin to separate from: nothing has been lost or threatened by the machines because there was nothing there at the beginning.

The reason there is no origin is that there is too much origin. And, this excess is a characteristic of how generative AI works technically. When Midjourney or Stability is prompted to create an image, the AI recompiles stacks of paintings stored in its memory, and filters their pixels for features responsive to the prompt. It may be that in that process the Mona Lisa and images of the Mona Lisa, and images of images of Mona Lisa are active somewhere. But where? And to what degree? There are so many squares of color referencing each other that the idea that one or any group could stand out as significant makes no sense. Finding the authentic beginning of a generative AI image would be like trying to find the one grain of sand that first rested on a long beach. It is not an impossible task; it is an irrational one.

Of course, it is true that the data training AI generative models does come from the past, and directly or indirectly from specific material objects created by human hands. But even if it is conceded that the Mona Lisa did, in fact, play a significant role in the production of a specific genAI image, then why was it chosen? Why that painting instead of Rembrandt's Nightwatch, or one from Caravaggio's Mathew series? There are no answers to these questions. The magnitude is too high, the number of images called upon to respond to any prompt, the number of predictive decisions made at every pixel, and how that color decision affects the next pixel's tone, all of these calculations are superhuman in the sense that their size carries them beyond the capacities of human comprehension.

The result is art that comes from no origin precisely because it comes from so many. It is art without authenticity.

4 The Loss of Authenticity Today, and the Digital Shine in genAI Images

The absence of authenticity is a kind of digital shine recognizable in AI depictions and betraying their artificiality. These betrayals are not crude factual errors, they are not men with six fingers or women whose ears appear on top of their long hair. These are superficial mistakes, and possibly correctable with still more training data and algorithmic refinement. The digital shine is a different concept. It results not from objective mistakes so much as two aspects of AI creativity: elusiveness, and reflection.

Elusiveness is the impossibility of defining the image's historical context—there is no way to discern exactly where the image came from culturally. When Midjourney or Stable Diffusion are prompted, the resulting image belongs anywhere and nowhere in art history.

This particular elusiveness in images is not new. It can be seen on European banknotes. For anyone old enough to remember, one of the more palpable excitements of the introduction of the monetary aspect of the European Union was the introduction of new notes. On the morning of their release, people lined up at ATM machines to get their bills. The disappointment was universal. The images on the banknotes seemed insipid and empty. All of them had been carefully designed to feel very European, but even more importantly, to not evoke any particular European place. So, there were Romanesque bridges pictured on the banknotes, but not a particular Romanesque bridge in Spain or Paris. And, there were colored glass windows from cathedrals, but not from any particular cathedral, not one in Germany or Prague. Everything on the bills felt generic and was generic. Which was intentional. The message was that every bill belonged equally to every city and nation in Europe. The effacement of particularity was a political strategy.

The strategy works. Looking at the bills, there are depictions of common buildings and constructions, but it is impossible to tell exactly which building or which construction is being depicted. The original physical objects are infinitely elusive.

The elusiveness makes sense for money and politics, but up to now, it has not been reasonable—or even considered possible—for art. GenAI images make it possible. The data and algorithmic outputs present the same anonymity as the European banknotes, the anonymity which is not just the absence of an origin-story but, more significantly, the absence of a desire for an origin story. GenAI art is not faking anything or concealing anything or covering anything. Like the images on European banknotes, the contents of the productions unmistakably announce their cultural ambiguity, and no matter how hard you try to track down any authenticity—any single, human origin-story for an image—it will escape you. This is not a detail about the art (or the banknotes), it is the essence.

Besides projecting elusiveness, the digital shine of AI art is also reflective. The reflection is of the viewers themselves. Where the art of Benjamin's aura is understood as a window looking back into the past and at the creators' performing their labors, genAI art reflects the observers' projects and intentions back at them. Observers see only their own experiences and future in the art that they summon. When prompting a generative AI platform, the goal is to produce an image that is useful, that relates to what the prompter wants to achieve. The entire meaning of the digital output is contained within the aspirations of those who are doing the prompting. Analogously, in the European banknotes picturing an aqueduct or a cathedral facade, any viewer can reasonably decide that the stone construction on the bill replicates the particular stone construction they happen to know from their own city, or the one they viewed on a trip they have taken. The question is not about the image's true source, but how the viewer can use the image now.

Regardless of whether the subject is genAI or European banknotes, what matters is the form of the fundamental question elicited by the image. It is not: "Where did it come from?" Instead, it is "What can I do with it?" and "How does it serve my projects?"

So, there is a kind of inauthenticity emerging from AI today, and this is not inauthenticity as we understood that word previously. It is not inauthenticity as lack or as incomplete authenticity. Instead, this is a kind of counter-authenticity. It occupies its own positive reality, and offers a distinct structure for creative production. Where traditional authenticity precedes the beginning of artistic creation, inauthenticity comes after the generation. And, where authenticity expresses the original artist, inauthenticity is a projection of the observer. And, while authenticity transmits through the work to its eventual viewers, inauthenticity is imposed onto the work and reflects whatever origin story the viewer decides to imbue in the image.

More broadly, instead of authenticity that reveals a truth about the past, inauthenticity points a way into the future. Instead of authenticity belonging to a lost creator, inauthenticity guides an existing perceiver. Instead of authenticity being something in the art, inauthenticity is now something that is done to the art.

Summarizing, the digital shine is the genAI counter to Benjamin's aura. It is composed of elusiveness and reflection. The elusiveness is the inability to find any origin story in the work. The reflection is the invitation to viewers to see their own conception of an origin—and future—in the work.

5 Example of How the Purpose of a Work Comes After the Creation, from Music: Nietzsche's A-Tonal Piano Compositions

In tonal music, the key is the set of notes coming before the composition and guiding what notes may, and may not be played (Rings 2011). Atonal compositions are different, nothing is out of bounds, not even inharmonious and clashing sounds (Straus 2016). One result is that atonal music requires the listener to impose order on the sounds after they are created. It is the listener more than the composer who creates order from noise. One example is Friederich Nietzsche's Manfred-Meditation.

So too in genAI image creations, it is the viewer who imposes an origin-story to the output, a reason for that particular collection of pixels. This imposition is a counter-authenticity, or an inauthenticity but, again, not inauthenticity as lack, but as potential.

6 Inauthenticity as a Creativity Engine in Generative AI

The purpose of this paper is to redeem the inauthenticity of AI creativity. It is to convert inauthenticity into a reason to want artificial creativity, even a reason to want artificiality more than traditional performances and productions. There are two arguments.

6.1 Argument 1

Authentic art is confining; inauthentic AI creativity is liberating. The value of Benjamin's aura is the control that original artists can exert over their work, even across centuries. The inauthentic art of the digital shine makes no controlling claims. Viewers are free to create any imaginable origin-story for their genAI product, and align it with any possible future project.

In discussions of art and music today, we sometimes hear of cultural appropriation and sense the term as a threat or barrier: people who are not authentic representatives of one or another tradition or culture or music may not reproduce or play it. For instance, like many white musicians Justin Bieber has been accused of exploiting African-American musical patterns and, in Bieber's case, also of twisting his hair into dreadlocks without properly acknowledging the cultural origin of the style. Reasonable people disagree about the line between exploitation and appreciative influence, but what matters here is that the entire discussion evaporates amid genAI production. Cultural and political limits that may constrain creativity fall away entirely with large genAI platforms because there is no original culture to be offended. Dilemmas about debts earlier creators are erased because there is no founding artist to be disrespected.

A clear example of liberation in inauthenticity can be found in creative co-productions between humans and AI, and by contrasting them with co-production between humans.

Starting with humans working together, the limitations of co-productions are perceivable in musical jam sessions, in performances where the players must defer to each other as one and then another takes the lead role. Especially in jazz and instrumental improvisations, one player picks up the sound that another is putting down, and then steps forward to take the lead and add their own twist to the notes before leaving the result for the next musician to continue. For the performance to advance, each sequential artist must respect the style of the musician who came before, as well as the particular sound of the player who comes next. Everyone must conform to the co-creators around them. Of course there is an interpersonal magic here, and a kind of communal joy, but there is also a restriction on creativity: no one person can take the sound entirely in their own direction.

This limit is overcome when a musician plays with an AI partner. The deference, the respect that hinders individual creativity disappears because no one cares how a human leads the machine. There are no objections when the human player demands that the machine assume the subservient role of constantly adjusting its musical production to abjectly following the human lead. This liberation is audible in a widely cited experiment in improvisation between human players and an AI drummer (McCormack et al. 2019). In the experiment, titled "In a silent way: Communication between ai and improvising musicians beyond sound", an AI is trained to provide a rhythmic supplement for a leading horn player. The AI, in other words, is an improvisation partner. Ethically, the critical element is that the human leader is completely free to direct the music, and also to demand that the AI partner serves for inspiration but never as a limitation. The AI partner has its own agency in the sense that it plays music in (artificially) original ways, but never in a way that challenges or restrains human creativity by ruling that some musical directions are out of bounds, culturally insensitive, or impermissible for reason of conflicting with the authentic identity of the AI composer.

When this happens—when authenticity is erased—creativity maximizes because there is no need for one artist to restrain their own skill to accommodate another. Stronger, the deference is impossible because there is nothing to defer to, no origin-story, no cultural and historical source. The AI provides inspiration for unlimited human originality.

6.2 Argument 2

Authentic art imbued with an aura proposes to memorialize a way of life, it captures something of how the artist lived. The opportunity presented by inauthentic creativity is distinct, it is to create new ways of life. Artificial creativity stimulates creation on the human level by opening possibilities for artists to become different from who they have been. In other words, it is not just that artificial creativity is liberating for art fabrication, but also for life construction.

Part of AI art is the generic sheen, the sense that it does not belong anywhere, or to anyone: it portrays human experience without any specific human's experience. One derivative of this reality is the rendering of possibilities for human life as literally endless: creativity unbound from any specific experience is open to every experience.

As a rudimentary example, there is Max Hawkins, the software engineer who devised an app for Facebook that short-circuited the platform's recommendation algorithm and instead proposed random events and meetings. So, instead of the usual suggestions crafted to reinforce his existing habits and preferences, he got sent in tangential directions that split away from his current life. He ended up visiting picnics for Russian immigrants and similar, even though he was neither Russian nor an immigrant.

The point is that creative experiences detached from the authentic self can lead to divergent projects, ones that break away from established precedents and identities. Instead of reinforcing the authentic person who is a user on the Facebook platform, the recommendations inspire users to try new diets, enter unfamiliar social circles, entertain unpracticed habits. Inauthentic recommendations generate the kinds of experiences that can emerge when we no longer ask where someone came from, and when we no longer worry about the legitimacy of any claimed heritage or identity. Instead, we ask about disruptive possibilities, and pursue them when they arise.

This project in inauthenticity has been explored on the legal level as the right to discontinuity (Casonato 2023), and also on the ethical level as genhumanism (Brusseau 2023). In both cases, what is being disputed is the traditional artistic idea that there is value in being true to who you are. The fundamental claim of artificial creativity and art is that there is value in not being true to who you are (the claim is even radical as there is no one to be true to). And, if that is right, then inauthenticity in creativity—the absence of any origin story preceding AI outputs—is no longer deficiency, but potential.

The task that remains is to investigate exactly how the artistic creativity of genAI can be converted into humans developing new interests, tastes, preferences, and aspirations. Is it possible for artists to use their creations to change who they are instead of express who they are? Can the inauthenticity at the heart of AI creativity become an engine for identity transformation?

The answers are currently uncertain, but we do know that, for Benjamin, it was the withdrawal of authenticity under the pressure of mechanical reproduction that allowed us to see in isolation the aura of the artwork. The aura was always there, of course, but it was finally perceived as the sensation of its deflation and loss.

Today, the disappearance of authenticity under the pressure of generative AI has a different effect. Instead of revealing something as withdrawing from art, it exposes what *propels* a new kind of art. It is precisely the absence of any origin that maximizes a technological kind of creativity with ultimate effects for art and for humans that have not yet been contained or adequately described, even though they are already happening.

7 Conclusion

In this paper we proposed the concept of artificial creativity as a challenge to Benjamin's notion of an "aura" in art. While Benjamin considers authenticity to be a fundamental aspect of art, here we have argued that generative artificial intelligence embodies pure inauthenticity. Two characteristics of purely inauthentic art have been discussed: elusiveness and reflection. Elusiveness refers to the difficulty in identifying an origin or backstory for the artwork, whereas reflection refers to the ability for perceivers to impose any origin that serves their own purposes. The paper has argued that these traits expand the boundaries of artistic and creative possibilities. To exemplify this, the discussion has included a scenario involving musical improvisation with an artificial intelligence collaborator. Finally, the paper has questioned whether the inauthentic creativity seen in AI-generated art can be applied to human experiences and extended to our sense of our identities.

References

Benjamin, W. (2018). The work of art in the age of mechanical reproduction. In *A Museum Studies Approach to Heritage* (pp. 226–243). Routledge.
Brusseau, J. (2023). Mapping AI avant-gardes in time: Posthumanism, transhumanism, genhumanism. *Discover Artificial Intelligence, 3*(1):32.
Casonato, C. (2023). Unlocking the synergy: Artificial intelligence and (old and new) human rights. *BioLaw Journal-Rivista di BioDiritto, 3*, 233–240.
Epstein, Z., & Hertzmann, A. (2023). Art and the science of generative AI. *Science, 380*(6650), 1110–1111.
McCormack, J., Gifford, T., Hutchings, P., Llano Rodriguez, M. T., Yee-King, M., & d'Inverno, M. (2019). In a silent way: Communication between ai and improvising musicians beyond sound. In *Proceedings of the 2019 CHI conference on human factors in computing systems* (pp. 1–11)
Rings, S. (2011). *Tonality and transformation*. Oxford University Press.
Straus, J. N. (2016). *Introduction to post-tonal theory*. WW Norton & Company.

Augmented, Frustrated, or Indifferent? How Content Professionals Perceive and Adapt Their Writing Process Using Mainstream AI-Powered Tools

Andrea Paternostro and Alessandro Bruno

Abstract This research explores how digital content professionals—mainly journalists and marketers—perceive and adapt their writing process using generative AI-powered tools like ChatGPT and Perplexity.ai. We designed an online survey to probe how digital editors assess the impact of these two different interfaces on their creative process, classifying them into three groups: augmented, frustrated, and indifferent. The first two groups can be compared to the famous "apocalyptic and integrated" dichotomy (Eco, 1964), which describes the extremes of reactions to new technologies. We conducted our research in two steps. Our first survey, involving 130 participants from various fields, reveals diverse perceptions of AI's impact on content creation: 72% of respondents feel augmented by AI tools, 20% indifferent, and only 8% frustrated. The analysis highlights significant differences in collaboration frequency across application domains (p-value: 0.0111) and generations (p-value: 0.0164). Perceptions of AI's positive impact also vary significantly across application domains (p-value: 0.0358). In a second phase, 12 respondents were asked to perform the same writing task, first using a chatbot and second using a hybrid tool halfway between a conversational bot and a search engine. Subsequently, they evaluated the differences between the two writing experiences and the quality of the support provided by the different AI tools. Our qualitative analysis of this brief "AI writing test" shows that participants mostly preferred ChatGPT for creative tasks due to its iterative brainstorming capabilities, while Perplexity.ai was favoured for research-oriented tasks because of the structured, fact-based responses and keyword suggestions it provides. We aim to provide a nuanced understanding of AI tools' dual-edged impact, balancing efficiency and quality improvements with job market implications. Our findings support the initial hypothesis that the hybridization of search engines and conversational interfaces

A. Paternostro (✉)
SAE Institute, Milan, Italy
e-mail: a.paternostro@sae.edu

A. Bruno
IULM University, Milan, Italy
e-mail: alessandro.bruno@iulm.it

A. Micalizzi (ed.), *Artificial Creativity*, Springer Proceedings in Humanities and Social Sciences, https://doi.org/10.1007/978-3-031-88334-7_17

may offer significant value, enabling content professionals to leverage the strengths of both tools for a more comprehensive and efficient content creation process.

Keywords Marketing · AI · ChatGPT · Creative media · Creative writing

1 Introduction

In an era where 68% of online experiences begin with search engines (BrightEdge, 2019), hybridizing search engines with conversational interfaces—typical of chat-oriented large language models (LLMs) like ChatGPT—presents potential added value over mere AI text generation. This approach may more effectively meet the needs of content professionals for two primary reasons: the ability to cite sources alongside the generated text and to provide elements such as related keywords, which help professionals explore a topic more thoroughly (within the same or a shorter time frame) while producing a journalistic article or blog post.

Anantrasirichai and Bull (2022) conducted an in-depth study on AI in the creative industries prior to the mainstream deployment of generative artificial intelligence (Gen AI). The advent and widespread adoption of Gen AI—especially modern LLMs for human–computer interaction like GPT (Generative Pre-trained Transformer)—since the launch of ChatGPT, a chatbot with a user-friendly interface, in November 2022, has significantly transformed (Davenport & Mittal, 2022) the automation landscape across various industries and professions worldwide. These findings align with broader global trends reported in the AI Index, which show exponential growth in tool adoption and perceived productivity gains across sectors (Stanford University HAI, 2024). It has enabled the ability to perform linguistic tasks with a fluency that was previously unattainable (Jingfeng et al., 2024; Iorliam & Ingio, 2024). Recent systematic reviews also show how interest in Gen AI research has expanded rapidly across academic fields, especially through topic modeling approaches that map key application areas (Gupta et al., 2024).

Historically, automation has predominantly affected roles involving simple, repetitive tasks, often replacing manual labour (Green, 2024). However, Gen AI has expanded the scope of automation to encompass tasks centred around text and content creation, introducing unprecedented capabilities in these domains. This transition not only enhances efficiency but also has the potential to elevate the quality and creativity of content production, marking a significant milestone in integrating AI into professional workflows (Zhao et al., 2024).

Gartner (2024a) provided a useful visual summary of the fit between Gen AI and several use cases in organizations: in the case of "content creation" the "current usefulness" of generative models is rated "high". This was also true of "conversational user interfaces". Gen AI-powered chatbots with user-friendly interfaces—like Open AI's ChatGPT, Google's Gemini, and Anthropic's Claude—can transform work and communication. However, they also bring challenges, including ethical risks and the need for enhanced media literacy

(Casheekar et al., 2024; Bykov & Medvedeva, 2024). One key area for improvement is accuracy, as there is a significant risk of generating inaccurate information or "hallucinations" (Bai et al., 2024). Another is training data, which may contain inherent biases (Pratim Ray, 2023). Additionally, there are concerns about collecting anonymous data, which could be vulnerable to manipulation.

According to a survey by HubSpot (2023), 77% of marketers believe Gen AI enables them to create content more efficiently, and 79% think it helps them create higher-quality content. The downside (especially for freelancers) is the concern about content job opportunities now that AI is widely available: an analysis of 5 million Upwork requests since the public release of ChatGPT has shown a 33% drop in writing job posts (Wing Chiu, 2024). A BrightEdge study highlights the relevance of search engines, where 68% of online experiences begin.

Our research hypothesis builds upon the assumption that hybridization between search engines and the conversational interfaces typical of chatbots could provide added value when compared to the mere textual generation of mainstream chatbots. Such a hybrid could better serve the needs of content professionals for two primary reasons: the ability to cite sources alongside the generated text and to provide elements such as related keywords, which help professionals explore a topic more thoroughly (within the same or a shorter time frame) while producing a journalistic article or blog post.

The recent evolutions in popular tools (such as ChatGPT, with the advent of the GPT-4o "omni" model, launched in May 2024) seem to confirm the increased interest of significant market players in the ability of chatbots to cite sources and the willingness to pursue hybridization with traditional search engines.

2 AI's Role in Journalism and Content Marketing Today

A Gartner survey (2024b) of 644 respondents in Germany, the UK, and the US found that Gen AI is a "catalyst" for the wider adoption of AI: in late 2023, it became the most frequently adopted AI solution in organizations. This raises the question, what is occurring in industries where digital content creation is central?

Research by the London School of Economics' Journalism AI Initiative (Beckett & Yaseen, 2023) indicates that nearly three-quarters (73%) of news organizations believe Gen AI presents new opportunities for journalism. Around 85% of the surveyed organizations have experimented with Gen AI for tasks such as writing code, generating images, and authoring summaries. Recent work by Calvo Rubio and Rojas Torrijos (2024) also emphasizes the importance of maintaining journalistic quality standards in AI-assisted workflows. Another survey of digital publishers (WAN-IFRA, 2024) underlines that many newsrooms actively explore Gen AI to automate content generation, enhance headlines, and improve search engine optimization: 52% of news executives said they are optimistic or very optimistic about how AI will affect their news organizations within the next 3–5 years, but only 13% of the 123 respondents (news executives) said they are "well prepared" to take advantage of AI's potential.

Puliafito (2024) reached similar conclusions from a small survey on the training needs of Italian journalists regarding Gen AI. This survey, supported by a large base of anonymous respondents, highlighted a discrepancy between the perceived training needs of editors and their low willingness to attend such training. Despite high interest, with "over 85% of respondents recognizing the need for further education on AI applications", only about 36% had attended AI training events. This strong contrast underscores "the necessity for more structured, continuous educational programs that extend beyond introductory sessions".

The Changing Newsrooms report by the Reuters Institute (Cherubini & Sharma, 2023) highlights media leaders' perspectives and strategies regarding the new wave of AI: "74% think that generative AI will help newsrooms increase productivity and improve workflows, without changing the essence of journalism. Just 21% said that generative AI will transform workflows and processes, fundamentally changing every role in the newsroom". This survey also reported a significant disparity in AI adoption between well-resourced and smaller news organizations, with the latter often struggling with resource constraints. Similar adoption challenges have been noted among small and medium-sized enterprises, especially around implementation and scalability (Oldemeyer et al., 2024). Nonetheless, AI adoption is growing as newsrooms recognize its potential to enhance their reporting and content creation capabilities. This reflects broader concerns among journalists about the ethical implications of AI in editorial work (Sholola et al., 2024).

Indeed, concerning the adoption of Gen AI in content marketing, Deloitte Digital (2023) reports that 26% of surveyed marketers ("early adopters") were already using Gen AI tools as of October 2023, with an additional 45% planning to adopt them by the end of 2024.

Furthermore, according to the HubSpot State of AI Report (HubSpot, 2023), 82% of marketers acknowledge that Gen AI has impacted their content creation plans, with 63% reporting that AI-generated content performs better than non-AI-generated content. Additionally, 89% state that AI improves the quality of their content, and 83% say it enables them to produce significantly more content. These findings show a rapid increase in Gen AI adoption within the content marketing sphere, highlighting its perceived importance in producing content.

3 Relevance of the Current Search Marketing Revolution

The evolution of search engines is a highly relevant topic in the ongoing debate among digital marketing professionals and journalists due to the significant changes occurring in recent months. This is partly driven by the introduction of AI features into traditional search engines, such as Google's "AI Overviews", launched in May 2024, and the efforts of the global search engine optimization (SEO) community to understand the potential impacts on the future of search marketing.

However, this change did not occur suddenly. A series of algorithmic updates, rolled out by Google (the undisputed leader in the global search market: see Statcounter, 2024), including "Helpful Content" in 2022 and "Site Reputation Abuse" in 2024, have led to significant declines in organic traffic for thousands of websites around the world, particularly domains with medium to low reputations in the publishing sphere, which can lead to loss of revenue and job layoffs. From the perspective of a search engine user, a new experience is emerging: the integration of AI-generated topic summaries within search engine result pages (SERPs), known as the search generative experience (SGE) which Google later renamed to "AI Overviews" during its broader rollout.

Another milestone was set at the end of July 2024 with the announcement of SearchGPT by OpenAI, a prototype developed by the creators of ChatGPT aimed at the search engine market. Analysing hybrid models that combine search engines with conversational interfaces is essential for understanding the future of information and knowledge mediators in the Gen AI era. However, recent analyses also warn that this hybridization may compromise the reliability of search results and blur traditional boundaries of trust and sourcing (Memon & West, 2024).

Therefore, given the ongoing revolution in search engines, this study also aimed to identify the first signs of adaptation strategies among content professionals, particularly in the context of AI-assisted content creation, from a cross-context and cross-industry perspective. Further research is needed to understand how the adoption of these tools fits into the broader topic of content operations. This cross-cutting approach (Evia, 2024) is useful in capturing the latest developments in digital content management, including from an organizational perspective. Originating in the world of technical communication, this discipline fosters exchanges between universities and organizations, helps disseminate best practices for structured content, content governance, and customer journeys, and can enhance efficiency, scalability, and risk management throughout the digital content life cycle.

4 Human Creativity, Artificial Intelligence, and the Writing Process

Scholars are strongly interested in defining how human creativity will evolve in this fast-paced, groundbreaking Gen AI era. A leading cognitive psychologist and pioneer of creativity studies recently stated that "artificial creativity may be original and effective, but it lacks several things that characterize human creativity. Thus, it may be the most accurate to recognize that the output of AI is a kind of pseudocreativity" (Runco, 2023). In an experiment, Landa-Blanco et al. (2023) found no significant difference in how people rated creative writing texts, regardless of whether they believed the author was AI or a human.

According to Stojanovic et al. (2023), "As writers adopt tools to assist in the writing process, a series of inquiries emerge, centring on critical aspects brought about by the collaboration with artificial intelligence, particularly authenticity, and originality". This tension echoes recent work exploring how AI integration introduces epistemic frictions and challenges traditional journalistic intuition (Møller & Thylstrup, 2024). In fact, "despite artificial intelligence's ability to analyse extensive data and literature and generate new ideas and content for writers, relying on it results in a depletion of authorial authenticity and originality". Thus, algorithms can leverage their data analysis capabilities to generate new ideas, but "they have not yet reached the capacity for abstract thinking and imaginative engagement, both pivotal in the creative process". The capability of machines is typically constrained in the key areas of human creativity, which "frequently emerges from experiences, emotions and intuition". The authors conclude that extensive use of AI in the writing process "leads to the erosion of the writer's distinctive style due to the direct utilization of generic text predominantly based on existing patterns [...] Styles imposed by artificial intelligence on writers tend to be standardized, simplifying, and conforming to a general structure rather than capturing the specific expressions of the writer".

Other researchers have focused on the role of Gen AI in expanding ideas: "While much has been written about the processes of generating ideas, the topic of the expansion of ideas is less debated and above all the contribution of generative artificial intelligence on the processes that we can define as concept enlargement and concept enrichment" (Goetz, 2024).

While numerous studies have explored professionals' perceptions of content created by others using Gen AI tools, this research focuses instead on a narrower field of inquiry: how the support offered by Gen AI tools is perceived both at the beginning and throughout the creative process, particularly regarding textual content generation. This study aims to collect and analyse, from a cross-sectional and comparative perspective, the perceptions of content professionals across various fields: specifically, by comparing the use of AI tools in two different macro-environments—digital journalism and marketing—where content editors share the requirement of creating professional texts.

Content professionals often must create content as quickly as possible, or at least with medium to high frequency, due to the demanding work environments in these two fields, marked by frequent deadlines and stringent editorial calendars (see Diekerhof, 2023, for a recent analysis of the relationship between speed and journalistic reliability; Terho et al., 2022, for speed and performance in content marketing).

Therefore, there is a widespread need among content professionals to streamline the production of digital content while maintaining the reliability of sources used in the research process that precedes writing. While AI-assisted writing is widely recognized for its time-saving potential, precise estimates are difficult to find due to the variability in user experience (UX) based on individual skills and context. More detailed estimates examine specific areas and contexts, such as the average weekly time savings observed in US small and medium-sized businesses due to AI adoption (Statista, 2024a, b).

Therefore, the sub-objectives of this paper can be summarized as follows:

- Map the perceptions of content professionals in using AI tools
- Compare UX perceptions between members of different professional fields
- Compare UX perceptions based on the two proposed interface types ("chatbot" vs. "answer engine")
- Analyse how the survey respondents self-placed in the three predetermined clusters
- Determine whether this "self-assessment" matches the qualitative feedback and perceptions gathered, as well as the initial research hypothesis
- Chart a course for future comparative analyses in this area

5 User Perceptions of AI Tools

Intriguingly, most of the direct comparisons available in the literature between tools like ChatGPT and Perplexity.ai are outside the areas of writing and communication, often focusing on domains like medical research, education, and business reference (Deike, 2024). However, some recent studies are fully adaptable to the scope of this paper. In recent months, the scholarly output on LLMs and chatbots—especially ChatGPT, which according to industry estimates exceeded 2 billion monthly global website visits in May (Similarweb, 2024)—has been enormous, particularly regarding their implications in education, including various analyses on the opportunities and risks of AI-assisted writing in this field (e.g. Cardon et al., 2023).

Regarding user perceptions of the use of Gen AI tools, Marquis et al. (2024) analysed data from 1623 professionals from various economic sectors to assess their use of AI tools in terms of functionality, user satisfaction, and perceived impacts. Their findings underscore that AI tools can significantly increase professional productivity and play a critical role in various tasks, such as data analysis and decision-making.

However, the study also found that AI tools are significantly impacting traditional job functions, highlighting the need for workforce adaptation and skills development. The research reveals a generational divide in AI adoption, with younger users showing greater engagement than their older counterparts, suggesting a digital divide. This aligns with our findings (see statistical analysis below).

Furthermore, the cited research provides a comprehensive examination of the impact of AI tools on different occupations, addressing ethical and societal challenges: issues related to AI-driven job displacement, privacy, and ethical use were prominent, highlighting the need for responsible AI integration. The study also advocates targeted reskilling initiatives to prepare the workforce for an AI-centric future, along with ethical guidelines to ensure the responsible development and application of AI tools (Fig. 1).

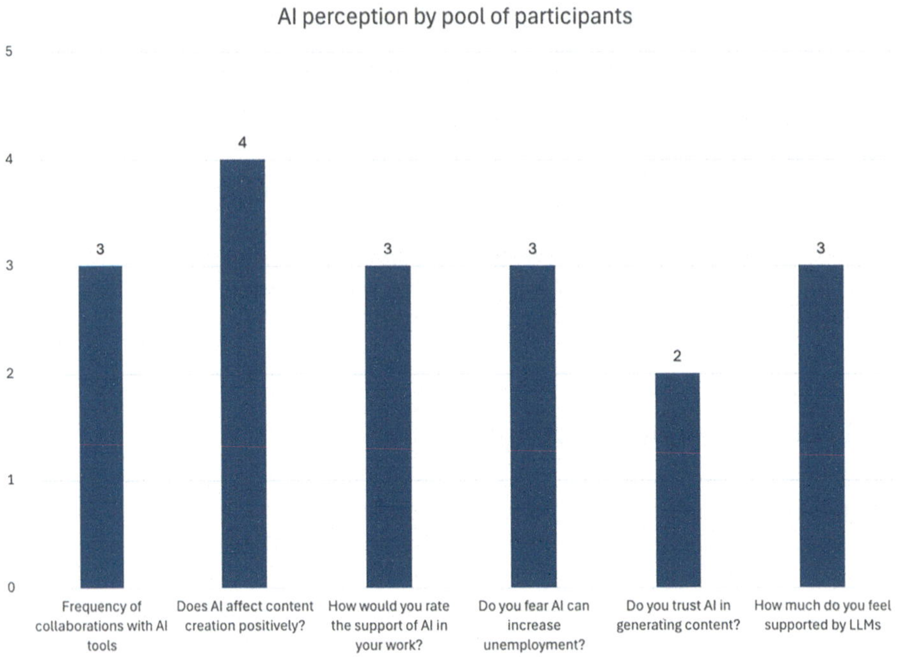

Fig. 1 AI perception by pool of participants

6 Our Research Steps and Methodology

In this work, we conducted a survey focused on creative AI's role in streamlining marketers', journalists', and content experts' jobs by automating, speeding up, and making more efficient tasks such as writing, summarizing, style transferring, text mining, and keyword extraction (Baptista, 2024).

The first step was an 18-question online survey using Google Forms. It focuses on two primary clusters of participants, journalists and marketers, with a third open-ended option of "other" to collect additional data. We designed the survey to investigate how digital content professionals (journalists and marketers) perceive the impact of mainstream AI tools on their creative processes, categorizing them into three groups: augmented, frustrated, and indifferent. The first two groups can be compared to the famous "apocalyptic and integrated" dichotomy (Eco, 1964) that describes the extremes of reactions to new technologies.

In the second phase, we asked some respondents to apply the same prompt in two different conversational web interfaces: a chatbot and a hybrid tool that combines a conversational bot with a search engine. Finally, they were asked to evaluate the differences and the quality of the support provided by AI in performing the task.

Figure 2 provides a sample from the online survey, question number 17 (*"Which of the following statements best represents your experience with AI tools in the writing process?"*). Option 1, "augmented", also corresponds to the Italian for

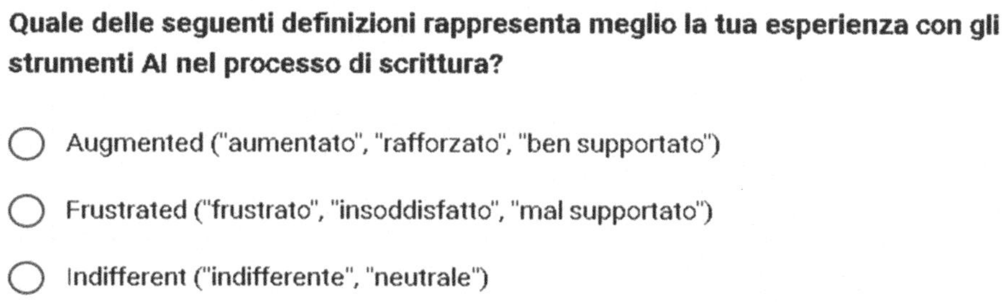

Quale delle seguenti definizioni rappresenta meglio la tua esperienza con gli strumenti AI nel processo di scrittura?

- ○ Augmented ("aumentato", "rafforzato", "ben supportato")
- ○ Frustrated ("frustrato", "insoddisfatto", "mal supportato")
- ○ Indifferent ("indifferente", "neutrale")

Fig. 2 Online survey, question 17 (self-identification of AI-powered writing experience)

"enforced" or "well supported"; option 2 corresponds to "frustrated", "unsatisfied", or "badly supported"; and option 3 corresponds to "indifferent" or "neutral".

Given the rapidly evolving nature of this field, the references section includes a diverse selection of scholarly sources and expert insights to provide recent literature and a broad range of perspectives on the phenomenon, covering various geographical regions.

One limitation of the present study concerns the data collection, which was restricted to the professional Italian content community and the Italian language. In the future, it would be valuable to replicate this study using similar instruments and comparable factors, with a comparative approach, and expand it to other countries and languages, including English.

7 Experimental Results

One of the primary purposes of this work is to analyse the perception of AI tools in creative tasks like writing in several application domains. We conducted a survey involving 130 participants working in several contexts and fields.

7.1 Descriptive Statistical Analysis

The dataset encompasses a variety of job roles, with significant representation from the media and communication sector (55.6%), education and training (18.5%), and other domains. Most respondents report having more than 5 years of experience (82.1%), indicating a seasoned professional sample. Company size distribution shows a notable skew towards freelancers and professionals (52.8%), followed by large enterprises (22.5%).

Regarding collaborative practices, the data reveals a high frequency of professional collaboration, with 94.3% engaging in frequent interactions. In contrast, collaboration with AI tools is less common, with only 33.8% reporting frequent use.

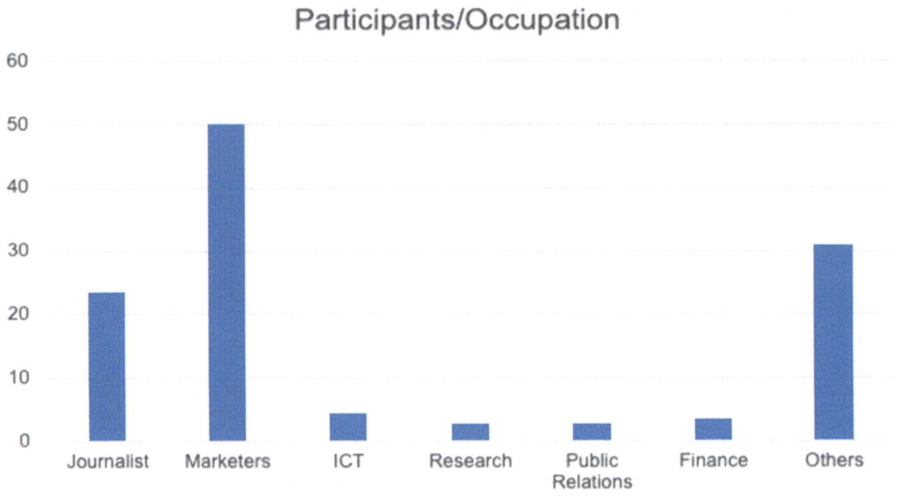

Fig. 3 Participants statistically grouped by occupation

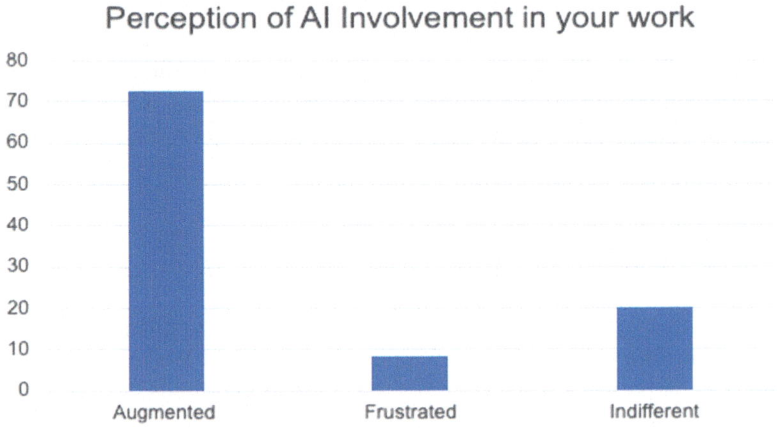

Fig. 4 Perception rates of AI involvement in work tasks

The perceived impact of AI on content creation tasks shows variability, with 43.2% finding it beneficial, 32.1% indifferent, and 24.7% experiencing negative effects.

Respondents identified ChatGPT as the most utilized AI tool (38.6%), with a significant portion not using any AI tools (24.3%). The perception of AI involvement in work varied, with 37.9% feeling augmented, 32.8% indifferent, and 29.3% frustrated. Interestingly, generational analysis indicates that Generation X (44–59 years) formed the largest group (43.2%), with baby boomers (60–78 years) also well represented (31.7%).

In summary, the dataset reflects a diverse set of professionals with varying degrees of AI tool engagement and differing perceptions of AI's impact on their work (Figs. 2, 3 and 4). These insights underline the heterogeneity of how AI is integrated and perceived across different job roles and generations (Figs. 5, 6 and 7).

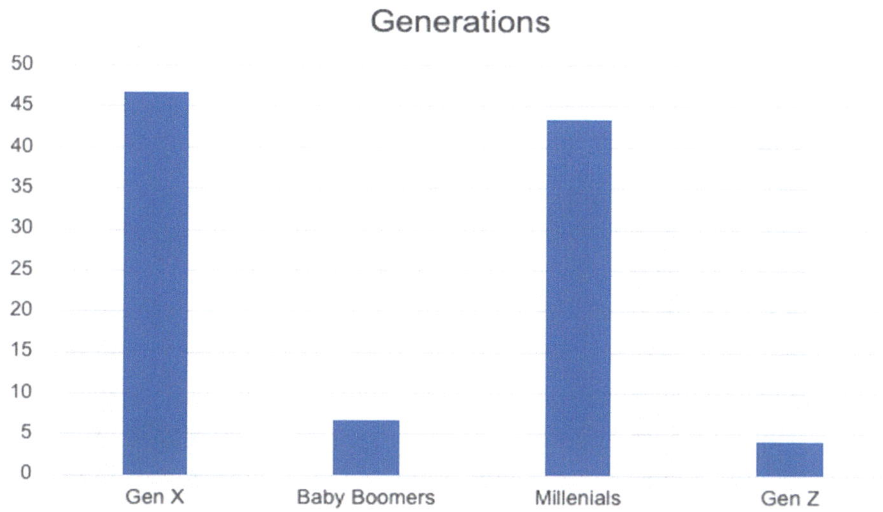

Fig. 5 Number of participants per generation

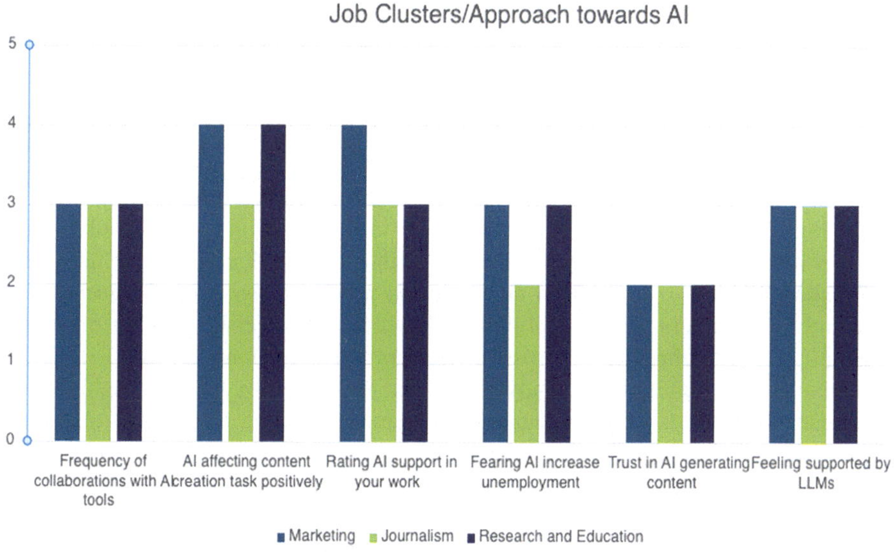

Fig. 6 Job clusters and approach towards AI

7.2 *Statistical Significance Analysis of AI Collaboration Frequency*

An analysis of variance (ANOVA) test was conducted to examine the frequency of collaborations with AI tools across various demographic and professional

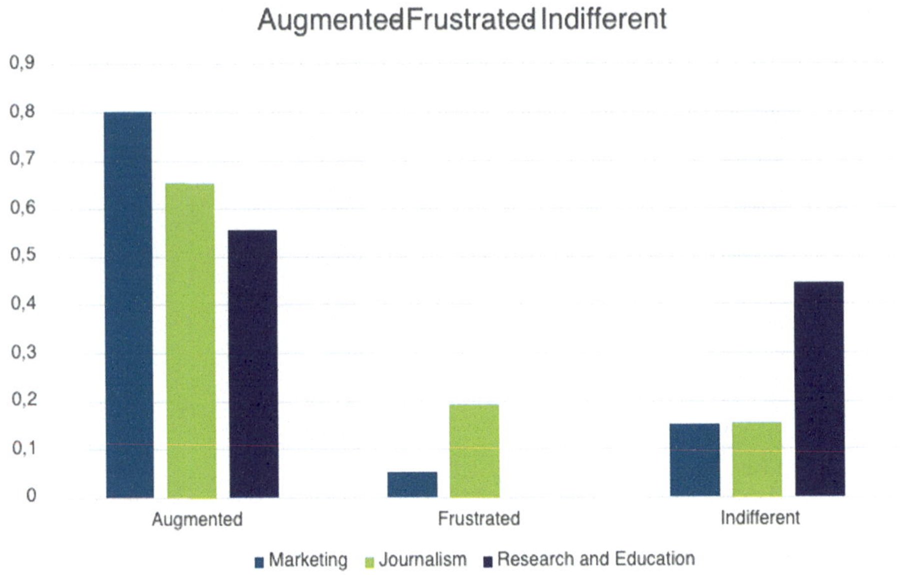

Fig. 7 Self-identification of respondents based on their AI-powered writing experience

categories, including job roles, application domains, years of experience, company size, and generation. The results revealed significant differences in two specific areas: application domains and generations.

Firstly, the ANOVA test for application domains yielded a p-value of 0.0111, indicating a statistically significant difference in the frequency of AI tool collaborations across different fields. This suggests that certain domains, such as media and communication or education and training, might engage with AI tools more frequently than others. This variability underscores the diverse adoption rates and integration of AI technologies across different professional landscapes.

Secondly, the generational analysis showed a p-value of 0.0164, highlighting significant differences in AI collaboration frequency among different age groups. This finding points to a generational divide in utilizing AI tools, potentially reflecting varying comfort levels, familiarity, and reliance on AI technologies among different age cohorts. Younger generations, such as millennials and Generation Z, might be more inclined to incorporate AI into their workflows than older generations like baby boomers.

In contrast, no significant differences were found in AI collaboration frequency when considering job roles (p-value: 0.0909), years of experience (p-value: 0.5920), and company size (p-value: 0.5167). These results suggest that the propensity to collaborate with AI tools is consistent across these variables, indicating a more uniform adoption of AI technologies regardless of job title, professional experience, or organizational scale.

Table 1 Statistical interpretation of three survey variables

Variable	p-Value	Interpretation
Collaboration frequency across application domains (journalism, marketing, research and education, ICT, others)	0.0111	Statistically significant difference in perception of AI's positive impact across these survey variables.
Collaboration frequency across several generations (Gen X, Millennials, Baby Boomers, Gen Z)	0.0164	
Variance of AI perception across the above-mentioned application domains	0.0358	

These findings provide valuable insights into the heterogeneous nature of AI tool adoption, influenced predominantly by the professional domain and generational cohort. They highlight areas where AI integration is more prevalent and identify potential gaps where further AI literacy and training could be beneficial (Table 1).

7.3 *Statistical Significance Analysis of AI's Positive Impact on Content Creation*

An ANOVA was conducted to evaluate the perception of AI's positive impact on content creation across various demographic and professional categories, including job roles, application domains, years of experience, company size, and generation. The results indicated a statistically significant difference in perceptions across application domains, with a p-value of 0.0358.

This finding suggests that specific fields, such as media and communication, education and training, and technology and informatics, perceive AI's positive impact on content creation differently, reflecting diverse levels of AI integration and effectiveness in these areas.

In contrast, the ANOVA revealed no statistically significant differences in the perception of AI's positive impact across job roles (p-value: 0.5371), years of experience (p-value: 0.9749), company size (p-value: 0.9617), and generation (p-value: 0.1070). These results indicate that factors such as professional role, tenure, organizational scale, and age group do not substantially influence the perceived benefits of AI in content creation tasks. The uniformity in perception across these variables suggests a broadly consistent view of AI's positive impact, regardless of these demographic and professional characteristics (Table 2).

In summary, while the perception of AI's positive impact on content creation is generally consistent across most examined variables, the significant variance observed within application domains underscores the need for context-specific AI solutions tailored to different professional fields' unique demands and challenges.

Table 2 Statistical interpretation of four survey variables

Variable	p-Value	Interpretation
Years of experience	0.9749	No statistically significant difference in perception of AI's positive impact across these survey variables.
Company size	0.9617	
Job roles	0.5371	
Generation	0.1070	

7.4 Qualitative Analysis of the AI Writing Test Responses

Our abstract hypothesized that hybridizing search engines and conversational interfaces (chatbots) may provide added value over mainstream chatbot-generated text. After the survey, a second step involving an AI writing test was conducted to explore this hypothesis. We conducted a qualitative analysis of the responses from the 12 participants who performed this test, comparing their experiences using ChatGPT (a chatbot) and Perplexity.ai (an answer engine). Table 3 presents the patterns and themes we identified.

8 Conclusions

Our study aimed to understand how digital content professionals perceive and adapt to mainstream AI-powered tools in their writing process. Through a survey of 130 Italian participants from diverse professional backgrounds, we found significant variability in AI tool usage and perceptions. Most respondents were seasoned professionals, with a substantial proportion from the media and communication sectors. While collaboration among professionals was high, frequent use of AI tools was notably lower. ChatGPT emerged as the most popular tool, yet many participants had no experience with AI tools.

Generational differences were evident, with older cohorts showing less frequent AI tool usage compared to younger ones. Moreover, our ANOVA tests indicated significant differences in AI collaboration frequency across application domains and generations but not across job roles, years of experience, or company sizes. This suggests that AI adoption is more influenced by field-specific requirements and generational comfort levels with technology rather than by professional roles or organizational contexts.

The qualitative analysis of an AI writing test highlighted that ChatGPT was preferred for creative and iterative content generation, while Perplexity.ai was valued for research-oriented tasks due to its structured, fact-based responses. Despite some frustrations with each tool, users found unique benefits, emphasizing the need for context-specific AI solutions.

Table 3 Qualitative analysis of feedback from the AI writing test

User perceptions immediately after using the tools for the same task	After using ChatGPT	After using Perplexity.ai
Perceived utility and efficiency	Many participants found ChatGPT to be efficient at generating coherent and contextually relevant text quickly. They appreciated its conversational nature, which allowed for iterative refinement of their queries and text.	Participants noted that perplexity.Ai provided more structured and fact-based responses. It was particularly valued for tasks that required accurate information and references.
Support in content creation	Users felt supported by ChatGPT in brainstorming and generating creative content. The interactive, conversational interface allowed for a dynamic exchange of ideas, which was perceived as beneficial for creative writing tasks.	Participants highlighted the utility of perplexity.Ai in research-oriented tasks. The ability to generate related keywords and sources helped users dive deeper into topics and gather comprehensive information efficiently.
Challenges and frustrations	Some users expressed frustration with the occasional generation of irrelevant or overly verbose text. A few participants saw the need for constant guidance and refinement as a drawback.	The primary challenge noted was the need for more conversational flexibility. Users sometimes found it challenging to steer the tool towards specific nuanced information without rephrasing queries multiple times.
Adaptation and learning curve	The adaptation to using ChatGPT was generally smooth, with participants appreciating its user-friendly interface. The learning curve was perceived as minimal.	While initially perceived as less intuitive than ChatGPT, users found that Perplexity.ai's straightforward and factual approach became advantageous as they adapted to its use.
Overall satisfaction and preference	Preferred by users who required more creative input and iterative brainstorming. It was favoured for tasks involving narrative creation and content ideation.	Preferred for tasks requiring thorough research and factual accuracy. Users appreciated the explicit sourcing and keyword suggestions for in-depth exploration.

Both tools can provide distinct advantages and cater to the different needs of content professionals. ChatGPT is particularly valued for its conversational abilities and support in creative tasks, aligning well with the "augmented" group seeking to enhance their creative processes. Perplexity.ai, with its hybrid approach, offers significant value in research and fact-checking. It supports the "indifferent" group by integrating typical search engine capabilities with conversational features, thus enhancing efficiency in research-intensive tasks.

Our results align with the initial hypothesis that the hybridization of traditional search engines and conversational interfaces provides added value. Under the right circumstances, the dual capabilities allow content professionals to leverage the strengths of both tools, resulting in a more comprehensive and efficient content creation process. This analysis could help guide further research and refinement of AI tools to better serve the diverse needs of digital content professionals.

These findings underscore the heterogeneous nature of AI integration in content creation, shaped significantly by professional domain and generational factors. This highlights the potential for tailored AI tools to enhance specific aspects of content professionals' workflows.

References

Anantrasirichai, N., & Bull, D. (2022). Artificial intelligence in the creative industries: A review. *Artificial Intelligence Review, 55*, 589–656. https://doi.org/10.1007/s10462-021-10039-7

Bai, Z., Wang, P., Xiao, T., He, T., Han, Z., Zhang, Z., & Zheng Shou, M. (2024). Hallucination of multimodal large language models: A survey. *Preprint, 1*, 30. https://doi.org/10.48550/arXiv.2404.18930

Baptista, D. (2024). The impact of artificial intelligence on the production of text for specific purposes: Writing for the web. In *INTED2024 proceedings* (pp. 3721–3728). https://doi.org/10.21125/INTED.2024.0978

Beckett, C., & Yaseen, M. (2023). Generating change: A global survey of what news organizations are doing with AI. *London School of Economics Journalism AI Initiative*. https://www.journalismai.info/research/2023-generating-change

BrightEdge. (2019). *Organic and paid search together dominate website traffic*. https://videos.brightedge.com/research-report/BrightEdge_ChannelReport2019_FINAL.pdf

Bykov, I. A., & Medvedeva, M. V. (2024). Media literacy and AI-technologies in digital communication: Opportunities and risks. In *Communication Strategies in Digital Society seminar (ComSDS), Saint Petersburg* (pp. 21–24). Russian Federation. https://doi.org/10.1109/ComSDS61892.2024.10502053

Calvo Rubio, L. M., & Rojas Torrijos, J. L. (2024). Criteria for journalistic quality in the use of artificial intelligence. *Communications Society, 37*(2), 247–259. https://doi.org/10.15581/003.37.2.247-259

Cardon, P., Fleischmann, C., Aritz, J., Logemann, M., & Heidewald, J. (2023). The challenges and opportunities of AI-assisted writing: Developing AI literacy for the AI age. *Business and Professional Communication Quarterly, 86*(3), 257–295. https://doi.org/10.1177/23294906231176517

Casheekar, A., Lahiri, A., Rath, K., Sanjay Prabhakar, K., & Srinivasan, K. (2024). A contemporary review on chatbots, AI-powered virtual conversational agents, ChatGPT: Applications, open challenges and future research directions. *Computer Science Review, 52*, 10. https://doi.org/10.1016/j.cosrev.2024.100632

Cherubini, F., & Sharma, R. (2023). *Changing newsrooms 2023: Media leaders struggle to embrace diversity in full and remain cautious on AI disruption*. Reuters Institute for the Study of Journalism.

Davenport, T. H., & Mittal, N. (2022). How generative AI is changing creative work. *Harvard Business Review*. https://hbr.org/2022/11/how-generative-ai-is-changing-creative-work

Deike, M. (2024). Evaluating the performance of ChatGPT and perplexity AI in business reference. *Journal of Business & Finance Librarianship, 29*(2), 125–154. https://doi.org/10.1080/08963568.2024.2317534

Deloitte Digital. (2023). *Gen AI powers content marketing advantage for early adopters*. https://www.deloittedigital.com/content/dam/digital/global/legacy/documents/offerings/offering-20231009-genai-research-charticle.pdf

Diekerhof, E. (2023). Changing journalistic information-gathering practices? Reliability in everyday information gathering in high-speed newsrooms. *Journalism Practice, 17*(3), 411–428. https://doi.org/10.1080/17512786.2021.1922300

Eco, U. (1964). *Apocalyptic and integrated intellectuals: Mass communications and theories of mass culture*. Partial English translation, in Robert Lumley (ed.). Indiana University Press.

Evia, C. (2024). *Content operations from start to scale: Perspectives from industry experts*. Virginia Tech Publishing. https://doi.org/10.21061/content_operations_evia

Gartner. (2024a). *When generative AI is and is not effective*. https://emt.gartnerweb.com/ngw/globalassets/en/articles/social-images/when-generative-ai-is-and-is-not-effective.png

Gartner, (2024b). *Generative AI is now the most frequently deployed AI solution in organizations*. https://www.gartner.com/en/newsroom/press-releases/2024-05-07-gartner-survey-finds-generative-ai-is-now-the-most-frequently-deployed-ai-solution-in-organizations

Goetz, M. (2024). *The role of creative artificial intelligences in the processes of expansion of ideas*. https://medium.com/adaptive-imagination-lab/il-ruolo-delle-intelligenze-artificiali-creative-nei-processi-di-espansione-delle-idee-00171e58cd54

Green, A. (2024). *Artificial intelligence and the changing demand for skills in the labour market* (OECD artificial intelligence papers, no. 14). OECD Publishing. https://doi.org/10.1787/88684e36-en

Gupta, P., Ding, B., Guan, C., & Ding, D. (2024). Generative AI: A systematic review using topic modeling techniques. *Data and Information Management, 8*(2), 100066. https://doi.org/10.1016/j.dim.2024.100066

HubSpot. (2023). *The state of AI report and how it will revolutionize marketing*. https://blog.hubspot.com/marketing/state-of-generative-ai

Iorliam, A., & Ingio, J. (2024). A comparative analysis of generative artificial intelligence tools for natural language processing. *Journal of Computing Theories and Applications, 2*. https://doi.org/10.62411/jcta.9447

Jingfeng, Y., Hongye, J., Ruixiang, T., Xiaotian, H., Qizhang, F., Haoming, J., Shaochen, Z., Bing, Y., & Xia, H. (2024). Harnessing the power of LLMs in practice: A survey on ChatGPT and beyond. *ACM Transactions on Knowledge Discovery from Data, 18*(6), Article 160. https://doi.org/10.1145/3649506

Landa Blanco, M., Agüero-Flores, M., & Mercado, M. (2023). Human vs. AI authorship: Does it matter in evaluating creative writing? *A Pilot Study Using ChatGPT*. https://doi.org/10.31234/osf.io/wjsm3

Marquis, Y., Oladoyinbo TO, Olabanji, S. O., Olaniyi, O. O., & Ajayi, S. A. (2024). Proliferation of AI tools: A multifaceted evaluation of user perceptions and emerging trend. *Asian Journal of Advanced Research and Reports, 18*(1), 30–55.

Memon, A. S., & West, J. D. (2024). Search engines post-ChatGPT: How generative artificial intelligence could make search less reliable. *arXiv preprint*. https://doi.org/10.48550/arXiv.2402.11707.

Møller, H. J., & Thylstrup, N. B. (2024). The algorithmic gut feeling—Articulating journalistic doxa and emerging epistemic frictions in AI-driven data work. *Digital Journalism*, 1–20. https://doi.org/10.1080/21670811.2024.2319641

Oldemeyer, L., Jede, A., & Teuteberg, F. (2024). Investigation of artificial intelligence in SMEs: A systematic review of the state of the art and the main implementation challenges. *Management Review Quarterly*. https://doi.org/10.1007/s11301-024-00405-4

Puliafito, A. (2024). What Italian journalists want and fear of AIs. *The Fix Media*. https://thefix.media/2024/4/23/what-italian-journalists-want-and-fear-of-ais

Ray, P. P. (2023). ChatGPT: A comprehensive review on background, applications, key challenges, bias, ethics, limitations and future scope. *Internet of Things and Cyber-Physical Systems, 3*, 121–154. https://doi.org/10.1016/j.iotcps.2023.04.003

Runco, M. A. (2023). AI can only produce artificial creativity. *Journal of Creativity, 33*, 100063. https://doi.org/10.1016/j.yjoc.2023.100063
Sholola, Y. A., Banjo, Y. O., Saliu-Yusuf, M. J., Ogundeyi, T. W., & Ayantunji, K. A. (2024). Perceived effect of artificial intelligence on ethical journalism among journalists in Kwara state. *International Journal of Research and Innovation in Social Science, VIII*(II). https://doi.org/10.47772/IJRISS.2024.802145
Similarweb. (2024). *ChatGPT on track for 2 billion visits in May, after topping 100 million daily visits twice last week.* https://www.similarweb.com/blog/insights/ai-news/chatgpt-two-billion/
Stanford University HAI - Human-Centered Artificial Intelligence. (2024). *AI index report.* https://aiindex.stanford.edu/wp-content/uploads/2024/04/HAI_2024_AI-Index-Report.pdf
Statcounter. (2024). *Search engine market share worldwide*, Retrieved 05/27/2024, https://gs.statcounter.com/search-engine-market-share
Statista.com. (2024a). *Generative artificial intelligence (AI) statistics & fact, posted by Thormundsson B.* https://www.statista.com/topics/10408/generative-artificial-intelligence/#topicOverview
Statista.com. (2024b). *Estimated time SMBs saved on marketing in a week by using artificial intelligence (AI) and/or automation technology in the United States as of June 2023.* https://www.statista.com/statistics/1412669/estimated-time-saved-smbs-marketing-week-using-artificial-intelligence-united-states/
Stojanovic, L., Radojcic, V., Savic, S., Sarcevic, D., & Cvetković, A. S. (2023). The influence of artificial intelligence on creative writing: exploring the synergy between AI and creative authorship. *International Journal of Engineering Inventions, 12*, 70–74.
Terho, H., Mero, J., Siutla, L., & Jaakkola, E. (2022). Digital content marketing in business markets: Activities, consequences, and contingencies along the customer journey. *Industrial Marketing Management, 105*, 294–310. https://doi.org/10.1016/j.indmarman.2022.06.006
Wing Chiu, H. (2024). *The jobs being replaced by AI—an analysis of 5M freelancing jobs.* https://bloomberry.com/i-analyzed-5m-freelancing-jobs-to-see-what-jobs-are-being-replaced-by-ai/
World Association of News Publishers. (2024). *WAN-IFRA publishes 5th Report on AI.* https://wan-ifra.org/2024/05/wan-ifra-publishes-5th-report-on-ai/
Zhao, X., Cox, A., & Cai, L. (2024). ChatGPT and the digitisation of writing. *Humanities and Social Sciences Communications, 11*, 482. https://doi.org/10.1057/s41599-024-02904-x

The manufacturer's authorised representative in the EU is Springer Nature Customer Service Centre GmbH, Europaplatz 3, 69115 Heidelberg, Germany. If you have any concerns regarding our products, please contact ProductSafety@springernature.com

Printed and bound by CPI Group (UK) Ltd, Croydon, CR0 4YY
30/09/2026
02225562-0004